YSEC Yearbook of Socio-Economic Constitutions

Volume 2023

The broad theme of the series revolves around the constitutional frameworks for economic activities and their interaction with the social sphere. It is this very interaction this Yearbook strives to focus on. At the same time, it is this focus which distinguishes it from other formats in the field. The reference to "constitutions" mirrors the Yearbook's ambition to contribute to a better understanding of those legal rules which provide the very foundations for our economic and social well-being within a community governed by a constitution, irrespective of whether on the local, national, regional, or global level. The Yearbook aims to, first and foremost, provide a forum for doctrinal legal treatment of the questions that various socio-economic constitutions are faced with in today's globalized context, while at the same time remain open to neighbouring disciplines to the extent that they inform the doctrinal treatment. For further information please visit https://www.ysec-yearbook.eu/.

Eduardo Gill-Pedro • Andreas Moberg
Editors

YSEC Yearbook of Socio-Economic Constitutions 2023

Law and the Governance of Artificial Intelligence

Springer

Editors
Eduardo Gill-Pedro
Faculty of Law
Lund University
Lund, Sweden

Andreas Moberg
Department of Law
University of Gothenburg
Gothenburg, Sweden

ISSN 2662-7124 ISSN 2662-7132 (electronic)
YSEC Yearbook of Socio-Economic Constitutions
ISBN 978-3-031-55831-3 ISBN 978-3-031-55832-0 (eBook)
https://doi.org/10.1007/978-3-031-55832-0

This Springer imprint is published by the registered company Springer Nature Switzerland AG
The registered company address is: Gewerbestrasse 11, 6330 Cham, Switzerland

Contents

Part III

Law and the Governance of Artificial Intelligence

Andreas Moberg and Eduardo Gill-Pedro

Contents

When the Editorial Board of the Yearbook of Socio-Economic Constitutions decided, at the start of 2022, to dedicate the 2023 Yearbook to 'Law and the Governance of Artificial Intelligence', we did not fully anticipate just how timely this publication would be. The year 2023 can be described as the year in which the governance of artificial intelligence (AI) became a matter of global concern. It is the 'breakout year' for generative AI.[1] ChatGPT, the much-talked-about large language model from OpenAI, might have been launched at the end of 2022, but it was in 2023 that it became the fastest-growing app on the Internet.[2] Together with its successors and other generative AI systems, these large language models form the

[1]Editorial 'A Breakout Year for Artificial Intelligence' Financial Times, 3 January 2023 https://www.ft.com/content/1a329ad3-f696-4ee2-a730-2f8b700f15a1, See also Chui et al. (2023), Market Trends "Why 2023 is a Breakout Year for Generative AI" Analytics Insight, 6 January 2023. Available at: https://www.analyticsinsight.net/why-2023-is-a-breakout-year-for-generative-ai/ and and Sideco (2023).

[2]Hu (2023).

A. Moberg
University of Gothenburg, Gothenburg, Sweden
e-mail: andreas.moberg@law.gu.se

E. Gill-Pedro (✉)
Lund University, Lund, Sweden
e-mail: eduardo.gill-pedro@jur.lu.se

E. Gill-Pedro, A. Moberg (eds.), *YSEC Yearbook of Socio-Economic Constitutions 2023*, YSEC Yearbook of Socio-Economic Constitutions (2024) 2023: 1–14,
https://doi.org/10.1007/16495_2024_69, Published online: 23 February 2024

foundation for hundreds of different applications and underpin the development of dozens of new startups.[3] Many analysts and business leaders see these remarkable developments as just the start of the transformation to the economy and society brought about by emerging AI technologies. In a recent survey, a majority of business leaders expected AI 'to cause significant or disruptive change in the nature of their industry's competition in the next three years'.[4] The Financial Times affirmed that '[j]ust as machines augmented muscle in the industrial revolution, so AI can augment brainpower in the cognitive revolution'.[5]

The articles presented in this volume certainly point to the enormous potential that AI brings to a range of technical, social and economic issues facing our world. Naarttijärvi explains how the use of law enforcement represents a clear example of 'shifting technological affordances' that provide law enforcement authorities with possibilities for the identification and location of individuals who did not previously exist. Müllerová highlights how new technologies are facilitating the expansion of quick and affordable mental healthcare to Europe's ageing possibilities, alleviating the pressure on overloaded healthcare services. In a similar vein, Lau notes how AI technology underpins significant advances in physical rehabilitation programmes, in diagnostic techniques and in biomedical developments. In the field of recruitment, Schloetzer and Yoshinaga describe how companies are increasingly aware of the opportunities that AI can bring to improve the speed, accuracy and effectiveness of hiring and employee evaluation processes. More generally, Colonna acknowledges the central role of scientific research, including research on AI, in addressing major societal problems in contributing to economic growth.

At the same time as the enormous transformative potential of AI, and the economic opportunities that these new technologies provide became increasingly apparent, 2023 was also the year where the risks posed by AI became much more widely acknowledged. In March 2023, an open letter demanding a pause to the development of powerful AI systems was signed by hundreds of AI experts, entrepreneurs and thinkers, including leading names such as Stuart Russel, Yoshua Benjio and Steve Wozniak. It noted that '[a]dvanced AI could represent a profound change in the history of life on Earth, and should be planned for and managed with commensurate care and resources' and therefore '[p]owerful AI systems should be developed only once we are confident that their effects will be positive and their risks will be manageable'.[6] The historian and philosopher Yuval Noah Harari argued in April 2023 that AI has already 'hacked the operating system of human civilization'[7] and poses a threat to the survival of humanity, and in May 2023, Geoffrey Hinton,

---

[3]For an updated table of startups deploying generative AI see https://airtable.com/shrBeWpMlxf3e14E8/tblS4TkbJbm0cqT0o.

[4]Mackinsley Consultancy 'State of AI', p. 4.

[5]Editorial, FT.

[6]'Pause AI Experiments: An Open Letter' *Future of Life Institute,* 23 March 2023, available at: https://futureoflife.org/open-letter/pause-giant-ai-experiments/.

[7]Harari (2023).

whom many regard as 'the godfather of AI' and whose team invented the technology behind the current large language models, left Google, calling for companies developing these technologies to stop scaling up AI models until they have understood whether they can control it.[8] Even Sam Altman, the CEO of OpenAI, the company behind ChatGPT, testified before the US congress in May 2023 that generative AI technologies could 'cause significant harm to the world'.[9]

1 AI Governance

These different voices highlighting the need for greater control over the development and deployment of AI can be said to be calling for better governance. The governance of artificial intelligence (AI) can be defined as *the array of institutions, practices and standards which are intended to guide the development and deployment of artificial intelligence systems and applications in a way that avoids negative outcomes and promotes positive outcomes.*

This definition seeks to encapsulate the range of definitions of AI governance that we identified in the literature but that we considered had some limitations. Butcher and Berdize define AI governance as 'a variety of tools, solutions and levers that influence AI development and deployment'.[10] This is somewhat overbroad – we suggest that governance refers to measures or processes that are intended to influence AI development, not to all those that might in fact influence it. Taeihagh describes governance as structures that 'enhance the benefits of AI while minimising the adverse risks they pose'.[11] This is perhaps the desired output of successful governance. But measures that intended to enhance the benefits of AI but that do not succeed would still be called governance—ineffective or failed governance but governance none the less. Erman and Furendal refer to governance (in their case global governance) as 'the coordination of collective action in order to provide public goods and avoid public bads'.[12] This is nicely concise but perhaps too vague to be helpful as a definition. Allan Defoe, then of the influential Future of Life Institute, defined the field of AI governance as '[the study of] how humanity can best navigate the transition to advanced AI systems'.[13] This is an important facet of AI governance, which is concerned with the potential development of advanced general intelligence (AGI), but there are other facets of AI governance that concern

[8] 'Godfather of AI' quits Google (https://www.youtube.com/watch?v=LWiM-LuRe6w&t=2s) and gives warning about the future of technology' *The Independent*, 30 May 2023, available at: https://www.independent.co.uk/tech/geoffrey-hinton-leaves-google-artificial-intelligence-b2331367.html.

[9] 'OpenAI's Sam Altman Urges Regulation of AI in Senate Hearing' New York Times, 16 May 2023, https://www.nytimes.com/2023/05/16/technology/openai-altman-artificial-intelligence-regulation.html.

[10] Butcher and Beridze (2019), p. 88.

[11] Taeihagh (2021), pp. 137–157.

[12] Erman and Furendal (2022), pp. 267–291.

[13] Defoe (2018).

AI systems that are currently being developed and that have not reached AGI level. Floridi sets out a helpful definition of digital governance: 'the practice of establishing and implementing policies, procedures and standards for the proper development, use and management of the infosystem'.[14] However, as will be shown below, he adopts a narrower understanding of the term than that proposed here.

2 Law as a Governance Tool

Law is one such 'institution, practice or standard' that can form part of the governance of AI. However, the governance of AI is not limited to the legal regulation of AI, that is to say, by the setting down of binding rules, backed by sanctions, mandating, prohibiting or permitting specific conduct on specific actors. The governance of AI can be achieved by legal regulation,[15] but it can also be achieved by other means. Lessig famously argued that there are four modalities to the governance of digital environments—law, the market, social norms, and the design and architecture of the digital environment. Market forces, such as supply and demand or the presence of competition from other companies, limit and constrain the action of market actors. Social norms about the acceptability of certain uses of AI may constrain providers and users, even in the absence of binding legal rules. And the limitations and path dependencies of AI systems, and the way in which the technology is developing, impose constraints on how AI systems can be developed.

It should be remembered that law is still at play, even in these modes of governance that are not dependent on direct legal regulation. Markets are not wholly spontaneous natural orders – modern markets are created by law and are dependent on a highly sophisticated legal superstructure to function.[16] Social norms also evolve alongside a legally constructed social world—social norms both shape the law and are shaped by it.[17] And technological and resource limitations are the outcome of political choices that have been codified in law and that in turn shape and limit law.[18] Technological and design choices made now will guide and constrain the range of technological and design choices available in the future.[19]

Up until recently, the attitude of many engaged in AI research or AI policy was that governance was a matter of lesser concern. There was a 'race to AI', where

[14] Floridi (2018), p. 3.

[15] C.f. Floridi, who defines digital regulation as a separate and distinct normative approach from digital governance, rather than as a subset of governance (Floridi, 'Soft Ethics').

[16] For an overview, see Brazeal (2023).

[17] See classically, Posner (2002).

[18] Lessig (1999).

[19] Araujo and Harrison (2001), p. 5. It should be noted that, as Araujo and Harrison insist "path dependency does not imply that the future is in any way closed and technological development predetermined" (p. 7).

corporations, states and institutions strived to advance the development of AI systems and to become leaders in the technology.[20] In the rush to develop better and more sophisticated AI, scholarly attention to questions of governance of AI in order to avoid the potential adverse effects of such AI remained negligible.[21] The 2016 Report of the 100 Year Study of Artificial Intelligence found that there was ‘no cause for concern that AI is an imminent threat to mankind’ and emphasised the need to approach AI technologies ‘without fear and suspicion’ so as not to slow AI development.[22] In a 2018 Opinion piece, Chris Reed asserted that ‘[m]asterly inactivity in regulation is likely to achieve a better long-term solution than a rush to regulate in ignorance’.[23] According to Brian Krzanich, then CEO of the chip manufacturer Intel, AI was in its infancy, and it was too early to regulate. Instead, according to Krzanich, the focus should be on fostering innovation and allowing the development of AI to grow.[24] Straub argued that, in light of the great potential of AI technologies, and the great benefits it could deliver, the work of AI scientists ‘should be free from concern that some AIs might be banned, and from the delays and costs associated with new AI-specific regulations’.[25]

The governance initiatives that emerged at this time were primarily voluntary codes of conduct promulgated by leading tech companies[26] and non-binding principles promulgated by governments[27] and international organisations.[28] Standard-setting bodies began developing certification procedures that would allow companies to demonstrate their efforts to deliver safe and trustworthy AI.[29] Binding regulations were seen either as too difficult and costly or as counterproductive.

This relaxed attitude began to change, and in 2021, the Commission of the European Union proposed a binding regulation for AI, to be known as the AI

---

[20] For an overview of this ‘race’ dynamic, see Smuha (2021), pp. 57–84.

[21] Dafoe (2018).

[22] Stone et al. (2016). Doc: http://ai100.stanford.edu/2016-report, Executive Summary. It should be noted that the panel’s recommendation was not that AI should not be regulated, but that “policies should be designed to encourage helpful innovation, generate and transfer expertise, and foster broad corporate and civic responsibility for addressing critical societal issues”. Nonetheless, the overall tenor of the Report is that one should be slow to impose regulatory constraints on the development of AI technology.

[23] Reed (2018).

[24] Kharpal (2017) at: https://www.cnbc.com/2017/11/07/ai-infancy-and-too-early-to-regulate-intel-ceo-brian-krzanich-says.html.

[25] Straub (2017).

[26] Such as Google’s AI Principles of 2018 (https://blog.google/technology/ai/ai-principles/).

[27] For example, Australia’s AI Ethics Framework of 2019, available at: https://www.industry.gov.au/publications/australias-artificial-intelligence-ethics-framework.

[28] OECD AI Principles, adopted on 22 May 2019, available at: https://oecd.ai/en/ai-principles.

[29] See for instance the IEEE SA CertifAIEd™, at https://engagestandards.ieee.org/ieeecertifaied.html?_gl=1*11fzjeg*_ga*MTQxOTMyMjAzNC4xNjkxNjY4MDc1*_ga_XDL2ME6570*MTY5MzIzNTc2Mi4yLjEuMTY5MzIzNTgwNC4xOC4wLjA.

Act.[30] If the regulation is enacted, it will be the world's first binding legal framework governing the development and use of artificial intelligence. It is likely that it will influence the governance of AI not only in Europe but also around the world, perhaps for years to come.[31] Other important actors have also realised the need for AI regulation. The UN Secretary General launched a Global Digital Compact[32] affirming the need for resolving the 'governance gap', insisting that industry self-regulation would not be sufficient and that a 'global, multi-disciplinary conversation' was necessary. The Council of Europe is developing a binding Framework Convention on AI and Human Rights, and the Working Draft published in July 2023[33] stated that the parties to the Convention were:

> [convinced] of the need to establish, as a matter of priority, a globally applicable legal framework setting out common general principles and rules governing the design, development, use and decommissioning of artificial intelligence.

Even in the United States, calls for binding regulatory intervention are growing, with one Congressman insisting that Congress 'must create a binding regulatory framework',[34] and in China, the concern about the need to maintain control over fast-developing technologies has led to extensive regulatory measures being recently proposed.[35]

The year 2023 can therefore be seen as the year where binding regulation of AI became the focus of the AI governance debate and the 'race to AI' became the 'race to AI governance'.[36]

3 The Challenges of Regulating AI

Nonetheless, while there may be a critical mass of actors acknowledging the necessity of a binding regulation, the difficulties associated with creating such a regulation have not gone away. This volume of the Yearbook highlights some of the challenges and particularities that are entailed when using law in the governance of artificial intelligence. The challenges present themselves in various contexts. Two key contexts that are rendered visible in the chapters of this Yearbook are, first, a set

---

[30] Proposal for a Regulation Laying Down Harmonised Rules on Artificial Intelligence (Artificial Intelligence Act), SEC(2021) 167 final.

[31] Gill-Pedro (2021).

[32] UN Secretary General Policy Brief "A Global Digital Compact" May 2023, available at: https://www.un.org/sites/un2.un.org/files/our-common-agenda-policy-brief-gobal-digi-compact-en.pdf.

[33] Committee on Artificial Intelligence *Consolidated Working Draft of the Framework Convention on Artificial Intelligence, Human Rights, Democracy and the Rule of Law* CAI(2023)18, available at: https://www.caidp.org/app/download/8468539363/CAI(2023)18%20-%20Consolidated%20Working%20Draft%20Framework%20Convention.docx.pdf?t=1693605881.

[34] Ted Lieu 'I'm a Congressman who codes: AI freaks me out!' NYT 23 Jan 2023.

[35] Zheng and Zhang (2023).

[36] Smuha 'From a 'race to AI' to a 'race to AI regulation' (*supra*, n. 13).

of challenges derived from the emergence and development of the new technology in our society and, second, a challenge that stems not only from the technology itself but also from the introduction of the new regulation in the existing legal system. The disruption caused by AI in society is quite easy for everyone to register, but ripples on the surface caused by the introduction of the new technology make their way into the legal system.[37]

3.1 *AI as the Subject of Governance*

One challenge that falls in the first category and is inherent in the nature of the technology itself is that governing AI entails governing a moving target. This has been made painfully obvious in the context of the proposed EU AI Act. In the draft first proposed by the Commission, generative or foundational AI applications were not listed as high risk nor subject to any specific regulatory requirements. Following the release of ChatGPT in November 2022, and the impact of that system, it became clear that such systems posed particular challenges that needed to be accounted for in the text of the Regulation.[38] As Schütte points out, in her contribution to this volume, developments in the technology can happen very rapidly and leave existing legislative solutions obsolete. Furthermore, AI is a broad term that covers a wide range of technologies, which can be applied in a wide range of contexts. A regulation that might be appropriate for an AI controlling the use of electricity in a building would not be appropriate for the same technology controlling a nuclear power station. As Schütte points out, a 'one-size fits all' approach risks under- or over-regulating. The breadth of applicability of the technology also means that several aspects of AI technology might fall under already existing regulations.

Another challenge posed by AI as a subject of governance, and perhaps the key distinguishing feature of modern AI, is that it can make decisions, at least to some degree, autonomously, that is to say, without human intervention.[39] That makes AI systems of great potential value.[40] However, as Carretta points out in her chapter, such autonomy can result in opacity and unpredictability. It might be impossible for humans to predict how a machine will decide in a particular case, and it may not even be possible to fully explain the decision ex post facto. In her contribution, Lau sets out the implications of such a lack of explainability in the context of the use of AI in healthcare: the rights of patients to informed consent and to be actively involved in

---

[37] On a meta-level, it is quite feasible that future legislation already today is prepared by, or with the use of, AI technology in some way, shape or form.

[38] Both the Council and the European Parliament proposed versions that included a section on regulating what the Council referred to as 'General Purpose AI' and the European Parliament 'Foundational Models'. The fact that the institutions could not even agree on what these kinds of AI systems should be called perhaps tells its own story about the difficulties of governing AI.

[39] See generally Chesterman (2020), p. 210.

[40] See generally Agrawal et al. (2018).

decisions about their care may be undermined. This opacity can be a challenge to governance as it can be difficult or impossible to specify what measures to take to prevent particular outcomes.[41] In his contribution, Granmar discusses how the use of artificial intelligence in automated decision-making may well be economically viable but potentially difficult to reconcile with the right not to be subjected to automated decisions stipulated in Article 22 of the EU's General Data Protection Regulation (GDPR). Furthermore, Müllerová explains, the opacity can also make it difficult to hold the developers or deployers of AI systems accountable for the harm suffered as a result of outputs generated by the AI system as proving the causal link may be increasingly difficult.

Closely connected to autonomous decision-making, accountability is one of the challenges highlighted by Córcoles in the field of public procurement law as the authorities procuring AI systems need to acknowledge that the acquisition of artificial intelligence systems is different from procuring traditional technology. Córcoles highlights the difficulties in ensuring adequate human supervision of systems that can otherwise make decisions autonomously of human control.

3.2 *AI and the Disruption of Current Governance Regimes*

The development of AI technologies is leading to what many consider as a 'worrying concentration of power', particularly in the hands of a handful of private companies that have the resources and knowledge to develop and control advanced AI systems.[42] The power imbalance between these companies and other actors in the field, such as academia or the public sector, is being entrenched as such companies are able to dominate what has been described as 'the three key ingredients of AI research: computing power, large datasets and highly skilled researchers'.[43] Such dominant actors are able to not only shape the direction in which AI develops but also play a leading role in shaping the regulatory measures that are contemplated by governments and institutions.[44] In this volume, Laukyte argues that AI technologies are not merely the subjects of governance, but they can also be used as tools for governance—tools that are in the hands of private actors that do not have the democratic legitimacy to exercise such power. Carretta goes further and argues that the accumulation of personal data and algorithmic decision-making capacities in the hands of private corporate actors not only undermines the fundamental rights of individual data subjects but can also undermine the rule of law as it can leave individuals vulnerable to arbitrary decisions over which they have no control. In this new regulatory landscape, the private corporations that develop and deploy AI are

[41] Taeihagh (2021), p. 137.

[42] See for instance Murgia (2023), Mahendra (2023).

[43] Ahmed et al. (2023), pp. 884–886.

[44] See David (2023).

given significant responsibilities to ensure not only that the AI is safe and in conformity with regulatory demands but also that it protects fundamental rights. Viljanen develops the legal theoretical implications of this new governance landscape. He calls this the meta-horizontal effect of fundamental rights, whereby private actors are obliged to identify potential fundamental rights impacts and to take appropriate measures to mitigate these through the development of internal processes.

Another example of the implications of AI governance that challenge current legal theoretical conceptions is presented in Carretta's piece, which identifies a need to re-conceptualise our understanding of the principle of the rule of law in light of the super-dominant position in both data collection and technology development that large private corporations are creating for themselves.

This blurring of the distinction between public and private, regulated and regulator, which governance approaches that are emerging to address AI risks entail, is a theme that recurs in several of the contributions. Colonna zooms in on a very specific aspect of the proposed EU AI Act—the way in which AI research may be exempted from the regulatory burdens that companies engaged in the development of AI technologies might otherwise face. Colonna highlights how *private* actors, pursuing private ends, will collaborate with public institutions in order to reap the benefits from exemptions that originally were designed to protect *public* goods – innovation, the development of socially or environmentally beneficial AI or simply the expansion of human knowledge.

4 Engaging with the Governance Challenge: This Volume's Contribution

As Geoffrey Hinton warned, we need to understand the implications for our societies of developing advanced AI if we are to have a chance of being able to control it. In this volume, we have collected 11 contributions to the ongoing process of collectively trying to understand AI governance better.

The volume is divided into three parts. Part I takes a closer look at the proposed AI Act and consists of two chapters written by Beatrice Schütte and Liane Colonna. In her chapter, Schütte analyses the EU's proposed AI Regulation and examines how it will interact with other EU regulatory frameworks, in particular the GDPR, proposed data governance measures and the product liability regime. Schütte identifies significant gaps and inconsistencies between these different regulatory frameworks and the conceptual and definitional apparatus that they rely on and calls for greater coherence.

Colonna's contribution is focussed on the proposed AI Act's research exemption. This is an important provision for researchers, both in industry and academia, but one that has not received much attention from legal scholars. Colonna points out how the provisions in the AI Act may allow the blurring of the distinction between public and private actors and allow private actors to create mechanisms for regulatory arbitrage that would allow them to circumvent the obligations that the AI Act would impose on them.

In Part II of the volume, the authors discuss challenges to AI governance from a system perspective rather than challenges to AI governance brought by the introduction of AI technology in fields already regulated—which is the focus of Part III. The four contributions that make up Part II are written by Migle Laukyte, Mika Viljanen, Silvia Carretta and Claes Granmar. Laukyte shows how the current human rights framework may be insufficient to address the challenges posed by AI and in her contribution presents ideas on how to bring existing human rights provisions up to date to ensure that the development and use of advanced AI technology under the control of governments, private companies or its own agency continues to respect these fundamental values.

In his contribution, Viljanen also focuses on human rights protection but highlights how the proposed AI Act is an example of an emerging EU regulatory practice that transforms the nature of fundamental rights. They are no longer subjective rights that individuals can invoke against the state or against each other. Nor are they mere programmatic instruments that need to be implemented by additional legislative measures. Instead, fundamental rights are given, what Viljanen calls, a 'meta-horizontal effect' by transforming them into obligations imposed on (primarily) private actors, which must incorporate them into their internal decision-making processes.

Silvia Carretta's contribution to the volume invites us to rethink our conception of the rule of law in light of societal changes such as the emergence of powerful private actors that hold super-dominant positions like data collectors and technology developers. Although traditionally associated with the relation between the state and the individual, the concept of the rule of law may be given a new meaning in the age where personal data are a commodity.

Concluding Part II, Claes Granmar's contribution highlights several challenges brought by the integration of artificial intelligence in human life but focusses on the particular phenomenon of automated decision-making and the potential conflict between the economic interests behind such decision-making and the right expressed in Article 22 of the EU's GDPR not to be subjected to automated decisions. As such, Granmar's contribution also works as a bridge to Part III of the volume, where we revisit the challenges to AI governance brought by automated decision-making in several contributions.

The five contributions that make up Part III span a wide range of legal issues. All of the contributions deal with disruptions to various practices caused by the introduction of new AI technology. The first contribution of Part III is written by Jason D. Schloetzer and Kyoko Yoshinaga. They examine the use of algorithmic hiring systems from the perspectives of both organisations and policymakers in Japan and the United States. Dr. Schloetzer and Ms Yoshinaga examine these systems primarily from the perspectives of data protection and the potential reproduction of selection bias and present recommendations to mitigate risks associated with both the development and use of such systems.

The second contribution to Part III is written by Pin Lean Lau, and in her chapter, she focusses on biases encountered by women in the context of AI-driven healthcare. Lau notes that data and algorithms are not neutral entities but inevitably carry biases and subjective perspectives that affect their creators and the societal and historical context in which they were developed. Lau highlights the urgent need to develop strategies to develop gender health equality in the face of rapidly advancing AI technologies. The proposed strategies are multifaceted and include data feminism, enhanced regulatory frameworks and strengthened informed consent practices.

Petra Müllerová's contribution also draws on examples from the healthcare sector, as it is focused on the role of artificial intelligence in mental health applications. Müllerová's contribution confronts the thorny problem of liability and the proposed changes to the EU's product liability regime in the context of AI applications. As she notes, the specific nature of AI makes it difficult to determine causation between the harm suffered and any defect in the AI system.

The fourth chapter in Part III is written by Isabel Gallego Córcoles, and in it, Córcoles examines how public procurement rules in the EU may or may not need to be adapted to the specific situation of procuring AI systems. Based on the analysis of a number of soft law instruments, she proposes a series of guidelines for the procurement of AI systems.

In the final chapter of Part III, and thus the volume, Markus Naarttijärvi returns to the question of the interaction of the different EU regulatory frameworks highlighted by Schütte in the first chapter. Naarttijärvi shows how the EU data protection legislation can complement the proposed AI Act in providing meaningful limits to the use of AI technology in law enforcement. Nonetheless, he points out that the conflation of the concept of effectiveness and efficiency in the application of the principle of necessity, which has been in evidence in the case law of the CJEU, may weaken the protection of fundamental rights. His conclusion, that the real potential of the AI Act and other regulatory measures lies in the evolving interpretation and application of fundamental principles such as privacy and human dignity, may also serve as a conclusion for this volume – law will play a key role in the successful governance of AI, but it will require us to engage with what is truly at stake for individual human beings and human communities when we share our world with AI.

4.1 Conclusion

As the leading AI researcher Stuart Russell put it in his influential book *Human Compatible*, the development of AI might require us to confront what could be 'the most important question facing humanity'.[45] He was considering the possibility of the emergence of human- or super-human-level artificial intelligence. We may never develop such systems. Nonetheless, today there are a few who would not agree that

[45] Russell (2019).

artificial intelligence (AI) is set to be 'one of the most transformative forces of our time, and is bound to alter the fabric of society'.[46]

The challenge of governing the development and deployment of such systems, and of navigating the transformations that these technologies will bring about, is a key challenge facing humanity. This volume of the Yearbook of Socio-Economic Constitutions has brought together legal scholars who tried to think through the role that law plays and can play in the governance of AI.

References

Agrawal A, Gans J, Goldfarb A (2018) Prediction machines: the simple economics of artificial intelligence. Harvard Business Review Press

Ahmed N et al (2023) The growing influence of industry in AI research. Science 379:884–886

Araujo L, Harrison D (2001) Technological trajectories and path dependence. Technol Anal Strategic Manage 14:5

Brazeal G (2023) Markets as legal constructions. Univ Cincinnati Law Rev. 91595–679

Butcher J, Beridze I (2019) What is the state of artificial intelligence governance globally? RUSI J 164:88–96

Chesterman S (2020) Artificial intelligence and the problem of autonomy. Notre Dame J Emerging Technol 2:210

Chui M et al (2023) The State of AI in 2023: Generative AI's Breakout Year. MacKinsley Consultancy, 1 August 2023, Available at https://www.mckinsey.com/capabilities/quantumblack/our-insights/the-state-of-ai-in-2023-generative-ais-breakout-year#research

Dafoe A (2018) AI governance: a research Agenda. Future of Humanity Institute. Available at: https://www.fhi.ox.ac.uk/wp-content/uploads/GovAI-Agenda.pdf

David E (2023) AI regulation is taking shape, but startups are being left out. The Verge, 8 August 2023. https://www.theverge.com/2023/5/19/23728174/ai-regulation-senate-hearings-regulatory-capture-laws

Defoe A (2018) Governance of AI: A Research Agenda. FHI Working Paper. Available at: https://cdn.governance.ai/GovAI-Research-Agenda.pdf

Erman E, Furendal M (2022) The global governance of artificial intelligence: some normative concerns. Moral Philosophy Polit 9:267–291

Floridi L (2018) Soft ethics, the governance of the digital and the general data protection regulation. *Phil.Trans.R.Soc. A*376

Gill-Pedro E (2021) The most important legislation facing humanity? The proposed EU regulation on artificial intelligence. Nordic J Eur Law 4

Harari YN (2023) AI and the Future of Humanity. Frontiers Forum, Keynote speech delivered 29 April 2023, Available at: https://www.youtube.com/watch?v=LWiM-LuRe6w&t=2s

High Level Expert Group (2018) Draft ethics guidelines for trustworthy AI. European Commission, p i

Hu K (2023) ChatGPT sets record for fastest-growing user base Reuters, 2 February 2023. Available at: https://www.reuters.com/technology/chatgpt-sets-record-fastest-growing-user-base-analyst-note-2023-02-01/

Kharpal A (2017) A.I. is in its 'infancy' and it's too early to regulate it, Intel CEO Brian Krzanich says. CNBC TechTransformers 7 November 2017

[46] High Level Expert Group (2018), p. i.

Lessig L (1999) Code and other laws of cyberspace. Basic Books
Mahendra S (2023) Dangers of AI – Concentration of Power. AIPlus Info, 31 August 2023
Murgia M (2023) Risk of 'industrial capture' looms over AI revolution. Financial Times 23 March 2023
Posner E (2002) Law and social norms. Harvard University Press
Reed C (2018) How should we regulate artificial intelligence? Philosophical Transactions of the Royal Society
Russell S (2019) Human compatible: artificial intelligence and the problem of control. Viking
Sideco F (2023) The Dawn of Creation: 2023 Rise of Generative AI. Forbes, 12 April 2023. Available at: https://www.forbes.com/sites/tiriasresearch/2023/04/12/the-dawn-of-creation-2023-rise-of-generative-ai/?sh=6f29ac851a7f
Smuha N (2021) From a 'race to AI' to a 'race to AI regulation': regulatory competition for artificial intelligence. Law Innov Technol 13:57–84
Stone P et al (2016) Artificial Intelligence and Life in 2030. In: One hundred year study on artificial intelligence: Report of the 2015-2016 Study Panel. Stanford University, Stanford
Straub J (2017) Does regulating AI save humanity or just stifle innovation? The Conversation
Taeihagh A (2021) Governance of artificial intelligence. Policy Soc 40:137–157
Zheng J, Zhang S (2023) China Wants to Regulate its AI Sector Without Crushing it. Time Magazine 14 August 2023, Available at: https://time.com/6304831/china-ai-regulations/

Part I

AI Regulation in the EU: The Future Interplay Between Frameworks

Béatrice Schütte

Contents

Abstract The purpose of this contribution is to analyse existing and proposed AI regulations and to identify the critical implications of their future interplay, that is, how the regulatory framework as a whole will function in the future. Given the abundance of legislation, it is essential that all measures dovetail into each other; otherwise, legal uncertainty, fragmentation, and regulatory gaps would be inevitable.

This research has been conducted with the help of project funding granted by the Academy of Finland, decision number 330884 (2020). All online sources were last accessed on 09 October 2023.

B. Schütte (✉)
University of Helsinki, Faculty of Law, Legal Tech Lab, Helsinki, Finland

University of Lapland, Faculty of Law, Rovaniemi, Finland

Information Society Law Center (ISLC), University of Milan, Milan, Italy
e-mail: beatrice.schutte@helsinki.fi

E. Gill-Pedro, A. Moberg (eds.), *YSEC Yearbook of Socio-Economic Constitutions 2023*, YSEC Yearbook of Socio-Economic Constitutions (2024) 2023: 17–50,
https://doi.org/10.1007/16495_2023_64, Published online: 16 December 2023

1 Introduction

The technological development of artificial intelligence (AI) is advancing at an ever-faster pace, and it influences almost every aspect of our lives. Wearable devices track whether we get enough sleep, facial recognition features integrated in CCTV cameras can identify offenders and our smartphones are the gateway to the answer to almost any question we might have. While these tools certainly make many tasks easier, there are also significant inherent risks for fundamental rights. Many existing laws date from the pre-digital era and are thus often ill-suited to address these risks and to remedy harm if these risks materialise. Against this background, the regulation of AI has been on the agenda of the EU institutions for some time now. They have acknowledged the potential benefits of digitalisation in addressing societal challenges that are related to climate change, health care, education, and transport.[1]

In the last few years there have been several proposals for laws that tackle the challenges that the emergence of AI poses. These proposals should not be examined in isolation. It is important to focus on general matters and to scrutinise the fit between instruments. This is so because an AI system can be subject to multiple legal regimes, such as the General Data Protection Regulation (GDPR),[2] the Artificial Intelligence Act (AI Act)[3] and the Digital Services Act (DSA).[4] Therefore, it is important that the terms that are used in them have the same meaning or that different usages be explained clearly. It is equally crucial to ensure that the applicable legal rules are not contradictory.

The purpose of this contribution is to analyse existing and proposed AI regulations and to identify the critical implications of their future interplay, that is, how the regulatory framework as a whole will function in the future. Given the abundance of legislation, it is essential that all measures dovetail into each other; otherwise, legal uncertainty, fragmentation, and regulatory gaps would be inevitable.

The foregoing propositions accord with the 'Better Regulation' system that the Commission and other EU institutions have adopted. Its aim is to ensure that the quality of legislation is high and that it is accessible and transparent.[5] The Commission has stated its intention is to establish an 'ecosystem of excellence' and an

---

[1] Georgieva et al. (2022), p. 697.

[2] Regulation (EU) 2016/679 of the European Parliament and of the Council of 27 April 2016 on the protection of natural persons with regard to the processing of personal data and on the free movement of such data (General Data Protection Regulation), OJ L 119, 4.5.2016, pp. 1–88.

[3] Proposal for a Regulation of the European Parliament and of the Council laying down harmonised Rules on Artificial Intelligence (Artificial Intelligence Act) COM(2021) 206 final.

[4] Regulation (EU) 2022/2065 of the European Parliament and of the Council of 19 October 2022 on a Single Market for Digital Services and amending Directive 2000/31/EC (Digital Services Act), OJ L 277, 27.10.2022, pp. 1–102.

[5] Communication from the Commission to the European Parliament, the Council, the European Economic and Social Committee and the Committee of the Regions 'Better regulation: Joining forces to make better law' COM(2021) 219 final, pp. 3, 6.

'ecosystem of trust' for AI.[6] The pursuit of excellence and trust should not be restricted to technological matters; it is also important that the legislation that governs new technologies be optimal. In general, effective governance can mitigate the risks that are associated with AI. Those risks, as indicated above, may be related to fundamental rights, including the ones that pertain to personal data, privacy protection, and non-discrimination. Safety and the effective functioning of the liability regime are also important desiderata.[7] In addition, many AI systems are opaque, which causes information asymmetries between their developers and other stakeholders such as consumers, authorities and businesses.[8] Therefore, one of the main goals of contemporary EU policy is to implement trustworthy AI and to avoid legal fragmentation across Member States. It is only in this way that developers, public authorities, companies or consumers, and all other affected stakeholders can reap the benefits of legal certainty.[9]

This contribution examines a selection of frameworks in detail. Section 2 points to some of the challenges for the regulation of AI. Section 3 overviews the AI Act, which can be considered the centrepiece of contemporary regulation of technology. Section 4 presents other relevant pieces of legislation in this domain. Section 5 highlights the critical features of interplay between these frameworks.

2 The Challenges of Regulating AI

It is difficult to futureproof regulations on AI and other rapidly developing technologies. Significant developments can necessitate amendments to existing legislation or delay the development of new laws. These tendencies were in evidence after the launch of ChatGPT by Open AI in 2022. That launch prompted EU regulators to engage in a thorough reassessment of the risk that generative AI poses and of its regulation in the AI Act.[10] An additional obstacle is the fact that currently, the law in this domain is in flux. Several regulations and directives are work in progress and constantly being amended. If corresponding amendments in related legislative proposals are omitted, this will lead to confusion and legal uncertainty.

In the AI race, the aim of the EU is to achieve digital sovereignty, regardless of the difficulties of competing with technological giants that operate outside of the EU.[11] The notion of digital sovereignty is relatively new, and the term has no official

---

[6] European Commission 'White Paper On Artificial Intelligence - A European approach to excellence and trust', COM(2020) 65 final, p. 3. (Hereafter: White Paper).

[7] Wirtz et al. (2022), p. 2; White Paper, pp. 10–13.

[8] Gasser and Almeida (2017), p. 58.

[9] White Paper, p. 3.

[10] See, e.g. Volpicelli (2023).

[11] Stix (2022), p. 11.

definition.[12] The German Ministry for Economic Affairs and Energy formulated a definition when presenting its 'GAIA-X' project, which has the development of a strong, competitive, secure, and trustworthy data infrastructure for Europe as its purpose. In that presentation, digital sovereignty was defined as follows:

> the 'possibility of independent self-determination by the state and by organisations' with regard to the 'use and structuring of digital systems themselves, the data produced and stored in them, and the processes depicted as a result'.[13]

In short, the concept of digital sovereignty refers to 'Europe's ability to act independently in the digital world'.[14] The pursuit of digital sovereignty is a consequence of the growing concerns about the economic and social influence of non-EU technology companies, which makes it difficult for EU citizens to control their personal data, for EU high-tech companies to grow, and for the EU and its Member States to enforce their laws.[15] Digital technologies and competition in the technological industries are becoming increasingly important for internal affairs.[16] In the pursuit of a comprehensive and integrated approach to AI governance, all efforts must be directed towards the regulatory landscape. If the contemplated ecosystem of excellence materialises, the emergence of an infrastructure for the development, deployment, and use of AI will increase ownership of the technology. Such a development would also make it possible shape AI through regulation, which will make the EU less dependent on external actors.[17]

There are high hopes that AI can contribute to solutions to the gravest problems that humanity faces. Those who entertain such hopes have been said to disregard the human factor in both origins of the problems in question and the prospective solutions. The underlying expectation, the argument runs, is that technology alone will tackle climate change, pandemics, and the likes. However, the influence of AI on societal structures is often underestimated, particularly in the context of Big Data.[18] At the same time, certain properties that are attributed to AI, such as opacity and complexity as well as its supposedly inherent biases and fluidity are said to pose difficulties for legal certainty, transparency, explicability, and equal treatment under the law. These clashes can lead to harm, undermine trust, and hinder the development and use of AI.[19] Nonetheless, the functioning of legal measures has been challenged by technical development for centuries.[20]

---

[12] Celeste (2021), pp. 216, 217.

[13] Federal Ministry for Economic Affairs and Energy (BMWi) (2019), p. 7.

[14] Madiega (2020), p. 1.

[15] Ibid.

[16] Monsees and Lambach (2022), p. 377.

[17] Stix (2022), p. 11.

[18] Ruschemeier (2023), p. 362.

[19] Ibid., p. 363.

[20] Ibid., p. 362.

The regulation of technology also poses problems of scope. This is so due to the variety of use-cases for AI and the wide array of capabilities that AI systems possess. The impact of an AI system on society or particular individuals can vary dramatically, depending on its purpose. An AI-enabled system that a law-firm uses to manage appointments cannot be compared to AI that is used for autonomous driving or for facial (or emotional) recognition technologies. AI systems that can interact with their physical environments may even cause injuries.[21] Therefore, one-size-fits-all-regulation is hardly feasible or desirable—over- and under-regulation are obvious risks.[22]

A coherent framework can also be important for achieving first-mover advantage in what Smuha called the 'race to AI regulation'.[23] If the EU does end up a first-mover, the main pieces of legislation are likely to exhibit the 'Brussels Effect', that is, they are likely to have significant de facto or de jure influence in jurisdictions outside of the EU.[24] The EU has a long track record in passing on emerging technologies, the GDPR being a paradigmatic example.[25] When a regulatory regime can balance the needs and interests of stakeholders and provide legal certainty, it is likely to also engender trust in the technology that is being regulated and thus to facilitate its uptake.[26] If the framework as a whole lacks coherence, fragmentation and legal uncertainties are likely to manifest across the globe. The worst-case consequences include a slower uptake of AI and new technologies as well as the abuse of loopholes on the part of powerful economic or state actors that find that it is in their interest to undermine Fundamental Rights.

The regulatory efforts of the Commission are thus directed at enabling innovation while increasing trust and designing a regulatory framework that is 'flexible enough to promote innovation while ensuring high levels of protection and safety' for the citizens of the EU.[27]

3 The AI Act as the Heart of the Regulatory Framework

The proposal for an AI Act that the Commission issued in April 2021 is the first attempt to regulate AI comprehensively.[28] It is one of the centrepieces of regulation of new technologies. So much is in evidence from the fact that proposals for laws

[21] See also, e.g. Schuett (2023), pp. 3, 14, 15, 16.

[22] See, e.g. Wheeler (2023).

[23] Smuha (2021), pp. 59, 60.

[24] The term 'Brussels Effect' describes 'the EU's unilateral power to regulate global markets', meaning that EU legislation influences policies and laws in third countries (Bradford 2020).

[25] Kolt (2023), p. 24.

[26] Smuha (2021), p. 59.

[27] Stuurman and Lachaud (2022), p. 2.

[28] See, e.g. Dempsey et al. (2022), p. 8.

that have been issued after April 2021 refer to the AI Act for the definitions of important terms.[29] However, the AI Act remains to be aligned with existing legislation such as the GDPR.

The AI Act is a form of specialised product safety legislation.[30] It accords with the product safety *acquis* from the New Legislative Framework (NLF).[31] The NLF posits that manufacturers must complete pre-marketing controls to ensure that their products are safe and perform well. These controls take the form of conformity assessments and the exact requirements for these assessments are prescribed by law. When a product passes the conformity assessment, a CE marking may be affixed to it, and it may move freely within the Internal Market thereafter. One of the assumptions of the NLF is that the manufacturer is best placed to complete this assessment because their employees are familiar with the design and the making of the product.[32]

The AI Act aims to ensure that only safe AI systems that users can trust are placed on the market. Since there are no means of guaranteeing that all AI systems are completely safe *ex ante*, the proposal also includes provisions for *ex post* market surveillance.[33] The Explanatory Memorandum to the AI Act implies that the latter is meant to be a form of product safety legislation.[34] In addition, Article 6 of the AI Act, which is on risk classification, refers to AI systems as safety components of products or AI systems being the product.

Is the AI Act genuinely a piece of specialised product safety legislation? The Commission's websites on product safety focus on consumer protection and health and safety. The same is true of the EU legislation on product safety.[35] Conversely, Recital (1) to the AI Act mentions health, safety and fundamental rights.[36] Presumably, these objectives take precedence over product safety or consumer protection. A similar conclusion can be drawn from the newly introduced Recital (2) (c), which posits that AI systems in the EU are subject to product safety legislation. This

[29] See, e.g. Proposal for a Directive of the European Parliament and of the Council on adapting non-contractual civil liability rules to artificial intelligence (AI Liability Directive) COM(2022) 496 final, Article 2.

[30] See also, e.g. Kop (2021), p. 2.

[31] Mazzini and Scalzo (2022), p. 27.

[32] Veale and Zuiderveen Borgesius (2021), p. 102.

[33] Mazzini and Scalzo (2022), p. 27.

[34] See AI Act, Explanatory Memorandum, p. 13.

[35] See, e.g. European Commission, 'What is the General Product Safety Regulation?' <https://commission.europa.eu/business-economy-euro/product-safety-and-requirements/product-safety/general-product-safety-regulation_en>; Directive 2001/95/EC of the European Parliament and of the Council of 3 December 2001 on general product safety OJ L 11, 15.1.2002, pp. 4–17, Recitals 1, 3, 4; Directive 2006/42/EC of the European Parliament and of the Council of 17 May 2006 on machinery, and amending Directive 95/16/EC, OJ L 157, 9.6.2006, pp. 24–86, Recital 3.

[36] European Parliament, Artificial Intelligence Act, Amendments adopted by the European Parliament on 14 June 2023 on the proposal for a regulation of the European Parliament and of the Council on laying down harmonised rules on artificial intelligence (Artificial Intelligence Act) and amending certain Union legislative acts (COM(2021)0206 – C9-0146/2021 – 2021/0106(COD)).

formulation might lead to the conclusion that the AI Act is not a piece of product safety legislation. Clarifying the exact classification of the Act would be desirable.

The starting point of any discussion of the regulation of AI should be its legal definition. In the latest version of the AI Act, which was adopted by the European Parliament (EP) in June 2023, an AI system is defined as follows:

> a machine-based system that is designed to operate with varying levels of autonomy and that can, for explicit or implicit objectives, generate outputs such as predictions, recommendations, or decisions, that influence physical or virtual environments.[37]

Recital (6) sets out that the definition of AI must be clear, and that it should accord with the definitions that have been adopted by international organisations that are involved with the matter. Such consistency would foster legal certainty and avoid contradictions between the AI Act and future international instruments. At the same time, the definition should be capable of accommodating rapid technological developments. It should refer to key characteristics such as learning ability, in order to enable AI to be distinguished from simpler software systems.[38] The contemporary definition reflects the criticism of the first definition of an AI system, which was part of the proposal that was issued in April 2021.[39] It was allegedly too broad and covered almost every computer program.[40] The definition adopted in the AI Act version adopted by the EP in June 2023 is similar to that presented by the OECD, which states that

> an AI system is a machine-based system that is capable of influencing the environment by producing an output (predictions, recommendations or decisions) for a given set of objectives. It uses machine and/or human-based data and inputs to (i) perceive real and/or virtual environments; (ii) abstract these perceptions into models through analysis in an automated manner (e.g., with machine learning), or manually; and (iii) use model inference to formulate options for outcomes. AI systems are designed to operate with varying levels of autonomy.[41]

The AI Act is underpinned by a risk-based approach, which is consistent with the earlier policy discussions that were described in the White Paper.[42] Devices or programs that are defined as AI are allocated to one of four different risk levels: unacceptable risk, high-risk, low risk and minimal risk. AI systems that pose unacceptable risks will be banned. Conversely, minimal-risk AI will not be subject to any specific regulation. Low-risk AI will be subject to certain transparency obligations.[43] The AI Act focuses chiefly on high-risk AI systems, and much of the draft is dedicated to setting out obligations that apply to them as well as to related

---

[37] Ibid.

[38] Ibid.

[39] See AI Act, Article 3 (1), Annex I.

[40] Ebers et al. (2021), p. 590.

[41] See OECD AI Principles Overview, available at <https://oecd.ai/en/ai-principles>.

[42] See, e.g. White Paper, p. 17.

[43] Ebers (2021), p. 335.

administrative matters.[44] The risk-based approach prioritises centralisation because it is the European legislator that determines which AI systems are to be classified as high-risk. The goal is to establish thresholds of risk to health, safety, and fundamental rights. Exceeding those thresholds will trigger regulatory (or legislative) intervention.[45]

The AI Act stipulates that high-risk AI systems must meet specific requirements. These requirements pertain to risk management (Article 9), data and data governance (Article 10), drawing up technical documentation (Article 11), record-keeping (Article 12), transparency (Article 13), human oversight (Article 14) and accuracy, robustness and cybersecurity (Article 15). The AI Act does not elaborate on the information that must be provided to meet the transparency requirement and does not indicate whether users should be capable of interpreting the output of the systems properly.[46] The requirement of human oversight has been criticised for lacking feasibility.[47] This criticism may be justified in relation for highly complex and autonomous systems, which to date do not exist. Throughout the legislative process concerning the AI Act, it seems to have been taken into account, as the version adopted in June 2023 by the EP presents a slightly more elaborate version of Article 14: the provision now sets out more precise requirements as to the persons in charge of the human oversight, such as an adequate degree of AI literacy in relation to the AI system in question. However, the AI Act still is not very precise in defining when and how human oversight is required and what makes it effective and meaningful.[48]

The requirements for high-risk AI systems can shape liability: failure to comply with them can be indicative of fault. The AI Act has been criticised for failing to address important issues, such as social media or private enforcement, sufficiently.[49] Some such matters are expected to be regulated by the implementing measures that should be issued in the future. Technical standards are yet to be established. Compliance with these standards will result in a presumption of conformity. More problematically, standardisation will be outsourced to private organisations. Although those organisations are not mentioned in the proposal, they might be decisive for the operation of the law in practice.[50] Reliance on harmonised standards is a core feature of the NLF. Standards might contribute to the establishment of uniform principles for the implementation of legal requirements and ethical values. There are also hopes that standards can foster the transfer of technologies from research settings to real life and that they can ensure the interoperability of AI systems.[51] Critics have suggested that it will be very difficult to develop effective

---

[44] See also, e.g. De Cooman (2022), p. 52.

[45] Gellert (2021), p. 19.

[46] See also, e.g. Varošanec (2022), p. 103.

[47] Ebers et al. (2021), pp. 596, 597.

[48] See also, e.g. Laux (2023), pp. 5, 6.

[49] See, in more detail, Sect. 5.1.

[50] Kolt (2023), p. 25.

[51] Ebers (2021), p. 331.

standards, particularly for highly complex systems such as neural networks, which may behave unpredictably.[52] Yet, these highly complex systems are in general difficult to regulate, also in view of future technological developments. More problematic is the fact that private organisations will be given significant power in shaping the law. Even though standards are not legally binding, they can have significant power in defining, for instance, product safety or compatibility.[53]

4 Other Relevant Pieces of Legislation

This section examines a selection of legislative measures that are relevant to the regulation of AI will be examined. The fields to which those pieces of legislation pertain are data, safety, and liability.

4.1 Data

4.1.1 The GDPR

The GDPR entered into force in May 2018. AI is not explicitly mentioned in the GDPR, but many of the provisions of the latter are relevant to the former.[54] Recital 15 states that, in order to protect natural persons, the Regulation should be technology-neutral. The GDPR applies when personal data is processed by automated means wholly or partially and to the non-automated processing of data other than by automated means of personal data that forms or is intended to form part of a filing system.[55] The focus of the Regulation is on the effects of processing data and on the attendant impact on risks for fundamental rights, not on the technologies that are used for data processing.[56] The GDPR applies to the development of AI systems and to their use for analysis and decision-making about individuals.[57]

Article 4 (1) GDPR defines personal data as follows:

> any information relating to an identified or identifiable natural person ('data subject'); an identifiable natural person is one who can be identified, directly or indirectly, in particular by reference to an identifier such as a name, an identification number, location data, an online identifier or to one or more factors specific to the physical, physiological, genetic, mental, economic, cultural or social identity of that natural person.

---

[52] Pouget (2023).

[53] See, e.g. Rühlig (2022).

[54] Sartor and Lagioia (2020), p. II.

[55] See Article 2 (1) GDPR.

[56] Mitrou (2018), p. 26.

[57] Ibid., p. 27.

Many AI systems process personal data,[58] therefore, they must be designed and programmed to conform with the GDPR. Personal data can be used for the training of machine learning systems, as well as to analyse, predict, and influence human behaviour.[59] In simple terms, AI and personal data are interrelated—AI is fed by personal data and produces inferred data.[60]

Articles 5 and 6 GDPR establish the core principles of data processing. Most importantly, data processing must be lawful, that is, it must have an actual legal basis. Furthermore, data must be processed fairly, and the interests that are involved must be balanced. The other core principles are transparency, purpose limitation, data minimisation, accuracy, and storage limitation.[61]

Transparency as defined in Article 5 (1) (a) GDPR is related to the data subject. This relationship is clarified further in Recital 39, which indicates that 'it should be transparent to natural persons that personal data concerning them are collected, used, consulted or otherwise processed and to what extent the personal data are or will be processed'. There is a duty to inform the data subject of data processing in advance, and it must be possible for them to determine how certain decisions have been reached.[62] The addressees of the transparency requirement are developers and data controllers. The former are required to reduce the opacity of algorithms; the latter must inform data subjects about the manner in which their data is processed.[63] Importantly, transparency is defined differently in the GDPR and in the AI Act.

Under the GDPR, the data controller must implement measures for compliance with the aforementioned principles, and they must be able to demonstrate compliance accordingly as per Article 5 (2) GDPR.[64]

In addition, data processing must be lawful. Article 6 includes six grounds for the lawful processing of data: the consent of the data subject (Article 6 (1) (a)), the performance of a contract (Article 6 (1) (b)), the controller's legal obligation(Article 6 (1) (c)), the vital interests of the data subject (Article 6 (1) (d)), the performance of a task carried out in the public interest or the exercise of official authority (Article 6 (1) (e)), and the legitimate interest of the controller or another third party (Article 6 (1) (f)).[65]

The principles that were outlined in the preceding paragraphs must be integrated into the programming and training of AI systems. As far as the transparency requirement is concerned, relevant information must be provided to the user of the AI system or to any other person whose data is processed by the system. The

[58] Sartor and Lagioia (2020), p. I.

[59] Ibid.

[60] Mitrou (2018), p. 19.

[61] Feiler et al. (2018), pp. 73, 74.

[62] Felzmann et al. (2019), p. 3.

[63] Mitrou (2018), pp. 54, 55.

[64] Ibid., p. 19.

[65] Article 6 GDPR; Gil González and de Hert (2019), p. 599.

information in question can be provided through the interface of the system or by any other means of communication.

Like the AI Act, the GDPR reflects the adoption of a risk-based approach. However, it does not contain any definitions of risk.[66] Instead, risk evaluation and mitigating measures are left chiefly to the discretion of data controllers and processors, a bottom-up approach.[67] The principle of accountability is considered to be at the core of the risk-based approach in the GDPR. So much is evident from Article 24, which, in describing the responsibilities of the controller, stipulates that they 'shall implement appropriate technical and organizational measures to ensure and to be able to demonstrate that processing is performed in accordance with this Regulation'.[68]

4.1.2 The Data Governance Act

The Data Governance Act[69] (DGA) and the Data Act[70] (DA) are part of the European Strategy for Data. That strategy is intended to create a single market for data in order to ensure that Europe retains its global competitiveness and data sovereignty. The establishment of common European data spaces will enable more data to become available for use in the economy and in society. At the same time, those who generate the data in question, be they companies or individuals, must retain control over it.[71] In general, the Commission strives to increase trust in data sharing and to improve tools for large-scale data sharing for the common good.[72]

The DGA has been applicable since September 2023. Article 1 (1) lays down the conditions for the re-use of certain categories of data that is held by public sector bodies within the Union. It also creates a notification and supervision framework for the provision of data intermediation services, and a framework for the voluntary registration of entities that collect and process data made available for altruistic purposes. A European Data Innovation Board is also to be established. At the same time, Article 1 (2) notes that the DGA 'does not create any obligation on public sector bodies to allow the re-use of data, nor does it release public sector bodies from their confidentiality obligations under Union or national law'.

---

[66] Gellert (2021), p. 20.

[67] Dunn and De Gregorio (2022), p. 3.

[68] Gellert (2021), p. 20.

[69] Regulation (EU) 2022/868 of the European Parliament and of the Council of 30 May 2022 on European data governance and amending Regulation (EU) 2018/1724 (Data Governance Act), OJ L 152, 3.6.2022, pp. 1–44.

[70] Proposal for a Regulation of the European Parliament and of the Council on harmonised rules on fair access to and use of data (Data Act), COM(2022) 68 final.

[71] European Commission, 'A European Strategy for Data', <https://digital-strategy.ec.europa.eu/en/policies/strategy-data>.

[72] Kruesz and Zopf (2021), pp. 569, 570.

The DGA also purports to facilitate the sharing of personal data by introducing the concept of data altruism. The reuse of data that is held by public sector bodies is another important element of the regime.[73] Article 2 (16) of the DGA defines data altruism as follows:

> the voluntary sharing of data on the basis of the consent of data subjects to process personal data pertaining to them, or permissions of data holders to allow the use of their non-personal data without seeking or receiving a reward that goes beyond compensation related to the costs that they incur where they make their data available for objectives of general interest as provided for in national law, where applicable, such as healthcare, combating climate change, improving mobility, facilitating the development, production and dissemination of official statistics, improving the provision of public services, public policy making or scientific research purposes in the general interest.

This definition has been criticised for its lack of clarity.[74] The wording is indeed long and unclear. What can additionally be problematic is the blurred line between personal and non-personal data, particularly in mixed datasets. In addition, with regard to data subjects, the DGA requires 'consent', whereas data holders must give a 'permission'. While consent must meet the requirements set out in the GDPR as per Article 2 (5) DGA, the threshold for the permission as per Article 2 (6) DGA in relation to non-personal data is lower. However, the DGA fails to clarify whether the permission is subject to any further formal requirements. Neither does it set out any requirements for mixed datasets. It would be appropriate to apply the stricter requirements for personal data. It would be helpful if the legislator explicitly stipulated this in the Regulation.

The DGA refers to the GDPR for the definitions of key terms, such as 'personal data', 'data subject' or 'consent', in order to ensure coherence. Similarly to the GDPR, which contains principles for data processing, the DGA sets out conditions for data re-use. Article 5 (2) refers to the principles of non-discrimination, transparency, and proportionality, and it requires objective justifications that should refer to the categories of data, the purposes of re-use, and the nature of the data for which re-use is allowed. Those conditions must not be used to restrict competition.[75] Data is defined in Article 2 (1) as 'any digital representation of acts, facts or information and any compilation of such acts, facts or information, including in the form of sound, visual or audio-visual recording'.

The DGA does not define the terms 'general interest', 'public services' or 'scientific research purposes'. Some examples of purposes of general interest are given in Recital 35 to the draft Regulation. Those purposes include improving healthcare, combating climate change, and expanding mobility.[76] The definitional parsimony of the DGA is likely to cause legal uncertainty. In any event, it should be noted that the 'purposes of general interest' remain limited by the principles of data

[73] Ruohonen and Mickelsson (2023), p. 2.

[74] See, e.g. ibid., p. 7.

[75] See also, e.g. ibid., p. 3.

[76] See also, Kruesz and Zopf (2021), p. 570.

processing, as per Articles 5 and 6 of the GDPR.[77] As far as 'scientific research purposes' are concerned, one can refer to the GDPR due to the close relationship between the two legislative measures. Recital 159 to the GDPR indicates that the notion of scientific research purposes should be interpreted broadly to include, for instance, fundamental research and technological development.[78]

The DGA is relevant to AI when data is used to develop or to train AI systems.[79]

4.1.3 The Data Act

The Data Act (DA) lays down harmonised rules for the availability of data, which shall eradicate obstacles to data access for private and public sector bodies.[80] It is expected that the Regulation will boost the European data economy as an estimated 80% of the data that is generated by devices is never used.[81] The DA will complement the DGA, but also the Digital Markets Act (DMA). It contains basic rules on the right to use data that apply to all sectors, including the manufacture of smart machinery or consumer goods.[82] It determines who can extract value from data and under what conditions. Businesses and individuals will enjoy an enhanced right to data portability. For instance, consumers will be able to transfer data that a digital product generates to a provider of repair services other than the manufacturer of the product.[83]

Central terms to the DA are 'data', 'data holder', 'data recipient' and 'product'. The definition of data in Article 2 (1) DA is identical to the one in the DGA. The 'data holder' and 'data recipient' are defined in Article 2 (6) and (7) DA. Data holders are natural or legal persons that have the right, obligation or, in the case of non-personal data, the ability to make certain data available. Data recipients are the natural or legal persons to whom the data holder makes data available. For example, the manufacturer of an IoT product is a data holder and the provider of repair or maintenance services for that product, if it is a party other than the manufacturer, is a data recipient.

Furthermore, it defines a 'product' as follows:

> a tangible, movable item, including where incorporated in an immovable item, that obtains, generates or collects, data concerning its use or environment, and that is able to communicate

---

[77] EDPB-EDPS Joint Opinion 03/2021 on the Proposal for a regulation of the European Parliament and of the Council on European data governance (Data Governance Act), pp. 41, 42.

[78] Kruesz and Zopf (2021), p. 571.

[79] Fischer and Piskorz-Ryń (2021), p. 426.

[80] European Commission, 'Data Act – Questions and Answers', online, 23 February 2022, <https://ec.europa.eu/commission/presscorner/detail/en/qanda_22_1114>.

[81] Haeck (2023).

[82] Proposal for a Regulation of the European Parliament and of the Council on harmonised rules on fair access to and use of data (Data Act) COM(2022) 68 final, Explanatory Memorandum, pp. 4, 5.

[83] https://ec.europa.eu/commission/presscorner/detail/en/qanda_22_1114.

data via a publicly available electronic communications service and whose primary function is not the storing and processing of data.

Pursuant to Recitals 14 and 15, the DA covers physical products, such as home equipment, consumer goods, and vehicles, that obtain, generate or collect data by means of their components. In contrast, devices that are primarily designed to display, play or transmit content, such as personal computers or mobile phones, are outside the scope of the proposed Regulation. The notion of product that is used in the DA differs considerably from its counterparts in the Product Liability Directive (PLD) or the Regulation on General Product Safety (GPSR).[84] It is emphasised that the products that fall under the scope of the proposed Regulation must be tangible; evidently, standalone software and other purely digital products are not covered. Surprisingly, the proposal does not define the terms 'manufacturers of products' or 'providers of related services' despite those entities being among its addressees.

Article 3 DA sets out the obligation to design and manufacture products and to provide services so that data that is generated from their use is easily, securely and, where relevant and appropriate, directly accessible to the user by default. The user must be given the right to access and to use data that is generated by IoT products and to share it with third parties.[85] The user must also be informed clearly and comprehensibly about the data that is generated, the means of accessing it, the identity of the data holder, and of the intentions of the manufacturer or the service provider to use the data or to provide it to a third party. If the manufacturer intends to use the data or to provide it to another entity, it must also identify the purpose that underlies this intention. This obligation is reminiscent of the transparency obligation from Article 13 AI Act, according to which AI systems must be designed so that users can understand their output and use it properly. At the same time, the Article 3 DA obligation contains elements of the transparency principle from the GDPR. The difference is that the DA refers to 'data' and not only to 'personal data'. In the context of the DA, the 'user' is a natural or legal person who owns, rents or leases a product or who receives a service.

The Regulation sets out further rights and obligations for stakeholders pertaining to the availability of data and its sharing with third parties. For instance, Articles 4 and 5 introduce a non-waivable right for users to access and share the data that they have generated through products or related services. The users in question can obtain access to all generated data and use it for all legal purposes. They may also share the data with third parties, which may employ it for purposes for which they have reached an agreement with the users. However, this principle applies only to the generated (raw) data, not to derived or inferred data.[86] Problematically, the data in question can be both personal and non-personal—often the datasets will be mixed. While personal data is already covered by the GDPR, no rights have been specified

[84] See below Sects. 4.2 and 4.3.2.

[85] Leistner and Antoine (2022), p. 340.

[86] Kerber (2023), p. 122.

in relation to non-personal data.[87] The DA has been criticised for its unclear terms[88] and provisions as well as for the compliance costs that it entails. Critics argue that the new terms and concepts that the Act introduces as well as several of its general clauses will require clarification in the future.[89] In addition, questions remain about the relationship between the Act and data protection and trade secrets law, and the need for such a far-reaching horizontal regulation may be doubted.[90] However, it is not the first time that legislation containing general clauses and new terms and concepts is introduced. What is more, the DA and other frameworks examined in this contribution are addressing aspects of digitalisation, which would not be feasible without new concepts. General clauses shall facilitate the accommodation of future developments without having to amend legislation continuously. More problematic is the notion of product, which differs from product liability and product safety legislation.

4.2 Safety: The General Product Safety Regulation

As mentioned previously, the AI Act as the core of AI regulation is a form of specialised product safety legislation. Therefore, to the present ends, it is important to examine product safety legislation in general. The applicable framework at the time of writing is the General Product Safety Directive (GPSD),[91] which dates from 2001. In June 2021, the European Commission published a proposal for a Regulation on General Product Safety (GPSR).[92] In the Impact Assessment that accompanies the GPSR Proposal, the European Commission acknowledges that it is not clear if and to what extent the GPSD applies to new technologies, particularly AI-related devices. It does not explicitly address the impact of digital features, such as AI, impact on product safety.[93]

---

[87] Ibid.

[88] For selected issues regarding terminology, see below.

[89] Leistner and Antoine (2022), p. 343.

[90] Kerber (2023), p. 120.

[91] Directive 2001/95/EC of the European Parliament and of the Council of 3 December 2001 on general product safety (Text with EEA relevance) OJ L 11, 15.1.2002, pp. 4–17.

[92] Proposal for a Regulation of the European Parliament and of the Council on general product safety, amending Regulation (EU) No 1025/2012 of the European Parliament and of the Council, and repealing Council Directive 87/357/EEC and Directive 2001/95/EC of the European Parliament and of the Council, COM(2021) 346 final (Hereafter: GPSR Proposal).

[93] European Commission, "COMMISSION STAFF WORKING DOCUMENT: IMPACT ASSESSMENT accompanying the document 'Proposal for a Regulation of the European Parliament and of the Council on general product safety, amending Regulation (EU) No 1025/2012 of the European Parliament and of the Council, and repealing Council Directive 87/357/EEC and Directive 2001/95/EC of the European Parliament and of the Council'", SWD(2021) 168 final, p. 12.

In May 2023, the GPSR[94] was finally adopted and published in the official journal and it will be applicable from December 2024.[95] In the GPSR Proposal the Commission had specified four main objectives, namely to update and modernise the general framework for the safety of non-food consumer products, to serve as a safety net for consumers, to meet the challenges that new technologies and online selling pose, and to ensure a level playing field for businesses.[96]

The GPSR contains a new definition of a 'product'. According to Article 3 (1), a product is

> any item, whether or not it is interconnected to other items, supplied or made available, whether for consideration or not, including in the context of providing a service, which is intended for consumers or is likely, under reasonably foreseeable conditions, to be used by consumers even if not intended for them.

The new Regulation thus refers clearly to interconnected devices. Furthermore, the term 'movable', which is used in Article 2 of the current PLD, is replaced by 'item'. Although this modification accounts for the technological progress to a certain extent, it remains unclear whether an 'item' can only be tangible or whether intangibles, such as standalone software or data, are also included.

The GPSR adds cybersecurity to the factors that must be considered in assessing the safety of products, as per Article 6 (1) (g). Likewise, Article 6 (1) (h) refers to the evolving, learning, and predictive functionalities of products. These additions reflect the elevated importance of products with digital elements and awareness of the possibility that contemporary products are likely to change during their life cycles.

The Regulation further creates obligations for providers of online marketplaces, in line with the Digital Services Act (DSA), in particular Article 9 (2).[97] Those obligations are evidently relevant to AI and digitalisation. Online marketplaces must provide a single point of contact for market surveillance authorities and apply voluntary measures on the basis of notifications in the Safety Gate. The market surveillance authorities can order the removal of specific illegal content referring to dangerous products, disable the access to it, or display explicit warnings without undue delay, within two working days. In general, online marketplaces will have to institute appropriate internal processes for product safety in place in order to comply with the regulation.[98]

---

[94] Regulation (EU) 2023/988 of the European Parliament and of the Council of 10 May 2023 on general product safety, amending Regulation (EU) No 1025/2012 of the European Parliament and of the Council and Directive (EU) 2020/1828 of the European Parliament and the Council, and repealing Directive 2001/95/EC of the European Parliament and of the Council and Council Directive 87/357/EEC, OJ L 135, 23.5.2023, pp. 1–51.

[95] European Commission, 'What is the General Product Safety Regulation?', <https://commission.europa.eu/business-economy-euro/product-safety-and-requirements/product-safety/general-product-safety-regulation_en>.

[96] GPSR Proposal, Explanatory Memorandum, p. 3.

[97] See Article 22 (4), GPSR.

[98] GPSR Proposal, Explanatory Memorandum, p. 6.

4.3 *Liability*

The central pieces in the field of liability are the proposals for the AI Liability Directive and the Product Liability Directive, which were published in September 2022. These proposals are particularly relevant to the AI Act and the GPSR proposal as the rules on safety and liability are complementary. The former are intended to ensure that only safe products or AI systems enter the market ex ante, while the latter provide ex post remedies in cases where damage occurs.

4.3.1 The AI Liability Directive

Article 1 AILD provides that the Directive contains

> common rules on the disclosure of evidence on high-risk artificial intelligence (AI) systems to enable a claimant to substantiate a non-contractual fault-based civil law claim for damages, and on the burden of proof in the case of non-contractual fault-based civil law claims brought before national courts for damages caused by an AI system.

The scope of application of the proposed Directive is described precisely in Recital 15 and Article 1, according to which it applies to claims for damage caused by the output of an AI system, or its failure to produce output due to wrongdoing on the part of a human actor. The Directive will not apply in cases in which damage is caused by a human assessment that is followed by a human act or omission, if the AI system only provides information or advice that the human actor takes into account. For example, no liability would accrue if an AI-enabled software provides a doctor with several diagnostic options on the basis of test results, and the doctor decides which of the options to examine more closely.

At the core of the proposal lie the rules on the disclosure of evidence in Article 3, which are accompanied with a presumption of non-compliance and a presumption of causation in Article 4. The presumptions alleviate the burden of proof that an injured party must discharge in cases in which an AI system is involved. According to the Commission, the current national rules on tort liability cannot accommodate technological development.[99]

The AILD proposal does not contain any rules on the substance of liability; instead, it refers to the national laws of the Member States.[100] For instance, if German law applies to a case, the question of whether a person is liable for the damage that the output of an AI system causes, or for its failure to produce a given output, would be answered by reference to § 823 BGB (the German Civil Code). In contrast, the European Parliament proposal for a Regulation from October 2020 contained a comprehensive civil liability regime that would regulate the liability of

---

[99] AILD Proposal, Explanatory Memorandum, p. 1.

[100] Ibid., Article 1; Explanatory Memorandum, p. 11.

the operator of an AI system.[101] That proposal introduced strict liability for damage caused by high-risk AI systems, and fault based liability for damage caused by AI systems that are not classified as high-risk.[102] However, in the Impact Assessment accompanying the AILD the European Commission indicates that the European Commission favours a staged approach to liability. As a first step, it will regulate matters such as the burden of proof and the disclosure of evidence. When the AILD has been in force for some time, the Commission will carry out a targeted review to reassess the need for harmonised rules on liability.[103]

Given the information asymmetry between the providers of AI systems and injured parties, the procedural matters are key. If the injured party does not possess specialised knowledge about the functioning of an algorithmic system, it would be difficult or even impossible for them to prove causation or fault.

In order to mitigate this information asymmetry, Article 3 of the proposed Directive introduces the possibility of Member State courts ordering—upon the request of the claimant or, before a claim is lodged, the potential claimant, that providers and persons subject to the obligations of a provider pursuant to Article 24 or Article 28(1) of the AI Act, or users, disclose relevant evidence at their disposal, which pertains to the specific high-risk AI system that is suspected of having caused the damage that is in dispute. The courts may not order such disclosure at their own initiative. Failure to comply with such an order triggers the application of a rebuttable presumption of non-compliance on the part of the defendant. While these rebuttable presumptions do provide relief to the injured parties, it is possible that the actual harmonisation of liability rules, as suggested in the EP proposal, would yield superior results. However, the harmonisation of private law at the EU level has always proven difficult in practice. Projects such as the Principles of European Tort Law or the Draft Common Frame of Reference, which were meant to serve as models for a harmonised European Tort Law or a European Civil Code, never bore fruit. By and large, the Member States are reluctant to harmonise.

Nonetheless, it does not seem particularly likely that a liability framework in name only, such as the current AILD, will contribute to levelling the playing field in liability for AI. Furthermore, the risk-based approach should be reflected not only in the allocation of the probative onus but also in the substantive rules of liability—damage that is caused through the use of prohibited or high-risk AI should

[101] European Parliament, Civil liability regime for artificial intelligence, European Parliament resolution of 20 October 2020 with recommendations to the Commission on a civil liability regime for artificial intelligence (2020/2014(INL)), 2021/C 404/05, OJ C 404/107 October 6, 2021, <https://eur-lex.europa.eu/legal-content/EN/TXT/?uri=CELEX:52020IP0276>.

[102] European Parliament resolution of 20 October 2020 with recommendations to the Commission on a civil liability regime for artificial intelligence, Annex B, Article 4 and Article 8.

[103] European Commission (2022) COMMISSION STAFF WORKING DOCUMENT IMPACT ASSESSMENT REPORT Accompanying the document Proposal for a Directive of the European Parliament and of the Council on adapting non-contractual civil liability rules to artificial intelligence, COM(2022) 496 final, pp. 57 et seq.

be subject to stricter rules than damage caused by AI systems with a lower risk profile.

4.3.2 The Product Liability Directive

The PLD[104] establishes a regime of no-fault liability for certain economic operators. In contrast to the proposed AILD, the PLD contains substantive liability rules rather than focusing purely on procedure.[105] An economic operator, that is, the 'producer' in the language of the current version, is liable if a defective product causes personal harm or property damage.

To make product liability fit for the digital age, the Commission issued a proposal for a revised Directive. [106] In the PLD proposal, the set of potentially liable persons has been amended. According to Article 1, the Directive 'lays down common rules on the liability of economic operators for damage suffered by natural persons caused by defective products'. The concept of an 'economic operator' is more expansive than that of the 'producer' under the 1985 PLD. This expansion reflects the increasing complexity of value chains: nowadays, it is common for the different components of a product to be provided by different economic operators. The 1985 PLD was already intended to provide injured parties with defendants that they could sue. This tendency is even more pronounced in the new PLD proposal.

In Article 4 of the PLD proposal, the term 'product' is defined so as to include software and digital manufacturing files. Only free and open-source software supplied outside a commercial activity should be excluded from the scope.[107] The developers of open-source software often work on those programs during their spare time and without remuneration. The risk of liability under the PLD would discourage these important activities.[108] Unlike the GPSR, the PLD Proposal does not use the term 'item', and there is no requirement that products must be tangible.[109]

For an injured party to have a claim under the PLD, it must establish defectiveness. According to Article 6 (1) of the PLD proposal, a product is defective when it does not provide the safety that the public at large are entitled to expect, taking all circumstances into account. The factors mentioned in the proposal are the presentation of the product, including the instructions for its installation, use, and maintenance; the reasonably foreseeable use and misuse of the product; the effect on the

---

[104] Council Directive 85/374/EEC of 25 July 1985 on the approximation of the laws, regulations and administrative provisions of the Member States concerning liability for defective products, OJ L 210, 7.8.1985, pp. 29–33.

[105] Hacker (2022), p. 7.

[106] Proposal for a DIRECTIVE OF THE EUROPEAN PARLIAMENT AND OF THE COUNCIL on liability for defective products, COM(2022) 495 final. Hereafter: PLD Proposal.

[107] See Recital 13 PLD Proposal.

[108] Hacker (2022), p. 15.

[109] The issue related to the differing terminology will be discussed below in Sect. 5.3.

product of any ability to continue to learn after deployment; the effect on the product of other products that can reasonably be expected to be used together with the product; the moment in time when the product was placed on the market or put into service or, where the manufacturer retains control over the product after that moment, the moment in time when the product left the control of the manufacturer; product safety requirements, including safety-relevant cybersecurity requirements, as well as any intervention by a regulatory authority or by an economic operator referred to in Article 7 relating to product safety; and the specific expectations of the end-users for whom the product is intended.

The concept of defectiveness has been adapted to increasingly complex value chains and to the tendency of contemporary products with digital features to nowadays change throughout their life cycles. Defects can manifest even after the product is placed on the market, for instance due to faulty updates. The proposal also considers interconnected products, for instance in smart home environments. In that setting, a defect in one product can spread to the other products that interact with it.

The AILD is applied to AI systems as defined in the AI Act, the new PLD will have an even wider scope: it will apply to products with AI features, but also to consumer products without any digital components, such as conventional home appliances such as toasters and vacuum cleaners. Similarly to the AILD, the PLD Proposal alleviates the burden of proof on the claimant in order to remedy the information asymmetry between injured parties and economic operators.

5 Interplay Issues

This section examines several matters that can affect the interplay between the frameworks that were presented above. It is not appropriate to consider each piece of legislation in isolation: they do not operate in a vacuum. The term 'interplay' refers to the interaction, be it observed or expected, between different frameworks. The matters that are discussed in this section are gaps in regulation, inconsistencies, and terminological issues. These factors can significantly affect the coherence of the regulatory framework that governs AI and technology regulation.

5.1 Regulatory Gaps

Gaps can jeopardise the efficiency of a regulatory framework. For this contribution, the term 'regulatory gap' refers to issues that are relevant to AI and which are not addressed in legislation, be it current or proposed, or which are not addressed sufficiently. When new and potentially disruptive technologies are being regulated, gaps create risks of misuse and harm to fundamental rights. Legal uncertainty might also have a chilling effect on the uptake of technologies. The main focus of this subsection is on gaps in the AI Act because it is at the core of the entire regulatory framework. The AI Act has been criticised for its focus on high-risk AI. As a result, the proposal fails to target large technology companies, despite the growing concerns about the use of AI-driven algorithms. Commonly used services such as social media, online search engines, app stores and online retailers do not seem to play any role, despite their ability to use techniques that can be manipulative. In addition, the transparency obligations in the AI Act might be insufficiently comprehensive. While users must be informed when they interact with an AI system, when an AI system recognises their gender, race, ethnicity or sexual orientation or when they encounter deep fakes, no such obligation applies to algorithmic assessments that determine eligibility for, among others, education, employment or social benefits.[110]

The AI Act creates large gaps in the regulation of social media. First, the proposal is silent on the risk classification of platforms such as Facebook, LinkedIn, and X (formerly Twitter), despite the amount of data that those services gather and the potential of the algorithms that they use to undermine fundamental rights. Most other aspects of social media are likewise unaddressed. These include content moderation and the deep analysis of users' behaviour, which create risks of discrimination and harm to the right to freedom of speech. Related questions about transparency and fairness also remain unanswered.[111] While the DSA and the DMA regulate social media platforms, they focus on some of the obligations of providers. They do not regulate the design of the mechanisms of those platforms, the algorithms that they use, the data they gather or the data they use to train their algorithms. The items that appear on individual user timelines, be they posts by friends, posts by pages that the users follow, or targeted advertisements can influence beliefs and even actions significantly. This said, the latest version of the AI Act classifies recommender systems used by social media platforms classified as Very Large Online Platforms (VLOP's) in the DSA as high-risk.[112] Other recommender systems, for instance those that online shops use, will remain unregulated under the AI Act. The DSA cannot close this gap as it is limited to the obligations of VLOP providers and—as already mentioned—does not include any rules on their design and functioning. In addition, recommender systems used in platforms that do not fall under the notion of VLOP's are neither addressed by the DSA nor by the AI Act. This legal lacuna could lead to smaller platforms getting significant power over their users, as their providers are neither subject to the obligations set out in the DSA nor will they be classified as high-risk under the AI Act.

The legislative procedure has enabled some progress to be made in the context of emotion recognition AI systems and their risk classification. Article 3 (1) (34) of the latest version of the AI Act defines emotion recognition AI systems as being designed 'for the purpose of identifying or inferring emotions, thoughts, states of mind or intentions of individuals or groups on the basis of their biometric and

[110] MacCarthy and Propp (2021), p. 6.

[111] Stuurman and Lachaud (2022), p. 5; Ruschemeier (2023), p. 369.

[112] European Parliament, Artificial Intelligence Act, Amendments adopted by the European Parliament on 14 June 2023, Annex III (1) (8) (ab).

biometric-based data'. Pursuant to Article 5 (1) (dc), emotion recognition AI cannot be used in law enforcement and border management, at educational institutions, and in workplaces. The emotion recognition AI systems that are not caught by these provisions are classified as high-risk. In the earlier versions of the proposal, these systems were classified as posing minimal risk, which meant that there would only be a duty to inform individuals that they are interacting with an AI system that can recognise their emotions. Depending on the context, in which it is used, an emotion recognition AI system can be manipulative. The prospect of manipulation can have a chilling effect on human behaviour, and it may cause individuals to deviate from their normal behaviour and decision-making. Therefore, the revised risk-classification is more appropriate for the harm that these technologies can cause. Further clarification remains necessary. The ban on emotion recognition AI is not completely explicit. For instance, in the context of workplace environments, it is not obvious if the legislator meant to refer to offices, or to any space where humans work. Many publicly accessible spaces, such as train stations or shopping centres are also workplaces. If the more expansive interpretation is favoured, the ban on emotion recognition AI systems would be very wide in its scope. Similarly, it remains unclear whether the ban on emotion recognition AI applies to all educational institutions, or only to educational institutions for minors.

Stuurman and Lachaud criticised the risk-based approach for being purely linear and for disregarding the risks that interactions between AI systems pose to individuals and to society as a whole.[113] Indeed the AI Act seems to focus on assessing each AI system in an isolated way and does not mention possible consequences of interactions between different systems, especially when they have different risk levels. However, one must also consider the difficulty of regulating all the possible interactions of AI systems, especially with regard to future technological developments. One way of addressing the issue could be the development of guidelines on how to react to certain impacts caused by interactions between AI systems.

It is also unclear how mixed-risk AI systems, that is, systems that have high- and low-risk components, should be treated. One option would be to assess the components separately, if feasible. The other option would be to treat the high-risk component as being decisive for the entire system.[114] In practice, the latter option is likely to be preferrable. A separate assessment of components might be more burdensome and there is a risk that certain matters will be overlooked.

Criticism has also been directed towards the treatment of general-purpose AI systems in the AI Act. The initial proposal from April 2021 did not mention such systems at all. In the General Approach that was issued by the Council of the EU, a new title that refers to general purpose AI systems was added to the proposal.[115]

---

[113] Stuurman and Lachaud (2022), p. 4.

[114] Sartor and Lagioia (2020), p. 56.

[115] Council of the European Union, General Approach Interinstitutional File: 2021/0106(COD) of 25 November 2022, p. 6. <https://data.consilium.europa.eu/doc/document/ST-14954-2022-INIT/en/pdf>.

General purpose AI systems are defined in Article 3 (1b) as AI systems which—irrespective of how they are placed on the market or put into service—are intended by the provider to perform generally applicable functions such as image and speech recognition, audio and video generation, pattern detection, answering questions, translation and others; a general purpose AI system may be used in a plurality of contexts and integrated in multiple other AI systems. Evidently, an open-source system can also be caught by this definition. The requirements for general purpose AI are specified in Articles 4 (a)-(c). Pursuant to Article 4 (b), general purpose AI systems that may be used as high-risk systems, must meet the corresponding requirements as per Title III, Chapter 2 of the AI Act. Other general purpose AI systems do not seem to be subject to any specific requirements. The critics say that the proposed regulations are ambiguous because it is not entirely clear which entity will be responsible for complying with the legal requirements.[116] What makes the regulation of general purpose AI challenging is that the risk-classification of an AI system depends on its intended purpose and not on the underlying foundational models—which might create a loophole—if an AI system that is based on, say, a biased model, is capable of being deployed in different contexts, it can affect many different sectors.[117]

Article 4 (c) of the AI Act stipulates that the obligations from Article 4 (b), which provides that general purpose AI that can be used as a high-risk system must comply with the high-risk requirements from the AI Act, do not apply when the provider explicitly excludes all high-risk uses in the instructions of use or in accompanying information. This approach has been criticised for being too lax because it makes it easy for the provider to evade responsibility.[118] It is questionable whether the good-faith requirement in Article 4 (b) (2) is a sufficient safeguard given the wide reach of the exemption. It might be difficult to prove bad faith on the part of the provider.

The AI Act has been criticised for its failure to mitigate misuse, as well for the blanket exception that it grants to systems for scientific research and development. The criticism is based on the argument that all types of AI systems, including those that are developed for research and the benefit of society, can be abused if they fall into the wrong hands.[119] However, as the AI Act is meant to be a safety framework, the omission of—at least private law—rules mitigating misuse might have been a conscious choice by the legislator, with the intention to cover that area with the AILD.

Likewise, the AI Act does not apply to that is AI developed or used for military purposes, as per Article 2 (3). The limitation is problematic because of the dual-use functions of many AI systems. AI systems that were originally developed for military purposes can likely be used for civil ones and vice versa. It might be

[116] Kolt (2023), pp. 32, 33.

[117] Ruschemeier (2023), p. 369.

[118] Kolt (2023), pp. 32, 33.

[119] Ibid., pp. 36, 37.

difficult or impossible to determine whether an AI system is exclusively designed or used for one purpose or the other.[120]

Additionally, it should be noted that end-users and those who are affected by the decisions or output of AI systems hardly feature in the AI Act. They are granted no rights or obligations under the most recent version of the proposal. For those affected by automated decision-making, the GDPR provides certain safeguards in Articles 13, 14 and 22, in addition to what is set out in Article 14 of the AI Act. The exclusion of non-professional (end-) users from the scope of the AI Act could be explained with its classification as product safety legislation intended to ensure that only safe AI systems are on the market. At the stage where this is relevant, end-users naturally do not play a role. However, one may want to ask why end-users should not be obliged to ensure human oversight when using AI systems.

The decision to focus on product safety has been said to reflect a regulatory paradigm that is excessively individualistic. Kolt has suggested that it would be more appropriate to target the broad and long-term implications of technologies rather than the immediate risks to individual consumers.[121]

Leaving out end-users and those affected by decisions or outputs of AI systems can—just like the omission of rules to mitigate misuse—also be a consequence of the envisioned division of labour between safety frameworks on the one hand and liability frameworks on the other hand. However, it is highly doubtful whether the AILD, at least in its current shape, is able to provide effective remedies for those who suffered harm as a consequence of an AI system's output, as it does not establish any substantial liability rules. Affected parties would have to rely on the applicable national laws, which, depending on the respective AI strategy, might lead to different outcomes across Member States.

5.2 Inconsistencies Between Frameworks

The frameworks that have been presented above are occasionally inconsistent with each other, which may jeopardise legal certainty and hinder efforts to create a level playing field.

The relationship between the AI Act and the GDPR supplies a salient example. Recital 41 to the AI Act states that operators of AI systems must comply with the rules set out in the GDPR. The AI Act can hardly be said to address data protection and privacy. One exception is Article 10 (5), which stipulates that the GDPR continues to apply. The GDPR has been criticised for not offering sufficient protection in the context of Big Data, and that the AI Act fails to close this legal lacuna.[122] Zarsky stated that the GDPR 'fails to properly address the surge in Big Data

[120] Bogucki et al. (2022), p. 4.

[121] Kolt (2023), p. 41.

[122] Ruschemeier (2023), p. 373.

practices' and that it is 'incompatible with the data environment that the availability of Big Data generates'.[123] Conversely, Sartor and Lagioia argue that despite some tension between the traditional data protection principles, such as purpose limitation or data minimisation, and the need to ensure that the power of AI and Big Data is harnessed fully, AI and the GDPR remain compatible.[124] Yet, compatibility does not necessarily mean that the GDPR is able to close the gaps left by the AI Act for instance in the regulation of social media. As regards the requirement to observe data protection principles such as data minimisation and purpose limitation, the platform providers will in most cases be able to find arguments to support the necessity of their data gathering and processing, even if it may be excessive in fact. Due to the phenomenon of consent fatigue,[125] even that requirement is not a reliable safeguard in practice.

While the AI Liability Directive refers to high-risk AI systems for some of the rebuttable presumptions, it never mentions prohibited AI systems. That a system is prohibited does not mean that it will never be used by anyone, and prohibited systems can still cause severe damage. The reference to national laws for the substantial rules on liability does not draw any distinctions between the risk classifications. It remains to be seen whether this liability regime will be as effective as envisioned by the drafters of the policy papers. Given the deterrent effect of liability rules, a gradational approach that reflects the risk-based rules from the AI Act should be considered. There should also be a difference between damage caused by a prohibited or high-risk system and a low- or minimal-risk system. However, most Member States impose strict liability only in limited circumstances, such as road traffic accidents or accidents that occur at dangerous installations, such as nuclear power plants.

Data portability is also covered by different and inconsistent frameworks. The right to data portability is enshrined in Article 20 (1) of the GDPR, which provides that 'the data subject shall have the right to receive the personal data concerning him or her, which he or she has provided to a controller, in a structured, commonly used and machine-readable format and have the right to transmit those data to another controller without hindrance from the controller to which the personal data have been provided, where the processing is based on consent pursuant to point (a) of Article 6(1) or point (a) of Article 9(2) or on a contract pursuant to point (b) of Article 6(1); and the processing is carried out by automated means'. That Article does not apply to non-personal data, to data that is processed lawfully, and to data that is used in real-time in digital ecosystems.[126] These exceptions make the right

[123] Zarsky (2017), p. 996.

[124] Sartor and Lagioia (2020), p. II.

[125] Consent fatigue describes the state of consumers being so used to ticking boxes in privacy notices online that they have lost their actual function of information and warning. See, e.g. Turton (2016).

[126] Commission Staff Working Document Impact Assessment Report Accompanying the document Proposal for a Regulation of the European Parliament and of the Council on harmonised rules on fair access to and use of data (Data Act), SWD(2022) 34 final, pp. 16, 128.

rather theoretical, also because interpretations concerning the type of data falling under this scope tend to differ.[127] The DA is likewise unclear, in that it indicates that its provisions complement the right to data portability from the GDPR.[128] However, the concept of data portability from the GDPR and the concept of data access from the DA may differ in scope. If that is correct, then it is not clear which framework will take precedence.[129] Further clarification as to the difference between data portability and data access on the part of the legislator would be helpful. Data access under the scope of the DA seems to have a wider scope as there are no exceptions similar to those in the GDPR. The exclusion of non-personal data under the GDPR might prove difficult, especially in mixed datasets and in borderline cases. Both the DSA and the DMA contain rules on data access, however, these Regulations target gatekeepers and large providers and do not aim for portability between cloud providers.[130] Therefore, they are unfit to close the gap.

The GPSR and the PLD Proposal should also be aligned. While the PLD includes refurbishers in the set of potentially liable economic operators, they are not mentioned in the GPSR. Since a product is considered defective, when it does not provide the safety the public at large is entitled to expect, the circumstances to take into account when assessing defectiveness should also be synchronised with the criteria that determine whether a product is safe.

The latest version of the AI Act is also ambiguous. Article 4 (a) contains principles that apply to all AI systems that fall under the scope of the Act. These principles correspond to the requirements for trustworthy AI enshrined in the Ethics Guidelines that were mentioned previously, namely human agency and oversight, technical robustness and safety, privacy and data governance, transparency, diversity, non-discrimination and fairness, societal and environmental wellbeing, and accountability.

As indicated by their names, some of these principles correspond to the requirements for high-risk AI systems. For instance, transparency also features in Article 13 of the AI Act, human oversight appears in Article 14, and data governance is mentioned in Article 10. Further explanations are needed to determine whether and to what extent these principles are identical to the requirements for high-risk AI. This point reflects the general criticism that the AI Act often defines terms loosely or not at all.[131]

---

[127] European Parliament Research Service Briefing, October 2022, 'The Data Act', pp. 2, 3. https://www.europarl.europa.eu/RegData/etudes/BRIE/2022/733681/EPRS_BRI(2022)733681_EN.pdf.

[128] Recital 31 Data Act.

[129] Graef and Husovec (2022), p. 1.

[130] European Parliament Research Service Briefing, October 2022, 'The Data Act', 2 https://www.europarl.europa.eu/RegData/etudes/BRIE/2022/733681/EPRS_BRI(2022)733681_EN.pdf.

[131] Gyevnar et al. (2023), pp. 5, 6.

5.3 Terminology

Terminology is also important for the efficient interplay between frameworks. Misunderstandings and diverging interpretations must be avoided by using the same terms for the same concepts. Some of the existing and planned measures, use terms consistently or refer to each other. In other cases, terminology is inconsistent. There are also instances in which the legislator has failed to explain the different definitions that were used. As mentioned previously, a single all-encompassing regulatory framework is neither feasible, nor particularly desirable. However, terminological divergence creates the risk that connected legal and ethical challenges are perceived as unrelated. In any event, there is much common technical ground between AI systems and other technologies, as reflected in the widespread use of algorithms and, on occasion, of hardware or software.[132] This section highlights several examples of the adequate and inadequate use of terminology in the relevant legislation.

Laudably, the proposals that have been issued since the GDPR, such as the one for a DGA refer to the GDPR for the definition of 'personal data'. Similarly, the AI Liability Directive refers to the AI Act for the definition of an AI system. However, there is no uniform definition of the term 'data' as such in EU law.[133] The GDPR does not contain one. The DGA, DA and the DMA provide the same definition for 'data'. The EU Regulation on the free flow of non-personal data[134] defines in Article 3(1) 'data' as all data other than personal data as defined in Article 4(1) GDPR. Because 'data' is a critical notion, it would be desirable for its definition to be unified across frameworks. The difficulty of discerning which definition applies in which context can jeopardise legal certainty.

Turning to product safety and product liability, it is currently problematic that the PLD proposal and the GPSR contain different definitions of the term 'product'. As noted previously, Article 3 (1) of the GPSR defines a product as

> any item, whether or not it is interconnected to other items, supplied or made available, whether for consideration or not, including in the context of providing a service, which is intended for consumers or is likely, under reasonably foreseeable conditions, to be used by consumers even if not intended for them.

It is unclear whether this definition captures intangibles such as software. Moreover, the definition differs from the one in the PLD proposal, according to which the term 'product' is said to include all movables, even if integrated into another movable or into an immovable. The term also includes 'electricity, digital manufacturing files and software'.[135] The PLD proposal thus clarified that software is a 'product' in the purview of the Directive. Therefore, they provide differing

[132] Gasser and Almeida (2017), p. 58.

[133] Baloup et al. (2021), p. 9.

[134] Regulation (EU) 2018/1807 of the European Parliament and of the Council of 14 November 2018 on a framework for the free flow of non-personal data in the European Union (Text with EEA relevance.), OJ L 303, 28.11.2018, pp. 59–68.

[135] Article 4 (1) PLD Proposal.

definitions of the term 'product', which is central to both. This disparity is suboptimal. The EU institutions should either change the definition of 'product' in the GPSR so that it is identical to the one in the PLD proposal, or they should reformulate both provisions to ensure uniformity.

The term 'product' also features in the proposal for a DA. As mentioned above,[136] its definition differs significantly from the one proposed in the PLD proposal, according to which software is also a product. That the Explanatory Memorandum and the recitals to the DA proposal refer repeatedly to 'products connected to the internet of things'[137] suggests that the definition may be narrower. A clarification that indicates that the notion of product is meant to be different from the one that appears in the PLD would be helpful, especially if this disparity is intended and not due to a failure of co-ordination.

The term 'user' is also employed in different ways in the legislation applicable to AI. In Article 3 (4) of the first version of the AI Act, 'user' meant 'any natural or legal person, public authority, agency or other body using an AI system under its authority, except where the AI system is used in the course of a personal non-professional activity'. However, in the latest version of Article 3, which contains the definitions of several important concepts, the term 'user' has been replaced with 'deployer'. On first impression, this change could remedy the ambiguity of the previous drafts. However, the latest version of the AI Act still contains the term 'user' in various passages.[138] Since the term 'user' is no longer defined in the proposal, its meaning has become unclear. It is difficult to tell whether a lapse of editorial attention meant that the old term 'user' was retained by accident or whether 'user' refers to a stakeholder other than a deployer, say, an end user.

The replacement of 'user' with 'deployer' also generates inconsistency between the AI Act and the AILD. The latter still contains 'user' and refers to the definition of that term in the AI Act. A 'deployer' is not mentioned at all in the AILD, a deficiency that must be addressed in the future.

From the viewpoint of the GDPR, the user as defined in the first version of the AI Act is the same as the data controller. However, in the GDPR, the 'user' is the data subject.[139] In addition, it is surprising that the data controller under the GDPR is a user and not a provider for the purposes of the AI Act.[140] Providers are subject to much stricter obligations than users under the AI Act. This discrepancy can be problematic when AI systems fall under the scope of both regulations: the terminology should be adjusted or explained more clearly. In addition, the term 'user' is also relevant to the DA. If the data collected by a product or service is personal, the 'user'

[136] See above Sect. 4.1.3.

[137] Proposal for a Regulation of the European Parliament and of the Council on harmonised rules on fair access to and use of data (Data Act) COM(2022) 68 final, Explanatory Memorandum, 1, 7; Recitals 1, 19, 22.

[138] See, e.g. Recitals 9 (b), 12 (a), 45 (a), 50; Articles 4 (a), 7 (2) (f), 13, 14 (4), 52, 55.

[139] Bogucki et al. (2022), p. 9.

[140] See also, e.g. Sartor and Lagioia (2020), p. 75.

seems to correspond to the data subject of the GDPR. In the first version of the AI Act, the term ‘user’ seemed to correspond to its counterpart, unless the product is used in a personal non-professional activity. It appears that the DA does not distinguish between consumer-users and professional users. In any case, the decision to replace the term ‘user’ with ‘deployer’ in the AI Act, which is the core of the regulatory framework, might produce confusion.

6 Concluding Remarks

The selection of gaps, inconsistencies, and terminological divergences presented above demonstrates how important and how challenging it is to coordinate a regulatory framework that is highly dynamic due to the rapid development of technology.

The legislation, both current and prospective, that was presented in this paper represents only a small part of the regulation of AI and technology, which is still in the making and will be expanded further in the coming years.

However, already this limited selection presents considerable gaps and inconsistencies. Some of these, particularly in frameworks that are still work in progress, might be due to the ongoing legislative procedures. It is therefore crucial, that the legislator keeps track of changes and ensures that they will be coherently incorporated into related pieces of legislation.

Ensuring that the applicable measures interact efficiently will increase legal certainty for all stakeholders and, as a result, will also promote the uptake of AI across society, which is in line with the plans of the EU institutions.

In view of the different legal proposals that the EU institutions have presented in the past years by EU institutions, one must also inquire what the division of labour between the EU and Member States will be in the future. So far, it seems that the Member States are waiting for the EU to regulate.[141] The decision to delegate substantive liability rules to national laws seems questionable. Different interpretations might emerge, and court decisions might come to reflect a variety of approaches, particularly to basic concepts such as causation or fault. This proliferation of interpretations can add another dimension to the interplay between frameworks, which may jeopardise the efforts to level the playing field.

In light of the foregoing, it will be more important than ever to monitor technological developments constantly and to re-evaluate the core concepts enshrined in the legislation continuously. It may become necessary to amend regulations on technology more often than other domains of law. When new positive or negative impacts of AI and the technologies that are related to it are discovered, new rights and obligations might need to be granted to the affected stakeholders, and the EU legislator must be capable of responding swiftly and efficiently to such

[141] Schütte et al. (2021), p. 33.

developments. So much to make and keep AI trustworthy. As Margrethe Vestager pointed when the AI Act was first introduced, 'on Artificial Intelligence, trust is a must, not a nice to have'.[142]

References

Baloup J et al (2021) White Paper on the Data Governance Act, CiTiP Working Paper Series, 23 June 2021. https://papers.ssrn.com/sol3/papers.cfm?abstract_id=3872703

Bogucki A et al (2022) The AI Act and emerging EU Digital Acquis: overlaps, gaps and inconsistencies, CEPS In-Depth Analysis. https://www.ceps.eu/ceps-publications/the-ai-act-and-emerging-eu-digital-acquis/

Bradford A (2020) The Brussels Effect: how the European Union rules the world. OUP

Celeste E (2021) Digital sovereignty in the EU: challenges and future perspectives. In: Fabbrini F et al (eds) Data protection beyond borders: transatlantic perspectives on extraterritoriality and sovereignty. Bloomsbury, pp 211–228

De Cooman J (2022) Humpty dumpty and high-risk AI systems: the ratione materiae dimension of the proposal for an EU Artificial Intelligence Act. Market Compet Law Rev 6(1):49–88. https://doi.org/10.34632/mclawreview.2022.11304

Dempsey M et al (2022) Transnational digital governance and its impact on artificial intelligence. In: Bullock J et al (eds) The Oxford handbook of AI governance. OUP. https://doi-org.libproxy.helsinki.fi/10.1093/oxfordhb/9780197579329.013.16

Dunn P, De Gregorio G (2022) The ambiguous risk-based approach of the artificial intelligence act: links and discrepancies with other union strategies. IAIL 2022 Imagining the AI Landscape after the AI Act. https://ceur-ws.org/Vol-3221/IAIL_paper7.pdf

Ebers M (2021) Standardizing AI – the case of the European Commission's Proposal for an Artificial Intelligence Act. In: DiMatteo LA et al (eds) The Cambridge handbook of artificial intelligence: global perspectives on law and ethics, pp 321–344. https://papers.ssrn.com/sol3/papers.cfm?abstract_id=3900378

Ebers M et al (2021) The European Commission's Proposal for an Artificial Intelligence Act—a critical assessment by members of the Robotics and AI Law Society (RAILS). J 4:589–603. https://doi.org/10.3390/j4040043

European Commission (2020) 'White Paper On Artificial Intelligence – A European approach to excellence and trust', COM(2020) 65 final

European Commission (2021) Communication from the Commission to the European Parliament, the Council, the European Economic and Social Committee and the Committee of the Regions 'Better regulation: Joining forces to make better law' COM(2021) 219 final

European Commission (2021) Commission Staff Working Document: Impact Assessment accompanying the document 'Proposal for a Regulation of the European Parliament and of the Council on general product safety, amending Regulation (EU) No 1025/2012 of the European Parliament and of the Council, and repealing Council Directive 87/357/EEC and Directive 2001/95/EC of the European Parliament and of the Council', SWD(2021) 168 final

European Commission (2022) Commission Staff Working Document: Impact Assessment Report Accompanying the document Proposal for a Regulation of the European Parliament and of the Council on harmonised rules on fair access to and use of data (Data Act), SWD(2022) 34 final

[142] European Commission, Press Release, 21 April 2021, 'Europe fit for the Digital Age: Commission proposes new rules and actions for excellence and trust in Artificial Intelligence', <https://ec.europa.eu/commission/presscorner/detail/en/IP_21_1682>.

European Commission (2022) Commission Staff Working Document: Impact Assessment Report Accompanying the document Proposal for a Directive of the European Parliament and of the Council on adapting non-contractual civil liability rules to artificial intelligence, COM(2022) 496 final

European Data Protection Board (2021) EDPB-EDPS Joint Opinion 03/2021 on the Proposal for a regulation of the European Parliament and of the Council on European data governance (Data Governance Act)

European Parliament Research Service (2022) Briefing, October 2022, 'The Data Act' https://www.europarl.europa.eu/RegData/etudes/BRIE/2022/733681/EPRS_BRI(2022)733681_EN.pdf

European Parliament Research Service (2023) Briefing of 08 February 2023, General Product Safety Regulation. https://www.europarl.europa.eu/thinktank/en/document/EPRS_BRI(2021)698028

Federal Ministry for Economic Affairs and Energy (BMWi) (2019) Project GAIA-X. A Federated Data Infrastructure as the Cradle of a Vibrant European Ecosystem

Feiler L et al (2018) The EU General Data Protection Regulation (GDPR): a commentary. Globe Law & Business

Felzmann H et al (2019) Transparency you can trust: transparency requirements for artificial intelligence between legal norms and contextual concerns. Big Data Soc 6(1). https://doi.org/10.1177/2053951719860542

Fischer B, Piskorz-Ryń A (2021) Artificial intelligence in the context of data governance. Int Rev Law Comput Technol 35(3):419–428. https://doi.org/10.1080/13600869.2021.1950925

Gasser U, Almeida VAF (2017) A layered model for AI governance. IEEE Internet Comput 21(6): 58–62. Available via https://ieeexplore.ieee.org/document/8114684

Gellert R (2021) The role of the risk-based approach in the General Data Protection Regulation and in the European Commission's proposed Artificial Intelligence Act: business as usual? J Ethics Leg Technol 3(2):15–33. https://jelt.padovauniversitypress.it/2021/2/2

Georgieva I et al (2022) From AI ethics principles to data science practice: a reflection and a gap analysis based on recent frameworks and practical experience. AI Ethics 2:697–711. https://link.springer.com/article/10.1007/s43681-021-00127-3

Gil González E, de Hert P (2019) Understanding the legal provisions that allow processing and profiling of personal data—an analysis of GDPR provisions and principles. ERA Forum 19: 597–621. https://link.springer.com/article/10.1007/s12027-018-0546-z

Graef I, Husovec M (2022) Seven things to improve in the data act. https://ssrn.com/abstract=4051793

Gyevnar B et al (2023) Bridging the transparency gap: what can explainable AI learn from the AI act? https://doi.org/10.48550/arXiv.2302.10766

Hacker P (2022) The European AI Liability Directives – critique of a half-hearted approach and lessons for the future. Working Paper. arXiv:2211.13960v3

Haeck P (2023) Europe's new data law, explained. Politico, 28 June 2023. https://www.politico.eu/article/europe-new-data-act-explained/

Kerber W (2023) Governance of IoT data: why the EU data act will not fulfill its objectives. GRUR Int 72(2):120–135. https://doi.org/10.1093/grurint/ikac107

Kolt N (2023) Algorithmic Black Swans. Wash Univ Law Rev 101, forthcoming. https://ssrn.com/abstract=4370566

Kop M (2021) EU Artificial Intelligence Act: The European Approach to AI. Stanford – Vienna Transatlantic Technology Law Forum, Transatlantic Antitrust and IPR Developments, Stanford University, Issue No. 2/2021. https://law.stanford.edu/publications/eu-artificial-intelligence-act-the-european-approach-to-ai/

Kruesz C, Zopf F (2021) The concept of data altruism of the draft DGA and the GDPR: inconsistencies and why a regulatory sandbox model may facilitate data sharing in the EU. Eur Data Prot Law Rev 7(4):569–579. https://doi.org/10.21552/edpl/2021/4/13

Laux J (2023) Institutionalised distrust and human oversight of artificial intelligence: toward a democratic design of AI governance under the European Union AI Act, Revised Working Paper Oxford Internet Institute August 2023. https://doi.org/10.2139/ssrn.4377481
Leistner M, Antoine L (2022) Attention, here comes the EU Data Act! Critical in-depth analysis of the Commission's 2022 Proposal. J Intellect Prop Inf Technol Electron Commerce Law 13(3): 339–349
MacCarthy M, Propp K (2021) Machines learn that Brussels writes the rules: the EU's new AI regulation. https://www.brookings.edu/blog/techtank/2021/05/04/machines-learn-that-brussels-writes-the-rules-the-eus-new-ai-regulation/
Madiega T (2020) Digital sovereignty for Europe. EPRS Ideas Paper Towards a more resilient EU
Mazzini G, Scalzo S (2022) The proposal for the Artificial Intelligence Act: considerations around some key concepts. In: Camardi (ed) La via europea per l'Intelligenza artificiale, 2023. https://doi.org/10.2139/ssrn.4098809
Mitrou L (2018) Data Protection, Artificial Intelligence and Cognitive Services: Is the General Data Protection Regulation (GDPR) 'Artificial Intelligence-Proof'? https://doi.org/10.2139/ssrn.3386914
Monsees L, Lambach D (2022) Digital sovereignty, geopolitical imaginaries, and the reproduction of European identity. Eur Secur 31(3):377–394. https://doi.org/10.1080/09662839.2022.2101883
Pouget H (2023) The EU's AI act is barreling toward AI standards that do not exist. Lawfare, January 12, 2023. https://www.lawfaremedia.org/article/eus-ai-act-barreling-toward-ai-standards-do-not-exist
Rühlig T (2022) The rise of tech standards foreign policy, German Council on Foreign Relations Online Commentary, 03 February 2022. https://dgap.org/en/research/publications/rise-tech-standards-foreign-policy
Ruohonen J, Mickelsson S (2023) Reflections on the Data Governance Act. https://arxiv.org/abs/2302.09944
Ruschemeier H (2023) AI as a challenge for legal regulation – the scope of application of the artificial intelligence act proposal. ERA Forum 23:361–376. https://doi.org/10.1007/s12027-022-00725-6
Sartor G, Lagioia F (2020) The impact of the General Data Protection Regulation (GDPR) on artificial intelligence. European Parliamentary Research Service Study. https://www.europarl.europa.eu/thinktank/en/document/EPRS_STU(2020)641530
Schuett J (2023) Defining the scope of AI regulations. Law Innov Technol. https://doi.org/10.1080/17579961.2023.2184135
Schütte B, Havu K, Majewski L (2021) Damages liability for harm caused by artificial intelligence – EU law in flux. University of Helsinki Legal Studies Research Paper Series Paper No 69. https://papers.ssrn.com/sol3/papers.cfm?abstract_id=3897839
Smuha N (2021) From a 'race to AI' to a 'race to AI regulation': regulatory competition for artificial intelligence. Law Innov Technol 13(1):57–84. https://doi.org/10.1080/17579961.2021.1898300
Stix C (2022) The ghost of AI governance past, present, and future: AI governance in the European Union. In: Bullock J et al (eds) The Oxford handbook of AI governance. OUP. https://doi-org.libproxy.helsinki.fi/10.1093/oxfordhb/9780197579329.013.56
Stuurman K, Lachaud E (2022) Regulating AI. A label to complete the proposed act on Artificial Intelligence. Comput Law Secur Rev 44. https://doi.org/10.1016/j.clsr.2022.105657
Turton F (2016) Shifting the burden of consent under the GDPR. Online, Society for Computers and Law, 18 February 2016. https://www.scl.org/articles/3598-shifting-the-burden-of-consent-under-the-gdpr
Varošanec I (2022) On the path to the future: mapping the notion of transparency in the EU regulatory framework for AI. Int Rev Law Comput Technol 36(2):95–117. https://doi.org/10.1080/13600869.2022.2060471

Veale M, Zuiderveen Borgesius F (2021) Demystifying the Draft EU Artificial Intelligence Act. Analysing the good, the bad, and the unclear elements of the proposed approach. Comput Law Rev Int 4:97–112. https://arxiv.org/abs/2107.03721

Volpicelli G (2023) ChatGPT broke the EU plan to regulate AI. Politico (Online 3 March 2023). https://www.politico.eu/article/eu-plan-regulate-chatgpt-openai-artificial-intelligence-act/

Wheeler T (2023) The three challenges of AI regulation. Commentary. Brookings. Online, 15 June 2023. https://www.brookings.edu/articles/the-three-challenges-of-ai-regulation/

Wirtz BW et al (2022) Governance of artificial intelligence: a risk and guideline-based integrative framework. Gov Inf Q 39(4). https://doi.org/10.1016/j.giq.2022.101685

Zarsky TZ (2017) Incompatible: the GDPR in the age of big data. Seton Hall Law Rev 47(4 (2)):995–1020. https://scholarship.shu.edu/cgi/viewcontent.cgi?article=1606&context=shlr

The AI Act's Research Exemption: A Mechanism for Regulatory Arbitrage?

Liane Colonna

Contents

Abstract This paper argues that by failing to acknowledge the complexity of modern research practices that are shifting from a single discipline to multiple disciplines involving many entities, some public, some private, the proposed AI Act creates mechanisms for regulatory arbitrage. The article begins with a semantic analysis of the concept of research from a legal perspective. It then explains how the proposed AI Act addresses the concept of research by examining the research

---

This work was partially supported by the Wallenberg AI, Autonomous Systems and Software Program—Humanities and Society (WASP-HS) funded by the Marianne and Marcus Wallenberg Foundation and the Marcus and Amalia Wallenberg Foundation. Additionally, I would like to express my gratitude to Associate Professor John Gerard Dinsmore for inspiring me to write this paper and providing helpful comments on the manuscript, or parts thereof, at various stages in its development. I would also like to thank the blind peer reviewers for their extremely helpful feedback. As far as shortcomings are concerned, they are all attributable to the author.

L. Colonna (✉)
Department of Law, Stockholm University, Stockholm, Sweden
e-mail: liane.colonna@juridicum.su.se

E. Gill-Pedro, A. Moberg (eds.), *YSEC Yearbook of Socio-Economic Constitutions 2023*, YSEC Yearbook of Socio-Economic Constitutions (2024) 2023: 51–94,
https://doi.org/10.1007/16495_2023_59, Published online: 28 October 2023

exemption that is set forward in the forthcoming law as it currently exists. After providing an overview of the proposed law, the paper explores the research exemption to highlight whether there are any gaps, ambiguities, or contradictions in the law that may be exploited by either public or private actors seeking to use the exemption as a shield to avoid compliance with duties imposed under the law.

To address whether the research exemption reflects a coherent legal rule, it is considered from five different perspectives. The paper begins by examining the extent to which the research exemption applies to private or commercial entities that may not pursue research in a benevolent manner to solve societal problems, but nevertheless contribute to innovation and economic growth within the EU. Next, the paper explores how the exemption applies to research that takes place within academia but is on the path to commercialization. The paper goes on to consider the situation where academic researchers invoke the exemption and then go on to provide the AI they develop to their employing institutions or other public bodies for no cost. Fourth, the paper inspects how the exemption functions when researchers build high-risk or prohibited AI, publish their findings, or share them via an open-source platform, and other actors copy the AI. Finally, the paper considers how the exemption applies to research that takes place "in the wild" or in regulatory sandboxes.

1 Introduction

The value of scientific research is universally recognized. Not only does it have an internal epistemic value, but it can also be used to address major societal problems as well as contribute to economic growth.[1] While the university often represents "the classic image of a research institution," the reality is that scientific research is conducted by a wide variety of actors, including private entities, ranging from small startups to powerful tech giants, as well as governmental and nonprofit organizations.[2] The role of non-university actors, especially large commercial

[1] Quinn (2021), p. 1.

[2] Id. at p. 22 (explaining, "Whilst the traditional image of research is that of a university research group or university hospital, the reality is that research has always and will always be conducted by a variety of actors. A large range of private entities, varying from small organisations (sic) to large and powerful tech and social media giants are continuously engaged in research. Whilst the motives of such research may often be more commercial in nature, it is nonetheless indispensable for innovation and economic growth."); see also European Data Protection Supervisor (2020), p. 7 ("Research is clearly no longer the preserve of academia, if indeed it ever was. The interface, including the exchange of data, between research organisations and the wider research ecosystem is highly complex. Scientific publishers, designers and developers, entrepreneurs, commercial, governmental and non-profit funding sources in the commercial, governmental and non-profit sectors all have a stake. Also playing a role are big data analytics firms and cloud service providers, and platforms and apps whose business models involve the accumulation and monetisation of as much data as possible.").

entities with significant resources, in the field of Artificial Intelligence (AI) research is likely to increase as these entities have the resources to collect, store and process huge quantities of data on an ongoing basis[3] as well as subsidize and sponsor academic research on a scale that is simply unprecedented.[4] The increasing complexity of AI research where there is often a multiplicity of actors working across various sectors and disciplines, some publicly funded, some privately funded, raises important legal questions about who should benefit from certain research exemptions found in national and European Union laws.

The focus of this paper is on the research exemption in the Proposal for a Regulation laying down harmonized rules on artificial intelligence ("AI Act"). The central argument is that the assumption in the AI Act's exemption that there exists a pure form of research detached from commercial interests is antiquated in today's dynamic research environment where many actors collaborate for different ends in a complex supply chain.[5] It contends that by failing to acknowledge the sophistication and heterogeneousness of modern research practices that are shifting from a single discipline to multiple disciplines involving numerous entities, some operating with public interests and others with private interests, the AI Act may create mechanisms for regulatory arbitrage.

Broadly, the concept of regulatory arbitrage is understood to be an avoidance strategy of regulation that is exercised because of a regulatory inconsistency.[6] It might occur, for example, when regulators lower safeguards and requirements to attract innovators.[7] In the context of the AI Act, it would involve a "perfectly legal" technique used to eschew regulatory compliance under the law by exploiting the research exemption as a facade.[8] Colloquially, it means "complying with the letter but avoiding the spirit of the law."[9]

The article begins with a semantic analysis of the concept of research as it is understood in European Union law to better understand the precise meaning of the term as well as the extent to which the AI Act's conceptualization of "research" aligns with the broader legal framework. It then explains how the AI Act addresses the concept of research by examining the research exemption that is set forward in the forthcoming law as it currently exists, *de lege lata*. After providing an overview of the existing, positive law, the paper explores the research exemption to highlight whether there are any gaps, ambiguities, or contradictions in the law that may be

---

[3] Quinn (2021), p. 24.

[4] European Data Protection Supervisor (2020), p. 6.

[5] Id. at 5 ("The distinction between, on the one hand, genuine research for the common good and, on the other, research which serves primarily private or commercial ends, has become ever more blurred.").

[6] See Willesson (2017); see also Partnoy (1997), p. 227 (defining "Regulatory Arbitrage" as the process of designing transactions or business practices "specifically to reduce costs or capture profit opportunities created by differential regulation or laws."); see generally Fleischer (2010).

[7] European Parliamentary Research Service (2022).

[8] For more see García (2019), p. 203; see also Burk (2016), pp. 15–16; Cohen (2017), p. 184.

[9] Allen (2020), p. 309.

exploited by either public or private actors to avoid compliance under the law in ways that are inconsistent with the research exemption's teleological purpose to foster innovation and knowledge development within the EU single market.

To address whether the research exemption reflects a coherent legal rule, it is considered from five different perspectives, involving various stakeholders and different scenarios. The goal of this methodological approach is to provide a comprehensive view of how the research exemption can be used as a mechanism for regulatory arbitrage by various actors in the AI supply chain. These perspectives also highlight the blurred private-public, profit-nonprofit boundaries in AI research.

The paper begins by examining the extent to which the research exemption applies to private or commercial entities that may not pursue research in a benevolent manner to solve societal problems, but nevertheless contribute to innovation and economic growth within the EU. Next, the paper explores how the exemption applies to research that takes place within academia but is on the path to commercialization. The paper goes on to consider the situation where academic researchers invoke the exemption and then provide the AI they develop to their employing institutions or other public bodies for no cost. Fourth, the paper inspects how the exemption functions when researchers build high-risk or prohibited AI, publish their findings, or share them via an open-source platform, and other actors copy the AI. Finally, the paper considers how the exemption applies to research that takes place "in the wild" or in regulatory sandboxes.

2 The Concept of Academic Research

At the outset, the concept of academic research must be made clear, even if defining what should qualify as genuine science most certainly involves confronting a "foundational epistemic problem."[10] Indeed, there is no universally agreed definition of research or scientific research.[11] Perhaps it is for this reason that the AI Act chooses to avoid setting forward a definition of research, despite its lengthy section on definitions.[12]

As a starting point to unpacking the notion of "research" in EU law, it is useful to consider the common usage of the term. The Oxford dictionary defines research as "a careful study of a subject, especially in order to discover new facts or information about it."[13] This definition implies that research involves an advancement in the state of the art or some creation of knowledge. Another way to conceptualize "research" is

[10] Marelli et al. (2021).

[11] European Data Protection Supervisor (2020).

[12] But c.f. Konečná et al. (2022) (proposing to define "scientific research and development" as "any scientific development, experimentation, analysis, testing or validation carried out under controlled conditions.").

[13] Oxford Advanced Learner's Dictionary, Research (n.d.).

to define it as being "basic" ("blue sky research") or applied research.[14] More controversially, research might further only be considered to be an activity that is subject to peer review, defined as "a process of subjecting an author's scholarly work, research or ideas to the scrutiny of others who are experts in the same field."[15] Google suggests that, in addition to the advancement of the state of the art, research is about the development of new products or services, or perhaps the development of new concepts and technologies that can be applied to existing products or services, therefore showing the close nexus between research activities, innovation and market activities.[16]

There are numerous examples whereby EU primary law refers explicitly to "research," although out the outset it must be specified that the concept of scientific research is "far from being settled or harmonized" at the EU level.[17] For example, the EU's 2019 Copyright Directive[18] explains that "it is important to have a common understanding of research organisations (sic)" which "should for example cover, in addition to universities or other higher education institutions and their libraries, also entities such as research institutes and hospitals that carry out research."[19] Importantly, it distinguishes between organizations that are "not-for-profit" or serve "a public-interest mission" and "commercial undertakings" which "have a decisive influence allowing such undertakings to exercise control because of structural situations, such as through their quality of shareholder or member, which could result in preferential access to the results of the research..."[20] Only the former should be considered research organizations under the law.[21] Similar language is repeated in the recently proposed Data Act.[22]

---

[14] Booth et al. (2016), pp. 51–65.

[15] Kelly et al. (2014), p. 228 citing "What Is Peer Review?" (2014). Int J Comput Appl. Web. Retrieved July 02, 2014, from http://www.ijcaonline.org/peer-review.

[16] Spector et al. (2012).

[17] See Comandè and Schneider (2022), p. 568; Richter (2018), p. 53; Slokenberga (2022), p. 139 (stating, "(the) borders of the scientific research regime – and consequently, possibilities to take advantage of the rules set forth therein – remain undefined.").

[18] Directive (EU) 2019/790.

[19] Id. recital 12.

[20] Id. recital 12, Article 2 (1) (defining "'research organization' as a university, including its libraries, a research institute or any other entity, the primary goal of which is to conduct scientific research or to carry out educational activities involving also the conduct of scientific research: (a) on a not-for-profit basis or by reinvesting all the profits in its scientific research; or (b) pursuant to a public interest mission recognised by a Member State; in such a way that the access to the results generated by such scientific research cannot be enjoyed on a preferential.").

[21] Directive (EU) 2019/790, recital 12; see also Comandè and Schneider (2022), pp. 567–568 (explaining "... contrary to the Recommendation or the Open Data Directive, the Copyright Directive appears to implicitly draw a distinction between not-for-profit and public interest-oriented research entities, on the one hand, and organizations operating for commercial purposes on the other.").

[22] Proposal for a Regulation of the European Parliament and of the Council on Harmonised Rules on Fair Access to and Use of Data (Data Act) COM(2022) 68 final, 23 February 2022 (Data Act), Recital (68), Article 21.

While the General Data Protection Regulation (GDPR) does not set forward a formal definition of scientific research[23], it explains that the term must be interpreted in a comprehensive way.[24] Recital 159 of the GDPR states that "processing of personal data for scientific research purposes should be interpreted in a broad manner including for example technological development and demonstration, fundamental research, applied research and privately funded research."[25] It is further stated that scientific research purposes should include studies conducted in the public interest in the area of public health.[26] The recital makes explicit reference to Article 179(1) of the Treaty on the Functioning of the EU, which encourages "the objective of strengthening its scientific and technological bases by achieving a European research area in which researchers, scientific knowledge and technology circulate freely." However, this guidance is provided in the recitals which are not legally binding, although still relevant where it comes to interpreting the meaning of a given legal rule.[27]

The European Data Protection Supervisor (EDPS), the EU's independent data protection supervisory authority, has provided further guidance on the concept of research in its guidelines on consent.[28] Here, it has followed the previous advice of the ex-Article 29 working party, an independent advisory group established at the EU level with the purpose to provide advice on issues related to the processing of personal data, and stated that the notion of "scientific research" "may not be stretched beyond its common meaning."[29] It further explains that "scientific research" in the context of the GDPR means "a research project set up in accordance with relevant sector-related methodological and ethical standards, in conformity with good practice."[30]

It is important to note that, unlike the Copyright Directive, the definition of "scientific research" in the GDPR does not distinguish between research for private or public purposes which means that the research exemption could theoretically be applicable to commercial research as well. Marelli et al. explain that the GDPR's approach to understanding the concept of research is tied to its ambition to take an omnibus approach to regulation that covers a wide range of processing activities as well as honor EU science policy priorities that seek to construct a European

---

[23] Buttarelli (2018) (stating "While the GDPR does not provide a formal definition, it embraces a wide view of what scientific research is. It covers 'technological development, fundamental research, applied research and privately funded research.'").

[24] GDPR, Recital 159.

[25] Id.

[26] Id.

[27] C-215/88 Casa Fleischhandel ECLI:EU:C:1989:331, para 31 (stating "whilst a recital in the preamble to a regulation may cast light on the interpretation to be given to a legal rule, it cannot in itself constitute such a rule.").

[28] European Data Protection Board (2020), para 153.

[29] Id.

[30] Id.; see also Article 29 Working Party (2020), para 153, p. 130.

knowledge society that integrates public and private resources.[31] They further suggest the GDPR's approach to understanding research is connected to a desire to open up the innovation process to individuals located outside of academia.[32] That said, if private researchers avail themselves to the research exemption found in the GDPR, there may be an obligation to publish the research or make it "available outside of the private entity."[33]

More recently, in its Preliminary Opinion on data protection and scientific research, the EDPS has explained that scientific research "applies the 'scientific method' of observing phenomena, formulating and testing a hypothesis for those phenomena, and concluding as to the validity of the hypothesis."[34] It has further emphasized that "relevant sectorial standards of methodology and ethics apply" when seeking to benefit from the GDPR research regime.[35] Additionally, for the research exemption to apply, it has stated that "the research . . . (must be) carried out with the aim of growing society's collective knowledge and wellbeing, as opposed to serving primarily one or several private interests."[36] Thus, while the EDPS does not preclude commercial purposes from constituting scientific research, the criteria set forward in the opinion suggest a more narrow approach to understanding "research" then for example, the recently proposed "Draft guidance on the research provisions within the UK GDPR and the DPA 2018" by the United Kingdom's Information Commissioner's Office.[37] De Vries explains, "(c)ertain types of research performed by a commercial company like Google Health might very well fall within the EDPS definition of 'scientific research'" but ". . .research that is only commercial and does not follow relevant ethical or medical standards, will fall outside."[38] Essentially, the idea behind the research exemption found in the GDPR is to relax the requirements under the law, at least in situations where the research is subject to high ethical standards, to "streamline and de-bureaucratize research practices" to support innovation.[39]

The European Commission has explained that the objectives of the EU's research and innovation policies are "opening up the innovation process to people with

---

[31] Marelli et al. (2021).

[32] Id.

[33] GDPR, Recital 159 (referring to Article 179(1) of the Treaty on the Functioning of the EU); Schneider (2019), p. 268.

[34] European Data Protection Supervisor (2020), p. 10.

[35] Id. at 12.

[36] Id.

[37] The UK Information Commissioner (2018), p. 11 (explaining, "The purpose of scientific or historical research is to produce new knowledge or to apply existing knowledge in novel ways, often with the aim of benefiting the public interest. Scientific or historical research aims to: advance the state of the art in a given field or provide innovative solutions to human problems; generate new understandings or insights that add to the sum of human knowledge in a particular area; or produce findings of general application that can be tested and replicated.").

[38] de Vries (2022), p. 122.

[39] Marelli et al. (2021).

experience in fields other than academia and science," "spreading knowledge as soon as it is available using digital and collaborative technology" and "promoting international cooperation in the research community."[40] In fact, the concept of research is at the center of the European Commission's Strategy for data which aims to create and consolidate a single market for data.[41] The nonbinding "Recommendation on access to and preservation of scientific research" emphasizes how public data can help drive innovation and envisages the re-use of public research data by commercial actors.[42] The Open Data Directive[43] also emphasizes the reuse of research data[44] by commercial actors.[45] The Data Governance Act further explains the how "pools of data" should be "made available on the basis of data altruism that have a sufficient size in order to enable data analytics and machine learning…"[46] The proposed Data Act[47] and the European Health Data Space Regulation[48] are also focused on data-driven innovation and making data more accessible for all.[49] Comandè and Schneider explain that a new principle of free movement of research data is emerging under EU policy which includes, among other categories, the use of public data employed for commercial-related research purposes.[50]

At the national level, Sweden, for example, defines research as "(s)cientifically experimental or theoretical work intended to result in new knowledge and development outcomes on a scientific basis, excluding work that is performed within the framework of higher education on the basic or advanced level" in the Act concerning Ethical Review of Research Involving Humans.[51] In understanding the concept of

---

[40] European Commission (2016); see also European Commission (2020).

[41] European Commission (2020).

[42] Commission Recommendation (EU) 2018/790.

[43] Directive (EU) 2019/1024, Recital 27.

[44] Id., Article 2(9) (stating that "research data" means "documents in a digital form, other than scientific publications, which are collected or produced in the course of scientific research activities and are used as evidence in the research process, or are commonly accepted in the research community as necessary to validate research findings and results.").

[45] Id., Article 2(11) (stating that "re-use" means "the use by persons or legal entities of documents held by: (a) public sector bodies, for commercial or non-commercial purposes other than the initial purpose within the public task for which the documents were produced, except for the exchange of documents between public sector bodies purely in pursuit of their public tasks.").

[46] Proposed Data Governance Act, recital 35.

[47] Proposed Data Act.

[48] Proposed Regulation on the European Health Data Space.

[49] European Commission (2022).

[50] Comandè and Schneider (2022), p. 567 (further distinguishes different categories of data "1) public data employed for public interest-related research purposes, 2) public data employed for commercial-related research purposes, 3) private data employed for public-interest related research purposes, and ultimately, 4) private data employed for commercial-related research and innovation purposes.").

[51] The Swedish Ethical Review Act, para 2 ("forskning: vetenskapligt experimentellt eller teoretiskt arbete eller vetenskapliga studier genom observation, om arbetet eller studierna görs för att hämta in ny kunskap, och utvecklingsarbete på vetenskaplig grund, dock inte sådant arbete eller sådana

research in the Swedish context, there is an emphasis on the existence of a methodologically sound scientific approach.[52] The Swedish Academy of Sciences points out that common characteristics of research are the existence of a scientific question, systematic working method, transparent methodology, intention to publish in a scientific journal and funding with research grants.[53]

Contemporary philosophers have also set forward definitions of research. For example, Floridi et al. have proposed the notion of "*bona fide* research," whereby "research qualifies as *bona fide* whenever its ultimate goal is to discover new knowledge intended for the general interest in health and to be made publicly accessible (e.g., published in scientific journals or disseminated through digital media) without undue delay."[54] *Bona fide* research should only be carried out by "*bona fide* research organizations," which are defined as "any organization appointed or accredited or funded to undertake bona fide research, and/or which has made public its commitment to adhere to recognized research governance principles."[55] Marelli et al. consider Floridi's approach as valuable insofar as it focuses "on what research organizations do instead of what they are" and "avoids simplistic dichotomies and binary framings (such as public vs private) that . . . do not largely stand the test of contemporary research practices."[56] They also highlight that this understanding of research is better since it is focused on the "governance context of research" rather than "ill-suited considerations on sectoral epistemic standards."[57]

Ultimately, there appear to be several critical factors to decipher whether a certain work will constitute research in the context of EU law. These factors include, first, whether the research is being conducted by a not-for-profit or commercial entity. Relatedly, another critical factor concerns the source of funding and more specifically, whether the funding comes from public sources or private sources. The third factor concerns whether the research is subject to recognized ethical standards for scientific research, ensuring that research activities adhere to appropriate methodological approaches. If there is an ethical assessment, it may also be relevant to understand who conducts the ethical oversight such as an independent ethical review authority or some "in house" corporate Research and Development authority.

studier som utförs endast inom ramen för högskoleutbildning på grundnivå eller på avancerad nivå.").

[52]See, e.g., Regeringens proposition 2018/19:165 (n.d.), p. 9 ("Att forska på människor utan etikprövningstillstånd eller i strid med ett sådant tillstånd kan innefatta forskningsmetoder som medför risk för att en forskningsperson kommer till skada eller att någons personliga integritet kränks.").

[53]Regeringens proposition 2018/19:165 (n.d.), p. 34 ("Kungl. Vetenskapsakademien påpekar att vanliga kännetecken på forskning är förekomsten av vetenskaplig frågeställning, systematiskt arbetssätt, transparent metodik, avsikt att publiceras i vetenskaplig tidskrift och finansiering med forskningsanslag.").

[54]Floridi et al. (2019), p. 361.

[55]Id.

[56]Marelli et al. (2021).

[57]Id.

Another critical factor to consider is whether the research is in the public interest rather than serving primarily one or several private interests. Finally, it is important to understand whether the research results are made publicly available to spread knowledge and support innovation.

It is clear research that research that serves the public interest and is conducted by public actors who openly publish their findings and subject their work to ethical review by independent authorities has the highest level of protection in the law. However, other forms of research are granted a special legal protection, such as purely commercial research that follows relevant ethical standards, at least under the GDPR. As noted above, the EU legal framework is not yet harmonized[58] and, the AI Act only adds further complexity to what is an already convoluted legislative environment.

3 The AI Act and the Research Exemption

The AI Act is a proposed regulation based on Article 114 of the Treaty on the Functioning of the European Union (TFEU), which concerns the approximation of laws to improve the functioning of the internal market.[59] A central purpose of the AI Act, as explained in the explanatory memorandum of the Commission's proposal, is to "to ensure the proper functioning of the single market by creating the conditions for the development and use of trustworthy AI systems in the Union."[60] The European Parliamentary Research Service has also reiterated that, "The general objective of the proposed AI act is to ensure the proper functioning of the single market by creating the conditions for the development and use of trustworthy AI systems in the Union."[61] Considering the legal basis of the proposal alone and its focus on ensuring the well-functioning of the internal market, it is logical that academic research is excluded from the scope of the proposed Regulation, at least insofar as the research is conducted in a non-commercial capacity.[62]

In the Commission's original proposal, Article 2(1)(a) states that the proposed Regulation applies to "providers placing on the market or putting into service AI systems in the Union, irrespective of whether those providers are established within

[58] Comandè and Schneider (2022), p. 568; Richter (2018), p. 53.

[59] TFEU, Article 16(1).

[60] Commission proposal AI Act, explanatory memo section 2.1; see also, Commission proposal AI Act, explanatory memo section 1.1 (explaining that the Commission has four goals, namely to "ensure that AI systems placed on the Union market and used are safe and respect existing law on fundamental rights and Union values; ensure legal certainty to facilitate investment and innovation in AI; enhance governance and effective enforcement of existing law on fundamental rights and safety requirements applicable to AI systems; facilitate the development of a single market for lawful, safe and trustworthy AI applications and prevent market fragmentation.").

[61] European Parliamentary Research Service (2023), p. 3.

[62] Smuha et al. (2021), pp. 15–16.

the Union or in a third country."[63] Essentially, under the Commission's approach, research only falls within the scope of the law if the researcher qualifies as a provider. The concept of "provider" is defined in Article 3(2) as "a natural or legal person, public authority, agency or other body that develops an AI system or that has an AI system developed with a view to placing it on the market or putting it into service under its own name or trademark, whether for payment or free of charge."[64] The concept of "placing on the market" is defined as "the first making available of an AI system on the Union market"[65] and the concept of "putting into service" is defined as "the supply of an AI system for first use directly to the user or for own use on the Union market for its intended purpose."[66] The Commission's proposal further defines the concept of "making available on the market."[67] This language is modeled off product regulation like the Medical Device Regulation which also refers to "placing on the market," "making available on the market," or "putting into service" medical devices for human use and accessories for such devices in the EU.[68]

Very basically, under the aforementioned definitions, a provider can be understood to be "the last entity to develop or integrate an AI system into a product or software before it is either sold or used."[69] If the provider sells the AI system then "a user is any purchasing entity that then uses the software or product for any non-personal use."[70] While the Commission's proposal also mentions additional entities such as importers and distributors, they are secondary to the importance of providers and users.[71]

It is further important to mention that in the Commission's proposal, Recital 16 sets forth an exception to the prohibition on AI systems which deploy subliminal techniques. It explains that "research for legitimate purposes" in this area may still occur if "such research does not amount to use of the AI system in human-machine relations that exposes natural persons to harm and such research is carried out in accordance with recognized ethical standards for scientific research."[72] The inclusion of Recital 16 confuses the relationship between research and the law, raising a question of whether research is completely exempted from the requirements of the proposal, or whether the requirements somehow apply but can be regarded as not

[63] Commission proposal AI Act, Article 2(1)(a).

[64] Id at Article 3(2).

[65] Id at 3(9), see further article 3(10).

[66] Id at 3(11).

[67] Commission proposal AI Act, 3(10) (defining the concept of "making available on the market" as "any supply of an AI system for distribution or use on the Union market in the course of a commercial activity, whether in return for payment or free of charge.").

[68] Regulation (EU) 2017/745 on medical devices, Article 1 (the MDR also applies "to clinical investigations concerning such medical devices and accessories conducted in the Union.").

[69] Engler and Renda (2022), p. 4.

[70] Id.

[71] Id.; Commission proposal AI Act, Article 3(5)–(8).

[72] Smuha et al. (2021), p. 16.

applicable under certain circumstances such as where rigorous ethical vetting takes place.

In an early draft of the Council's Compromise Text, it defined which areas should fall outside the parameters of the Act and, unlike the Commission's proposal, it explicitly excluded AI systems used solely for the purpose of scientific research within the main body of the legislative text.[73] In this Council text, Article 2(6) and (7) highlighted the special status of AI research and development. Article 2(6) made plain that research must be the "sole purpose" of any activity included within the scope of the exemption.[74] Article 2(7) added that any activity that leads to or entails placing an AI system on the market or putting it into service would not fall within the scope of the research exemption.[75] Additionally, Recital 12(a) in this draft further explained that the AI Act should not apply to AI systems, which are used "for the sole purpose of scientific research and development" to ensure that the Act "does not otherwise affect scientific research and development activity on AI systems."[76] This Council text also introduced the requirement into recital 12(a) that "any research and development activity should be carried out in accordance with recognized ethical standards for scientific research."[77]

In subsequent drafts of the Council's Compromise Text, language was added to recital 12(b) to include that any research and development activity should be carried out in accordance with not just ethical standards but also "professional standards for scientific research."[78] It is also noteworthy that the mention of "scientific research" found in Recital 16 of Commission's draft was dropped from the Council Compromise Texts. The removal of this language eliminated the confusion about whether there were limitations for research or a complete exemption.

In the Council's General Approach (its final internal position), the Czech Presidency has retained much of same language as that described above.[79] However, in recital 12(b), it explicitly refers to "product-oriented research" conducted by providers and explains that this type of activity should fall within the scope of the exemption. Recital 12(b) also states that the rules regarding the research exemption are "without prejudice... to the application of provisions on regulatory sandboxes and testing in real world conditions." Furthermore, in Article 3(2) where the definition of a provider is included, the phrase "with a view" to placing AI on the market or putting it into service is removed, possibly to provide greater legal

[73] 29 November 2021 Council Compromise text, Article 2(6), Article 2(7).

[74] 29 November 2021 Council Compromise text, Article 2(6) reads: "This Regulation shall not apply to AI systems, including their output, specifically developed and put into service for the sole purpose of scientific research and development."

[75] 29 November 2021 Council Compromise text, Article 2(7) reads: "This Regulation shall not affect any research and development activity regarding AI systems in so far as such activity does not lead to or entail placing an AI system on the market or putting it into service."

[76] 29 November 2021 Council Compromise text, recital 12(a).

[77] 29 November 2021 Council Compromise text, recital 12(a).

[78] Fourth Presidency compromise text, recital 12(b).

[79] Council General Approach.

certainty for researchers.[80] That is, by removing the language "with a view" it is clearer that even if a researcher has some hypothetical ambition or hope of putting AI into service, they could nevertheless still utilize the exemption.[81]

In the Parliament's General Approach, its definition of "provider" is completely aligned with the Commission's definition. In other words, it is in support of the language "with a view" proposed by the Commission, making its definition broader than the Council's General Approach. The Parliament also utilizes the word "deployer" instead of "user," although it does not suggest any other changes to Article 3(4).

In Article 2(5)(d) of the Parliament's General Approach, it provides for a research exemption, explaining that the AI Act "shall not apply to research, testing and development activities regarding an AI system prior to this system being placed on the market or put into service, provided that these activities are conducted respecting fundamental rights and the applicable Union law."[82] Article 2(5d) states that the Commission is empowered to adopt delegated acts to specify the research exemption with the specific aim of preventing its abuse. It also explains that the AI Office can provide guidance on the governance of research.

Unlike the Council, there is no explicit reference to ethical review provided for in the research exemption set forward in the Parliament's General Approach. That said, a requirement for ethical review may be encompassed by the requirement to respect fundamental rights and applicable Union law.[83] Recital 16 retains the Commission's reference to ethical reviews in the context of research on AI-based subliminal techniques.

Importantly, Article 2(5)(d) states that the research exemption does not cover "testing in real world conditions" which significantly limits its scope. It defines "testing in real world conditions" to mean "the temporary testing of an AI system for its intended purpose in real world conditions outside of a laboratory or otherwise simulated environment." This issue will be discussed in greater detail below.

Finally, Article 54(a) sets forth a separate article on the promotion of AI research and development in support of socially and environmentally beneficial outcomes. Such research and development include but are not limited to "development of AI-based solutions to increase accessibility for persons with disabilities, tackle

---

[80] Council General Approach, Article 3 (2) ("provider" means a natural or legal person, public authority, agency or other body that develops an AI system or that has an AI system developed and places that system on the market or puts it into service under its own name or trademark, whether for payment or free of charge).

[81] See Smuha et al. (2021), p. 21 (stating, "While an academic researcher may not be a 'provider' who places an AI system on the market in the course of a commercial activity (Article 3(10)), they might be accurately described as "a natural person" who "develops an AI system with a view to" supplying it "for first use directly to the user or for own use" "free of charge." The text of the Proposal seems to suggest that in such a case, the proposed Regulation would apply to academic researchers.").

[82] Parliament General Approach, Article 2(5)(d); see also Recital 2(f).

[83] Id.

socioeconomic inequalities, and meet sustainability and environmental targets." Support could be provided by, for example, giving priority access to regulatory sandboxes to certain projects, and earmarking public funding for AI research and development in support of socially and environmentally beneficial outcomes. Recital 72(b) emphasizes that such projects "should be based on the principle of interdisciplinary cooperation between AI developers, experts on inequality and non-discrimination, accessibility, consumer, environmental, and digital rights, as well as academics."

4 Research Conducted for Commercial or Financial Reasons

This section will explore the research exemption from the perspective of private entities that conduct research for commercial or financial reasons. As already highlighted at the outset of this article, the role of private entities in the context of research is expanding because of their ability to collect, process and store huge amounts of data in a manner and on a scale that is generally unimaginable to university research groups.[84] It is further important to note how the commercial sector is able to hire swarms of expert researchers, competing directly with universities,[85] which means that they have not just the technical capacity to collect and process data but also the human talent to, for example, run experiments on large databases of variously aggregated information.[86] This ability, for example, makes it possible for these private firms to be in a position to build resource intensive General Purpose AI (GPAI) which is becoming foundational to AI research and development of AI throughout the supply chain. Additionally, private companies are increasingly partnering with public institutions which further obfuscates the scope of the research exemption. Referring to algorithmically driven health research, Becker et al. highlight the sophisticated and heterogeneous nature of modern research which is "... characterized by a deep interconnection between traditional research centres (sic) and large high-tech corporations."[87]

An initial issue concerns the extent to which private or commercial actors can rely on the exemption where there has not been any ethical assessment conducted by an independent review board. In the Commission's draft of the AI Act, the only mention of an explicit requirement for ethical review of scientific research occurs in Recital 16 which explains that one of the conditions to research about AI systems that are intended to distort human behavior is that the research should be carried out

[84] Quinn (2021), p. 24.
[85] European Data Protection Supervisor (2020), p. 7.
[86] Schneider (2019), p. 256.
[87] Id. at 270.

in accordance with recognized ethical standards for scientific research.[88] Since Recital 16 only addresses AI systems intended to distort human behavior, there is a question about whether other types of high-risk or prohibited AI would fall within its scope. The language of Recital 16 was removed in the EU Council's first compromise text on the AI Act draft and an explicit requirement that research and development activities should be carried out in accordance with recognized ethical standards for scientific research was added to Recital 12(a).[89] As noted above, further Council drafts have also referred to adhering to "professional standards for scientific research."[90]

While the Parliament's General Approach includes a research exemption, it does not contain an explicit requirement for independent ethical review. However, it states in both Recital 2(f) and Article 2(5)(d) that any activity falling under the research exemption should be conducted respecting fundamental rights and the applicable Union law. This development is interesting since not all member states may require ethical approval under national law.[91] Recital 16 is the only provision to explicitly refer to ethical review in the Parliament's General Approach, requiring one in the context of research on AI-based subliminal techniques.

Taking a critical perspective, it is unclear whether the reasoning for including ethical assessment as a condition to claim the research exemption should apply in the context of AI, or if some alternative approach is more suitable. Here, it can be questioned whether ethical oversight provides "sufficient bite" to govern data-intensive research, especially where there is a lack of well-established guidelines and regulatory tools to help guide ethical oversight committees.[92] Marelli and Van Hoyweghen have expressed doubts about whether research ethics committees are capable of confronting "the lack of well-established guidelines and regulatory tools for providing adequate ethics assessment for non-traditional types of data-intensive research (e.g., AI, social companion robots)."[93] They also make the important point that these bodies have been "traditionally appointed with the aim to review clinical research on human subjects" and may be "devoid of the epistemic as well as ethical expertise required to master recently established research fields and deal with the ethical quandaries raised by new data-intensive technologies and research practices."[94] Ultimately, they worry whether reliance on these types of bodies might

[88] Commission proposal AI Act, Recital 16.

[89] 29 November 2021 Council Compromise text, recital 12(a).

[90] See Council General Approach, recital 12(a).

[91] Slokenberga (2022), p. 140 (explaining, "While ethical approval has long been an essential feature in biomedical research, not necessarily all countries have adopted that as a requirement for purely data-driven research" and comparing approaches in Sweden and Latvia).

[92] Marelli et al. (2021); see also Brightman et al. (2019); see also European Commission (2021a), p. 13 (stating, "Authorities do not have the powers, procedural frameworks and resources to ensure and monitor AI development and use complies with applicable rules.").

[93] Marelli et al. (2021).

[94] Id.

paradoxically lead to lower standards of ethical oversight in research.[95] The issue of the "integrity, impartiality and credibility" of AI research, especially research conducted by large technology companies demands further attention, especially given the challenges with ethical assessments in the AI context.[96]

Related to the issue of the adequacy of ethical oversight, it is unclear whether public and private ethical review standards are comparable, and what this means for the applicability of the research exemption. Quinn explains how ". . . private entities are unlikely to have as rigorous procedures of ethical review as public research entities" and how ethical review committees are unlikely to have as "as strong an institutional underpinning" as exist within public institutions.[97] He is also concerned that, even where strong ethical review requirements exists, they may not be as transparent as they are in their public sector counterparts like universities where "ethics committees have an extremely powerful role in deciding whether research can go ahead."[98] The lack of a level playing field where it concerns ethical review may create a situation where private entities can more easily avail themselves to the research exemption, and therefore create a mechanism for regulatory arbitrage.

Another issue that arises when research is conducted for commercial purposes concerns the relationship between commercial secrecy, open science requirements and the research exemption. Private companies often demand that their employees sign non-disclosure agreements and protect their research results under a cloak of commercial secrecy.[99] Arguably, it is inequitable for these entities to invoke the research exemption in situations where their research results will not be made publicly available, especially if one considers the EU's push towards an open science model and the increasing demands placed on public researchers financed by taxpayers to share their research data and disseminate knowledge quickly in an effort to foster scientific progress, meet humanitarian goals, and maximize the impact of their work.[100] Questions about unfair competition and regulatory arbitrage arise where both private and public researchers can invoke the research exemption but the demands of open science are only placed on public researchers. At the very least, it creates confusion about whether the EU's broader policy goal is to promote commercialization of research through, e.g., licensing and patenting or whether it is to promote open science.[101]

The growing role of private actors in the research environment raises a wider issue about how the research exemption should function in cases where an entity may not pursue research in support of socially and environmentally beneficial

[95] Id.

[96] European Data Protection Supervisor (2020), p. 7.

[97] Quinn (2021), p. 30.

[98] Id.

[99] European Data Protection Supervisor (2020), p. 38.

[100] Caulfield et al. (2012), p. 1.

[101] Id.

outcomes, but nevertheless contributes to innovation and economic growth.[102] There is a related question about whether the exemption should apply to research that serves *both* commercial and public interests. For example, Facebook has funded biomedical research that, on the one hand, may be very beneficial for people with communication disabilities, thus serving the public good.[103] At the same time, this research also serves Facebook's self-proclaimed financial goal to develop a commercial non-invasive brain-computer interface that allows customers to type via brain activity.[104]

If a central purpose of the exemption is to promote and protect innovation and knowledge development within the EU's single market then there is at least some support, based on the teleological purpose of the exemption, for the idea that the actual motivation of an entity for invoking the exemption is irrelevant so long as innovation is promoted in one form or another. On this point, it is worth highlighting again that the EU Parliament has explicitly called for the promotion of AI research and development in support of socially and environmentally beneficial outcomes.[105] On the other hand, companies like Google and IBM have made major headlines and sparked controversy for their partnerships with public institutions in realms like AI-based health research. For example, the cases of Google DeepMind and the English National Health System as well as IBM Watson Health Centre and the Italian government highlight the challenges associated when data-intensive research activities are carried out by major technology companies.[106] The concern is that powerful companies will use available research exemptions and their collaboration with public institutions to exclude their work and activities from regulatory oversight. In other words, they may use the exemption as a mechanism to circumvent AI Act requirements by structuring work as research and development.[107]

Based on a plain reading of the various proposals of the AI Act, it appears that the critical factor concerning the applicability of the research exemption is whether research is the "sole purpose" of the activity being claimed under the exemption. To put it differently, the research exemption will likely not apply to any activity that leads to or entails placing an AI system on the market or puts AI into service, unless possibly if it takes place in a sandbox, an issue discussed more below. Article 2 of the Council and Parliament's General Approaches to the AI Act implies that research

[102] Quinn (2021), p. 21.

[103] Ienca and Malgieri (2022), p. 13.

[104] Id.

[105] Parliament General Approach Recital 72(b) and Article 54(a).

[106] For an excellent and complete discussion of these cases in relation to the research exemption in the GDPR, see Schneider (2019), pp. 261–266.

[107] See Bogucki (2022), p. 28 (stating, "There is a need to ensure that the AI Act does not undermine R&D around AI systems. This regulation should apply only when scientific projects are expected to lead to or entail placing an AI system on the market. AI systems developed for the sole purpose of scientific research should not be constrained by the same regulatory framework. Yet, the exemption needs to be drafted so as to prevent it being used a means to circumvent AI Act requirements by structuring work as R&D.").

within the scope of the exemption should be performed for a purpose that benefits society and serves the public good as opposed to being performed in the economic interest of the party performing the research. However, the language in Article 2 leaves room for purely for-profit activities to fall within the exemption so long as they are, for example, at the proof-of-concept stage or the prototype phase. Recital 12b of the Council's General Approach also explicitly refers to "product-oriented research" which is a vague term but one that implies some kind of market or user analysis for a particular product, rendering the line between research and commercial activities even more complicated to discern.[108] Ultimately, as will be emphasized throughout this article, the complexity of modern AI research makes distinguishing between what AI systems are developed for the "sole purpose of scientific research and development" a difficult task, if at all possible.[109]

5 Academic Research on the Path to Commercialization

Article 2 of the Council's General Approach as well as the Parliament's General Approach suggest that AI systems that are developed purely for research purposes and which are wholly disconnected from commercialization will fall within the scope of the exemption. de Vries states that the "...the AI Act only excludes AI systems that are completely disconnected from practice, whose sole purpose is research and development."[110] However, it can be difficult to define research clearly and succinctly as a purely nonprofit activity, or from something that can be totally separated from commercialization. Although universities often carry out research to, for example, advance scientific understanding or to address societal concerns, it is erroneous to assume that universities do not seek any financial return on their research, even if it is understood that the return may not be immediate.[111] While universities do not typically "hold" CE mark certification or place products on the market,[112] the reality is that commercialization is often a means to drive scientific advances forward.[113] Indeed, universities have moved from "knowledge producers" and "knowledge transmitters" towards engines for economic growth and development.[114]

[108] The United Nations Environment Programme (1989) (explaining "Product-oriented research is the exercise of evaluating the nature of the market for a particular product, the relative merits of different marketing strategies for that product and so forth.").

[109] Kazim et al. (2022), p. 386 (stating, "...the determination of which AI systems are for the "sole purpose of scientific research and development" is not an easy task.").

[110] de Vries (2022), p. 121.

[111] Quinn (2021), p. 22.

[112] Shrourou (2020).

[113] Slokenberga (2021), p. 21.

[114] Caulfield et al. (2012), p. 2.

This section will continue to explore whether AI systems are ever developed for "the sole purpose of research and development" within the meaning of the proposal and how the ambiguity of this language may create legal loopholes that can be exploited by various actors. Particularly, it will examine the situation where research is on the pathway to commercial exploitation from the perspective of the research exemption set forth in the AI Act. It questions whether a more holistic approach to understanding the concept of research in general, and the research exemption specifically, is required to recognize the social and political forces that pressure publicly funded researchers to commercialize their work.[115]

It is unclear how the research exemption should apply to researchers who are not *per se* "putting AI onto the market" but are developing it with the possibility that it may be placed onto the market eventually. For example, in many research projects there is close collaboration with one or more industrial partners who perhaps would like to commercialize the research once the exploratory research is completed and a profit-oriented purpose is defined. Here, there is a question concerning the exact point (either theoretically or temporally) that the research exemption stops to apply, particularly in situations where academic research is entangled with commercial exploitation.

Imagine the situation where a major European university is developing an AI-based technology to improve and advance home-based self-management and integrated care for older adults with multimorbidity. Using computer vision techniques, the technology can assist in formulating certain diagnoses and recommending certain treatment options. As such, the technology will likely be subject to regulation under the Medical Device Regulation but also under the AI Act as a high-risk AI.

While the research occurring within this project is likely covered by the research exemption found in the AI Act since there is no ambition to commercialize the research by the university itself and the research is just in the exploratory phase, it nevertheless remains a question about whether there is a need to meet legal requirements in the early life cycle of the system, while, for example, the AI-based service is still squarely being researched and developed in the academic context. While a detailed discussion of these provisions is outside the scope of this article, the AI Act sets forth strict rules for high-risk AI that include, among others, risk management (Article 9), data governance (Article 10), technical documentation (Article 11 and annex IV), record keeping (Articles 12 and 15), transparency and information (Article 13), and human oversight (Article 14). Additionally, there are rigorous demands set forth in laws like the Medical Device Regulation for, among other things, the handling of clinical data. Without preparing to meet these requirements early in the technology's lifecycle, it may be very difficult for the commercial entity that ultimately seeks to obtain the CE mark because it will not have all the information it needs, at least not quickly or easily. In other words, in addition to the rigorous demands set forth in laws like the Medical Device Regulation, there are

[115] Id.

additional and quite burdensome requirements in the AI Act that may slow the system's path to commercialization.

It may be sufficient for the researcher to conduct clinical studies in accordance with academic ethical requirements. However, the moment that the researcher attempts to commercialize the technology it will likely be required to go through a lengthy, heavily regulated clinical trial under the MDR, depending on which risk class it is assigned. With a limited number of certification bodies in the EU, the process can take years. There may be further delays because of the added complexities of the AI Act, especially given that there may be a limited number of notified bodies as well as different risk classifications, risk management requirements and safety requirements under each of the respective laws.[116] Here, the point is that the complexity of the legal environment may hinder the exploitation of the results of academic research and the transfer of knowledge to a commercial context, which is a distinct advantage of advanced economies.[117] It may also create confusion about who bears responsibility for compliance with legal and regulatory requirements as well as attendant opportunities to exploit the legal rules.

The critical point whereby researchers may lose their privileged position is when they try to commercialize the project by placing it into the market or putting it into use. However, the point at which a researcher seeks to commercialize their results can be hard to determine, especially when the researcher works closely with commercial partners in a project or has other links to the market. It is easy to imagine the situation whereby a project coordinator heading up a large research consortium involving a mix of public and commercial entities finds themselves in an unfortunate situation where the law applies to them, but they lack an awareness of this reality.

If a researcher makes a strategic exit and allows the research to be commercialized through, for example, establishing a "spin out" company or entering into a licensing agreement with a private entity they should be in theory "off the hook" for meeting legal requirements under laws like the AI Act.[118] The problem with this logic is that it will drastically slow down innovation pathways if early-stage researchers ignore the legal requirements found in laws like the AI Act because when the commercial entity that wants to exploit the research results attempts to apply for a CE mark, it will be difficult to collect all of the relevant information from scratch, or it might take a significant amount of time to do so. Here, it is unclear as to what extent the exemption serves the goal of fostering innovation within the EU, especially when failure to begin compliance efforts early in the AI's lifetime may ultimately delay its entry into the market to a significant extent, reducing the competitive advantage of the AI provider. Paradoxically, it may be the case that the research exemption impairs innovation within the EU, unless new ways are developed to address the legal challenges.

---

[116] Ake-Kob et al. (2022), p. 9.

[117] Abramo et al. (2021), p. 2 (stating, "The ability of industry to exploit the results of academic research is a distinctive competence of advanced economies.").

[118] Shrourou (2020).

There are several responses to the dilemma. First, universities could support academic researchers to develop quality management systems, even if the requirements will be resource demanding. As Shrourou explains, there is a "…pressing need for a change in research culture and practice that addresses the need for appropriate technical documentation in the early life cycle of medical devices."[119] At the very least, universities should support academic researchers to make their AI systems more translational by improving knowledge of regulatory requirements and presenting project coordinators "with both pragmatic and the least onerous solutions to satisfy regulatory compliance in early-stage device projects and facilitate commercialisation."[120] Letourneur et al. make the point that universities should support academic researchers to transfer their innovative ideas into "industry-produced marketable products" but the increasing complexity of the legal framework is likely to limit technology transfers unless resources are devoted to overcoming the challenges.[121]

Second, academics could partner with industry to meet legal requirements and overcome regulatory hurdles. Letourneur et al. explain, "The barriers and threats to successful translation in academia can be overcome by strong clinical partnerships, close-industrial collaborations, and entrepreneurial programs, enabling continued product development to overcome regulatory hurdles…"[122] However, as discussed above, if the partnership is too close, it may be the case the research exemption will not apply in the first place, perhaps unbeknownst to the project coordinator in charge of the research. Worse, it could be used as a mechanism for regulatory arbitrage by commercial firms who structure their project with academic partners to avoid compliance obligations.

Third, policymakers can define the concept of academic research in such a way that makes explicit reference to trial design and funding.[123] For example, in Ireland, the Commercialization Fund is available to support both proof of concept and ready to develop technology.[124] Researchers can access two separate levels of sequential funding.[125] First, commercialization feasibility funding is available which is intended to help researchers validate the potential market opportunity before development.[126] Second, commercialization funding is available which is intended to de-risk the technology through development for real world application.[127] Here,

---

[119] Id.

[120] Id.

[121] Letourneur et al. (2020), p. 1.

[122] Id. at abstract.

[123] This idea came from Associate Professor John Dismore at Trinity College Dublin during our discussions on this paper.

[124] Enterprise Ireland (n.d.).

[125] Id.

[126] Id.

[127] Id.

funding could be provided to meet legal requirements in anticipation of regulatory approvals.

Ostensibly, one of the central purposes of the research exemption is to support innovation. Academic research on topics like AI-based medical devices is key not only to provide patient-focused medical devices but also to develop "the next generation of industry-relevant, publicly engaged researchers to become an anchor for applicable industry research."[128] Even if a researcher wants to make a clean exit and avoid meeting early stage compliance obligations, it may hard for the researcher to understand the exact point at which they will be perceived as someone who puts AI into service, especially if they work closely with commercial partners. At the same time, if a researcher can exit before their work is commercialized and can avoid legal responsibility, this may delay an AI-based technologies "CE-readiness" and ultimately, hamper innovation in the EU.[129]

6 Researchers Provide AI to Their Employing Institutions or Other Public Bodies

It is easy to imagine that many universities have talented researchers available with the skills and knowledge about AI to promote in-house development of certain needed systems. This raises an interesting legal question about what happens when academics build AI-based technology that is to be used by the university where they are employed. More broadly, there is also a question about what happens when publicly funded researchers provide AI to other public bodies free of cost. Set forth below is an example of the legal challenges provided concerning the development of an AI-based Educational Technology (Ed Tech).

Imagine that there is a researcher, relying on a grant for internal research, which embarks on a project to utilize the massive amounts of data collected from a learning platform like Moodle with AI. More specifically, this researcher seeks to develop an AI-based tool that can help predict when students are likely to drop out of a given course so that early intervention can be provided to any struggling students.[130] The basis for the application is a learner model or profile that allows for predictions.[131] After applying for the relevant ethical approvals, the researcher successfully develops a protype. Subsequently, the university where the researcher works is

---

[128]Letourneur et al. (2020), p. 2.

[129]Shrourou (2020).

[130]Zawacki-Richter et al. (2019), p. 11 (explaining "The basis for many AI applications are learner models or profiles that allow prediction, for example of the likelihood of a student dropping out of a course or being admitted to a programme, in order to offer timely support or to provide feedback and guidance in content related matters throughout the learning process. Classification, modelling and prediction are an essential part of educational data mining.").

[131]Id.

interested in fueling it with new data and applying the AI system in a broader context, namely in a course with several hundred students where drop-out rates are high. The university is also interested in adapting the model to make decisions about what students are admitted to the university in the first place.

The law is unclear concerning the applicability of the research exemption in situations where a university develops its own high-risk software in house which can, for example, be used to assess students, and maybe even be used to determine whether they are admitted to the university in the first place. While it is unlikely that the university is entirely exempted by way of the research exemption set forth in the AI Act, it is confusing to squarely locate a responsible provider. In many situations it can be difficult to distinguish between pure research subject to the exemption, on the one hand, and the organization of managerial activities, including the provision of public services like education, on the other hand.[132] This is especially true because implicit in the idea of "pure research" is that it serves the common good or has beneficial public purposes which overlaps with the mission of many public administrations who exist to serve the inhabitants of a given community and to support their welfare by providing services "effectively and efficiently."[133]

An initial question is who exactly is entitled to claim the research exemption: is it the university or the researcher or both? On one hand, it seems obvious that the researcher must be the party to invoke the exemption since, of course, they are the party to conduct the work. Yet, the university is responsible for the researcher by way of the employment relationship and through the concept of vicarious liability. In other words, the concept of "researcher" under the AI Act includes not just the university but also natural persons within the university such as instructors, even if it is hard to distinguish the different roles and levels of accountability that exist in an institutional context.[134] Ostensibly, if the university is the party that claims the research exemption, then it may be able to use the exemption as a mechanism for regulatory arbitrage. That is, it might be able to claim the exemption to avoid compliance obligations under the AI Act when developing AI inhouse, for example, to develop certain educational technologies.

The compliance obligations under the AI Act are triggered when either the researcher or the university puts the high-risk AI system into service, albeit free of charge. In this case the university will likely constitute both a provider and a user under the AI Act. The university may be the "provider" to the extent that it

---

[132] Quinn (2021), p. 23.

[133] Parlak and Dogan (2022), p. 6.

[134] See also Kiseleva (2021), p. 3 (stating, "It seems that the concept of the 'user' suggested in the proposed regulation has a dual character and applies both to organizations applying AI systems and natural persons doing so inside the organization. In this case, the roles and obligations of these subjects have to be clearly distinguished. Otherwise, their proper accountability can be difficult to ensure (internal citation omitted);" see further, Herrmann and Pfeiffer (2022), p. 1523 (emphasizing institutional perspectives and arguing that the binary of "human and technology" does not consider "the use of technology and the decisions generated in this interplay of humans and technology are embedded in human organizations.").

constitutes a public authority that puts an AI system into service under its own name, albeit free of charge. It may also be the user which is defined under the Commission's proposal as "any natural or legal person, public authority, agency or other body using an AI system under its authority, except where the AI system is used in the course of a personal non-professional activity."[135] While the Commission's version of the AI Act refers to "public authorities" in both the definition of "provider" and the definition of "user," it is ambiguous whether the same public authority can act as a provider and a user simultaneously. If the university is found to be both the provider and the user at the same time then it will find itself in the strange position by, for example, needing to provide instructions to itself for its own use.[136]

The European Ombudsman has explained that it is possible to be both a provider and a user of an AI system at the same time, at least in the context of the EU administration.[137] This may occur if a governmental agency develops a system in house (i.e., it does not buy the system off the shelf as a finalized product from the market) and it puts the system into service for its own use.[138] In the event that an entity is both a provider and user then it must comply with the requirements in title III, chapter II and undergo conformity assessment procedures.[139] Relevant procedural obligations are also applicable like obligations to have in place a quality management system and a system for post-market monitoring.[140]

A central difficulty with the AI Act is the assumption built into the law that there is an end-to-end, fixed "provider" which can be squarely identified for purposes of liability.[141] The development of AI is a highly complex task that has a modular nature, often moving from one actor to another, some private, some public, in a complex supply chain where different types of knowledge-sharing models are employed.[142] The definitions of a "provider" and a "user" under the law lack nuance, create confusion about how to allocate responsibility between different entities in the AI supply chain and create a binary that potentially excludes other important actors from bearing responsibility such as, for example, backend operators who provide data and "essential backend support service."[143] It may further force certain actors to

[135] Commission proposal AI Act, Article 3(4).

[136] Colonna (2022), pp. 40–41.

[137] European Ombudsman (2021), p. 8.

[138] Id. (stating, "The EU administration can be both a provider and a user of AI systems. If EU institutions, bodies, offices and agencies are developing the systems in-house (not 'buying them off the shelf as a finalised product' from the market), the EU administration will be considered 'provider' when putting those systems into service for its own use.").

[139] Id.

[140] Id.

[141] Osborne Clarke (2021).

[142] See Engler and Renda (2022).

[143] See European Parliament resolution (2020) (defining "backend operator" as "any natural or legal person who, on a continuous basis, defines the features of the technology and provides data and an essential backend support service and therefore also exercises a degree of control over the risk connected with the operation and functioning of the AI-system.").

"wear many hats," especially in bureaucratic and institutional contexts, as they find themselves taking over the dual role of provider and user, creating not just a heavy compliance load but also conflicts of interests that must somehow be recognized and managed to ensure trust and confidence in the law (as well as the AI being developed!). It may also be the case that there is a nonsensical replication of compliance in the situation where an entity finds itself as both a provider and a user under the AI Act, particularly as the AI Act seeks to create a risk-based and proportionate distribution of responsibility under the law.[144]

7 Researchers Build High-risk or Prohibited AI and Other Actors Copy It

It is at least plausible that a researcher may develop software that falls within the high-risk AI category, publish their findings in a free distribution service like arXiv, and then allow it to be shared under an open-source license. It is also plausible that a researcher may develop and openly share non-high-risk software that winds up being a component in high-risk AI. This raises a question about whether a researcher may be regarded as a provider subject to the high-risk requirements of the AI Act in these contexts. While publishing research results and distributing software under open-source licenses promotes innovation by allowing developers to build on the work of others, it creates legal complexity in the AI value chain by increasing the number of potentially responsible parties. More specifically, it is unclear whether compliance obligations should rest with the researcher who develops the software or the entity that subsequently uses it downstream, ostensibly for commercial purposes.

Globalization and digitalization have transformed the way that knowledge and information are disseminated. Where it concerns publicly funded data financed by taxpayers' money, the general consensus is that it should be distributed for free (or low costs) and with no restrictions concerning how the information may be used.[145] Indeed, the Commission's nonbinding "Recommendation on access to and preservation of scientific information" recognizes the increasing importance of open science and calls for more mechanisms at the EU and Member State level to ensure that scientific publications and research data are widely disseminated through open access channels.[146]

Additionally, open-source software (OSS) is a critical part of the research ecosystem, supporting collaboration and knowledge sharing across a diverse range of communities and individuals.[147] Broadly, the concept of OSS is used to signify

[144] Osborne Clarke (2021).

[145] Richter (2018), p. 52.

[146] European Commission (2018).

[147] Richter (2018).

"innovations that are jointly developed by different contributors."[148] OSS can emerge from a wide range of actors, including academia, and it can enable other technologies.[149] The deployment of OSS can also support a cheaper way to introduce technology to society, lowering the digital divide between industrialized and developing countries.[150]

When it comes to a researcher's decision to publish their software code as OSS on a platform like GitHub for example, it becomes possible for other developers to download the source code and use or modify it.[151] de Laat notes that "this move is not mere altruism" since the "code involved may get better because of modifications contributed in return; the code may become a de facto standard; and it may help the company to attract clients to their commercial products."[152] It can also ensure that the resulting AI is more fair, transparent and trustworthy AI, leading to scientific advancement.[153]

Concerning the commercial nature of OSS, Blind et al. explain, "Although Open Source outputs such as software code can be included in products that are sold, royalty fees are seldom paid to contributors and there are usually no significant restrictions on how these outputs are used."[154] Basically, the developer and copyright holder allows anybody the right to edit, modify, and distribute the software for no cost.[155] Engler succinctly expounds that open source models are "freely available for use by anyone, rather than being sold or otherwise commercialized."[156]

It is unclear whether a researcher who uploads materials to a platform like GitHub will be viewed as a provider to the extent they "put into service" the system within the EU and therefore, whether the research exemption applies to them. Yordanova explains that the Commission's definition of "provider" is "...problematic in practice because its scope is so large it encompasses big tech companies such as Microsoft but at the same time individual FOSS developers."[157] She further explains that there is a lack of clarity about whether "uploading software to GitHub would constitute "placing it on the market" or "putting it into service" according to the regulation's terminology."[158] Ebers et al. explain that "classifying any release of an OSS as "putting into the market/into service" and imposing conformity assessment

148 European Commission (2021b), p. 31.

149 Centre for Information Policy Leadership (2021).

150 Krakowski (2006), p. 321 (explaining "Free and open source software enables a cheaper way to introduce information and communication technologies to citizens of the developing world and by doing so, reducing the digital divide between and within these countries.").

151 de Laat (2021), p. 1154.

152 Id.

153 Engler (2022).

154 European Commission (2021b), p. 31.

155 Seide Bretthauer (2002).

156 Engler (2022).

157 Yordanova (2022), p. 3.

158 Id.

requirements on it will simply be detrimental to the entire scientific research ecosystem."[159] Engler contends that the research exemption will not protect OSS because they tend not to be used solely for research and development but rather to build things that people use.[160] The situation is even more vexing when one considers what happens when a researcher publishes proof-of-concept code in an academic paper which is often a condition of receiving public funding.

During the negotiations over the AI Act there has been a lively debate surrounding whether OSS requires its own exemption and whether those who publish their findings in an open-source manner should fall within the definition of provider under the law. Recital 60 of the Commission's original proposal notes the complexity of the software value chain and implies that suppliers of "software, software tools and components" should not constitute providers. In the Council's General Approach, it refers to open source where it defines GPAI, stating that the provisions concerning GPAI will apply irrespective of whether the GPAI is open-source software or not.[161] This means OSS is regulated, at least to the extent that it involves GPAI.

In the Parliament's General Approach, it provides for an explicit open-source exemption, albeit one subject to several exceptions. Article 2(5)(e) states that the regulation shall not apply to OSS except to the extent that they are placed on the market or put into service by a provider as part of a high-risk AI system or of an AI system that constitutes prohibited AI under Title II or as an AI system that falls under the transparency obligations set forth in Title IV.[162] The Parliament's General Approach clarifies in Recital 12(b) that "(n)either the collaborative development of free and open-source AI components nor making them available on open repositories should constitute a placing on the market or putting into service." However, it continues to explain that "charging a price" for "a free and open-source AI component" as well as "charging a price for technical support services" might constitute a commercial activity, at least where micro enterprises are not involved. Essentially, the idea is to shift the liability from the creator of OSS to the entity bringing it to the market, making sure that the fundamental regulatory objectives of the law cannot be circumvented by open-source AI development.

Article 2(5d) further explains that the open-source exemption "shall not apply to foundation models" which are defined in Article 3(1)(c) as "an AI system model that is trained on broad data at scale, is designed for generality of output, and can be adapted to a wide range of distinctive tasks." This point is echoed in Article 28(b)(1) which states that the rules regarding foundation models must apply regardless of whether the AI is "provided under free and open source licences." In other words,

[159] Ebers et al. (2021), p. 591.

[160] Engler (2022) (explaining, "The Council's draft of the AIA includes two exemptions that circumstantially apply to open-source GPAI models, but both have serious problems. The first exemption excludes all AI models that are only used for research and development from the entirety of the AIA. Yet open-source developers are most motivated by the idea of building things that people use, meaning this restriction decreases the incentive to contribute to open-source AI.")

[161] Council General Approach, Article 3(1)(b).

[162] See also Parliament General Approach recitals 12(a)(b).

open-source foundation models appear to be regulated under the AI Act, although it is important to note that there is an ambiguity about whether the research exemption could be still applied when open-source foundational models are shared for research purposes. There is also an ambiguity raised by Recital 12(b) insofar as it implies that all types of AI, including foundational models, can be shared freely as open-source without falling into the scope of the law.

The debate around the role of OSS raises questions about how research results should be understood and shared. Richter suggests that "Research information can be broadly divided into research data and publications."[163] There may also be a need to further distinguish between publication of results in journals and publication of OSS. This is because there are different interests involved which may be necessary to distinguish from a legal perspective. Here, there is a need for guidance on what kind of publishing models fall within the scope of the law.[164]

Ultimately, it may be reasonable to expect researchers and providers of OSS to provide the requisite information to help control errors and unexpected behavior in the AI as well as support compliance with the AI Act further along in the value chain.[165] For example, model cards can be required which are short documents that outline the performance traits of certain AI models to limit their usage in contexts in which they are not well suited to be deployed.[166] Related concepts include data sheets[167], data set nutrition labels[168], system cards[169] and fact sheets[170] which also support model and data documentation to improve explainability and transparency early in the AI development process.

In fact, Recital 12(c) of the Parliament's General Approach suggests the use of "documentation practices, such as model and data cards, as a way to accelerate information sharing along the AI value chain, allowing the promotion of trustworthy AI systems in the Union." Importantly, the Parliament does not mandate OSS suppliers to provide this information but merely "encourages" them to do so to support technology providers who use the OSS further down the supply chain to meet their requirements under the Act, at least where it concerns non-foundational models.[171] While thorough documentation of the data used in model creation is no

[163] Richter (2018), p. 56.

[164] Bogucki et al. (2022), p. 9 (explaining, "The AI Act could, for instance, clarify that publishing models and putting them online to access for free (making them open source) would not constitute putting them on the market (thus not triggering the requirements).").

[165] *See* Bender et al. (2021), p. 615 (arguing that model documentation is necessary "to understand training data characteristics in order to mitigate some of these attested issues or even unknown ones" and that a solution "is to budget for documentation as part of the planned costs of dataset creation, and only collect as much data as can be thoroughly documented within that budget.").

[166] Mitchell et al. (2019).

[167] Gebru et al. (2018).

[168] Holland et al. (2018).

[169] Alsallakh et al. (2022).

[170] Arnold et al. (2019).

[171] Parliament General Approach, Recital 12(c).

doubt critical to minimizing risks, from a practical perspective, researchers, especially academics, may lack sufficient resources to manage additional obligations. Therefore, if additional information-sharing requirements are ultimately deemed necessary, new forms of funding schemes or other mechanisms should be developed to support researchers to meet these supplementary compliance burdens.

8 Research that Takes Place "in the Wild" or in Regulatory Sandboxes

Ensuring the accurate, accountable, efficient, and robust performance of various forms of AI is challenging because certain AI models may meet unexpected challenges once they are released in a real-world setting that may negatively affect how they function.[172] As one commentator puts it: "...even carefully designed and developed AI systems tend to act in ways that their developers never predicted."[173] In an effort to account for the open-ended encounters that happen in the real world, "in the wild" studies and testing are performed outside of a lab[174] to, for example, consider the way the AI functions when it is operating for its end users.[175]

There are different methods and approaches available to improve model performances in the real world. Testing may, for example, focus on the technology alone by employing numerous technical approaches to enhancing the accountability and robustness of complex algorithmic decisions.[176] Testing may also focus on socio-technical issues such as acceptability, usability and fitness for purpose.[177] Chamberlain and Crabtree explain that there are "a range of approaches" available in the field of Human Computer Interaction "that focus upon carrying out research-based studies reporting on user behavior (sic) in 'natural', 'situated' contexts, in distinction to lab-based studies."[178] Rooksby et al. further notes that testing is

[172] AI TechPark (2020) (providing examples of situations where AI has "gone wrong.").

[173] Id.

[174] Björling et al. (2020), p. 3 (stating "Lab studies cannot adequately account for the open-ended encounters that happen between people and robots that are context-dependent. Studies in HRI often privilege the technological capabilities of robots over important factors such as social context and needs of a diverse group of users or stakeholders (internal citations removed).").

[175] Tschider (2021), p. 714.

[176] National Science and Technology Council (2016), p. 32 (explaining "There are several technical approaches to enhancing the accountability and robustness of complex algorithmic decisions. A system can be tested "in the wild" by presenting it with situations and observing its behavior"); Rooksby et al. (2009), p. 561 (explaining, "Testing now also goes well beyond mitigating defects in programs, looking at issues such as their performance, reliability, internationalisation, and security.").

[177] Rooksby et al. (2009), p. 561.

[178] Chamberlain and Crabtree (2019), abstract.

becoming more system focused as opposed to simply focusing on the software in isolation.[179]

Although "in the wild" testing is increasingly recognized as critical to ensuring responsible AI, the legal regulation of "in the wild" testing is murky at best, particularly given the conceptual muddle surrounding the concept. Smuha et al. argue that while it is vital that in-the-wild testing of AI applications are subject to appropriate legal regulation, such regulation is currently lacking under the law.[180] One important issue to consider from a legal perspective is whether testing or experimentation with AI by public or private actors in a real-world context constitutes research that may fall within the exemption. If it does then this may significantly limit the applicability of a harmonized AI regulation to certain software that is tested in real-world conditions, potentially commercially viable technology very close to market readiness, presenting risks to individual's health, safety, and fundamental rights, as well as broader societal concerns. This argument might be more colloquially framed as a "race to the bottom" approach. On the other hand, omitting real-world testing from the scope of the research exemption might significantly limit its application, harming rapid innovation in Europe.

According to the Commission's proposal, if an academic researcher tests his or her own AI "in the wild" for the sole purpose of research then the exemption should apply, at least in so far as this activity does not lead to or entail placing an AI on the market. The scope of the exemption is less clear when a researcher relies on a professional tester such as a specialist consultancy agency or relies on a software test center to do the testing for them[181] because there may be a commercial advantage to the third-party tester. However, the research exemption probably continues to apply, even when relying on a professional tester. Under the Commission's proposal, what is most difficult to understand is the scenario where a commercial researcher tests their AI "in the wild" and whether they may claim the research exemption. Here, the temporal aspect of Article 2 comes to the fore as it is not at all clear at what point an entity places an AI on the market or puts it into service, especially when they edge closer to market readiness by testing model performance in real-world settings.

The Council acknowledges that although "in the wild" testing is critical for ensuring responsible AI, there nevertheless remain serious risks that may require regulatory action. It provides an entire provision in Article 54(a) devoted to the

[179] Rooksby et al. (2009), p. 561 (explaining, "Testing no longer simply focuses on the technology alone but on socio-technical issues such as acceptability, usability and fitness for purpose. Testing is also increasingly focused on systems rather than software in isolation.").

[180] Smuha et al. (2021), p. 17.

[181] Rooksby et al. (2009), p. 561 (explaining, "Initially programmers were encouraged to test other programmers' work rather than their own because they may be unwilling to admit to their own faults, but the increasing scope and complexity of testing is now serving to make testing a profession in its own right. Many larger software teams include professional testers. Specialist consultancies are often used to supply expertise, particularly in specialist tasks such as performance testing. We are also seeing the emergence of software test centres to which testing can be outsourced.").

testing of high-risk AI systems in real world conditions as well as defines "testing in real world conditions"[182] Basically, it allows for testing in real world conditions to take place for a period of 12 months if specific conditions are met, most notably creating a testing plan and informing the market surveillance authority.[183] Recital 12 (b) explains that the research exemption does not apply when doing testing in real world conditions.

An issue with the Council's approach is that it is unclear why any individual or entity would follow the requirements of Article 54(a), unless they can be defined as a provider, and therefore responsible under the law. The Council's General Approach refers to the concept of "prospective providers" thirteen times in Article 54(a). Yet, it does not define this concept in its extensive definition section. Furthermore, it narrows the scope of the definition of "provider" by dropping the language "with a view" which might have included "prospective providers." While the definition of "testing in real world conditions" states that "testing in real world conditions shall not be considered as placing the AI system on the market or putting it into service" provided that the conditions in Article 54(a) are met, this logic is circular and leads back to the definition of provider.

The Parliament defines "testing in real world conditions" to mean "the temporary testing of an AI system for its intended purpose in real world conditions outside of a laboratory or otherwise simulated environment."[184] Rather than relying on a recital like the Council, it has included language in the body of the research exemption provided for in Article 5(d) that explicitly states, "(t)he testing in real world conditions shall not be covered by this exemption." In other words, according to the Parliament's General Approach, if a researcher tests AI in the wild, even if he or she has no intention to place that AI on the market or put it into service, the researcher must still meet all the requirements of the law. Unlike the Council, the Parliament retains the language "with a view" in its definition of provider, ostensibly allowing the provisions on "real world testing" to apply to "prospective providers."

The distinction between "research" and "in the wild" testing is further muddied when one takes into consideration the concept of regulatory sandboxes which the AI Act introduces as a mechanism to bridge the gap between innovation and compliance. Broadly, a regulatory sandbox is a mechanism which affords innovators with a safe environment for trial and error. Regulatory sandboxes also help to ensure an even playing field between the smaller firms and the larger ones. Madiega and Van De Pol explain that "...regulatory sandboxes generally refer to regulatory tools

---

[182]Council General Approach, Article 3(48) ("'testing in real world conditions' means the temporary testing of an AI system for its intended purpose in real world conditions outside of a laboratory or otherwise simulated environment with a view to gathering reliable and robust data and to assessing and verifying the conformity of the AI system with the requirements of this Regulation; testing in real world conditions shall not be considered as placing the AI system on the market or putting it into service within the meaning of this Regulation, provided that all conditions under Article 53 or Article 54a are fulfilled.").

[183]Council General Approach, Article 54(a).

[184]Parliament General Approach, Article 3(44n).

allowing businesses to test and experiment with new and innovative products, services or businesses under supervision of a regulator for a limited period of time."[185] They highlight that regulatory sandboxes have "a double role," first, to support "business learning" by allowing for the development and testing of technologies in a real-world environment and, second, to support "regulatory learning" by creating a space where regulators can better understand new technologies within the context of an "experimental legal regime."[186]

Regulatory sandboxes have emerged as testbeds for various types of AI-powered technology like that employed in autonomous cars and smart meters and, represent a tool to support "a more agile approach to innovation and regulation in the high-tech sector."[187] While it would make sense that research and development that goes on in a sandbox is not a proverbial "get out of jail free card," it is important to consider how the research exemption may be invoked in this context.[188] Particularly, it is interesting to consider whether there is a legal presumption that any AI that is tested in a sandbox will be considered to be AI that will be placed on the market or put into service and therefore within the scope of the law.

Article 53 of the Commission's proposal includes a provision on AI regulatory sandboxes to provide a controlled environment that facilitates the development, testing and validation of innovative AI systems.[189] The Commission's proposal does not specify the exact requirements for participation in the sandbox, although it does call on Member States to give start-ups and small-scale providers priority access.[190] Article 53 further explains that "(t)he AI regulatory sandboxes shall not affect the supervisory and corrective powers of the competent authorities," implying that the legal requirements of the law apply in full.[191] The failure to include any regulatory leniency allowing national authorities to deviate from the requirements of the AI Act (or even EU law more generally) has raised concerned that the inclusion of Article 53 by the Commission is merely symbolic.[192]

---

[185] European Parliamentary Research Service (2022).

[186] Id.; see also Kelly (2023) (Defining the four key benefits of AI Regulatory sandboxes as (1) reducing the time and cost of commercializing AI products and services (2) supporting improved regulation via regulatory learning (3) improving AI standards development processes and enabling the development of standards alongside regulation (4) enabling increased market participation by small and medium sized enterprises (SMEs)); see further Undheim et al. (2023); see also Parliament General Approach Recital (72) and Article 53(1)(d).

[187] European Parliamentary Research Service (2022).

[188] See further Grady (2022) (acknowledging that sandboxes should not create a "wild west" of AI development but arguing for experimentation clauses to "allow authorities to act with a degree of discretion when enforcing or implementing rules.").

[189] AI Act Commission Proposal, Article 53(1).

[190] Id. at Article 55(1)(a).

[191] Id. at Article 53(3).

[192] Ringe (2023) (stating, "The proposed AI Act does mention the idea of a sandbox on the margin. However, the proposed text resembles more of a symbolic marketing trick rather than a serious utilization of the potential of a sandbox.").

The Council's General Approach retains the provision on regulatory sandboxes but substantially modifies it. It clarifies that authorities have the possibility to "exercise their supervisory powers in a flexible manner."[193] Additionally, if the participant(s) respect the sandbox plan and follow in good faith the guidance given by the authorities, then no administrative fines shall be imposed by the authorities for infringement during the testing period.[194] Unlike the Commission, the Council defines the concept of "AI regulatory sandbox."[195]

In the Parliament's General Approach, it also defines a "regulatory sandbox"[196] as well as "testing in real world conditions."[197] Its definition of "regulatory sandbox" diverges from the Council's General Approach where it concerns making an explicit reference to the entity that utilizes the sandbox. That is, while the Council refers to "providers or prospective providers" as the entities that shall use regulatory sandboxes, the Parliament drops this language. The Parliament's definition of "testing in real world conditions" is aligned with the Council's definition, albeit significantly shortened to remove the Council's circular language described above.

Article 53(1)(d) of the Parliament's General Approach further explains that AI regulatory sandboxes shall "provide for a controlled environment that fosters innovation and facilitates the development, testing and validation of innovative AI systems for a limited time *before* their placement on the market or putting into service pursuant to a specific plan agreed between the prospective providers and the establishing authority." This may motivate why the Parliament has retained the language "with a view to placing it on the market or putting it into service" in its definition of provider. Otherwise, the definition of provider, such as that set forth by the Council which excludes the "with a view" language[198], may not cover entities that utilize a sandbox (i.e., "prospective providers").

---

[193] Council General Approach, Article 53(3).

[194] Id.

[195] Id. at Article 3(52) ("AI regulatory sandbox" means "a concrete framework set up by a national competent authority which offers providers or prospective providers of AI systems the possibility to develop, train, validate and test, where appropriate in real world conditions, an innovative AI system, pursuant to a specific plan for a limited time under regulatory supervision.").

[196] Parliament General Approach, Article 3(44g) ("regulatory sandbox" means "a controlled environment established by a public authority that facilitates the safe development, testing and validation of innovative AI systems for a limited time before their placement on the market or putting into service pursuant to a specific plan under regulatory supervision.").

[197] Parliament General Approach, Article 3(44n) ("testing in real world conditions" means "the temporary testing of an AI system for its intended purpose in real world conditions outside of a laboratory or otherwise simulated environment.").

[198] Council General Approach, Article 3 (2) ("provider" means a natural or legal person, public authority, agency or other body that develops an AI system or that has an AI system developed and places that system on the market or puts it into service under its own name or trademark, whether for payment or free of charge); *but see also* Council General Approach, Recital 72 (stating, "The supervision of the AI systems in the AI regulatory sandbox should therefore cover their development, training, testing and validation *before* the systems are placed on the market or put into service,

According to the Parliament's General Approach, if an AI system complies with the guidance and supervision provided by the sandbox, it will be presumed to be in conformity with the AI Act when exiting the sandbox.[199] However, Article 53 (3) states that the sandboxes shall not affect the supervisory and corrective powers of the competent authorities.[200] Article 53(4) adds that "prospective providers" that utilize an AI regulatory sandbox shall remain liable under applicable Union and Member States liability legislation for any harm inflicted on third parties as a result of the experimentation taking place in the sandbox. That said, if the "prospective provider" respects the specific plan developed with the authorities as well as the terms and conditions for their participation and follow in good faith the guidance given by the establishing authorities, no administrative fines shall be imposed by the authorities for infringements of the AI Act.[201]

Ultimately, clarification is necessary to explain the relationship between the regulatory lenience afforded under the research exemption and potentially under rules governing real world testing both within and outside of regulatory sandboxes. If technology providers can claim the research exemption, then they may not have to follow the additional requirements such as those set forward in Article 53 and 54 of the Council's General Approach that require the provider to obtain approval from the market surveillance authority if they want to do real-world testing outside of a regulatory sandbox. If researchers do not place AI on the market or put it into service, then they can argue they are not "providers" under the law and therefore, not subject to any of the provisions, including those concerning regulatory sandboxes and real-world testing.

It is necessary to distinguish the various actors more clearly in the AI supply chain such as researchers that qualify under the exemption, "prospective providers" and "providers." It is difficult to understand how "prospective providers" are regulated under the AI Act, if at all, and how this concept relates to the research exemption. On this point, the importance the language "with a view to placing it on the market or putting it into service" in the definition of a provider comes to the fore. While the Commission and the Parliament include this language, it is dropped in the Council's approach.

---

as well as the notion and occurrence of substantial modification that may require a new conformity assessment procedure.").

[199] Parliament General Approach Article 53(1)(g) ("Insofar as the AI system complies with the requirements when exiting the sandbox, it shall be presumed to be in conformity with this regulation.").

[200] Parliament General Approach Article 53(3) ("The AI regulatory sandboxes shall not affect the supervisory and corrective powers of the competent authorities, including at regional or local level.").

[201] Parliament General Approach Article 53(4).

9 Discussion

This paper has examined whether there are any responsibility gaps or ambiguities set forward in the AI Act's research exemption that may be used as mechanisms for regulatory arbitrage by either public or private actors, seeking to use the exemption as a shield to avoid compliance with duties imposed under the law. First, it can be observed that when private companies partner with public entities, the scope of the research exemption expands, raising concerns that it may be used as a mechanism to exclude commercial activities that are otherwise subject to requirements under the proposed AI Act from regulatory oversight. While the exemption only applies where research is the "sole purpose" of the activity being claimed under the exemption, the determination of when research is the "sole purpose" of an activity can be difficult to make in the context of modern AI research which increasingly involves close collaborations between traditional research institutions and for-profit entities along a complex supply chain.

Relatedly, it is necessary to more clearly define the scope of the research exemption so that publicly funded researchers can understand whether the law applies to them and appropriately define their relationships with commercial entities. If the AI Act applies to research that is on the path to commercialization within the academic context, then publicly funded researchers and project coordinators should be prepared to meet the rigorous requirements of the law. If researchers are expected to meet the requirements of the AI Act, there must be ways to support them to achieve their compliance obligations in ways that do not hinder publicly funded research, especially to the unfair advantage of the private sector. Even if research that takes place at the exploratory phase is exempted from the requirement of the proposed AI Act, policymakers should consider ways to support compliance with the regulatory requirements at this point to allow for the quicker introduction of socially useful knowledge and products on the EU market.[202]

There is a further question about how the exemption should apply in situations where researchers invoke the exemption and then provide the AI they develop to their employing institutions or other public bodies for no cost. Here, there is an ambiguity in the law concerning whether these activities are for the "sole purpose" of research or rather for the provision of public services. Allowing public institutions such as universities to claim the research exemption for in-house development of systems can create a major responsibility gap. Conversely, if public entities cannot avail themselves to the exemption, then they may find themselves in the position of being a provider and a user of AI, creating a duplication of compliance in some instances and a lack of legal certainty concerning how to allocate responsibility between its different roles. Ultimately, there is a need to clarify the understanding of "provider" in situations where universities, research institutions, or other public authorities develop AI systems within the research environment and then put them into use within the same context.

---

[202] Caulfield et al. (2012).

Likewise, it is unclear how the exemption should function in situations where researchers build high-risk or prohibited AI, publish their findings, or share them via an open-source platform, and other actors use the AI. If publishing proof-of-concept code in a paper or uploading it online as OSS constitutes "placing AI on the market" or "putting AI into service" then the exemption will have a very narrow scope. On the other hand, excluding these activities from the scope of the exemption may serve as an end run around the requirements of the regulation in certain cases. A middle ground appears to be to require researchers who share their results as OSS to provide documentation like model cards to entities who use the software further down the supply chain to increase explainability and transparency throughout the development and deployment of the AI.

Research in the wild is critical in the context of AI development. It not only engages the individuals and communities that are ultimately impacted by the technology, but it can also uncover unexpected behaviors in the algorithms that may create unfair or unjust outcomes. A major problem is that it can be difficult to demark when AI is being researched and developed from when it is being tested in the wild and in sandboxes from when it is being placed on the market, creating opportunities for regulatory arbitrage. While the AI Act sets forward several bold proposals seeking to regulate real world testing, it is important to clearly demark the regulatory flexibility provided by the research exemption and possibly under rules governing real-world testing both within and outside of regulatory sandboxes.

Finally, it is challenging to determine whether all the possible mechanisms for regulatory arbitrage explored in this paper raise equal legal, regulatory, or practical concerns, or whether one or more of them poses especially imminent threats. Future studies might deploy empirical research methods to assess the practical ramifications of how the research exemption operates "on the ground" to help inform policy decisions and support compliance.[203] While the discussions around open-source software, regulatory sandboxes, and real-world testing have recently sparked significant debate, signalling an awareness by policymakers of the potential practical problems, other mechanisms for regulatory arbitrage discussed herein, remain under looked. These include, for example, mechanisms found in the academic research environment.

10 Conclusion

Ultimately, the paper highlights that the boundaries between public and private actors and their respective domains of operation are blurred which creates challenges, especially regarding legal responsibility as a provider under the law. Pinpointing a provider as the entity squarely responsible to meet the obligations of the AI Act becomes even more complicated in the research context because AI

[203] See generally, Cane and Kritzer (2010).

research often involves a nonlinear process, involving an amalgamation of different methods which are deployed during various phases and performed across sectors by numerous actors such as government agencies, universities, research institutions, and commercial entities. It can be concluded that the normative distinction between research, on the one hand, and other purposes subject to the rules under the AI Act breaks down considering modern research practices which are conducted by public and private actors for commercial and non-commercial reasons alike in a complex, entangled, and diaphanous process.

If EU policymakers want to support AI innovation, a more nuanced approach must be taken that better acknowledges how research is conducted and disseminated in the Digital Age. Otherwise, the result of the AI Act may just be the worst of both worlds: heavy regulation that still allows AI to threaten health, safety, and fundamental rights. Policymakers should clarify the role of ethical oversight and open science in this context, especially where the research may not serve socially and environmentally beneficial outcomes. They should also specify the value chain in more detail so that there could be greater understanding about who is in the best position to, first, meet regulatory requirements, and second, to ensure the safe and responsible use of AI.[204] Additional clarification about how the research exemption should function in the context of the OSS, in the wild testing and regulatory sandboxes is also necessary.

Legislation

Consolidated Version of the Treaty on the Functioning of the European Union ("TFEU") (2008) OJ C 115/47.

Directive (EU) 2019/790 of 17 April 2019 on copyright and related rights in the Digital Single Market and amending Directives 96/9/EC and 2001/29/EC (2019) OJ L-130/92.

Directive (EU) 2019/1024 of the European Parliament and of the Council of 20 June 2019 on Open Data and the Re-Use of Public Sector Information (2019) OJ L 172.

Regulation (EU) 2016/679 of the European Parliament and of the Council of 27 April 2016 on the protection of natural persons with regard to the processing of personal data and on the free movement of such data, and repealing directive 95/46/EC (General Data Protection Regulation, "GDPR")(2016) OJ 2016 L 119/1.

Regulation (EU) 2017/745 of the European Parliament and of the Council of 5th April 2017 on medical devices, amending Directive 2001/83/EC, Regulation (EC) No 178/2002 and Regulation (EC) No 1223/2009 and repealing Council Directives 90/385/EEC and 93/42/EEC (2017) OJ EU 2017, No. L 117/1.

[204] For more, see Engler and Renda (2022).

Commission Recommendation (EU) 2018/790 of 25 April 2018 on access to and preservation of scientific information (2018) C/2018/2375 OJ L 134.

Sw. Lag (2003:460) om etikprövning av forskning som avser människor (the "Swedish Ethical Review Act").

Proposed Legislation

Proposal for a Regulation of the European Parliament and of the Council Laying Down Harmonized Rules on Artificial Intelligence ("Commission proposal AI Act") and Amending Certain Union Legislative Acts COM/2021/206 final. https://eur-lex.europa.eu/resource.html?uri=cellar:e0649735-a372-11eb-9585-01aa75ed71a1.0001.02/DOC_1&format=PDF. Accessed 12 Sept 2023.

Council of the European Union, Interinstitutional File: 2021/0106, 29 November 2021, 14278/21, Proposal for a Regulation of the European Parliament and of the Council laying down harmonised rules on artificial intelligence (Artificial Intelligence Act) and amending certain Union legislative acts—first Presidency compromise text, ("29 November 2021 Council Compromise text"). https://data.consilium.europa.eu/doc/document/ST-14278-2021-INIT/en/pdf. Accessed 12 Sept 2023.

Council of the European Union, Interinstitutional File: 2021/0106(COD), 19 October 2022, Proposal for a Regulation of the European Parliament and of the Council laying down harmonised rules on artificial intelligence (Artificial Intelligence Act) and amending certain Union legislative acts ("Fourth Presidency compromise text"). https://artificialintelligenceact.eu/wp-content/uploads/2022/10/AIA-CZ-4th-Proposal-19-Oct-22.pdf. Accessed 12 Sept 2023.

Council of the European Union, Interinstitutional File: 2021/0106(COD), Brussels, 25 November 2022 ("Council General Approach"). https://artificialintelligenceact.eu/wp-content/uploads/2022/12/AIA-%E2%80%93-CZ-%E2%80%93-General-Approach-25-Nov-22.pdf. Accessed 12 Sept 2023.

European Parliament, Artificial Intelligence Act Amendments adopted on 14 June 2023 on the proposal for a regulation of the European Parliament and of the Council on laying down harmonised rules on artificial intelligence (Artificial Intelligence Act) and amending certain Union legislative acts (COM(2021) 0206—C9-0146/2021—2021/0106(COD))1 ("Parliament General Approach"). https://artificialintelligenceact.eu/wp-content/uploads/2023/06/AIA-%E2%80%93-IMCO-LIBE-Draft-Compromise-Amendments-14-June-2023.pdf. Accessed 12 Sept 2023.

Kateřina Konečná, Pernando Barrena Arza, Cornelia Ernst, Elena Kountoura (June 2022), Proposed Amendment to the AI Act 1105, Article 3—paragraph 1—point 44 a. https://parltrack.org/activities/197699/type/amendments. Accessed 12 Sept 2023.

Proposal for a Regulation of the European Parliament and of the Council on Harmonised Rules on Fair Access to and Use of Data ("Data Act") COM(2022)

68 final. https://eur-lex.europa.eu/legal-content/EN/TXT/?uri=COM%3A2022%3A68%3AFIN. Accessed 12 Sept 2023.
Proposal for a Regulation of the European Parliament and the Council on European Data Governance ("Data Governance Act") COM/2020/767 final. https://eur-lex.europa.eu/legal-content/EN/TXT/PDF/?uri=CELEX:52020PC0767&from=EN. Accessed 12 Sept 2023.
Proposal for a Regulation of the European Parliament and of the Council on the European Health Data Space ("European Health Data Space") COM(2022) 197 final. https://eur-lex.europa.eu/legal-content/EN/TXT/PDF/?uri=CELEX:52022PC0197&from=EN. Accessed 12 Sept 2023.

Case Law

C-215/88 Casa Fleischhandel ECLI:EU:C:1989:331.

References

Journals and Articles

Allen HJ (2020) Sandbox boundaries. Vanderbilt J Entertain Technol Law 22:299–321
Björling EA, Thomas K et al (2020) Exploring teens as robot operators users and witnesses in the wild. Front Rob AI 7(5):1–15
Burk DL (2016) Perverse innovation. William Mary Law Rev 58:1–34
Caulfield T, Harmon S, Joly Y (2012) Open science versus commercialization: a modern research conflict? Genome Med 4(17):1–11
Cohen J (2017) Law for the platform economy. UC Davis Law Rev 51:133–204
Colonna L (2022) Artificial intelligence in higher education: towards a more relational approach. Loyola Univ Chic J Regul Compliance 8:18–54
Comandè G, Schneider G (2022) Differential data protection regimes in data-driven research: why the GDPR is more research-friendly than you think. German Law J 23(4):559–596
De Laat PB (2021) Companies committed to responsible AI: from principles towards implementation and regulation? Philos Technol 34:1135–1193
Ebers M, Hoch V et al (2021) The European Commission's proposal for an Artificial Intelligence Act—a critical assessment by members of the Robotics and AI Law Society (RAILS). Multidiscip Sci J 4(4):589–603
Fleischer V (2010) Regulatory arbitrage. Tex Law Rev 89:227–289
Floridi L, Luetge C et al (2019) Key ethical challenges in the European Medical Information Framework. Minds Mach 29(3):355–371
García K (2019) Copyright arbitrage. Calif Law Rev 107:199–266
Herrmann T, Pfeiffer S (2022) Keeping the organization in the loop: a socio-technical extension of human-centered artificial intelligence. AI Soc 38:1523–1542
Ienca M, Malgieri G (2022) Mental data protection and the GDPR. J Law Biosci 9(1):1–19
Kazim E, Güçlütürk O et al (2022) Proposed EU AI Act—presidency compromise text: select overview and comment on the changes to the proposed regulation. AI Ethics 3:381–387

Kelly J, Sadeghieh T et al (2014) Peer review in scientific publications: benefits, critiques, and a survival guide. EJIFCC 25(3):227–243
Letourneur D, Joyce K et al (2020) Enabling MedTech translation in academia: redefining value proposition with updated regulations. Adv Healthc Mater 10(1):1–9
Marelli L, Testa G, Van Hoyweghen I (2021) Big tech platforms in health research: re-purposing big data governance in light of the general data protection regulation's research exemption. Big Data Soc 8(1)
Partnoy F (1997) Financial derivatives and the costs of regulatory arbitrage. J Corp Law 22:211–256
Quinn P (2021) Research under the GDPR – a level playing field for public and private sector research? Life Sci Soc Policy 17(4):1–33
Richter H (2018) Open science and public sector information, reconsidering the exemption for educational and research establishments under the directive on re-use of public sector information. Inf Technol E-Commerce Law 9(1):51–74
Rooksby J, Rouncefield M, Sommerville I (2009) Testing in the wild: the social and organisational dimensions of real world practice. Comput Supported Coop Work 18:559–580
Schneider G (2019) Disentangling health data networks: a critical analysis of Articles 9(2) and 89 GDPR. Int Data Privacy Law 9(4):253–271
Seide Bretthauer MD (2002) Open source software: a history. Inf Technol Libr 21(1):3–11
Slokenberga S (2022) Scientific Research Regime 2.0? Transformations of the research regime and the protection of the data subject that the proposed EHDS regulation promises to bring along. Technol Regul 2022:135–147
Tschider CA (2021) Beyond the "Black Box". Denver Law Rev 98:683–724
Undheim K, Erikson T, Timmermans B (2023) True uncertainty and ethical AI: regulatory sandboxes as a policy tool for moral imagination. AI Ethics 3:997–1002
Zawacki-Richter O, Marín V et al (2019) Systematic review of research on artificial intelligence applications in higher education – where are the educators? Int J Educ Technol High Educ 16(39):1–39

Books and Chapters

Booth W, Colomb G et al (2016) The craft of research, 4th edn. University of Chicago Press, London
Brightman A, Beever J, Hiles M (2019) Next-generation ethical development of medical devices: considering harms, benefits, fairness, and freedom. In: Abbas A (ed) Next-generation ethics: engineering a better society. Cambridge University Press, Cambridge, pp 387–410
Cane P, Kritzer H (2010) The Oxford handbook of empirical legal research. Oxford Academic. online edition
Chamberlain A, Crabtree A (2019) Research 'in the wild'. In: Chamberlain A, Crabtree A (eds) Into the wild: beyond the design research lab. Studies in applied philosophy, epistemology and rational ethics. Springer, Cham, pp 1–6
De Vries K (2022) A researcher's guide for using personal data and non-personal data surrogates: synthetic data and data of deceased people. In: De Vries K, Dahlberg M (eds) De Lege 2021: law, AI and digitalization. Iustus förlag, Uppsala, pp 117–140
Krakowski P (2006) ICT and free open source software in developing countries. In: Berleur J, Nurminen MI, Impagliazzo J (eds) Social informatics: an information society for all? In remembrance of Rob Kling. HCC 2006. IFIP International Federation for Information Processing, vol 223. Springer, Boston, pp 319–330
Parlak B, Dogan K (2022) The handbook of public administration, vol 1. Livre de Lyon

Slokenberga S (2021) Setting the foundations: individual rights, public interest, scientific research and biobanking. In: Slokenberga S, Tzortzatou O, Reichel J (eds) GDPR and biobanking, Law, governance and technology series, vol 43. Springer, Cham, pp 11–30
Willesson M (2017) What is and what is not regulatory arbitrage? A review and syntheses. In: Chesini G, Giaretta E, Paltrinieri A (eds) Financial markets, SME financing and emerging economies. Palgrave Macmillan, Cham, pp 71–94

Proceedings and Conference Papers

Bender E et al (2021) On the dangers of stochastic parrots: can language models be too big? In: Proceedings of the 2021 ACM conference on fairness, accountability, and transparency. Virtual Event Canada, pp 610–623
Mitchell M et al (2019) Model cards for model reporting, In: FAT* '19: Proceedings of the conference on fairness, accountability, and transparency, pp 220–229

Online Publications

Abramo G, Apponi F, D'Angelo C (2021) Do the propensity and drivers of academics' engagement in research collaboration with industry vary over time? arXiv:2102.05364. https://arxiv.org/pdf/2102.05364.pdf. Accessed 12 Sept 2023
AI TechPark (2020) Halloween special: how unbridled AI can give enterprises the scares (26 October 2020). https://ai-techpark.com/halloween-special-how-unbridled-ai-can-give-enterprises-the-scares/. Accessed 12 Sept 2023
Ake-Kob A, Aleksic S, Alexin Z et al (2022) Position paper on ethical, legal and social challenges linked to audio- and video-based AAL solutions. https://zenodo.org/record/7326184#.Y5HeNnbMKUk. Accessed 12 Sept 2023
Alsallakh B et al (2022) System-level transparency of machine learning, technical report; Meta AI: New York, NY, USA. https://ai.facebook.com/research/publications/system-level-transparency-of-machine-learning. Accessed 12 Sept 2023
Arnold M et al (2019) FactSheets: increasing trust in AI services through supplier's declarations of conformity. arXiv:1808.07261. https://arxiv.org/abs/1808.07261. Accessed 12 Sept 2023
Article 29 Working Party (2020) Guidelines on consent under Regulation 2016/679. https://edpb.europa.eu/sites/default/files/files/file1/edpb_guidelines_202005_consent_en.pdf. Accessed 12 Sept 2023
Bogucki A et al (2022) The AI Act and emerging EU digital acquis: overlaps, gaps and inconsistencies. CEPS in Depth analysis, Brussels, pp 1–32. https://www.ceps.eu/download/publication/?id=37468&pdf=CEPS-In-depth-analysis-2022-02_The-AI-Act-and-emerging-EU-digital-acquis.pdf. Accessed 12 Sept 2023
Buttarelli G (2018) Speech at the fifth world congress for freedom of scientific research (12 April 2018). https://edps.europa.eu/data-protection/our-work/publications/speeches-articles/fifth-world-congress-freedom-scientific_en. Accessed 12 Sept 2023
Centre for Information Policy Leadership (2021) Response to the EU Commission's consultation on the Draft AI Act (29 July 21). https://ec.europa.eu/info/law/better-regulation/have-your-say/initiatives/12527-Artificial-intelligence-ethical-and-legal-requirements/F2663366_en. Accessed 12 Sept 2023

Engler A (2022) The EU's attempt to regulate open-source AI is counterproductive (Wednesday, August 24, 2022). https://www.brookings.edu/blog/techtank/2022/08/24/the-eus-attempt-to-regulate-open-source-ai-is-counterproductive/. Accessed 12 Sept 2023

Engler A, Renda A (2022) Reconciling the AI value chain with the EU's Artificial Intelligence Act, CEPS, pp 1–31. https://www.ceps.eu/download/publication/?id=37654&pdf=CEPS-In-depth-analysis-2022-03_Reconciling-the-AI-Value-Chain-with-the-EU-Artificial-Intelligence-Act.pdf. Accessed 12 Sept 2023

Enterprise Ireland (n.d.) Enterprise fund. https://globalambition.ie/commercialisation-fund/. Accessed 12 Sept 2023

European Commission (2016) Open innovation, open science, open to the world: a vision for Europé. https://digital-strategy.ec.europa.eu/en/library/open-innovation-open-science-open-world. Accessed 12 Sept 2023

European Commission (2018) Recommendation 2018/790 of 25 April 2018 on access to and preservation of scientific information. https://digital-strategy.ec.europa.eu/en/library/recommendation-access-and-preservation-scientific-information. Accessed 12 Sept 2023

European Commission (2020) Communication from the Commission to the European Parliament, the Council, the European Economic and Social Committee and the Committee of the Regions, A European Strategy for Data, Brussels, 19.2.2020 COM(2020) 66 final, pp 1–93. https://eur-lex.europa.eu/legal-content/EN/TXT/PDF/?uri=CELEX:52020DC0066&from=EN. Accessed 12 Sept 2023

European Commission (2021a) Staff working document impact assessment accompanying the proposal for a regulation of the European Parliament and of the Council Laying Down Harmonized Rules on Artificial Intelligence (Artificial Intelligence Act) and Amending Certain Union Legislative (COM(2021) 206. https://digital-strategy.ec.europa.eu/en/library/impact-assessment-regulation-artificial-intelligence. Accessed 12 Sept 2023

European Commission (2021b) Directorate-General for Communications Networks, Content and Technology, Blind K, Pätsch S et al. The impact of open source software and hardware on technological independence, competitiveness and innovation in the EU economy: final study report, Publications Office. https://data.europa.eu/doi/10.2759/430161. Accessed 12 Sept 2023

European Commission (2022) Press release – Data Act: Commission proposes measures for a fair and innovative data economy. https://ec.europa.eu/commission/presscorner/detail/en/ip_22_1113. Accessed 12 Sept 2023

European Data Protection Board (2020) Guidelines 05/2020 on consent under Regulation 2016/67 (version 1.0). https://edpb.europa.eu/sites/default/files/files/file1/edpb_guidelines_202005_consent_en.pdf. Accessed 12 Sept 2023

European Data Protection Supervisor (2020) A preliminary opinion on data protection and scientific research. https://edps.europa.eu/sites/default/files/publication/20-01-06_opinion_research_en.pdf. Accessed 12 Sept 2023

European Ombudsman (2021) Report on the meeting between European Ombudsman and European Commission representatives. https://www.ombudsman.europa.eu/en/doc/inspection-report/en/149338. Accessed 12 Sept 2023

European Parliamentary Research Service (2022) Madiega T and Van De Pol AL, Artificial Intelligence Act and regulatory sandboxes, pp 1–12. https://www.europarl.europa.eu/RegData/etudes/BRIE/2022/733544/EPRS_BRI(2022)733544_EN.pdf. Accessed 12 Sept 2023

European Parliamentary Research Service (2023) Madiega T, Briefing EU Legislation in Progress: Artificial Intelligence Act. https://www.europarl.europa.eu/RegData/etudes/BRIE/2021/698792/EPRS_BRI(2021)698792_EN.pdf. Accessed 12 Sept 2023

Gebru T et al (2018) Datasheets for datasets. arXiv:1803.09010. https://arxiv.org/abs/1803.09010. Accessed 12 Sept 2023

Grady P (2022) EU's AI regulatory sandboxes need fixing, Center for Data Innovation. https://datainnovation.org/2022/10/eus-ai-regulatory-sandboxes-need-fixing/. Accessed 12 Sept 2023

Holland S, Hosny A et al (2018) The dataset nutrition label: a framework to drive higher data quality standards. arXiv:1805.03677. https://arxiv.org/abs/1805.03677. Accessed 12 Sept 2023

Kelly D (2023) Towards an AI regulatory sandbox: emerging research and pilots, AI Standards Hub. https://aistandardshub.org/toward-ai-sandbox. Accessed 12 Sept 2023

Kiseleva A (2021) Comments on the EU proposal for the Artificial Intelligence Act, pp 1–8. https://ssrn.com/abstract=3949585 or https://doi.org/10.2139/ssrn.3949585. Accessed 12 Sept 2023

National Science and Technology Council (2016) Executive Office of the President National Science and Technology Council Committee on Technology, preparing for the future of artificial intelligence, pp 1–48. https://obamawhitehouse.archives.gov/sites/default/files/whitehouse_files/microsites/ostp/NSTC/preparing_for_the_future_of_ai.pdf. Accessed 12 Sept 2023

Osborne Clarke (2021) Debate continues over the pros and cons of regulating artificial intelligence. https://www.osborneclarke.com/insights/debate-continues-pros-cons-regulating-artificial-intelligence. Accessed 12 Sept 2023

Oxford Advanced Learner's Dictionary, Research (n.d.). https://www.oxfordlearnersdictionaries.com/definition/american_english/research_1. Accessed 12 Sept 2023

Regeringens proposition 2018/19:165 (n.d.) Etikprövning av forskning – tydligare regler och skärpta straff Prop. 2018/19:165. https://data.riksdagen.se/fil/1C9078D3-DAA7-430F-BCAB-0EEC6FBB82DE. Accessed 12 Sept 2023

Ringe WG (2023) Why we need a regulatory sandbox for AI. https://blogs.law.ox.ac.uk/oblb/blog-post/2023/05/why-we-need-regulatory-sandbox-ai. Accessed 12 Sept 2023

Shrourou A (2020) Medical Devices Regulation (MDR) 2021 – implications for the Devices Academic Community, University College London (UCL) Translational Research Office Blog. https://blogs.ucl.ac.uk/translational-research/2020/09/09/mdr-2021-implications-for-devices-academic-community/. Accessed 12 Sept 2023

Smuha N, Ahmed-Rengers E et al (2021) How the EU can achieve legally trustworthy AI: a response to the European Commission's proposal for an Artificial Intelligence Act, pp 1–59. https://papers.ssrn.com/sol3/papers.cfm?abstract_id=3899991. Accessed 12 Sept 2023

Spector A, Norvig P, Petrov S (2012) Google's hybrid approach to research, communications of the ACM, 55(7):34–37. https://static.googleusercontent.com/media/research.google.com/en//pubs/archive/38149.pdf. Accessed 12 Sept 2023

UK Information Commissioner (2018) Draft guidance on the research provisions within the UK GDPR and the DPA 2018. https://ico.org.uk/media/about-the-ico/consultations/4019614/research-provisions-draft-consultation-202202.pdf. Accessed 12 Sept 2023

United Nations Environment Programme (1989) Technology, markets and people: the use and misuse of fuelsaving stoves - a project case study. https://www.nzdl.org/cgi-bin/library?e=d-00000-00%2D%2D-off-0cdl%2D%2D00-0%2D%2D%2D%2D0-10-0%2D%2D-0%2D%2D-0direct-10%2D%2D-4%2D%2D%2D%2D%2D%2D-0-1l%2D%2D11-en-50%2D%2D-20-about%2D%2D-00-0-1-00-0%2D%2D4%2D%2D%2D%2D0-0-11-10-0utfZz-8-00&cl=CL2.20&d=HASH014ac928c772f8a8f8f36abf.9&gc=1. Accessed 12 Sept 2023

Yordanova K (2022) The EU AI Act – balancing human rights and innovation through regulatory sandboxes and standardization. Competition Policy International, pp 1–9. https://kuleuven.limo.libis.be/discovery/fulldisplay?docid=lirias3708651&context=SearchWebhook&vid=32KUL_KUL:Lirias&lang=en&search_scope=lirias_profile&adaptor=SearchWebhook&tab=LIRIAS&query=any,contains,LIRIAS3708651&offset=0. Accessed 12 Sept 2023

Part II

Governance of AI or Governance by AI: Limits, New Threats, and Unnegotiable Principles

Migle Laukyte

Contents

Abstract This chapter analyses the dynamics of AI governance and advances a few ideas that should help us ensure an AI compliant with human dignity and freedom, human rights, democracy, and the rule of law. Human beings are shedding their ability to govern and exercise regulatory authority over their own affairs, ceding power to nonhumans, but as much as this trend may be owed to the advance of AI technology, also complicit in it is the regulatory activity of the companies that develop these technologies. On top of that, there is the question of AI in the hands of governments, whose use of the technology for their own (legal) regulation gives them over citizens a power that can be misused or abused. How, then, to confront this danger that AI and its use are posing? This chapter argues that one tool we can use to protect ourselves is that of human rights, but to that end—if we are to make these rights effective—we must bring them up to date considering the advancements made in AI. Due to the very nature of AI, the focus is on privacy and data protection, where I identify three cases—namely, group privacy, biometric psychography, and neurorights—and with each of these cases I show that AI can be governed by introducing a suite of rights designed to be AI-responsive or otherwise by reinterpreting existing rights to make them so.

M. Laukyte
Faculty of Law, Pompeu Fabra University, Barcelona, Spain
e-mail: migle.laukyte@upf.edu

E. Gill-Pedro, A. Moberg (eds.), *YSEC Yearbook of Socio-Economic Constitutions 2023*, YSEC Yearbook of Socio-Economic Constitutions (2024) 2023: 97–116,
https://doi.org/10.1007/16495_2023_58, Published online: 21 October 2023

1 Introduction

There have been and continue to be many debates on how to govern and regulate artificial intelligence (AI), which not only refers to autonomous and intelligent technologies broadly understood but also introduces a new paradigm in regulation where technologies are turning from objects to be regulated into regulatory tools.[1] What is most worrisome with these dynamics is that these tools of governance and regulation are coming from the private sector, which has no authority to govern or legislate, and no moral basis on which it might be legitimised to do so. The growth in the power of private industry over the last centuries is a threat that democracies will have to deal with sooner rather than later, considering that the corporate world has already started to expand into the public sector.[2]

In addition, governments, especially (but not only) authoritarian ones, are themselves often tempted to use AI to control and manipulate citizens so as to ensure the stability and continuity of the status quo, cut social entitlements, or infringe the fundamental rights of its citizens.[3] Indeed, as Mejias has commented, 'governments are not only failing to regulate the creation and deployment of these new types of codes/laws by corporations, but by going as far as using code from these corporations, governments are becoming partners in joint ventures that are motivated by profit, and that are sometimes racist and discriminatory'.[4]

This chapter argues that in dealing with these issues that we are facing in relation to the use of AI and other technologies, in an effort to hold back the threat of submission to these technologies, we can turn to the legal instrument of human rights. My argument is that human rights need to be sharpened and shaped to fit the challenges posed by AI, and I suggest that we do that by looking at three cases, or three new ways to see human rights from the AI perspective. The first has to do with group privacy: The rights to privacy and personal data protection should have to be expanded to include *groups* of individuals, the very groups that algorithms aggregate and organise as they see fit. The second case is that of biometric psychography, meaning the ability of certain AI-empowered technologies to read our (human) bodily and cognitive reactions to stimuli from the virtual environment without our realising it (and hence, obviously, without our informed consent). This loss of control over our most intimate emotions and interests is not just about revealing ourselves in commercial settings but is about much deeper revelations that human

[1] Abramowicz (2015); Brownsword (2021).

[2] See, for example, De Souza and Taylor (2021), who point out that big tech companies make inroads into new areas of interest and influence, such as healthcare, and that this could lead to a 'thinning out of expertise and capacity in the public sector'.

[3] Among many who have made this claim, see Eubanks (2018); Mejias (2023); Calo and Citron (2021).

[4] Mejias (2023), p. 2.

rights—particularly privacy and personal data protection—cannot properly address in their current form.[5]

Similarly, and this is the third case, human rights are ill-equipped to protect what newly created neurorights are designed to protect.[6] A recent creation, these rights signal the threats that AI—along with similar technologies that make it possible access to the brain's cognitive and intellectual dynamics—is posing to the very essence of human beings. In this case, human (neuro) rights would shield the human brain from commercial or governmental attempts to exploit our cognitive biases to turn us into pliant consumers or into compliant citizens, happy with the status quo and not so ready to demand change or accountability.

The examples just mentioned highlight a dual need: a need to regulate the use of AI and limit the ability of technology companies to set the rules governing that use, but also a need to ensure that the future governance of AI is human-rights oriented and that human rights address the new vulnerabilities. Hence the three areas of vulnerability selected for study, namely, group privacy, biometric psychography, and neurorights. These rights reflect the evolution of AI-empowered processing of human-generated data: Group privacy is already on the table of privacy scholars, thanks to social networks, e-commerce, and other digital environments, and biometric psychography is becoming part of the debate as well thanks not only to advancements of Metaverse but also to the European Parliament's awareness of it and reference to biometrics-based data in its version of Artificial Intelligence Act that is currently being negotiated. Biometric psychography is closely related to the non-invasive brain interfaces that link virtual reality headsets to the virtual environment. However non-invasive brain interfaces could soon by eclipsed by invasive brain interfaces that should bring the discussion on neurorights into focus.

Furthermore, these three cases are also representative in clearly showing what we need to focus on to ensure that advancements in AI are in line with human rights in general, and personal data protection in particular. In the first case, that of group privacy, AI signals the need to introduce a new data subject: We should grant personal data protection not only to individuals but also to groups, and particularly to those assembled by algorithms. The second case, that of biometric psychography, requires that we update the concept of sensitive data, which should not be limited to idea of biometric data as static data only (such as fingerprints) but should also include dynamic data, such as our bodily and mental reactions to stimuli, reactions which are understood to be beyond human control and which fall under the concept of biometrics-based data. The third case, that of neurorights, highlights the need to legally recognise a new source of data, namely, the brain as a source of sensitive data and as an extremely vulnerable organ, which cannot be put in jeopardy for the sake of commercial profits or government interests.

To be sure, the articulation of AI governance through these three cases has its weaknesses and shortcomings. Among these is the fact that all these cases relate to

[5] Heller (2021).

[6] Yuste et al. (2017); Ienca (2021a).

privacy and personal data protection only, but AI can undermine a whole range of other rights as well, such as the right to assembly, freedom of movement, freedom of expression, and freedom discrimination, none of which are addressed in this chapter. However, these and other rights could be affected because of—and through—the data that AI tools collect about us, and it therefore seems reasonable to deal with AI governance through the lens of privacy and personal data, as it is (personal) data that enables AI to govern us or be used to that end.[7]

Another critical aspect is the limited field of view this chapter affords on AI governance: The governance of such a complex technology is a multi-layered and multistakeholder endeavour that involves different levels of granularity in terms of norms and practices. This is why in addressing this governance by way of three yet-to-be-recognised rights within a broad understanding of the right to privacy and personal data protection, we are only looking at very small slice of the range of issues at stake, and even worse, we risk zooming in on one aspect of such a wide-ranging problem, thinking that in this way we can solve the whole of it.[8] That is not the idea behind this chapter. The point of zooming in is rather that this can be useful in shedding light on a particular aspect of this many-sided problem, in the hope that by figuring out how to deal with this particular aspect, we can also find a solution to some of the other aspects, too. For example, if we agree to protect group privacy, we would also provide new and additional protections to other groups that stand to be affected by AI, such as consumers.

Here, then, is how this chapter will be organised. I begin by explaining why we need a human rights-based approach in thinking about the governance *of* technologies, and as well as governance *by* technologies, and what kind of improvements we need to introduce to make this approach work. We will then turn to the cases that illustrate the argument that the new challenges posed by AI call for an updated vision of human rights and that this updated vision could enable us to govern AI in such a way as to fix the power asymmetries between stakeholders (businesses, governments, and citizens): These cases are group privacy (Sect. 2.1), biometric psychography, (Sect. 2.2) and neurorights (Sect. 2.3). In Sect. 3, I briefly introduce the role that courts—particularly the European Court of Human Rights (ECtHR)—could play in advancing a human-rights-based AI governance, and finally in Sect. 4 I

---

[7] In response to the Supreme Court's 2022 decision in *Dobbs v. Jackson Women's Health Organization*, depriving American citizens of the constitutional right to abortion they had previously enjoyed, President Biden commented that 'the fundamental right to privacy [the basis of the previously recognized constitutional right to abortion] has served as the basis for so many more rights that we have come to take [...] for granted that are ingrained in the fabric of this country' (Biden 2022). Although President Biden was referring specifically to the right to abortion, it is by all means possible to use these words to refer to a more extensive and inclusive interpretation of privacy and personal data protection.

[8] Another problem is the *how* question, namely, how to make these rights real and functional within the realm of AI governance and how to situate the challenges of AI governance within the wider framework of regulatory theory. This chapter leaves this *how* question unanswered, as it focuses on the *what* and *why* questions involved in this governance.

offer some closing remarks, with a few ideas on how this research could continue and evolve.

2 A Human-Rights-Based Approach

Human beings are shedding their ability to govern and exercise regulatory authority over their own affairs, ceding power to nonhumans, but as much as this trend may be owed to the advance of AI technology, also complicit in it is the regulatory activity of the companies that develop these technologies.[9] Indeed, legal systems have long been grappling with the abiding problem of the legal personhood of companies, their legal rights, and the clashes that pit these rights against human rights, in a continuing effort to strike a balance between these competing interests. This balancing act now has become more complicated: The technological advancements that technology companies are making are offering new ways to tilt this balance in their own favour much more powerfully than before.

In fact, from the private companies' perspective, technologies and humans are two kinds of tools with which to achieve their goals, and the fact that technology is being used as a tool with which to subdue humans into passivity is a threat that technology-enabled governance and regulation by business entities is posing for the future of humanity.

In addition, governments have quickly learned to use AI for purposes that negatively impact citizens, especially the most vulnerable social groups.[10] In this sense, the state fails twice: it fails in its own use of AI, and it fails in not regulating the use of AI by the private sector, in a sense turning into an 'aider and abetter' together with private companies—if the latter are abusing their newly acquired AI power, the former is doing the same,[11] or at least it is turning a blind eye on that abuse.[12] What this means for democracy, transparency, trust, the rule of law, and other basic principles of our societies is obvious: AI is in this sense destructive and antidemocratic.

The importance of human rights in governing and regulating technologies is nothing new: Many have argued that human rights should serve as a blueprint in choosing the regulatory and governance models for any technological innovation,[13]

---

[9] Nemitz (2018).

[10] See Eubanks (2018), Mejias (2023), Calo and Citron (2021), among many others.

[11] For instance, Calo and Citron (2021) claim that government agencies use these systems to mask choices that would be unpopular, such as cutting healthcare benefits for certain social groups.

[12] Particularly, Mejias (2023) addresses public-private partnerships under which AI systems developed in the private sector are then used by governments to deliberately discriminate against vulnerable social groups.

[13] Among many examples, see Lucchi (2014), arguing that any regulation of the Internet and its content should be compliant with human rights. Schneider (2022) addresses the implementation of human rights in blockchain technology.

that should be 'context-sensitive, adaptive, anticipatory, effective, agile and at the right level of ethical and legal granularity'.[14]

The governance of AI is no exception:[15] Bryson argues that human rights are 'the painstakingly agreed foundation of international law and the obligations of the state and should be treated as core to ethical AI systems',[16] while Donahue and MacDuffee Metzger argue that what we need is 'a shared global framework [...] to ensure that AI is developed and applied in ways that respect human dignity, democratic accountability, and the bedrock principles of free societies',[17] and this framework is represented by the existing universal human rights framework. Furthermore, Nemitz, considering the pervasiveness of AI on the one hand and the need to link AI to basic constitutional principles on the other, makes the case for 'a new culture of technology and business development for the age of AI which we call "rule of law, democracy and human rights by design"'.[18]

This culture should not be limited to the private sector: governments around the world must be accountable for the uses they put AI to, even more so that when we talk about human rights, we entrust our governments to make these rights real: no government can be non-transparent in its use of AI and at the same time claim compliance with and adherence to the ideal of human rights.

At the institutional level, the human rights-based approach, at least as concerns the EU, is aligned with AI: The Council of the European Union has concluded that the European approach to digitalisation in general and AI in particular 'should be human-centric and ensure the full respect and promotion of fundamental rights',[19] and a very similar position was also expressed by the EU Commission and other EU bodies.[20]

The position is very similar in other continents as well. Thus, in October 2022, the White House Office of Science and Technology Policy issued a 'Blueprint for an AI Bill of Rights' that highlights the threat that technology poses to 'the rights of the American public', making reference to civil rights, civil liberties, and privacy (even if this policy statement is not concerned with human or fundamental rights traditionally understood).[21] And China, without taking up the question of rights generally, includes privacy protection among the principles of AI development.[22]

The terminological differences in these policy statements across three continents are significant. For it is not an accident that the EU should be referring to

---

[14] Kellmeyer (2022), p. 424.

[15] For an overview, see Fjeld et al. (2020).

[16] Bryson (2020), p. 20.

[17] Donahoe and MacDuffee Metzger (2019), p. 116.

[18] Nemitz (2018).

[19] Council of the European Union (2020), p. 6. Here human rights are understood to be the same as fundamental rights.

[20] EU Commission (2020), EGE (2018), and many others.

[21] AI Bill of Rights (2022).

[22] Ministry of Science and Technology (2019).

fundamental rights, the US to civil rights and liberties, and China to the protection of privacy without mentioning rights at all. What we have here is evidence that, as has long been argued in connection with human rights, while these rights may have traditionally been presented as universal, they are in fact a Western conceit, a device of the Western liberal order—not universal but 'a contemporary, internationalized and universalized version of the liberal position on rights'.[23]

In a different take on the question of the universality of rights, it has been argued that there is a distinction to be made if we look at the development of rights over the course of history: We have the first two generations of human rights, namely, civil and political rights and social and economic rights, and these are in effect an entirely Western creation, but with the third generation, what are called solidarity rights, we do have something resembling the universal, as these rights represent 'the demand of *non*-Western countries for the right to economic and social development'.[24]

Even so, if Western societies should manage to address the negative effects of AI on the human rights-based approach and achieve success by turning AI development and applications into a more (even if only Western) human-centric endeavour, perhaps AI could help to universalise human rights in a way that is beneficial not only for Western societies but also, collaterally, for those countries that are sceptical of Western ideals.

Bryson links governance to redistribution and argues that excessive inequalities reflect a failure of governance,[25] and this reasoning can undoubtedly be applied to the AI domain as well. In what follows, I address three cases that risk making citizens more vulnerable, all the while strengthening the position of companies that develop AI and governments that deploy it, thus creating new power asymmetries between them or otherwise widening existing ones.

In what follows, the focus is on three cases which illustrate how human rights as they stand are inadequate to address the new situations brought into being by the development of AI, as well as by developments in other groundbreaking technologies. This is not to say that human rights as we know them are outdated: On the contrary, the argument these cases highlight is that human rights are not static but dynamic and 'living', which means that they need to be constantly reinterpreted to ensure the protection of human dignity and autonomy in the fullest sense of these terms.[26]

This reasoning falls in line with Habermas's idea that human rights are responses to specific violations of human dignity,[27] and a continuous flow of such violations stems precisely from the advancement of AI (notwithstanding the positive outcomes

---

[23] Brown (1997), p. 43. For a discussion of the different accounts of the universality of human rights, with a critical assessment, see Donnelly (2007), Wang (2002).

[24] Wang (2002), p. 172. Italics added.

[25] Bryson (2020), p. 19.

[26] For an overview, see Rosen (2012). On the Universal Declaration of Human Rights as a living document, see also Vasak (1977).

[27] Habermas (2010).

of that advancement). In our case, these violations take place when people are aggregated into groups without their even realising it, using the technology to enter into their minds or to accesses their most private emotions and probe for their interests, the ultimate purpose being to increase profits by selling more goods and services, where private companies are concerned, and to keep citizens under control, where states are concerned.

As noted, the focus in this chapter will be on some human rights (understood as rights ascribable to human beings, as opposed to rights that might be claimed for nonhuman entities), and the approach we will be taking draws on the idea that these rights are new and not new at the same time. The novelty often depends on the perspective through which it is addressed, but it is clear that new rights are intrinsically contested,[28] so it should come as no surprise that the new rights addressed in this chapter are subject to extensive criticism.[29]

In addition, these cases also serve as guideposts that we can use in finding our way through the complexities of AI governance and regulation: There are so many applications, uses, products, and services that more often than not it is unclear what needs to be regulated, what is already regulated, and what need not be regulated at all. These cases key in on applications and uses of AI that need to be addressed by regulation and cannot be left either to self-regulation by the market or to governments alone to solve, so much so that research shows that even within a single country, such as the United States, there are 'different political agendas in play when it comes to the use and regulation of algorithms'.[30]

In a way, all three cases deal with personal data, and this brings into focus the General Data Protection Regulation (GDPR).[31] Its importance for the governance of technology in general, and AI in particular, cannot be underestimated. Indeed, 'the GDPR is a modern example of technology neutral law, the meaning and relevance of which changes with the progress of technology, including through AI'.[32] The following examples show how challenging it is for the GDPR to go hand in hand with AI development and that legislative updates will probably have to be introduced to enable it to be functional in governing AI in the near future.

---

[28]von Arnauld et al. (2020), p. 2.

[29]Among many, see Griffin (2008), arguing that group rights that more often than not are either not rights in the first place or are individual rights, and Hertz (2023), arguing that there is no need to introduce new human rights to protect mental self-determination. Other authors claim that we already have rights that apply to communities and groups, such as the rights of indigenous people, but these rights are quite scarce. At the same time, as Wang (2002, p. 174) observes, it is worth bearing in mind that central to the modern idea of human rights is the 'connotation of individualism', or the idea that human rights are ultimately individual rights.

[30]Mejias (2023), p. 10.

[31]Regulation (EU) 2016/679 of the European Parliament and of the Council of 27 April 2016 on the protection of natural persons with regard to the processing of personal data and on the free movement of such data, and repealing Directive 95/46/EC (General Data Protection Regulation), available at https://gdpr-info.eu/.

[32]Nemitz (2018).

2.1 Group Privacy

AI-empowered big data algorithms pose a threat not only to individual privacy but also to groups, which too could be mistreated or discriminated against (and this may already be happening).[33] As Eubanks puts it: 'In his famous novel *1984*, George Orwell got one thing wrong. Big Brother is not watching *you*, he's watching *us*. Most people are targeted for digital scrutiny as members of social groups, not as individuals. People of color, migrants, unpopular religious groups, sexual minorities, the poor and other oppressed and exploited populations bear a much higher burden of monitoring and tracking than advantaged groups'.[34]

Group privacy is a right to privacy that an entire group enjoys *as a group*, rather than as a sum individuals each with their own right to privacy.[35] In this sense, group privacy is the privacy of an entity which is composed of individuals, but which is nevertheless viewed as a single whole. Groups can be created on the basis of consumer preferences, political ideas, or other characteristics under which that algorithms group individuals.[36] Group privacy has been around for a while, to be sure, but it is new in the sense that we have not felt the threat or need to address group privacy by law as we did with individual privacy.[37]

The speed of datification should, however, cause us to rethink that stance: It is no longer the threat of identification but rather the threat of aggregation and monitoring that should impel us to act. And the tools of aggregation and monitoring are all AI-based. As Radaelli et al. argue, 'the current individual-centric approach to privacy and data protection does not encompass the realities of modern life. This makes us—as a society—vulnerable to large-scale surveillance attacks which we need to develop protections against'.[38] And that suggests that one way to protect ourselves may be to get legal recognition for group privacy.

In light of the above, we should also rethink what we consider a group. In our everyday language, a group is usually made up of people who are aware of their belonging to the group or might have actively chosen to belong to it. AI changes that: Groups are created by algorithms; people are not even aware of their being placed into one group or another or—which is more likely—into many different groups at the same time, and they have no control over where the algorithms place them and why. The question is, why should this matter? If an algorithm, in a simplified

---

[33] In addition, individuals misclassified as part of a certain group could also be subject to specific treatment, of a kind that is undesirable, to say the least. Suh et al. (2018), p. 168.

[34] Eubanks (2018), p. 6. Italics in the original.

[35] Floridi (2014).

[36] In addition, grouping people on the basis of their ethnic origin or political ideas also involves the questions of discrimination and violation of political freedoms.

[37] For early ideas on group privacy, see Skinner et al. (2006, p. 391), who define group privacy as privacy that 'protects the personal information of the group and each member of the group'.

[38] Radaelli et al. (2018).

scenario, places me in a group comprising middle-aged foreign female academics living in Finland, why is that a problem?

It becomes a problem if as a middle-aged foreign female academic living in Finland, I am treated as such for any number of purposes, including the purpose of profiling me as a consumer, such that I am targeted with commercial offers that an algorithm has determined I should be interested in as a member of such a group. This treatment limits my freedoms and choices, and even if I am not identified as a specific person—making it difficult to talk about personal data, which usually means data by which one is identified—I am put into a box with a multi-layered label and treated accordingly, but not according to my individuality and personal preferences, which might be very different from those that algorithms perceive as belonging to middle-aged foreign female academics living in Finland.

But that is a bland example, to be sure. Much more concerning is the more complex situation in which I should also be put into other boxes with other labels that identify my political preferences, sexuality, skin colour, health problems, or income: Together with the rest of the group—and unbeknownst to me and to them—we may attract the attention of law enforcement (if, for example, the algorithm identified us as a group tending to espouse radical political views) or of health authorities and pharmaceutical companies (if, for example, the algorithm identified us as 'anti-vaxxers' or as particularly prone to certain diseases), or we may end up falling into some other risk class we are unaware of, affecting our employment prospects, credit scoring, insurance premiums, and the like.

Commenting on this potential for misuse of algorithmically processed data, Mittelstadt argues that such ad hoc groups ought to be granted an 'informational privacy right' or a 'right to inviolate personality', which may come into contrast with, but does not deny, individual privacy guarantees and protections from individual profiling, guaranteed by GDPR. Particularly, Mittelstadt defends a limited right for these groups—and not for AI—enabling them to manage their own identity and protect it from public or private entities that create knowledge about such groups, acting on such knowledge without the awareness or consent of the group's members.[39]

This line of reasoning—under which decisions about a group or its identity are for the group to take and not for an algorithm—aligns with privacy and personal-data-protection logic adopted in the EU: If we have placed citizens at the centre of decision-making when it comes to their personal data, it follows that the same should happen when it comes to the groups they are clustered into. It is clearly not so simple to put that principle into practice, since decision-making can easily turn into a complex endeavour where competing interests need to be balanced, but this complexity at least gives those concerned some agency, which they do not get when decision-making is left to algorithms and consequently to private companies or to governments. Under an open scenario in which group data is disclosed and transparent, citizens play an active role, and it is up to them to make it passive if they so

[39] Mittelsdadt (2017), p. 476, 483.

choose, whereas under a *closed* algorithmic scenario, human decision-making is passive by default: Passivity turns people into means to certain ends, where they can no longer be considered as ends in themselves in the Kantian sense.

In case of group privacy, what becomes obvious is that AI is used as a tool by which to control what people know about themselves, or what information has been collected about them as members of various groups, forcing them into a state of unawareness, which itself becomes a further tool by which to govern them. This means that before we can even address the question of consent in connection with group privacy, we have to address that of (human) awareness.[40] Hence the idea of protecting group privacy: We need that protection because, without it, we can be subjected to a kind of AI-enabled governance that we are not even aware of, and when we are so governed, without our knowledge, those who govern us, whether in the private or the public sector, gain over us an outsized amount of control that has no justification, precisely because it is exerted in the dark through the black box of algorithmic AI.

2.2 Biometric Psychography

Biometric psychography is a technique that combines biometrics with behavioural information to gain information about us: it is used not to identify us as named individuals (although it certainly *can* be used to that end) but to decode our interests, inclinations, and desires.[41] The purpose of this technology, in other words, is not to find out who someone *is* but what they like and prefer. In both cases there is an issue of privacy and personal data;[42] in both cases there is at stake our freedom to decide for ourselves who—or what, in case of algorithms—can access this information, for what purposes, when, and how; and in both cases, we would like this information to be protected and not available to anyone.

[40] The principle at stake here is simple enough when it comes to *individual* privacy: If data about us is being processed, we need to be made aware of that fact. This means being informed by the data processor or being informed that when we are accessing a service or buying a product, the cookies we consent to are data we are handing over to the entity providing that service or selling that product: Awareness precedes consent. But with algorithmically aggregated groups this isn't even a possibility: People are not even aware they have been made to belong to a group, so they cannot give any informed consent, because they cannot consent to that which they cannot be aware of.

[41] Heller (2020, 2021).

[42] Even if biometric data can be used to reveal someone's preferences, or what these preferences are likely to be, these preferences as such are not considered personal data in the law and so is not protected under any privacy and personal-data-protection legislation. But because the information that can be extracted from biometric data can be used to reveal personal preferences and can be used in combination with identifying information, I will consider it personal data (albeit in a broader sense than what the law usually grants).

The functioning of biometric psychography depends on how sophisticated the technologies in place are: The more virtual, augmented, and extended reality advances, and the more the Metaverse or an analogue comes into use,[43] the easier it becomes to use biometric psychography. Thanks to biometric tracking techniques—making it possible to measure pupil dilation, do facial scans, read galvanic skin response, and take measurements of electric activities of the human body (electromyography)—algorithms can discover what makes us sweat or alters our heartbeat, what we focus our eye on in a virtual environment, and how long, how we react to a variety of stimuli, and what constitutes a stimulus for us in the first place.

In this way, companies and governments gain access to data about individuals that is extremely revealing, making it possible to determine, for example, what someone's sexual orientation is, or what drugs they may be using, or whether they have an autistic spectrum disorder.[44] And as intimately granular and wide-ranging as the dataset is that companies and governments can collect about individuals through conventional digital means, as through social networks or apps, even more complete is the picture they can form about those who enter into virtual environments.

That is a critical change that can take place in virtual environments: The biometric data these environments give access to, including data about our physical and cognitive reactions in such environments, enable companies and governments to form a dramatically more comprehensive, multifaceted, and intimate picture about us, giving them insights about preferences and inclinations that we ourselves might not even be aware of. This augmented knowledge that companies and governments can now access in relation to individuals changes the paradigm in our understanding of privacy and personal data and what they mean for individuals and their personal development, dignity, and autonomy.[45]

And, as noted, it is not just the private sector that could have access to such information and knowledge: If people flock to the Metaverse, or something like it, and the public sector gets in as well, the same information and knowledge would become available to any public-sector entity. And indeed, as current uses of the Metaverse by the public sector seem to be suggesting, this may become a space in

[43] Mystakidis (2022), p. 486 define the Metaverse as a 'post-reality universe, a perpetual and persistent multiuser environment merging physical reality with digital virtuality', where our avatars will be able to move among different virtual worlds.

[44] We already can predict the risk of developing mental disease based on how we perform in videogames, an example being Sea Hero Quest, which has been used to discover that a player's abnormal spatial navigation correlates with a higher genetic risk of developing Alzheimer's disease. See Coughlan et al. (2019).

[45] Consider, for example, the kind of power that companies and governments, armed with this new algorithmic knowledge, can wield over children and minors, using the data so acquired to nudge them from a very early age into being specific kinds of consumers or citizens.

which citizens can interact with public-sector entities but in so doing end up giving these entities access to data that may not be necessary in facilitating the interaction at hand.[46]

What is worth underscoring is the gap between the advancement of AI and other disruptive technologies, on the one hand, and on the other hand the slow response of the human right to privacy, which cannot afford to play for time: Another way to put a limit on AI, in such a way as to govern its advancement and use, is therefore to revise the regulation of personal data protection in view of the possibilities offered by the new realities and digital environments that captivate and absorb our glances, faces, and bodily reactions.

This is why biometric psychography marks a new phase in the evolution of threats to privacy. This is no longer a question of our freedom to consent to others processing our personal data—and in this case, in GDPR terminology, our most sensitive data. For it isn't even possible to consent to such processing: We do not control our heartbeat, eye movement, perspiration, or reflexes, nor do we fully control our cognitive responses, and so all of this biometrics-based data is raw material of value that we unwittingly give over to algorithms so that they can process, classify, and build individual as well as group profiles that can subsequently be used to nudge us into doing something or into behaving in a certain way, or it could simply be used to keep an eye on us, as law enforcement would be able to do.[47]

Nor is that the end of it: We have electroencephalography that makes it possible to read brain waves, not only offering a more invasive means to probe the brain to see how it reacts to stimuli but also opening the door to possibilities to manipulate and monitor it. This is the possibility considered in the next section, where I discuss how this further threat might be prevented, to this end drawing on a newly conceived legal instrument intended to protect human integrity and autonomy, an instrument that has come to be known as neurorights.

2.3 *Neurorights*

The advancements made in neurotechnology are unquestionably beneficial, not only for the healthy but also, and especially, for those who have suffered serious brain injury and live at the margins of consciousness, in a penumbral area of consciousness

[46] Maciejewski (2023).

[47] There is also the possibility of misreading or misinterpreting the data our bodies communicate in virtual environments. For instance, an accelerated heartbeat might be caused by something that has nothing to do with our experience in a virtual environment. It may be owed, for example, to a brisk movement, our previous experience in the physical environment, or a surprise hug from a family member. In this case, a person would be mislabeled as having responded emotionally to stimuli unrelated to the response, and would accordingly be misattributed with interests he or she does not have.

which is complicated to explore, and which can represent an irreversible state for the patient.[48]

However, the technology can also be used for nonmedical, nontherapeutic purposes: the invasive brain-computer interfaces can be put to commercial uses,[49] and governments might soon realise the potential of these technologies as well. The risks are numerous: A widening gap between haves and have nots through human cognitive enhancement, side effects on the human brain and its cognitive and intellectual abilities, and new forms of manipulation, such as subconscious manipulation, [50] seem to be just behind the corner if it should become standard practice for private companies and governments to access our brains.[51]

This is why human rights have been put on the table, here too, and new rights have been proposed to protect the very essence of a human being and perhaps the most mysterious part of the human body, the brain.[52] These neurorights can be sorted into five groups: (a) the right to mental privacy, or the right to privacy of personal neurodata, with strict limitations on its use; (b) the right to agency, or freedom from manipulation in decision-making; (c) the right to identity, or the right to preserve one's idea of oneself; (d) the right to fair access to mental augmentation, which requires equality and justice in enabling citizens to access it; and (e) the right to protection against algorithmic bias, which could be further perpetuated through access to one's brain.[53]

As of today, these rights are widely discussed and contested: Some authors argue that already existing rights—such as the right to freedom of thought—can be broadly construed to include these rights, and that novel rights are therefore not needed at all.[54] But these considerations are specific to the problem of how to *formalize* these rights, translating them into legal language. They do not deny that there *is* a problem to be solved—in the form of the threats posed by the advancement of AI uses in

---

[48] A comprehensive overview is provided by Fins (2015).

[49] One of many uses the brain-computer interface can be put to is its use to control autonomous vehicles. See Choi (2014).

[50] Subconscious manipulation falls very much in line with what the EU already wants to prohibit within the wide domain of AI applications. Particularly, the EU has a ban on systems that 'manipulate persons through subliminal techniques beyond their consciousness or exploit vulnerabilities of specific vulnerable groups such as children or persons with disabilities in order to materially distort their behaviour in a manner that is likely to cause them or another person psychological or physical harm' (AIA 2021, 5.2.2). These systems, however, are not based on neural technologies, suggesting that there are limits the EU legislator may be unwilling to cross.

[51] Yuste et al. (2017), p. 160; Ienca (2021b).

[52] Kellmeyer (2022); Hansotia (2003), who among other particularities, also observes that although the brain is made from the same nucleated and mitochondria-filled cells as other organs, such as the liver, it is the only organ that can generate such an amasing phenomenon as the mind.

[53] Yuste et al. (2021); Bublitz (2022).To be sure, having in mind the focus of this Chapter, only four neurorights are relevant: the right to fair access to mental augmentation addresses a different problem and has nothing to do with this Chapter's perspective on AI governance.

[54] Hertz (2023). A similar position is argued for by Bublitz (2022) and Kellmeyer (2022).

neuroscience—nor is there any denying that rights can be an effective tool with which to respond to these threats.

It is not easy to figure out what the best way is to make neurorights effective, to be sure, but whether they are incorporated into exiting rights or are introduced as a new package of self-standing human rights, they have a fundamental role to play in tightening the use of AI in neurotechnology, with a focus on the extraction of personal, particularly sensitive, data and the consequent manipulation of the individual *in loco*, rather than a focus on human health, wellbeing, and the public good.

3 Living Human Rights, or the Role of the Courts

Having framed the governance of AI by suggesting how human rights might be developed moving forward, we now turn to the question of what might be done to implement this human-rights-based approach to AI governance and make effective the rights that are central to it.

One way to attack this problem is to start from the dynamic view of human rights introduced in Sect. 2. Human rights, it was suggested, are not static entities detached from the course of events, and whose meaning is fixed once and for all, but are instead woven into the fabric of the changing society out of which they emerge, and so, much like any legal rule or principle, they need to be constantly interpreted and reinterpreted to meet the challenges of that ever-changing social environment. And here the courts have a role to play, shaping human rights in response to those challenges and in keeping with national and international law, and with the spirit of the very conventions in which they are enshrined.[55]

For instance, the European Court of Human Rights (ECtHR) has been recognised as a court that often reflected the trends of international human rights law in its decisions. It also constantly updates its interpretation of the European Convention on Human Rights (ECHR) to extend it to do two things: first, to give it scope over rights that are not expressively included in it, such as the rights of sexual minorities; and second, to guarantee rights which are not yet fully acknowledged, as is the case with environmental rights; economic, social, and cultural rights; and the right to health.[56]

---

[55] Thus, in connection with neurorights, the draft constitution that Chile put to a popular vote 2022 contained provisions recognising a right to 'physical and mental integrity' and protecting 'cerebral activity and its data', and although this new constitution was ultimately voted down, it is in itself significant that these protections were even debated as part of a constitutional process (Ienca 2021b, p. 65).

[56] Viljanen (2008).

Going back to the three cases discussed in the previous section, there is an obvious link to Art. 8 ECHR (privacy) and its interpretation by the ECtHR.[57] In addition, Art. 8 has been interpreted by the ECtHR as not only a negative obligation of states not to interfere with citizens' private lives, but also as a positive obligation of states to adopt measures that secure that right.[58] From this perspective, then, if a case relating to the use of AI by a private or public entities should be brought before the ECtHR, the Court could interpret Art. 8 ECHR to cover group privacy, to prohibit the detection and processing of emotions and interests in alternative realities, and to recognise neurorights as legitimate claims. This reading of Art. 8 ECHR could, on the one hand, protect this expanded vision of privacy from state interference (and so from the use the state itself might make of commercial algorithms, the Metaverse, or neural technologies to get into its citizens' minds), and, at the same time, it could also oblige the state to prohibit private companies from doing that, too.

In this sense, the ECtHR could provide states with additional legal grounds and pressure to enact laws guided by human rights contained in the ECHR and reinterpreted by ECtHR, which in so doing would be taking a 'dynamic' and 'evolutive approach' as a 'necessary element of any human rights interpretation, either in the European context, or universally applied'.[59]

But if these rights, and consequently human-rights-based AI governance, are to be made effective, it will not be enough to rely on networks of national and international courts. We will also need to update the law itself and have the institutions in place that will undertake oversight and enforcement functions. That discussion, however, falls outside the scope of this chapter, so we will address it as a question for future research, the topic of the next section.

[57] Article 8 ECHR—Right to respect for private and family life:

1. Everyone has the right to respect for his private and family life, his home and his correspondence.
2. There shall be no interference by a public authority with the exercise of this right except such as is in accordance with the law and is necessary in a democratic society in the interests of national security, public safety or the economic well-being of the country, for the prevention of disorder or crime, for the protection of health or morals, or for the protection of the rights and freedoms of others.

[58] The relevant case here is *Von Hannover v. Germany*, no. 59320/00, ECHR 2004-VI, where the Court also comments as follows in the matter of positive and negative obligations: 'The boundary between the State's positive and negative obligations under this provision does not lend itself to precise definition. The applicable principles are, nonetheless, similar. In both contexts regard must be had to the fair balance that has to be struck between the competing interests of the individual and of the community as a whole; and in both contexts the State enjoys a certain margin of appreciation' (para 46).

[59] Viljanen (2008), p. 251.

4 Conclusions and Future Research

In this chapter, we looked at the advancements made in AI to argue that AI governance can be viewed through the lens of the novel threats to which it exposes humans, and so through the novel human rights it gives rise to. These new and still somewhat fuzzy rights may never come to fruition, to be sure, but if the argument stands and gains ground, they can be understood as outlining a future landscape for AI and its use—a legal future in which these activities will be regulated and the rules enforced.

AI has always been regulated to an extent, particularly as concerns its commercial applications. The question has always been how to craft this regulation considering the constant changes AI is undergoing. But it is not just the constant change of the AI landscape that should be of concern in regulating the development and use of AI, for the point of such regulation should be to make sure that AI serves a public good. The rules therefore must be robust, and they need to cast a wide net, applying not just to the private sector but also to the public sector, where the stakes and expectations are higher. And one reason why effective AI governance needs robust rules enacted into law is that ethical governance will not suffice in ensuring that we are protected from the most disruptive effects of AI. To this end we also need to rely on the courts, such as the ECtHR, which can play a crucial role in promoting AI governance by reshaping international human rights law in view of the march of events, its mission being 'to pass the torch to another [human rights] actor and let the dialogue [on human rights] continue; and maybe to return to the discourse in a later stage of the development processes'.

What I am suggesting, in short, is that for AI governance to work effectively—across the full spectrum of AI applications, seemingly as wide-ranging as human activity itself—we have to draw on a number of sources that need to be made to work together: legislation establishing rights protecting us from the many potentially harmful uses AI can be put to, a judiciary that can interpret that legislation in the face of the new challenges brought on by this quickly advancing technology, governmental bodies exercising oversight and ensuring compliance with the law, self-regulation by those who develop the technology and put it to use, with codes of professional conduct to be updated as the technology advances and control mechanisms that make sure that self-regulation has not turned into self-indulgence. The overarching goal is to make sure that the public good is (pre)served, and to determine what that public good means, and how it should be advanced, a broad conversation around the technology needs to be kept alive engaging all the stakeholders involved (AI developers, businesses, government, civil society and the citizenry), especially considering that the technology is changing our paradigms for thinking not just about privacy but about personhood and society at large. A human-rights-based AI governance, if it is to be effective, needs to take all these factors into account. This means implementing dynamic legal frameworks at once ‘stronger, responsive and imaginative’.[60]

The rights discussed in this chapter can be thought of as boundary markers that signal to legislators, civil society, and businesses what limits need to be observed in developing and using AI technology, limits crossing which we stand to suffer from that use and development, in a territory of open vulnerability where much is at stake. This is what human rights can do for the governance of AI: stop certain practices, limit certain uses, make more transparent certain operations, impose technological human-rights-by-design standards, enforce normative and technical compliance. And by developing and enforcing these standards and applying the laws meant to ensure responsible AI, we can importantly alert ourselves collectively to the specific dangers we expose ourselves to through a carefree, even compulsive use of apps, tools, and services whose operation we do not fully understand but which we nonetheless find appealing and entertaining.

The rights designed to protect us from an unregulated use of AI are rights that, as noted, I am classifying as human rights. This is meant to underscore, in the first place, that the risk we are exposed to with the spread and advancement of AI is potentially existential and can cross national boundaries (just like environmental risk, it is not limited to any single country or region) and, in the second place, that the same goes for the debate we need to be having in constructing a framework of legal protections around AI and its uses, a debate that needs to be global, because the risk is global and the solution accordingly needs a global consensus.

References

Abramowicz M (2015) Cryptocurrency-based law. GW L Sch Pub L Research Paper 2015-9. https://papers.ssrn.com/sol3/papers.cfm?abstract_id=2573788

AI Bill of Rights (2022). https://www.whitehouse.gov/ostp/ai-bill-of-rights/

AIA (2021) Proposal for a regulation of the European Parliament and of the Council Laying Down Harmonised Rules on Artificial Intelligence (Artificial Intelligence Act) and Amending Certain Union Legislative Acts. European Commission, Brussels, 21.4.2021, COM/2021/206 final. https://eur-lex.europa.eu/legal-content/EN/ TXT/?uri=CELEX:52021PC0206

Biden J (2022) Remarks by President Biden on the Supreme Court Decision to Overturn Roe v. Wade. https://www.whitehouse.gov/briefing-room/speeches-remarks/2022/06/24/remarks-by-president-biden-on-the-supreme-court-decision-to-overturn-roe-v-wade/

Brown C (1997) Universal human rights: critique. Int J Hum Rights 1(2):41–65

Brownsword R (2021) Law 3.0: rules, regulations, and technology. Routledge, Oxon and New York

Bryson J (2020) The artificial intelligence of the ethics of artificial intelligence. In: Dubber MD, Pasquale F, Das S (eds) The Oxford handbook of ethics of AI. Oxford University Press, New York, pp 3–25

Bublitz JC (2022) Novel neurorights: from nonsense to substance. Neuroethics 15:7. https://link.springer.com/article/10.1007/s12152-022-09481-3

[60] These are the adjectives used to describe the regulation that AI needs in Mejias (2023), p. 3.

Calo R, Citron DK (2021) The automated administrative state: a crisis of legitimacy. Emory Law J 70(4):797–845

Choi SJ (2014) Prototype design and implementation of an automatic control system based on a BCI. Wirel Pers Commun 79(4):2551–2563

Coughlan G, Coutrot A, Khondoker M, Minihane AM, Spiers H, Hornberger M (2019) Toward personalized cognitive diagnostics of at-genetic-risk Alzheimer's disease. Bio Sci 116(19): 9285–9292

Council of the European Union (2020) Presidency conclusions – The Charter of Fundamental Rights in the context of Artificial Intelligence and Digital Change, 11481/20. https://www.consilium.europa.eu/media/46496/st11481-en20.pdf

De Souza SP, Taylor L (2021) Should might make right? On data, norms and justice. Blog of the UN World Data Forum. https://unstats.un.org/unsd/undataforum/blog/should-might-make-right-on-data-norms-and-justice/

Donahoe E, MacDuffee Metzger M (2019) An intelligent human rights agenda for artificial intelligence. Power 3.0 Blog. https://www.power3point0.org/2019/04/23/an-intelligent-human-rights-agenda-for-artificial-intelligence/

Donnelly J (2007) The relative universality of human rights. Hum Rights Q 29(2):281–306

EGE (2018) Statement on artificial intelligence, robotics and 'autonomous' systems. https://op.europa.eu/en/publication-detail/-/publication/dfebe62e-4ce9-11e8-be1d-01aa75ed71a1/language-en/format-PDF/source-78120382

EU Commission (2020) White Paper on Artificial Intelligence – A European approach to excellence and trust. COM(2020) 65 final. https://commission.europa.eu/publications/white-paper-artificial-intelligence-european-approach-excellence-and-trust_en

Eubanks V (2018) Automating inequality. Picador, St. Martin's Press, New York

Fins JJ (2015) Rights come to mind. Cambridge University Press, New York

Fjeld J, Achten N, Hilligoss H, Nagy AC, Srikumar M (2020). Principled Artificial Intelligence: mapping consensus in ethical and rights-based approaches to principles for AI. Berkman Klein Research Pub No 2020-1. https://papers.ssrn.com/sol3/papers.cfm?abstract_id=3518482

Floridi L (2014) Open data, data protection, and group privacy. Philos Technol 27:1–3

Griffin J (2008) On human rights. Oxford University Press, Oxford

Habermas J (2010) The concept of the human dignity and the realistic utopia of human rights. Metaphilo 41(4):464–480

Hansotia P (2003) A neurologist looks at mind and brain: "The Enchanted Loom". Clin Med Res 1(4):327–332

Heller B (2020) Reimagining reality: human rights and immersive technology. Carr Center Discussion Paper, Spring 008

Heller B (2021) Watching androids dream of electric sheep: immersive technology, biometric psychography and the law. Vand J Ent Tech L 23:1. https://scholarship.law.vanderbilt.edu/jetlaw/vol23/iss1/1/

Hertz N (2023) Neurorights – do we need new human rights? A reconsideration of the right to freedom of thought. Neuroethics 16:5. https://doi.org/10.1007/s12152-022-09511-0

Ienca M (2021a) On neurorights. Front Hum Neurosci 15:-701258. https://www.frontiersin.org/articles/10.3389/fnhum.2021.701258/full

Ienca M (2021b) Common human rights challenges raised by different applications of neurotechnologies in the biomedical field. Report commissioned by the Committee of Bioethics of the Council of Europe

Kellmeyer P (2022) 'Neurorights' - a human rights–based approach for governing neurotechnologies. In: Voeneky S, Kellmeyer P, Mueller O, Burgard W (eds) The Cambridge handbook of responsible artificial intelligence. Cambridge University Press, Cambridge, pp 412–426

Lucchi N (2014) Internet content governance and human rights. Vand J Ent Tech L 16(4):809–856

Maciejewski M (2023) Metaverse. Policy Department for Citizens' Rights and Constitutional Affairs, DG IPOL, requested by the European Parliament's Committee on Legal Affairs. https://www.europarl.europa.eu/thinktank/es/document/IPOL_STU(2023)751222

Mejias U A (2023) The People vs. the Algorithmic State: how government is aiding Big Tech's extractivist agenda, and what we can do about it. Commissioned by PolicyLink. https://www.policylink.org/resources-tools/the-people-vs-the-algorithmic-state

Ministry of Science and Technology (2019) Governance principles for new generation AI – developing responsible AI. https://oecd.ai/en/dashboards/policy-initiatives/http:%2F%2Faipo.oecd.org%2F2021-data-policyInitiatives-24427

Mittelsdadt B (2017) From individual to group privacy in Big Data analytics. Philos Technol 30: 475–494

Mystakidis S (2022) Metaverse. Encyclopedia 2(1):486–497. https://doi.org/10.3390/encyclopedia2010031

Nemitz P (2018) Constitutional democracy and technology in the age of artificial intelligence. Philos Trans R Soc A 376:20180089. https://doi.org/10.1098/rsta.2018.0089

Radaelli L, Sapiezynski P, Houssiau F, Shmueli E, de Montjoye YA (2018) Quantifying surveillance in the networked age: node-based intrusions and group privacy. https://arxiv.org/pdf/1803.09007.pdf

Rosen M (2012) Dignity: its history and meaning. Harvard University Press, Cambridge

Schneider N (2022) How we can encode human rights in the blockchain. Noema, June 7, 2022. https://www.noemamag.com/how-we-can-encode-human-rights-in-the-blockchain/

Skinner G, Han S, Chang E (2006) An information privacy taxonomy for collaborative environments. Inf Manag Comput Secur 14(4):382–394

Suh JJ, Metzger MJ, Reid SA, El Abbadi A (2018) Distinguishing group privacy from personal privacy: the effect of group inference technologies on privacy perceptions and behaviors. Proc ACM Hum Comput Interact 2(CSCW):1–22. https://dl.acm.org/doi/abs/10.1145/3274437

Vasak K (1977) A 30-year struggle. The sustained efforts to give force of law to the Universal Declaration of Human Rights. The Unesco Courier: a window open to the world XXX:28–29. https://unesdoc.unesco.org/ark:/48223/pf0000048063

Viljanen J (2008) The role of the European Court of Human Rights as a developer of Internatioanl Human Rights law. Cuadernos constitucionales de la Cátedra Fadrique Furió Ceriol 62-63:249–265

von Arnauld A, von der Decken K, Susi M (2020) Introduction. In: von Arnauld A, von der Decken K, Susi M (eds) The Cambridge handbook of new human rights. Cambridge University Press, Cambridge, pp 1–3

Wang Z (2002) Towards a postmodern notion of human rights. Educ Philos Theory 34(2):171–183

Yuste R, Goering S, Agüera y Arcas B et al (2017) Four ethical priorities for neurotechnologies and AI. Nature 551:159–163. https://www.nature.com/articles/551159a

Yuste R, Genser J, Herrmann S (2021) It's time for neurorights. Horizons 18:154. https://www.cirsd.org/en/horizons/horizons-winter-2021-issue-no-18/its-time-for-neuro%2D%2Drights

A Horizontal Meta-effect? Theorising Human Rights in the AI Act and the Corporate Sustainability Due Diligence Directive

Mika Viljanen

Contents

Abstract The indirect horizontal effect of human and fundamental rights has dominated European constitutional practice. In recent years, fractures have appeared in its face in courts and in regulatory practice. The EU has introduced multiple legislative initiatives that have pushed the rights towards apparent direct horizontal effect.

This article analyses the AI Act and the Corporate Sustainability Due Diligence Directive as examples of a novel human and fundamental rights strategy. The article argues that the instruments first weaken the rights and then deploy them to normatively guide and condition intra-firm sense-plan-act cycles. The rights first create adverse human rights impacts and fundamental rights risks to serve as objects of concern in corporate information processing. The planning and acting stages transport the rights into real-world reduction in human and fundamental rights violations.

M. Viljanen (✉)
University of Turku, Turku, Finland
e-mail: mivevi@utu.fi

E. Gill-Pedro, A. Moberg (eds.), *YSEC Yearbook of Socio-Economic Constitutions 2023*, YSEC Yearbook of Socio-Economic Constitutions (2024) 2023: 117–136, https://doi.org/10.1007/16495_2023_65, Published online: 15 December 2023

While on its face weak, the novel strategy is likely an adaptation to political pressures, but contains the seeds of a possible progressive end-game.

1 Introduction

European scholars have debated the impact of fundamental rights in horizontal relationships between private parties for decades. While human and fundamental rights are legally binding on states, their reach within the private realm has been and remains contested. This debate commenced in post-World War II Germany. Günther Dürig contended that fundamental rights had an *indirect horizontal effect*. They were relevant in private relationships as far as state-issued regulations mediated and extended their influence into society.[1] Walter Leisner and Hans Carl Nipperdey disagreed, arguing for a direct horizontal effect where individuals could directly invoke the fundamental rights and demand that others respect them.[2]

The German post-World War II fracas[3] was not unique. The dispute has persisted in Germany and elsewhere in Europe, reaching also the EU and the Luxembourg Court. Dürig has largely held his ground, but fractures have appeared in the face of the long-dominant indirect effect as the Court has given the Charter of Fundamental Rights of the European Union[4] a limited direct effect in a few contexts in recent judgments.[5,6]

While progress towards a fully developed direct horizontal effect for fundamental rights within the EU constitutional practice has been slow and arduous,[7] the EU legislator has introduced new hybrid regulatory strategies to entrench the rights into horizontal relationships, particularly within the digital and transnational business domains.

The EU has, for example, required digital platforms to 'strike a balance between fundamental rights' when ruling on whether to refuse content takedown requests by content rightsholders[8] and mandating them to act 'with due regard to the [...] fundamental rights of the recipients of digital services' when enforcing the terms

[1]Dürig (1956).

[2]Leisner (1960); Nipperdey (1961).

[3]On the German debate and its stakes, see der Walt (2014).

[4]Charter of Fundamental Rights of the European Union (2012/C 326/02).

[5]CJEU Case C-414/16, 7 April 2018, Vera Egenberger v Evangelisches Werk für Diakonie und Entwicklung eV, ECLI:EU:C:2018:257; CJEU Case C-68/17, 11 September 2018, IR v JQ, ECLI: EU:C:2018:696; CJEU Joined Cases C-569/16 and C-570/16, 11 June 2018, ECLI:EU:C:2018: 871; CJEU Case C-684/16, 6 November 2018, Max-Planck-Gesellschaft zur Förderung der Wissenschaften eV v Tetsuji Shimizu, ECLI:EU:C:2018:874.

[6]For example, Ciacchi (2019); Frantziou (2019a); Krause (2021).

[7]For example, Walkila (2016); Frantziou (2019b).

[8]Article 17(9) and Recital 70 of the DSM copyright directive (EU) 2019/790.

and conditions in moderating speech on social media.[9,10] In effect, these digital acquis instruments deploy a 'quasi-judicial' approach where the platforms use private ordering tools to enforce corporate-modulated renderings of fundamental rights.[11]

The approach adopted for transnational value chain contexts has taken a different path from platform regulation. During the 2010s, the business and human rights movement[12] resulted in the UN Guiding Principles and OECD Guidelines that eschewed the standard legal imaginary of enforceable subjective rights and duties.[13] The instruments promote a framework where businesses should 'develop the institutional capacity to know and show that they do not infringe on others' rights'.[14] The two soft law instruments have inspired various European Union[15] and Member State initiatives[16] that retain the instruments' oblique human and fundamental rights regulatory strategy and coax businesses into developing intra-firm processes for identifying and managing human and fundamental rights impacts and risks.[17]

Regulatory action has thus pushed towards a direct horizontal effect. While De Gregorio has provided a theoretical account of the quasi-judicial direct effect strategy,[18] how the transnational value chain branch uses the rights remains under-theorised. Importantly, the value chain strategies have also found their way into the digital acquis in the GDPR rules for data protection impact assessments,[19] Digital Services Act Articles 34 to 36 and the Artificial Intelligence Act (the AI Act) proposal.[20] This article addresses the research gap by analysing how the EU proposes to deploy fundamental and human rights to govern business conduct under the 2022 Corporate Sustainability Due Diligence Directive (the Directive)[21] and the AI Act proposals. The two proposals contain the most sophisticated examples of what I will call the *horizontal meta-effect* human and fundamental rights strategy.

---

[9] Article 14(4) of the Digital Services Act (EU) 2022/2065.

[10] De Gregorio (2019, 2022); Celeste (2022); Celeste et al. (2023).

[11] For a critique, see e.g. Mylly (2021), pp. 69–70; De Gregorio (2022), pp. 199–203.

[12] Bird et al. (2014); Baumann-Pauly and Nolan (2016).

[13] United Nations (2011); OECD (2011).

[14] Ruggie (2013), p. 83.

[15] Timber regulation (EU) 2010/995; Non-financial reporting directive (EU) 2014/95; Conflict mineral regulation (EU) 2017/821.

[16] For example, the French loi n° 2017-399 du 27 mars 2017 relative au devoir de vigilance des sociétés mères et des entreprises donneuses d'ordre and the German Lieferkettensorgfaltspflichtengesetz vom 16. Juli 2021 (BGBl. I S. 2959).

[17] For an account of transnational sustainability laws, see e.g. Salminen and Rajavuori (2019).

[18] De Gregorio (2019), pp. 97–98; De Gregorio (2022), pp. 92–97.

[19] Regulation (EU) 2016/679 (GDRP).

[20] European Commission (2021); Permanent Representatives Committee (2022a); European Parliament (2023b).

[21] European Commission (2022); Permanent Representatives Committee (2022b); European Parliament (2023a).

The article will argue that the horizontal meta-effect approach uses human and fundamental rights in a novel way. The Act and the Directive use the rights to guide business conduct, but not as traditional rights. Before entering the firms, the rights are hollowed out and transformed into aspirational standards. The hollowing out does not entail that the rights would be insignificant. Even if the instruments do not force the firms to comply with, implement or enforce the rights or extend them as normative claims to individuals to invoke against the firms, they still matter.

The instruments transform the rights into objects of concern and normative inputs in intra-firm cognitive sense-plan-act-flows. The strategy first forces the firms to build processes that allow them to *sense* the adverse impact and risks to the rights as objects for management action. Second, the approach imposes the rights as normative inputs for corporate *planning* processes. Third, the behavioral effects emerge once the firms *act* on and implement the mandated and normatively conditioned plans and the plans result in desirable real-world changes in how the human and human rights are realised. The regulatory calculation is that if the rights can transform into objects of concern and function as normative inputs in intra-firm cognitive processes, human and fundamental rights will contribute to a decrease in human and fundamental rights violations. Hence, the name horizontal meta-effect: the rights affect the processes that determine action outcomes.

The following sections will outline the contours of the horizontal meta-effect. I will begin by shortly introducing the two instruments and their objectives. The third section outlines the human and fundamental rights the instruments impose on businesses. Section 4 tracks how the instruments relativise the rights and make them porous. Section 5 theorises how the weakened rights can still have a horizontal effect. Section 6 concludes the article by discussing the political underpinnings and trajectories of the horizontal meta-effect.

2 The Instruments

The Corporate Sustainability Due Diligence Directive proposal is a part of the EU sustainability regulation continuum.[22] As a corporate social and environmental responsibility instrument, the Directive would extend the EU's regulatory reach, fundamentally disrupting the distribution of regulatory power. Traditionally, the states' capability to regulate production has ended at their borders: states have set and enforced the rules for production taking place on their soil.[23] Once produced, goods and services have typically traversed borders easily, regardless of how and

[22] Timber regulation (EU) 2010/995; Non-financial reporting directive 2014/95/EU; Conflict mineral regulation (EU) 2017/821; Taxonomy regulation (EU) 2020/852; Sustainability reporting directive (EU) 2022/2464.

[23] Cf. on transnational environmental regulation Heyvaert (2018).

under what conditions they have been produced. This design has created an uneven playing field with low- and high-regulation jurisdictions,[24] creating an opening for regulatory arbitrage.[25] Businesses have been able to 'lift off' from production constraints imposed by their home jurisdictions[26] by locating production in low-regulation jurisdictions and importing the goods. The Directive seeks to limit this arbitrage play by mandating that large EU firms ensure their value chains and production activities keep to minimum human rights and environmental standards both in and outside the EU.

The AI Act proposal, in turn, emerged in 2021 as a response to algorithms' growing power over European societies and fears over existing and future AI-related harms. While a part of the expanding digital single market[27] instrument array,[28] the Act is a trailblasing effort by the EU. It is an opening gambit in the global AI regulation race and still largely lacks international peers. Drawing on work done by the High-level expert group on AI[29] and within the OECD,[30] the Act seeks to create and sustain a single market for artificial intelligence systems while simultaneously ensuring a high level of health, safety, and fundamental rights.[31] The Act regulatory design reflects its two-pronged objective set. The product safety regulation template allows the regulators to set flexible minimum standards for AI system safety, accuracy, and robustness, but the Act also creates a level-playing field for artificial intelligence systems providers seeking to place their offerings on the EU single market.

3 Human and Fundamental Rights at the Core

Fundamental and human rights sit at the core of both instruments. The Directive would force large EU businesses to prevent causing adverse impacts to a selection of human rights codified in international human rights documents. The AI Act would, in turn, require AI system providers to minimise risks to the EU Charter of Fundamental Rights when developing AI systems.

[24] Waller (1999–2000); Avi-Yonah (2003).

[25] Salminen and Rajavuori (2021).

[26] Wai (2002).

[27] European Commission (2020).

[28] Data Governance Act (EU) 2022/868; Digital Markets Act (EU) 2022/1925; Digital Services Act (EU) 2022/2065.

[29] High-Level Expert Group on Artificial Intelligence (2019).

[30] OECD (2019).

[31] European Commission (2021), p. 2.

3.1 Human Rights in the Directive

In the Directive, the link to human rights is explicit and hard to miss. In addition to preventing adverse impacts on a selection of environmental rights,[32] the objective of the Directive is to 'lay down rules [. . .] on obligations for companies regarding actual and potential human rights adverse impacts'. Despite the numerous recital references to the EU Charter of Fundamental Rights, the Directive however does not attempt to enforce the entire EU fundamental rights regime. Instead, it deploys a restrictive, pick-and-choose approach, collecting a limited roster of rights from international human rights documents to impose on firms.

The roster contains a selection of fundamental first-generation negative freedoms, some second-generation economic, social, and cultural rights, key rights of the child and minorities, and a selection of the most essential labour rights. The first-generation freedom rights include the Universal Declaration of Human Rights[33] freedom from torture, cruel, inhuman, or degrading treatment (Article 5); freedom from arbitrary arrest, detention, or exile (Article 9); and rights to life, liberty, and security of person (Article 3), privacy, family, home, correspondence, and reputation (Article 17) and freedom of thought, conscience, and religion (Article 18). The second-generation social and cultural human rights include the International Covenant on Economic, Social, and Cultural Rights[34] Article 7 rights to safe and healthy working conditions, fair wages, equal remuneration, and decent living, the Convention on the Rights of the Child[35] rights of children to have their best interest given primary consideration in all decisions affecting them (Article 3), develop to their full potential (Article 6), attain the highest attainable standard of health (Article 24), and have access to social security (Article 26), and an adequate standard of living (Article 27), and education (Article 28). Further, numerous ILO Conventions and other human rights instruments contribute to drawing the boundaries for acceptable value chain impacts. These instruments prohibit slave, forced, and child labour, establish rights to assembly, association, and collective bargaining, and affirm the workers' right to a fair wage, equal treatment, and non-discrimination in work contexts.

In sum, the Directive imposes a limited roster of human rights on large EU firms to work on within their organisations and value chains. The approach lays bare the production ethics the EU seeks to export. The ethics is minimalist, only seeking to curb the gravest violations of human rights and the worst forms of abuse.

---

[32] The proposal refers to the Paris Agreement (United Nations (2015)), Article 15, but the Agreement is not listed as a core environmental instrument. The Directive would instruct firms to 'adopt a plan to ensure that the business model and strategy of the company are compatible with the' 1.5-degree goal. However, adverse climate impacts give no one a right to damages due to the careful drafting of Article 22 and its liability rule.

[33] United Nations (1948).

[34] United Nations (1966).

[35] United Nations (1989).

3.2 Fundamental Rights in the Act

In contrast to the Directive, the AI Act deploys a maximalist approach to AI production ethics. as it will likely make all EU Charter fundamental rights govern AI development processes.

The original Commission proposal did not make the fundamental rights connection. While the recitals reference fundamental rights and the Charter, the rights were absent from the proposal's centrepiece Article 9 risk management rules. The rules simply required that providers identify, analyse, estimate, and evaluate *risks* and then adopt suitable measures to manage the *risks*. The rules provided no direct definition of the risks the providers were to target. Despite the omission, ample circumstantial evidence suggested that fundamental rights risks were covered. Article 7, for example, framed high-risk AI systems by referencing the risks they caused to fundamental rights. Article 67, in addition, explicitly pegged initiating supervisory action on compliant AI systems to the breaches of Union or national law provisions intended to protect fundamental rights]. The issue was resolved in the Council by the French presidency compromise proposal published in January 2022. An amendment to Article 9 made the fundamental rights connection explicit. Article 9(2)(a) now required that the first step in the Article 9 iterative risk management process was the 'identification and analysis of the known and foreseeable risks most likely to occur to health, safety, and fundamental rights in view of the intended purpose of the high-risk AI system'.[36] The explicit reference to fundamental rights persisted through the subsequent Council compromise proposals.[37] The Parliament also included equivalent language to its amendments.

While the Charter provides a seemingly fixed point of reference, the footing is fluid. First, the Charter contains dozens of fundamental rights ranging from dignity, fundamental freedoms, and equality rights to solidarity rights and citizen rights, many with unclear application potential in horizontal relations. Second, Recital 28 may add to the confusion. The recital contains a list of specific Charter rights. These rights are 'human dignity, respect for private and family life, protection of personal data, freedom of expression and information, freedom of assembly and association, and non-discrimination, consumer protection, workers' rights, rights of persons with disabilities, right to an effective remedy and a fair trial, right of defence and the presumption of innocence, right to good administration'. While entrenching some rights as relevant in the AI Act context, the list simultaneously omits several important rights, including the right to property and the freedom to conduct business. Despite the ambiguities in details, the thrust is clear. Providers should consider the Charter's fundamental rights when developing AI systems.

---

[36] La présidence française (2022), Article 9.

[37] Permanent Representatives Committee (2022a), Article 9(2).

4 Weak Rights Transformed

4.1 Fuzzy Rights for the Foreseeable Future

Taken at face value, the Directive and the Act signify a dramatic sea change in the balance between the direct and indirect effects of fundamental and human rights. The EU seems to be on the road to making direct horizontal effect true for a vast swath of private commercial activity. With the Directive, the EU would start exporting a minimum ethics for global production to jurisdictions that are either unwilling or incapable of ensuring even minimally decent conditions, thus sidestepping extra-EU governance deficiencies and subjecting firms to public human rights governance.[38] The AI Act would, at first glance, seek to ensure that providers comply with the rights emanating from the EU Charter of Fundamental Rights.

Several factors, however, modulate the apparent direct horizontal effect. The first set of factors is practical and temporal. The rights will be fuzzy and hard to pin down for the foreseeable future.

Rights fuzziness has multiple sources. The human rights in Annex 1 of the Directive and the fundamental rights in the Charter are typical fundamental and human rights provisions. They are semantically vague, deeply contextual, open to interpretation, and thus fiercely contested. The situation is, of course, not hopeless. For example, UN treaty body practice such as UN Human Rights Council Universal Periodic Reviews, ad hoc investigations, and decisions on individual complaints[39] may add detail to the bare language of the human rights provisions. At the same time, the EU courts will undoubtedly contribute to disambiguating the Charter.

However, the basic problem of direct horizontal effect complicates the situation. Human and fundamental rights best fit to constrain state action. To become relevant to businesses and other private actors, existing human rights treaty body practice, for example, would have to be repurposed and translated to the new landscape. Similar problems lie ahead when the EU Charter governs horizontal relationships. The Charter was initially designed to address EU institutions, bodies, offices, and agencies, as well as Member States when they implement Union law.

The repurposing process will constitute a fundamental challenge for the target firms, national supervisors, and, ultimately, the courts that rule on potential challenges to supervisory action and claims brought by aggrieved parties. Target firms and supervisors must develop strategies to navigate the uncertain landscape until courts, as the ultimate translators and arbiters of the rights, have had the opportunity to disambiguate the rule contents. Judicial disambiguation will inevitably take a long time, weakening the immediate horizontal bite of the rights. At the same time, the translation process keeps the future unlocked. While a future where supervisors take aggressive measures and get support from the courts is improbable, the possibility exists.

---

[38] Duval (2023).

[39] Keller et al. (2012); Bantekas and Oette (2020); Tistounet (2020).

4.2 *'Appropriate Measures' Instead of Human Rights*

Both instruments, however, also contain devices that weaken the force the rights could gain, perhaps handicapping the strategy permanently.[40]

In the Directive, two small words in Articles 5, 6, 7, and 8 do the heavy lifting. The rules require that firms take *appropriate measures* to prevent and bring to an end adverse human rights impacts. The words gain their meaning from Article 3(q). Point q reads: '"appropriate measure" means a measure that is capable of achieving the objectives of due diligence, commensurate with the degree of severity and the likelihood of the adverse impact, and reasonably available to the company, taking into account the circumstances of the specific case, including characteristics of the economic sector and of the specific business relationship and the company's influence thereof, and the need to ensure prioritisation of action'.

The point has consequences in three dimensions. First, the two words transform the obligation to prevent and mitigate adverse human rights and environmental impacts into the Directive's namesake due diligence obligation. Instead of implementing the rights, the Directive requires that firms take appropriate measures to prevent and mitigate adverse impacts. The transition is crucial. Without the two words, the firms would be under an *obligation de résultat,* but the language turns the obligations into an *obligation de moyens*, a due diligence obligation where the effort matters instead of results.

Second, the language that pegs the measures to the 'objectives of due diligence' further weakens the rights. The focus shifts once again. Instead of requiring firms to take steps to simply comply with the rights, the Directive requires action that aligns with the objectives of due diligence. The move seems bound to sap the Directive's normative force by abstracting the rights into their goals, less definite and articulated objects.

The third dimension arises from three framings that bring what is reasonable and commercially feasible into the picture. First, Article 3(q) allows businesses to modulate their prevention and mitigation efforts to make them 'commensurate with the degree of severity and the likelihood of the adverse impact'. Instead of requiring the companies to eliminate all rights violations, as within the usual logic of rights, the Directive seems to tolerate *some* rights violations. Second, Point q makes the rights also subject to resource constraints. When undertaking appropriate measures, the firms have to only take measures that are 'reasonably available to the company'. Finally, Point q also acknowledges that Annex I human rights have a deeply contextual existence. The reasonable measures are contingent upon the 'circumstances of the specific case, including characteristics of the economic sector and of the specific business relationship and the company's influence thereof, and the need to ensure prioritisation of action'.

As a result of the three transformations in Point q, the Directive concedes much of its normative demand for compliance, relativising the rights. Designing the

---

[40] On challenges, see Schilling-Vacaflor and Lenschow (2023).

appropriate measures is not about implementing the rights or achieving compliance. Instead, the design processes constitute a venue for abstracting the rights into due diligence objectives. The firms may further balance the due diligence objectives with their internal and external imperatives and pressures. As a result, the Directive accepts that rights cannot be absolute. Point q allows the firms to engage in impact triage to identify which rights deserve their attention and action and then take action deemed feasible given the circumstances.

4.3 Acceptable Fundamental Rights Violations

The AI Act also drives down the bite of its fundamental rights peg. The complicated mechanism runs through Articles 9(4)(1), 65 and 67. The mechanism has its point of origin in Article 9(4)(1). The original proposal and subsequent Council and Parliament versions set an identical target for providers' efforts to implement a person's fundamental rights. To comply with the risk management obligation, the Act directed providers to design the AI systems so that 'the residual risk associated with each hazard as well as the overall residual risk of the high-risk AI system *is judged acceptable*.'

The 'is judged acceptable' language thus calibrates the minimum ambition standard for providers' efforts to secure fundamental rights. The standard seems depressingly low for two reasons. The passive voice in the language first leaves undefined who will do the judging. A literal interpretation suggests that the provider should judge the acceptability of its system. Second, the provision is mum about which normative framework for acceptability, if any, the providers should use. A literal interpretation, again, suggests that the Act ascribes no normative external framework for acceptability. The language tasks the providers first to minimise and review the risks and then decide whether the residual risks are acceptable. As a result, the 'is judged acceptable' seems to hollow out the rights. An AI system would comply with the Act's fundamental rights risks management requirements if the provider can show that it analysed the residual risk levels and judged them acceptable sometime during development. The factual residual risk level seems to have no significance.

The story does not, however, end there. While Article 65 would deal with non-compliant systems, including those whose providers did not undertake minimisation efforts and judge the system acceptable, Article 67 contains the rules on supervisory action for AI systems where the providers complied with regulatory requirements. Under the original Commission language for Article 67, supervisory authorities would have been able to initiate enforcement action only if the system 'present[ed] a risk to the compliance with obligations under Union or national law intended to protect fundamental rights obligations'. The Commission standard would have essentially signified that the Act subscribed to the indirect horizontal effect for fundamental rights: only violations of secondary fundamental rights legislation would have resulted in enforcement action by supervisory authorities.[41] However, the Council language for Article 67 would impose a stricter standard for human rights compliance. The supervisors would have the right to initiate enforcement action if a compliant AI system merely 'present[ed] a risk to fundamental rights'. However, as Article 65(1) positions that a risk is 'present' only when the conditions set in Market Supervision Regulation[42] Article 3(19) are met, the threshold for supervisory action becomes potentially high but, in any case, fuzzy. Under Article 3(19), a risk to fundamental rights would only exist if the danger were to go 'beyond that considered reasonable and acceptable in relation to [the product's] intended purpose or under the normal or reasonably foreseeable conditions of use of the product concerned'. Consequently, the Council would like the supervisors to take action only if an AI system jeorardized fundamental rights beyond what is reasonable and acceptable, provided that the provider ticked the boxes.

As a result, two possible standards for fundamental rights compliance emerge from Article 9(4), 65 and 67. The first one is a hollow tick-the-box standard. The system will be deemed compliant if the provider goes through the motions mandated by Article 9(4), no matter the residual risk level is. Even the fallback standard in the Article 67 enforcement rules leaves much to desire. The language in the Commission and Parliament proposals would turn the budding horizontal direct effect back into an indirect effect, pegging enforcement action to the authorities finding that an AI system presents a 'risk to compliance' with Union and Member State legislation intended to protect fundamental rights. With such language, fundamental rights would take ordinary legislation to affect horizontal relationships. Even the more accommodative Council language would perform a distancing similar to what takes place in Directive Article 3(q), replacing the fundamental rights with the risks of jeopardising the right 'to a degree that goes beyond that considered reasonable and acceptable'.

5 Theorising the Horizontal Meta-effect

The 'appropriate measures' in the Directive and the AI Act's 'is judged acceptable' language contribute to hollowing out the rights in both instruments. Instead of forcing businesses to implement or 'respect' human rights, the Directive replaces the rights with an obligation to take appropriate measures to attain the objectives underlying the rights. The Act in turn relegates the rights to adjudication by the providers and either emasculates the direct effect altogether or only outlaws violating the rights 'to a degree that goes beyond that considered reasonable and acceptable'. After these transformations, the rights in both instruments seem soft and pliable at best. In addition, the recourse the instruments afford to the bearers of the rights

[41] The Parliament retained the approach in its amendments: European Parliament (2023b).

[42] Market Surveillance Regulation (EU) 2019/1020.

is limited. The Directive puts in place an extrajudicial remedial framework in Article 8. Article 22 further grants the aggrieved parties a weak right to compensation for rights violations that taking appropriate measures would have prevented.[43] The Act, in turn, is silent on how private parties can enforce their fundamental rights.[44]

Watering down the rights and curtailing the private enforcement mechanisms compromises the direct horizontal effect. It seems to wither away. So, how could the instruments have a horizontal human and fundamental rights effect given their softness? The answer lies in the regulatory strategy. The traditional rights- and enforcement-centric view may understate the significance of both instruments. The instruments work in a new space, using a novel strategy. Instead of employing the public enforcement channels, the novel strategy runs through meta-regulatory pathways[45] and uses intra-firm cognitive sense-plan-act-cycles to condition corporate action.

To implement the strategy, regulators first require that target firms establish processes for identifying, analysing, and evaluating the fundamental and human rights risks and impacts their activities create. In this *sensing* step, the rights serve as *epistemic and ontological devices*. They condition how the firms sense their environments, affecting what objects emerge as action targets.[46] The rules on sensing also guide the firms' attention, priming them for concerted action. Second and third, the firms must also devise plans to act on the risks and impacts and implement the plans. The latter planning step effectuates a process of normative cognitive programming. The sensing rules mandate firms to enact impacts and risks as objects of concern. These objects then become subject to required directional manipulation efforts. The firms have to devise and implement plans that actuate the normative agenda embedded in the rules.[47] In practice, the scheme is simple. In the Directive, firms must take appropriate measures to prevent and bring to an end the actual and potential adverse human rights impacts they sense to exist. In the Act, the normative programming materialises in the eliminate-reduce-mitigate-manage sequence that should lead to the firm producing an AI system that 'is judged acceptable'.

In the following, I will flesh out the building blocks of the horizontal meta-effect strategy in more detail, starting with sensing.

5.1 Sensing with Rights

Sensing is the first step in the sense-process-act cycles that both instruments impose on corporations. In the Directive, sensing is regulated by Article 6 rules. Here, the

[43] Pacces (2023), p. 11.

[44] See however Chamberlain (2023).

[45] Parker (2002, 2009); Chiu (2015); Viljanen (2017); Heyvaert (2018).

[46] Scott (1998).

[47] Taylor (1984).

frame for sensing rests on *adverse human rights impacts*. The Commission proposal would require that lead firms 'take appropriate measures to identify actual and potential adverse human rights impacts and adverse environmental impacts arising from their operations or those of their subsidiaries and, where related to their value chains, from their established business relationships'. The AI Act, in turn, guides the firms to sense fundamental rights risks. Article 9(2) in the Commission proposal would require the providers to build a process for 'identification and analysis of the known and foreseeable risks associated with each high-risk AI system' and 'estimation and evaluation of the risks that may emerge when the high-risk AI system is used in accordance with its intended purpose and under conditions of reasonably foreseeable misuse'.

It is important to note that the rules function as ontological and epistemic devices. They force objects on the firms in two directions. First, the rules mandate that the firms recognise the ontological categories of human rights impacts fundamental rights risks, forcing the firms to accept that their activities may have impacts and create risks. Second, the rules require firms to build epistemic processes to sense the risks. The rules may seem superficial, but I argue they are critical regulatory devices. Information alone may have behavioural consequences, even if isolated from other measures. At the same time, one should remember that differences in framing what the sensing should focus on may have significant downstream consequences. In the Directive, the impact framing creates a relatively open landscape for detecting human rights violations. Adverse impacts extend not only to how production affects individuals but may also encompass the harms communities experience. The AI Act instead focuses exclusively on *persons'* fundamental rights, which might lead to a myopic and restrictive view of harms.

5.2 Planning with and Acting on Rights

The second and third steps in the sense-plan-act cycle turn information into action. Separating the rules on planning and acting is, however, difficult in the rules.

The Directive lays out the high-level principle for both steps in Article 7(1): lead firms must 'take appropriate measures to prevent, or where prevention is not possible or not immediately possible, adequately mitigate potential adverse human rights impacts and adverse environmental impacts'. Article 7(2)(a) establishes that lead firms must 'develop and implement a prevention action plan, with reasonable and clearly defined timelines for action and qualitative and quantitative indicators for measuring improvement'. In contrast, Article 8(3)b adds an obligation to develop and implement a corrective action plan if the adverse impacts cannot be immediately brought to an end (Article 8(3)(b).

Article 8 of the Directive proposal contains a comprehensive roster of possible preventive actions. Lead firms may first seek contractual assurances (Article 7(2)(a)) where business partners undertake to comply with the lead firm's code of conduct and preventive action plan. As a technique, the assurances allow the lead firms to extend their reach to parties with whom they have no direct contractual relationships by requiring that their immediate partners force the instruments downstream. Second, the lead firms should invest in management or production processes and infrastructures that facilitate prevention and, third, provide targeted and proportionate support to partner SMEs if complying with the firm's code of conduct or prevention action plan would jeopardise the SME's viability. Fourth, the firms would be directed to collaborate with other entities to increase their ability to bring adverse impacts to an end. Implementing only the positive measures would not, however, be enough. Under Article 7(5), the Directive would force lead firms to 'refrain from entering into new or extending existing relations with partners that cause adverse impacts' if the partners cannot prevent or mitigate adverse impacts adequately. In addition, the Directive would require lead firms to temporarily suspend or terminate the relationships if other measures prove inadequate if the governing law allows it.

Article 8 turns the focus from prevention to 'bringing actual impacts to an end' and minimising them. The measures include neutralising the adverse impacts or minimising their extent. Minimising the impact could involve paying damages or financial compensation to affected persons or communities. As with prevention, the Directive would force the lead firms to seek contractual assurances that partners implement the corrective action plans under Article 8(3)(c), make investments in processes and infrastructures (Article 8(3)(d)), provide support for SMEs (Article 8(3)(e)), and cooperate with other actors to bring impacts to an end (Article 8(3)(f)). In addition, the obligation to refrain from expanding or starting new businesses with partners who cause adverse impacts is on the menu. If nothing else helps, the lead firms must suspend or terminate contractual relationships (Article 8(6)).

In the AI Act, the rules on processing are, in comparison, few. The Act requires providers to implement a three-layered risk management process in Article 9(4). After identifying and analysing the risks, developers should first work to either eliminate or reduce the risks. Second, the developers should take appropriate measures to mitigate and manage the risks they cannot stop. Third, the developers must inform the users of eventual residual risks.[48]

While the sensing step only provides normative guidance to the firms by requiring the firms to enact objects of concern, planning and action rules take on a clear normative direction. They force a normative frame for action. The businesses must start working on the adverse impacts and risks identified during the sensing step. Work is directional. The firms must eliminate, reduce, mitigate, and manage the adverse impacts and risks to align activity outcomes with fundamental and human rights. Planning turns human and fundamental rights into discrete actions. Once the processes are in place and appropriate, the results follow automatically. Affecting the meta-level processes that determine corporate behaviour improves rights outcomes.

Notably, the rules, however, shy away from dictating specific actions. Here, the Directive and the Act reproduce the strategy characteristic of management-based

[48] Mahler (2022).

regulation schemes. The regulators use a preexisting normative system to define the goals that the firms should reach. Still, the firms retain the power and responsibility to decide their actions.

6 Political Implications and Future Trajectories

Here, the traits of the novel horizontal fundamental and human rights effect and the underlying regulatory strategy emerge. The strategy first forces businesses as private actors to develop and entrench practices that produce information on the adverse impacts and risks their activities cause to human and fundamental rights. I referred to this as *sensing rights*. Second, the strategy forces the firms to plan and implement action under the normative guidance of human and fundamental rights. The firms must devise and implement plans to eliminate, reduce, mitigate, and manage the impacts and risks. While the rules on sensing enact objects of concern for planning action, the *planning and action* rules do most of the normative programming. The horizontal meta-effect strategy folds human and fundamental rights to govern business conduct by rigging intra-firm processes with human and fundamental rights inputs to produce desirable outcomes. The hope is that rights violations decrease as firms sense and work on reducing the impacts and risks they create.

One should note two dimensions at this juncture. First, within the horizontal meta-effect strategy, firms undertake *unilateral and unidirectional action*. Both instruments avoid allowing the rights to gain a traditional horizontal direct effect. The rights undoubtedly affect businesses, but the rights do not achieve their impact by entering the flows of the usual adversarial legal processes. The instruments deny the affected individuals the opportunity to appeal to their rights and challenge the firms' actions. Instead, private firms become the arbiters and enforcers of the rights within their business decision-making processes. This move makes the rights inherently conditional.

This conditionality is second reflected in the modality that rights gain in affecting corporate behaviour. The rights transform into conditional second-order *meta-obligations* that trigger and force the firms to build intra-firm cognitive processes. These processes mediate the rights into their real-world effects. The move changes the rights from direct behavioural commands and claim-rights into normative inputs in business decision-making. In the Act, the rights transform into inputs into the balancing exercises where firms strike compromises between fundamental rights and other concerns. In the Directive, a further shift takes place. Human rights are mediated by business prerogatives and transmogrify into 'objectives of due diligence' that guide the firms in designing the 'appropriate measures'.

Importantly, horizontal meta-effect strategies seem to be increasing in EU legislation. While the article discussed the Act and the Directive as the most sophisticated examples, other recent initiatives, such as the General Data Protection Regulation with its data protection impact assessments[49] and the Digital Services Act and its risk assessment and mitigation[50] rules contain similar regulatory devices.

Veerle Heyvaerth has traced the emergence of meta-regulation and other 'innovative' regulatory strategies to the perceived failures of the command-and-control paradigm and changes in venues of regulatory action and regulatory actors' capabilities.[51] Heyvaerth's reading provides a backdrop for understanding the EU meta-regulation developments. On the one hand, the new strategies are doubtless responses to the shortcomings of command-and-control approaches to using human and fundamental to guide business conduct in transnational value chains and AI development. Articulating and enforcing the standards for compliance within a command-and-control frame would be impossible. However, the other dimension of Heyvaert's reading seems to fail to account for the EU's adoption of the meta-regulatory strategies. Heyvaert suggests that the changes in regulatory modalities of transnational environmental regulation stem at least in part from the 'very different circumstances of the regulators' as to the drafting, credibility, and enforcement capabilities. The regulators' circumstances should not be a concern in the EU context. The EU institutions have clear-cut, if sometimes contested, regulatory powers, credibility, and enforcement mandates.

Consequently, the choice of strategy may flow from other reasons. The political constraints that the regulators face seem the most likely candidates. While the recitals state clearly what value orientations and objectives the Act and the Directive seek to attain, different stakeholders likely have variegated levels of commitment to their effective pursuit. For example, despite their professed support for responsible business, industry lobbies would probably fight tooth and nail any instrument that established firm, clear-cut obligations for corporates to comply with human or fundamental rights. The flexible, soft, and ambiguous duties that the Directive and Act establish may be what is politically feasible, a second-worst option of sorts. The compromises allow the progressives to argue that the EU is taking significant action to promote and secure human and fundamental rights in business contexts. In contrast, businesses retain much of the existing business-as-usual status quo.

The balance between the interests of the two camps is, however, precarious and hinges on what the supervisory authorities and the courts choose to do. While a cynical reading would suggest that the language in the instruments strongly favours a business-friendly endgame,[52] the same language could contain the seeds for a progressive win. Progressive interpretations and aggressive supervisory action by authorities with support from sympathetic courts could result in drastic changes to the cynic's bleak outlook. If admittedly unlikely, it is conceivable that the 'appropriate measures' standard in the Directive turns into an exacting requirement where business reasons are paid little heed. Similarly, the courts could rule that the 'is

[49] General data protection regulation (EU) 2016/679, Article 35.

[50] Digital Services Act (EU) 2022/2065, Articles 34 and 35.

[51] Heyvaert (2018), pp. 92–98.

[52] Patz (2022); Veale and Borgesius (2021).

judged acceptable' standard requires that the AI system risk outcomes meet a substantive ethical threshold and that mere tick-box exercises do not pass muster. Time will tell. The building blocks for a real, effective horizontal meta-effect are, nevertheless, in place.

References

Avi-Yonah RS (2003) National regulation of multinational enterprises: an essay on comity, extraterritoriality, and harmonisation. Colum J Transnatl Law 42:5–34

Bantekas I, Oette L (2020) International human rights law and practice, 3rd edn. Cambridge University Press, Cambridge

Baumann-Pauly D, Nolan J (2016) Business and human rights: from principles to practice. Routledge, Abingdon

Bird RC, Cahoy DR, Prenkert JD (eds) (2014) Law, business and human rights. Edgar Elgar, Cheltenham

Celeste E (2022) Digital constitutionalism: the role of internet bills of rights. Routledge, London

Celeste E, Palladino N, Redeker D, Yilma K (2023) The content governance dilemma: digital constitutionalism, social media and the search for a global standard. Springer, Cham

Chamberlain J (2023) The risk-based approach of the European Union's Proposed Artificial Intelligence Regulation: some comments from a tort law perspective. Eur J Risk Reg 13:1–13. https://doi.org/10.1017/err.2022.38

Chiu IH-Y (2015) Regulating (from) the inside: the legal framework for internal control in banks and financial institutions. Hart, Oxford

Ciacchi AC (2019) The direct horizontal effect of EU fundamental rights. Eur Const Law Rev 15: 294–305. https://doi.org/10.1017/S1574019619000154

De Gregorio G (2019) From constitutional freedoms to the power of the platforms: protecting fundamental rights online in the algorithmic society. Eur J Leg Stud 11:65–103

De Gregorio G (2022) Digital constitutionalism in Europe: reframing rights and powers in the algorithmic society. Cambridge University Press, Cambridge

der Walt J (2014) The horizontal effect revolution and the question of sovereignty. De Gruyter, Berlin

Directive (EU) 2014/95 of the European Parliament and of the Council of 22 October 2014 amending Directive 2013/34/EU as regards disclosure of non-financial and diversity information by certain large undertakings and groups

Directive (EU) 2019/790 of the European Parliament and of the Council of 17 April 2019 on copyright and related rights in the Digital Single Market and amending Directives 96/9/EC and 2001/29/EC

Directive (EU) 2022/2464 of the European Parliament and of the Council of 14 December 2022 amending Regulation (EU) No 537/2014, Directive 2004/109/EC, Directive 2006/43/EC and Directive 2013/34/EU, as regards corporate sustainability reporting

Dürig G (1956) Grundrechte und zivilrechtsprechung. In: Maunz T (ed) Vom Bonner Grundgesetz zur gesamtdeutschen zerfassung: Festschrift zum 75. geburtstag von Hans Nawiasky. Isa Verlag, Goldbach, pp 157–190

Duval A (2023) Ruggie's double movement: assembling the private and the public through human rights due diligence. Nord J Hum Rights. https://doi.org/10.1080/18918131.2023.2171633

European Commission (2020) Shaping Europe's digital future. Communication from the Commission to the European Parliament, the European Council, The European Social and Economic Committee and the Committee of the Regions. COM(2020) 67 final

European Commission (2021) Proposal for a Regulation of the European Parliament and of the Council laying down harmonised rules on artificial intelligence (Artificial Intelligence Act), COM(2021) 206 final

European Commission (2022) Proposal for a Directive of the European Parliament and of the Council on Corporate Sustainability Due Diligence and amending Directive (EU) 2019/1937, COM(2022) 71 final

European Parliament (2023a) Amendments adopted by the European Parliament on 1 June 2023 on the proposal for a directive of the European Parliament and of the Council on Corporate Sustainability Due Diligence and amending Directive (EU) 2019/1937 (COM(2022)0071, 2023

European Parliament (2023b) Amendments adopted by the European Parliament on 14 June 2023 on the proposal for a regulation of the European Parliament and of the Council on laying down harmonised rules on artificial intelligence (Artificial Intelligence Act) and amending certain Union legislative acts. (COM(2021)0206 – C9-0146/2021 – 2021/0106(COD)). P9_TA(2023) 0236, 14 June 2023

Frantziou E (2019a) (Most of) the Charter of Fundamental Rights is horizontally applicable. Eur Const Law Rev 15:306–323. https://doi.org/10.1017/S1574019619000166

Frantziou E (2019b) Horizontal effect of fundamental rights in the European Union: a constitutional analysis. Oxford University Press, New York

Heyvaert V (2018) Transnational environmental regulation and governance: purpose, strategies and principles. Cambridge University Press, Cambridge

High-Level Expert Group on Artificial Intelligence (2019) Ethics guidelines for trust-worthy AI. EU, Brussels

Keller H, Ulfstein G, Grover L (eds) (2012) UN human rights treaty bodies: law and legitimacy. Cambridge University Press, Cambridge

Krause R (2021) Horizontal effect of the EU Charter of Fundamental Rights: Bauer and Willmeroth. Common Mark Law Rev 58:1173–1206. https://doi.org/10.54648/COLA2021070

La présidence française (2022) Proposition de Règlement du Parlement européen et du Conseil établissant des règles harmonisées concernant l'intelligence artificielle (législation sur l'intelligence artificielle) et modifiant certains actes législatifs de l'Union - Texte de compromis de la présidence - Articles 8-15 et Annexe IV, 13 January 2022

Leisner W (1960) Grundrechte und Privatrecht. Beck, München

Mahler T (2022) Between risk management and proportionality: the risk-based approach in the EU's Artificial Intelligence Act proposal. Nord Yearb Law Inform:247–270. https://doi.org/10.53292/208f5901.38a67238

Mylly T (2021) The new constitutional architecture of intellectual property. In: Griffiths J, Mylly T (eds) Global intellectual property protection and new constitutionalism: hedging exclusive rights. Oxford University Press, Oxford, pp 50–79

Nipperdey HC (1961) Grundrechte und Privatrecht. Scherpe, Krefeld

OECD (2011) OECD Guidelines for Multinational Enterprises, 2011 Edition. OECD, Paris

OECD (2019) Recommendation of the Council on Artificial Intelligence. OECD, Paris

Pacces AM (2023) Civil liability in the EU Corporate Sustainability Due Diligence Directive proposal: a law & economics analysis. SSRN. https://doi.org/10.2139/ssrn.4391121

Parker C (2002) The open corporation. Cambridge University Press, Cambridge

Parker C (2009) Meta-regulation: legal accountability for corporate social responsibility. In: Kinley D (ed) Human rights and corporations. Routledge, London, pp 335–368

Patz C (2022) The EU's draft Corporate Sustainability Due Diligence Directive: a first assessment. Bus Hum Rights J 7:291–297. https://doi.org/10.1017/bhj.2022.19

Permanent Representatives Committee (2022a) General approach. Proposal for a Regulation of the European Parliament and of the Council laying down harmonised rules on artificial intelligence (Artificial Intelligence Act) and amending certain Union legislative acts. 25 November 2022

Permanent Representatives Committee (2022b) General Approach. Proposal for a Directive of the European Parliament and of the Council on Corporate Sustainability Due Diligence and amending Directive (EU) 2019/1937. 30 November 2022

Regulation (EU) 2010/995 of the European Parliament and of the Council of 20 October 2010 laying down the obligations of operators who place timber and timber products on the market
Regulation (EU) 2016/679 (GDRP) of the European Parliament and of the Council of 27 April 2016 on the protection of natural persons with regard to the processing of personal data and on the free movement of such data, and repealing Directive 95/46/EC (General Data Protection Regulation)
Regulation (EU) 2017/821 of the European Parliament and of the Council of 17 May 2017 laying down supply chain due diligence obligations for Union importers of tin, tantalum and tungsten, their ores, and gold originating from conflict-affected and high-risk areas
Regulation (EU) 2019/1020 of the European Parliament and of the Council of 20 June 2019 on market surveillance and compliance of products and amending Directive 2004/42/EC and Regulations (EC) No 765/2008 and (EU) No 305/2011
Regulation (EU) 2020/852 of the European Parliament and of the Council of 18 June 2020 on the establishment of a framework to facilitate sustainable investment, and amending Regulation (EU) 2019/2088
Regulation (EU) 2022/1925 of the European Parliament and of the Council of 14 September 2022 on contestable and fair markets in the digital sector and amending Directives (EU) 2019/1937 and (EU) 2020/1828 (Digital Markets Act)
Regulation (EU) 2022/2065 of the European Parliament and of the Council of 19 October 2022 on a Single Market For Digital Services and amending Directive 2000/31/EC (Digital Services Act)
Regulation (EU) 2022/868 of the European Parliament and of the Council of 30 May 2022 on European data governance and amending Regulation (EU) 2018/1724 (Data Governance Act)
Ruggie JG (2013) Just business: multinational corporations and human rights. Norton, New York
Salminen J, Rajavuori M (2019) Transnational sustainability laws and the regulation of global value chains: comparison and a framework for analysis. Maastricht J Eur Comp Law 26:602–627. https://doi.org/10.1177/1023263X19871025
Salminen J, Rajavuori M (2021) Private international law, global value chains and the externalities of transnational production: towards alignment? Transnatl Leg Theory 12:1–19. https://doi.org/10.1080/20414005.2021.1970470
Schilling-Vacaflor A, Lenschow A (2023) Hardening foreign corporate accountability through mandatory due diligence in the European Union? New trends and persisting challenges. Regul Gov. https://doi.org/10.1111/rego.12402
Scott JC (1998) Seeing like a state: how certain schemes to improve the human condition have failed. Yale University Press, New Haven
Taylor S (1984) Making bureaucracies think: the environmental impact statement strategy of administrative reform. Stanford University Press, Stanford
Tistounet E (2020) The UN Human Rights Council. Edward Elgar, Cheltenham
United Nations (1948) Universal Declaration of Human Rights
United Nations (1966) International Covenant on Economic, Social and Cultural Rights
United Nations (1989) Convention on the Rights of the Child
United Nations (2011) Guiding principles on business and human Rights. Implementing the United Nations 'protect, respect and remedy' framework. United Nations, New York
Veale M, Borgesius FZ (2021) Demystifying the Draft EU Artificial Intelligence Act — analysing the good, the bad, and the unclear elements of the proposed approach. Comput Law Rev Int 22: 97–112. https://doi.org/10.9785/cri-2021-220402
Viljanen M (2017) A cyborg turn in law? Ger Law J 18:1277–1308. https://doi.org/10.1017/S2071832200022331
Wai R (2002) Transnational liftoff and juridical touchdown: the regulatory function of private international law in an era of globalisation. Colum J Transnatl Law 40:209–274
Walkila S (2016) Horizontal effect of fundamental rights in EU law. Europa Law Publishing, Groningen
Waller SW (1999–2000) The twilight of comity. Colum J Transnatl Law 38:563–580

Everybody Wants To Rule the World: The Relevance of the Rule of Law for Private Law in the Context of Algorithmic Profiling of Online Users

Silvia A. Carretta

Contents

Abstract The rule of law is an elusive concept, and its fluidity lends itself to multiple interpretations. Different accounts connect various core elements—'-*desiderata'*—under this universally recognised concept. However, there is a consensus (albeit implicit) that the rule of law is essentially a public law concept, of only marginal concern to private law. This paper departs from this understanding and suggests that this presumption is a misperception. The rule of law does not concern

S. A. Carretta (✉)
Faculty of Law, Uppsala University, Uppsala, Sweden

Digital Life Initiative, Cornell Tech, New York, United States
e-mail: silvia.carretta@jur.uu.se

E. Gill-Pedro, A. Moberg (eds.), *YSEC Yearbook of Socio-Economic Constitutions 2023*, YSEC Yearbook of Socio-Economic Constitutions (2024) 2023: 137–180,
https://doi.org/10.1007/16495_2023_62, Published online: 14 December 2023

only the regulation of powers and arbitrariness between individuals and the State, but it operates also in the relationships between private individuals.

In particular, with the flare-up in recent years in the use of machine learning algorithms to profile online users (in order to predict their behaviour and tailor recommendations and searches to their preferences), private actors (i.e. online platforms) have obtained a super-dominant position both in the collection of data and development of the technology, in the digital (eco)systems in which they operate.

This paper aims to prospectively assess the duplicitous relevance that algorithmic profiling has for the protection of fundamental rights from a private law perspective (e.g. right to privacy, right to not be discriminated, freedom of expression) and for the self-appointed power of online platforms to self-regulate their contractual relationships with users, in the digital markets. Conversely, it also discusses the relevance of the rule of law for private law relationships in its function of stronghold for the protection of fundamental rights. This value, on one side, creates legal guardrails around private self-regulation of online platforms, and on the other side, it secures the respect of fundamental rights of users from algorithmic profiling by online platforms. The paper concludes with the need to re-evaluate the State's power to limit private freedom and interfere in parties' autonomy in cases where fundamental rights are seriously at stake.

1 Introduction

Machine learning (ML) algorithms[1] play an increasingly dominant role in contemporary society.[2] Their ability to solve complex problems by transforming input data into a desired output decision is what makes them extremely relevant. There are many fields in which we can see a fast-growing use of AI potential such as justice, policing, public welfare, hiring, banking, political elections, and so on. However, despite the promise to revolutionise the way we interact with each other and bring enormous potential to humanity, algorithms also convey risks and challenges. Some of the main concerns involve the high risks for biased and erroneous decisions taken autonomously by the algorithms, boosting of human biases, inequalities, discrimination, and unfair consequences, as well as concrete risks for fundamental rights,[3] such as the right to privacy, freedom of expression, the right not to be discriminated against, and right to equality.[4]

[1]When discussing the potentiality and challenges of machine learning algorithms, this paper will make use of the general term 'algorithm', for readability.

[2]See, e.g. Dourish (2016); Gillespie (2014); Mayer-Schoenberger and Cukier (2013).

[3]When referring generically to rights, this paper intends to make reference to fundamental rights.

[4]For an interesting overview of the constitutional limits of AI, see Simoncini and Longo (2021).

One of the most common moments where these concerns are experienced by many users is indeed when algorithms are developed and deployed by private actors to profile users online. Algorithms have become increasingly important to facilitate the meeting online between offers and requests for goods and services. The paper sets its analysis around the specific example of online profiling of users. These algorithms are used to predict users' behaviour, assess their consumption, tailor recommendations and searches to their preferences, offer extra services and identify groups' patterns for better economic gain.

First, the paper will show the problem connected to the use of algorithms to profile online users and the serious limitations that they cause to users' fundamental rights. Using algorithms, online platforms obtained a super-dominant position both in developing the technology and the (eco)systems in which they operate. This one-sided and overwhelming power to shape contractual relationships between users and online platforms through self-regulation contravenes the fundamental principles of equality and autonomy of the parties. Further, it nullifies the bargaining power of online users in these private contractual relationships where self-regulation by online platforms proved to be insufficient to guard user's rights. Furthermore, it negatively impacts users' fundamental rights by users and threatens the exercise of these rights as provided by the law.

Subsequently, the paper prospectively assesses the role that the rule of law takes as a stronghold in the European Union for the protection of fundamental rights in the context of private law relations. It discusses the double function of the rule of law from the perspective of private law. First, the law calls for a limit of any arbitrariness from the more powerful of the two parties over the other; the stronger cannot regulate the relationship with the weaker party so users are subjected to profiling and automated decision-making. Second, it must secure the respect of fundamental rights in private, online contractual relationships.

The rule of law is one of the fundamental values upon which the Union is built. At first glance, the readers might wonder where the connection lies between the rule of law and private law. As it will be described below, there is a consensus (albeit largely implicit) that the rule of law is essentially a public law concept, of only marginal concern to private law scholars. Based on this statement, the State's invasion of private spheres by way of the rule of law for the regulation of powers and arbitrariness is generally frowned upon.

On the contrary, this paper sets out from the opposite understanding assumption that this presumption can be contested. The importance of the function of the rule of law within private contractual relationships between parties cannot be underestimated. The argument is that law must guarantee non-arbitrariness when it comes to the deployment of artificial intelligence (AI) based technologies that have the potential to deeply impact the fundamental rights of private parties within the EU internal and digital markets.

Lastly, the paper presents some parallelism between the rule of law's '*desiderata*' and the principles of private law. It explains the need to keep questioning the use of algorithms that negatively impact fundamental rights and to delimit the discretion that tech companies have in imposing unilateral contractual terms on users based on the results of the profiling. At the same time, it re-evaluates the need for the State to interfere in private contractual relationships and limit their contractual freedom, in cases where fundamental rights are seriously at stake. At the end, conclusions are drawn.

One last clarification is in order. When discussing fundamental rights, this paper does not refer to national constitutional rights but focuses instead on the fundamental rights established at the European level and enshrined—among others—in the Treaty on European Union (TEU) and the Treaty on the Functioning of the European Union (TFEU);[5] the European Convention for the Protection of Human Rights and Fundamental Freedoms (ECHR),[6] and the European Charter of Fundamental Rights (Charter).[7]

2 The Problem Outline: The Erosion of Fundamental Rights in the Context of Algorithmic Profiling of Online Users

The incipit of this section introduces how ML algorithms work and describes in simple terms their ability to draw inferences from data to create meta-profiles of users. Subsequently, it briefly presents the current EU legislative framework on algorithmic profiling (and, more broadly, on AI systems) and pairs it with a discussion around the phenomenon of the rise of private self-regulation of contractual relationships between users and online platforms. In the end, it frames the threats to fundamental rights that private self-regulations of algorithmic profiling rise pose within the EU framework.

2.1 The Use of Algorithms for Online Profiling

The current online economy relies mostly on the commercial activities of online platforms, which operate in multi-sided markets. Users profiling and shaping users' behaviour are a huge business for data-driven firms. In simple terms, user profiling can be defined as the process of examining, analysing, and creating useful summaries of data related to online platforms' users.

Their main activities are twofold. On the one side, online platforms facilitate user access to their platforms to produce a 'network effect' between users allowing them

[5]Consolidated versions of the Treaty on European Union and the Treaty on the Functioning of the European Union (2016/C 202/01) 7.6.2016.

[6]European Convention for the Protection of Human Rights and Fundamental Freedoms, 1950. Expand on use for reference on RoL and not application from individuals.

[7]Charter of Fundamental Rights of the European Union (2016/C 202/02) OJ C 326, 26.20.2012).

to find and interact with each other. On the other side, online platforms facilitate matching users' and service providers' profiles to streamline the provision of goods and services. From these activities, the online platforms gain economic value and develop what has been referred to as a 'collaborative economy'.[8]

Notably, data is inherently relevant for the functioning of algorithms. Through the collection, acquisition or purchase from third parties of colossal amounts of raw data about users' interactions on their platforms, engineers train algorithms to extract knowledge from raw data and draw inferences to build 'meta-profiles' of users. [9] In fact, once labelled, data is stored in a compiled dataset that is fed to algorithms that proceed in creating the 'meta-profiles' of each user. These automated meta-profiles are used to carry out the function of profiling and create the best matching between users and service providers within the collaborative economy—or more generally to obtain the best matching between companies and users' profiles.

The 'meta-profiles' identify users' main characteristics that online platforms want to know to evaluate how to offer their goods or services in the best possible way. Users' profiling produces critical data insights that can be leveraged to the advantage of online platforms. For instance, to provide services for online booking of flights, a platform might want to know whether a user travels frequently, out of which airport (s), in which class, how many times they have checked a certain route in the past days/months, which services they usually buy in addition, as well as connected information that is inferred from the dataset such as in which neighbourhood a user lives, which job they have, gender and race, with whom do they interact the most on social media and where these connections are based, and so on. This data allows the algorithms to infer whether a user might be interested in booking a flight in the near future, predicting upcoming destinations to offer discounts that invite them to purchase, whether a user is undecided on booking and eventually showing more targeted advertisements that might convince them to book or offering a personalised price as a 'deal' to appeal to the users' shopping compulsion.[10]

Moreover, these algorithms also perform several other secondary tasks, such as predicting the behaviour of users, assessing their consumption patterns, producing search ranking, tailoring recommendations and searches to their preferences, setting the price for underlying services, offering extra services to meet consumers' needs (or general profile patterns), making predictions about future actions likely to be followed by specific groups of individuals (e.g. minorities or disadvantaged group living in poorer areas of the city) and so on.

There are various categories of data within the dataset used to train algorithms for profiling, and the collection and processing of some of these categories may clash

[8]Communication from the Commission to the European Parliament, the Council, the European Economic and Social Committee and the Committee of the Regions 'A European agenda for the collaborative economy' COM/2016/0356 final, p. 3.

[9]The term 'profiling' is used as defined in Article 4, point (4), of Regulation (EU) 2016/679.

[10]The topic of personalized advertisement and adv targeting is extremely relevant nowadays and raises a lot of discussion on the impact that it has on users' fundamental rights. It is advised to read more in depth into it, for instance: Neumann (2016), p. 13; Imana et al. (2021); Ali et al. (2021).

with fundamental rights. The extensive discussion on the functioning of algorithms does not fall under the scope of this paper. Here, it suffices instead to mention that data is the pivotal point around which online platforms can conduct the profiling of users and, therefore, perform activities on their platforms. Therefore, the following paragraphs briefly introduce the main categories of data that online platforms collect and process to train their algorithms for profiling purposes.

2.1.1 Personal Data

The first category of data includes any information which is related to an identified or identifiable natural person. It involves any data that makes directly or indirectly identifiable the data subject (i.e. the user), in particular by reference to any identifier such as name, identification number, location data, online identifier (e.g. IP address)[11] or to one or more factors specific to the physical, physiological, genetic, mental, economic, cultural or social identity of these users (Article 4 General Data Protection Regulation—'GDPR').[12] In practice, these data can be provided by users when they register on a platform and use their services, or be collected by websites through cookies[13] or any sort of online behaviour or even simply via forms (requesting info such as telephone number, credit card number, social security or personal number, account data, number plate, appearance, customer number or address, etc.).

In particular, for certain special categories of personal data, the GDPR prohibits the processing without specific grounds provided by the law (Article 9 GDPR). This data reveals racial or ethnical background, political opinions, religious or philosophical beliefs, or trade union membership, and it includes also genetic and biometric data to uniquely identify a natural person as well as data concerning health, medications, dietary preferences, data subject's sex life or sexual orientation.

It is worth mentioning also that any personal data that has been de-identified, encrypted or pseudonymised, but can still be used to identify a person, is still considered personal data, falling under the scope of the GDPR. Conversely, personal

---

[11] Under the EU General Data Protection Regulation and EU case law, IP addresses (both static and dynamic) are considered personal data, if it is legally and practically possible for the website operator to obtain additional data from the ISP to identify the visitor. See, among others, CJEU Case C-582/14, ECLI:EU:C:2016:779; CJEU Case C-70/10, ECLI:EU:C:2011:771.

[12] Regulation (EU) 2016/679 of the European Parliament and of the Council of 27 April 2016 on the protection of natural persons with regard to the processing of personal data and on the free movement of such data, and repealing Directive 95/46/EC.

[13] There is a specific sectoral legislation regulating the use of location data or the use of cookies: Directive 2002/58/EC of the European Parliament and of the Council of 12 July 2002 concerning the processing of personal data and the protection of privacy in the electronic communications sector (e-Privacy Directive), OJ L 201, 31.7.2002; Regulation (EU) 2017/2394 of the European Parliament and of the Council of 12 December 2017 on cooperation between national authorities responsible for the enforcement of consumer protection laws and repealing Regulation (EC) No 2006/2004.

data that has been rendered irreversibly anonymous is no longer considered personal data. [14]

2.1.2 Statistical Data

The second category of data includes information contained in any user's digital footprints that is necessary for statistical surveys or the production of statistical results. For instance, behavioural observations, consumers' attitudes and propensities, search histories and others.

The processing of data for statistical purposes is subject to the rules set out in the GDPR and includes processing for different purposes—including public interest, scientific or historical research purposes (Recital 162 GDPR)—and special safeguards and derogations relating to their processing ex Article 89 GDPR. It is worth mentioning that the result of processing for statistical purposes is not considered personal data, but 'aggregate data', not used in support of measures or decisions regarding any particular natural person.

Within this category it is possible to include also the so-called 'freemium': personal or generic data given away freely by users as a 'commodity' in exchange for digital content or digital services supplied by the trader (for instance to participate in a raffle for free tickets or in a lottery to win a prize, as well as to receive free content online or promotional material). [15]

The vast variety of data included as well as its disparate origins has led to referring to these data as part of so-called 'big data' (or 'mass data'). The latter refers to a large body of information that cannot be comprehended when used only in smaller amounts. This big data consists of many different types of data: both structured (like traditional data structured in a database) and new semi-structured and unstructured (such as text, audio, and video). This last is particularly relevant but it requires additional pre-processing and labelling before it can be used to derive meaning and offer greater statistical power.[16]

[14] Recital 26 and Article 4(5) GDPR. The GDPR protects personal data regardless of the technology used for processing that data (Recital 15 GDPR).

[15] However, the EU 'fully recognise(s) that the protection of personal data is a fundamental right and that therefore personal data cannot be considered as a commodity'. See Recital 24, Directive (EU) 2019/770 of the European Parliament and of the Council of 20 May 2019 on certain aspects concerning contracts for the supply of digital content and digital services, OJ L 136, 22.5.2019.

[16] Gartner's IT glossary defines 'Big data' as 'high-volume, high-velocity and/or high-variety information assets that demand cost-effective, innovative forms of information processing that enable enhanced insight, decision making, and process automation' (see https://www.gartner.com/en/information-technology/glossary/big-data).

2.1.3 Proxies Data

The third category of data on which algorithms can be trained or that they can acquire in their life cycle is the so-called 'proxies data'. This category includes data that is not personal data per se (under Article 4 GDPR). However, this data is enough to allow algorithms to infer information on the users that could then be used to translate them into personal characteristics of the users (e.g. Geographic location, employment status, behavioural observations, habitual routes via public transportation, saved shops on maps, etc.). This allows online platforms to become aware—reflectively—of the personal characteristics of users, without having to collect their data directly.

In short, as it is often said: data is the new oil. Data acts as the new currency which, due to its strategic relevance, characterises most relationships in the context of the online collaborative economy within the EU digital market.

Via the collection of all aforementioned categories of data, some online platforms have obtained a super-dominant position through the development of powerful algorithms—created through big data analytics such as machine learning—used to automate decision-making processes and for profiling users. Consequently, they can use said super-dominant position in the online ecosystem in which they operate. By feeding to algorithms an ever-greater body of 'big data' they are able to obtain meaningful, statistical information about users' 'meta-profiles' that can be used for their advantages, but more importantly, it can be used to the user's disadvantage.

Regardless of the benefits of online platforms, unintelligible ranking and rating of human beings through algorithmic profiling raises doubts and worries about the protection of users' fundamental rights. In some of the most extreme examples, algorithmic profiling could go as far as predict—with the risk of making it a self-fulfilling prophecy—whether a user could become physically or mentally ill (for insurance purposes), a lazy employee (for employment purposes), a failing student (for admission purposes), a criminal or a terrorist (for security purposes). However, as mentioned above, these assessments often reproduce stereotypes, generalisations and discriminatory outcomes ingrained within the data, conveying human biases and reinforcing social hierarchies and material inequalities.

Due to obscure (if not complete lack of) explicability and transparency in the automated decision-making processes of algorithms, users stand at a disadvantaged point and often lack information to comprehend or even challenge the decisions of algorithms which can have significant life consequences on their lives. They are, in practice, inherently vulnerable to the power and whims of big tech and online platforms, in as much as their persons' livelihoods, rights, and freedoms are impacted directly by these automated decision-making processes.

As we will see below, AI technologies bring positive effects to society, online platforms and users, thanks to the increased capacity of individuals to connect with each other, access information and exercise their rights and freedoms online. Despite this, however, there are still strong concerns over the serious negative consequences that algorithmic profiling brings and over the restriction of users' fundamental rights.

As a consequence, several scholars and policymakers argue for the need to regulate AI and set up effective procedural safeguards for the use of algorithms for profiling users, especially when the latter are made unaware of this (see Sect. 2.2). If algorithmic reasoning and decision-making processes cannot be explained in a narratively intelligible way and they lack the direct consent of the person being evaluated—especially when his/her understanding of the technical and societal implications of such profiling is suboptimal—it needs to be discussed whether these algorithms should be used at all in certain sectors.[17] We will see next the current legislative framework regulating algorithmic profiling, before moving on to the challenges it raises for fundamental rights of users.

2.2 The EU Legislative Framework of Algorithmic Profiling: Public Regulations v. Private Self-Regulation

Given the impact that algorithmic profiling has on users' rights and in shaping their behaviour, this application of AI technology has not escaped the attention of the EU legislator. Currently, there exist multiple legislations that regulate the use of algorithms to profile users. The discussions around these legislations—as interesting as they might be—have to be reserved and addressed elsewhere. Instead, what is relevant for the scope of this paper is to give a brief, general overview of the main legislation in the EU on automated profiling. This will help to set the basis of the discussion for the readers and connect with the central issue of this paper: the recent tendency of online platforms to issue self-regulation to govern their private relationship with users and sustain their super-dominant position through the development and deployment of powerful algorithms.

2.2.1 General Data Protection Regulation

The first regulation that includes provisions on profiling is the GDPR. Its Article 4(4) considers 'profiling' any form of automated processing of personal data that is used for the objective of evaluating the personal aspects of a natural person. The article adds a series of exemplifications of statistical deductions concerning, among others, performance at work, economic situation, health, personal preferences, interests, reliability, behaviour, location or movements.

As a consequence, it is considered profiling pursuant to the GDPR includes any processing activity that online platforms perform online to monitor the behaviour of users, by tracking them on the Internet in order to make decisions concerning them

[17] See, for instance, the discussion of Pasquale over the use of profiling in judicial cases and the reference to the COMPAS case. Pasquale (2017) (see https://www.technologyreview.com/2017/06/01/151447/secret-algorithms-threaten-the-rule-of-law/).

or for analysing or predicting their personal preferences, behaviours and attitudes.[18] Users have the right to be informed that profiling is happening.[19]

Furthermore, Article 22 GDPR establishes the right for data subjects to object to automated individual decision-making, including profiling and direct marketing purposes, which produces legal effects, or similarly significantly affects them.[20] Recital 71 GDPR provides some examples such as 'automatic refusal of an online credit application' or 'e-recruiting practices without any human intervention'.

2.2.2 Proposal for an AI Act Regulation

In 2021, the European Commission issued a proposal for a Regulation laying down harmonised rules on AI (AI Act)[21] which includes provisions that both prohibit or considerably limit the use of certain AI-based systems considered too dangerous for EU citizens' safety or too restrictive of their fundamental rights. The AI Act follows a risk-based approach, dividing AI systems into three main risk categories: (i) unacceptable risk (it prohibits their use—e.g. social scoring or for exploring vulnerabilities of specific groups); (ii) high risk (it permits the use under certain conditions of compliance—e.g. AI-based systems for civil aviation security, medical devices or the management and operation of critical infrastructure); and (iii) limited risk (it permits the use in compliance with certain transparency obligations—e.g. chatbots).

The proposal classifies as high-risk any manipulative or exploitative practices facilitated by AI systems based on profiling and intended for individual risk assessments, to detect the emotional state of natural persons, for the evaluation of the reliability of evidence in criminal proceedings, for predicting the occurrence of an actual or potential criminal offence, or assessing personality traits and characteristics or past criminal behaviour of natural persons.

Moreover the AI Act reiterates the enforcement of existing data protection, consumer protection and digital service legislation that guarantee that natural persons are properly informed and have free choice not to be subject to profiling or other

[18]Recital 24 GDPR. More explicitly, the Working Party 29 emphasizes in their guidelines that simply assessing or classifying individuals based on characteristics could be considered profiling, with or without predictive purpose. In any case, if online platforms profile users, the latter have the right to be informed of this and of the consequences of such profiling. Working Party 29, Guidelines on Automated individual decision-making and Profiling for the purposes of Regulation 2016/679, 17/EN WP251 rev. 01, 6 February 2018.

[19]Article 13 and 14 GDPR.

[20]Nevertheless, controllers can continue to process the data over a subject's objection if they additionally prove that the impact to the data subject is limited to the minimum necessary and the objective is critical for the organization. Article 22(2) GDPR.

[21]Proposal for a Regulation of the European Parliament and of the Council laying down harmonised rules on artificial intelligence (artificial intelligence act) and amending certain union legislative acts, COM/2021/206 final.

practices that might affect their behaviour. On this note, it established a transparency obligation to inform users that they may interact with an AI system or their emotions or characteristics are detected and recognised through automated means, in particular if in association with (social) categories based on biometric data.

Of most relevance is EU Parliament's vote expressed in June 2023 on its most recent version of the draft. Key proposals approved include substantial amendments to the list of banned AI-based systems, now expanded to include intrusive and discriminatory uses for remove biometric surveillance, emotion recognition, predictive policing and social-scoring. Also generative AI uses have been limited, making it mandatory to disclose when content is AI-generated. Moreover, high-risk AI systems now also include also systems used to influence voters in elections or used in online recommender systems of very large online platforms (e.g. social media). Now, the EU institutions will enter the trialogue negotiations to reach an agreement on the final text, which will hopefully enter into force by 2025.

2.2.3 Digital Services Act Regulation

The Digital Services Act (DSA) is a regulation that regulates obligations of digital services that act as intermediaries in their role of connecting consumers with goods, services, and content. It aims to protect online users and their fundamental rights, establish a powerful transparency and accountability framework for online platforms and provide a single, uniform framework across the EU.[22]

With regards to profiling (as defined in Article 4 GDPR), online platforms will no longer be able to present behaviourally targeted advertisements for minors (Article 28(2)) or ads to all users based on profiling that rests on special categories of personal data such as ethnicity, political views or sexual orientation (Articles 26(3), recalling Article 9(1) GDPR).

In addition, Article 38 give users the right to opt-out of recommendations based on profiling. It requires providers of very large online platforms and online search engines that use recommender systems to push content across to users their platforms to offer at least one option for each of their recommender systems which is not based on profiling.

Lastly, the DSA prohibits online platforms from manipulating users into choices they do not intend to make via 'dark patterns' (i.e. the practices of materially distorting, impairing or algorithmically suggesting, ranking and prioritising information, distinguishing through text or other visual representations, or otherwise curating information provided by recipients). [23] Online platforms cannot deceive

[22] Regulation (EU) 2022/2065 of the European Parliament and of the Council of 19 October 2022 on a Single Market For Digital Services and amending Directive 2000/31/EC.

[23] Recitals 67 and 70 DSA. Recital 67 mentions that the rules on dark patterns should be interpreted 'as covering prohibited practices falling within the scope of this Regulation to the extent that those practices are not already covered under GDPR'.

or nudge unaware users into using their services, by distorting or impairing their autonomy in making a choice, for instance with exploitative design choices or by giving more prominence to certain messages, stimulating online behaviour through visual, auditory, or other components or urging the recipient to change their choice via interfering pop-ups.

Consequently, the DSA reiterates how online platforms shall consistently ensure that users are appropriately informed about how recommender systems impact the way information is displayed and can influence how information is presented to them.

2.2.4 Digital Markets Act Regulation

Alongside, the new Digital Markets Act (DMA) aims to control how large online platforms (i.e. 'gatekeepers') operate to promote competition and give consumers more choices in the digital economy.[24]

The DMA prohibits online platforms to from perpetrating behaviours consisting in of discriminating against business users by using their gateway position and superior bargaining power and unilaterally setting unbalanced conditions for the use of their platform services. [25] Recital 72 reiterates the fundamental protection of the right to privacy of end-users, especially during the collection of large amounts of their data by online platforms for the purpose of ranking and profiling activities. The DMA refers to the GDPR regarding the definition of profiling methods in question.

Correspondingly, Article 6(5) sets a clear obligation for online platforms to ensure adequate transparency in their profiling practices, via fair and non-discriminatory conditions in ranking and related indexing and crawling, as well as not to treat more favourably services and products offered by themselves compared to those of third parties.[26]

In addition, Article 15 requires online platforms to undergo an annual audit of their profiling techniques over consumers across its core platform services. They shall share this data with the European Commission by submitting an independent report. This information is then transmitted to the European Data Protection Board. The aim is to keep under control ensure the compliance of gatekeepers with the objectives set out in Recital 72, including enhancing transparency and accountability

[24] Regulation (EU) 2022/1925 of the European Parliament and of the Council on contestable and fair markets in the digital sector and amending Directives (EU) 2019/1937 and (EU) 2020/1828 (Digital Markets Act) OJ L 265, 12.10.2022, pp. 1–66.

[25] Recital 33 DMA.

[26] Article 6(2) para 2 specifies that 'data that is not publicly available shall include any aggregated and non-aggregated data generated by business users that can be inferred from, or collected through, the commercial activities of business users or their customers, including click, search, view and voice data, on the relevant core platform services or on services provided together with, or in support of, the relevant core platform services of the gatekeeper'.

for the use of profiling techniques as well as facilitating fairness and contestability of core platform services.

In short, we have shown how there is are currently a number of existing legislations within the EU legal framework that are applicable to challenges raised by algorithms for user profiling. The collective impact of regulations such as the GDPR, the upcoming AI Act, the new DSA and DMA is likely going to be significant for the protection of online users, to ensure that digital technologies are safer, more respectful of fundamental rights and the law as well for their role in setting a global precedent.

However, as mentioned before, a new sort of regulation is emerging among private players in the digital environment. Online platforms that develop or deploy algorithms used to profile users have taken begun to issue private self-regulation to govern the private relationship between themselves and their users. The rationale behind these self-regulations is based on one side on a sort of a perception of self-accountability to third parties for their use of AI on users (e.g. human-centred principles, values and ethical guidelines).[27] On the other hand, a second rationale can be seen in the need for online platforms to issue their own private contractual terms that regulate their relations with the users and their access to the platforms' services and goods (e.g. Terms and Conditions or community guidelines).

This attitude of the private industry can be seen as a clear signal of its intent to provide policy-makers with a reason not to pursue new regulation.[28] Thanks to their auto-appointed power to regulate individuals' access to, and use of, digital technology instruments, they consequently can affect the way in which individuals exercise their rights online, access information and network with each other. An obvious example is the fact that users are incapable of exerting any influence over the contractual terms imposed by online platforms for their use of their services. This contractual imbalance contravenes the fundamental principle of equality of the parties and autonomy of will, and it nullifies the bargaining power of users as counterparts in private contractual relationships.

Despite the fact that violations of fundamental rights perpetrated by private actors is not a novelty but have been perpetrated for centuries offline, in the context of the digital society their likelihood has increased due to the dominant role in the hand of few, powerful big tech companies.[29] By claiming a commitment towards the issuing principles and guidelines for their use of AI-based algorithms, the private industry

[27] It suffices to see how this auto-imposed self-regulatory power of private industry has produced a plethora of vague, high-level documents containing value statements and promises of action. However, they very rarely contain specific, practical recommendations and often fail to address fundamental normative tensions embedded in conflicts between Principles (e.g. between Principles of fairness, privacy, and explainability). More on this topic can be read in: Fjeld et al. (2020); IEEE (2017) (see: https://iapp.org/resources/article/ethically-aligned-design-a-vision-for-prioritizing-human-wellbeing-with-artificial-intelligence-and-autonomous-systems/).

[28] Concerns have been raised over the fact that representatives of industry are being given too much leeway in shaping AI regulations. For instance, Benkler (2019).

[29] Celeste (2019).

has implicitly claimed for itself the right to define what it means to responsibly deploy these technologies, which actors should be held responsible, and when. Consequently, it has claimed the right to shape its version of AI for the rest of the world too, with the intent to delay regulation and pre-emptively focus only on abstract problems and technical solutions. As a consequence, these self-regulations deeply impact deeply the everyday life and choices of an unprecedented number of online users, as well as the expression of their rights, especially in the context of algorithmic profiling.[30]

In light of this, the possibility that these non-state actors interfere with users' fundamental rights has become more intense and ever-present in our daily lives. As Coeckelbergh points out, when dealing with the power unbalances of tech companies, 'it is hard to see how responsible innovation can really be implemented when there is a concentration of power in the hands of a relatively limited number of powerful actors, including a small number of large corporations: it seems that a handful of companies decide the future of AI'.[31]

Before, the State was the main dominant actor within the polity, bound by the obligation that limits its power to guarantee the respect of individual, fundamental rights. Now, with the rise of 'platform capitalism',[32] fundamental rights are regulated by private actors in contractual relationships that contain imperatives to be complied with by the signatory parties, but not legally binding for society. Thus, it is apparent the need for the EU legislator to concern itself with setting guardrails and limitations to algorithmic profiling, and indirectly on the self-regulatory power of Big Tech just as much as it became imperative that the State—and, more in generally, the EU—ensure that such private entities respect fundamental rights of users.[33]

To sum up, in accordance with the current outlook, while trying to catch up with technological developments and upcoming challenges, it is time for the law to embrace its role in the future of the relationship between AI and society, in order to act as an enabler and protector of fundamental rights and democratic values. In the next section, starting from three concrete examples, we will see how algorithmic profiling can negatively impact fundamental rights of users.

---

[30] Suzor believes that self-regulation of online platforms is legitimate, even if unilaterally established because users provide their consent to it. He argued that constitutional law plays a twofold role in the limitation of private power. Since these self-regulations could infringe on fundamental rights, they are to be subjected to the limitations imposed by contract law as well as by the principles established by the State (e.g. the rule of law) (Suzor 2018).

[31] Coeckelbergh (2019), p. 33.

[32] For instance, an interesting study on the impact that algorithms have on individuals access to education, access to credit (within the US credit score systems), job opportunities and health insurance coverage among other areas, see O'Neil (2016); or Pasquale (2016).

[33] As Celeste point out in his analysis of the new digital constitutional, citing Sartor, he underlined that there is not a precise hierarchy between private self-regulation and state law. Instead, these two sources as melding together 'in a "mesh" of public and private governance schemes' (Celeste 2019; Sartor 2017).

2.3 *Fundamental Rights Are Threatened by Algorithmic Profiling Online*

It should be clear by now how the use of algorithms for online profiling generates alterations in the digital ecosystem and has a deep impact on users' choices. Algorithms have the duplicitous role of amplifying the possibilities for users to exercise their fundamental rights, yet at the same time amplifying the risk of threats to these rights. Given these concrete risks of contrasting with the existing fundamental rights paradigm, eroding the procedural legitimacy of, and trust in, democratic institutions and the authority of the law, the following section discusses a few of the fundamental rights challenged by algorithmic profiling.

The criticalities connected to the act of profiling users for matching purposes—so that online platforms can obtain economical gains from their activities—come to light and threaten the protection of the fundamental rights of online users. Even if algorithms functions are questionably legal, they may still yield illegitimate or illegal results as well as plainly wrong outcomes. On the one side, they can enhanced fundamental rights based on the exchange of information—such as freedom of expression, religious freedom, freedom of assembly, freedom to conduct a business—while, on the other hand, they create new sources of threats to users' fundamental rights such as defamation, hate speech, cyberbullying, child pornography, limiting the transmission of certain information or monitoring individuals and the content transmitted (infringing e.g. the right to privacy, right to private life, secrecy of correspondence).

Algorithms that are poorly built, trained on incorrect data, or data collected via poorly designed processes will cause the algorithms to yield unexpected or wrong outcomes. It can be mentioned the clamorous example of Google Photos—an image recognition algorithm—that yielded a plainly wrong outcome when it identified two people of colour as 'gorillas' instead of as of black teenagers. [34] The same company received backlash when an online query for 'three white/black teenagers' on Google images presented an image of white teenagers with balls and being happy, while the black teenagers' image portrayed them in mug shots taken by the police. [35] These example illustrates in obvious terms how the discriminatory outcomes of a decision-making process are strongly connected to a poorly thought-out model.

Alongside to the collection of data and the effect of profiling on fundamental rights, it is necessary to point out the relevance that ownership of data has in the digital markets. Data gives its owner a relevant power over other parties of a contract, not only in economic terms but also as a commodity that can be used to improve the owner's services or products above competitors, or even to damage their reputation for their advantage (see e.g. The Cambridge Analytica scandal). [36] This

[34] Barry (2015) (see https://www.wsj.com/articles/BL-DGB-42522).

[35] Allen (2016).

[36] Confessore (2018) (see https://www.nytimes.com/2018/04/04/us/politics/cambridge-analytica-scandal-fallout.html).

asymmetry in data ownership can be translated into an asymmetry in the wealth of information as well as in bargaining power between the user and digital market operators. As a consequence, when subjected to algorithmic profiling online, the fundamental rights of users—just as much as the rights of other competitors—might be hindered by the stronger party.

As discussed previously, the ability to develop and deploy algorithms on users has vested an extraordinary amount of power in non-state actors, such as few, powerful online platforms, which own, commercialise or manage algorithms to the detriment of users and traditional actors (e.g. such as nation States).[37] AI-based algorithms for users profiling provide an unprecedented means for these private parties to limit and direct individuals' freedoms and fundamental rights 'from inside', through the exercise of a self-regulatory power.[38]

The diffuse use of algorithmic profiling challenges any democratic system due to their impact on public discourse, the lack of transparency in how automated decisions are made, and difficulty to explain the outcomes, as well as the struggles to ensure accountability of AI technology (or for AI technology) when it negatively affects individual rights and freedoms.[39] For these reasons, it is necessary to bind the development of algorithmic technologies with safeguards and democratic oversight in order to avoid the marginalisation of public actors and stop society from being controlled by techno-determinism.

Thanks to the horizontal effect of fundamental rights within the Union, these rights are autonomously applicable between private parties, without the need for reproduction within a general clauses of private law.[40] Even the fundamental rights codified in the Charter have horizontal effect among private parties.[41]

By way of example, the paper analyses three examples of fundamental rights that are clashing with algorithmic profiling deployed by private parties on users.

2.3.1 Right to Privacy

A first example of fundamental rights threatened by algorithmic profiling is the right to privacy. The main rational for profiling users, as we have seen before, is allowing companies to know better individuals' needs and desires, in order to build a positive

---

[37] Pagallo (2018).

[38] To read more about 'algorithmic capitalism'—which use AI to increasingly link economics and politics to certain forms of knowledge—see Bodei (2019).

[39] Among others, see Danaher (2016); Mittlestadt et al. (2016); Gillespie (2014).

[40] See, inter alia, four judgments by the CJEU from 2018, which definitively establish the direct effect of Article 21, Article 31(2), and Article 47 of the Charter in the adjudication of litigations between private parties.

[41] Karavas and Teubner (2005); Frantziou (2015).

connection with the users and between the services offered and potential new customers.[42]

From a data protection perspective, algorithms can access enormous amounts of data about individuals and process it with incredible speed to consistently identify individuals with a minimum degree of accuracy. Since most this data can be personal data 'tension between the need for identifiability of users and their data protection rights is unavoidable'.[43]

As seen in Sect. 2.2, the EU legislative framework protects personal data and the right to privacy as fundamental rights inter alia under Article 2 TEU, Article 16 TFEU, Articles 7 and 8 Charter, and the GDPR. The Court of Justice of the European Union (CJEU) case law has gone as far as stating that the processing of personal data requires appropriate safeguards so that personal data is not disclosed without consent and, in any case, in such a way that it would constitute a breach of the Charter.[44] Moreover, the CJEU has multiple time interpreted Article 6(1) GDPR requirements in a strict manner for lawful processing of personalised social network data.[45]

As a consequence, all type of personal data collected from a user can in theory be invasive of their privacy and a cause for users to alter their behaviour upon fear of being surveyed (so-called 'panoptic effects') or can also be used to manipulating users into choices they do not intend to make, nudging unaware users into choosing their services, impairing their autonomy in making a choice.[46]

Of relevance for the present discussion is also the question whether these rights apply also to the processing of non-personal data. The aforementioned rules do not seem to take into account the role played by proxies and the way platforms operate.

Since algorithms can make predictions about a person's behaviour, state of mind, identity and so on by collecting information that is not classified as falling under the category of personal data, it is not clear to what extent the right not to be subject to decisions based solely on automated processing of personal data—such as algorithms-based profiling and prediction—might also cover the use of proxies (see Sect. 2.2). In fact, the collection and use of apparently neutral data such as 'proxies' can still indirectly inform the algorithms of protected characteristics pertaining to said user.[47]

Reference can be made to the case of recurring itineraries booked via the Uber service, which has proved able to reveal users' sexual preferences and information about their private lives by tracking the location they often frequent or the neighbourhoods in which they stop (as the notorious scandal of Uber's 'rides of

---

[42] Wiedemann (2022).

[43] Cit. Wiedemann (2022), p. 2.

[44] CJEU Joined Cases C-92/09 and C-93/09, EU:C:2010:662. See also Tene and Polonetsky (2013).

[45] Inter alia, CJEU Case C-252/21; CJEU Case C-597/19 ECLI:EU:C:2021:492; CJEU Case C-645/19 ECLI:EU:C:2021:483.

[46] Lyon (2001).

[47] Newell and Marabelli (2015).

glory has shown),[48] or matching name and bodily measurement can be proxies for information on the user's gender just as much as the postal code or educational level could be proxies for race or minority status, and so on.

For these reasons, the right to privacy of users is clearly put at risk by the myriad of automated decisions taken by algorithms on online platforms for the profiling of users or the matching of users and service providers.

2.3.2 Right Not To Be Unlawfully Discriminated

Moving on to a second example, which involves the risks associated with profiling and the right not to be discriminated against, it is possible to build on top of the previous discussions to present how data used for training and decisions taken on how to build a model have a direct connection with the outcomes of the autonomous decision taken by the algorithms.

The EU legislative framework protects the right to not be discriminated against and the right to equal treatment as fundamental rights inter alia on the basis of the protected grounds set out in Article 21 of the Charter. Numerous case law by the CJEU have also reiterated the principle of equal treatment in various areas (e.g. employment, occupation, nationality etc) and the prohibition of all discrimination on the basis of special characteristics.[49]

Starting from a common saying within the data science community—'garbage in, garbage out'—it is possible to illustrate how algorithms draw patterns from data on which have been trained—and fed in the development phase—but also learn from data acquired autonomously during their decision-making processes throughout their life cycle. Consequently, by providing the algorithms with 'garbage' data—containing human bias or inequality patterns that are structurally recorded in the data process or in past data—data engineer and developers risk conveying human bias to the algorithms and reinforcing the existing social hierarchy and material inequalities.

Examples from previous algorithms fails have shown how using biased data can endanger the exercise of fundamental rights as well as be the cause of discrimination at a large scale. Mentions can be made to the chatbot Tay.AI which turned racist in as little as twenty-four hours, having learned sexist and hate speech from the interaction with its users,[50] or to gender-biased facial-recognition systems which have a high accuracy of recognition for white men but not black women.[51] Other examples of prejudiced outcomes come from wrongful labelling of data: in many cases it has been seen that, when asking an image recognition algorithm to recognise the

[48] Hill (2014) (see https://www.forbes.com/sites/kashmirhill/2014/10/03/god-view-uber-allegedly-stalked-users-for-party-goers-viewing-pleasure/).

[49] CJEU Case C-930/19, ECLI:EU:C:2021:430.

[50] Hunt (2016) (see https://www.theguardian.com/technology/2016/mar/24/tay-microsofts-AI-chatbot-gets-a-crash-course-in-racism-from-twitter).

[51] Buolamwini and Gebru (2018).

profession of a person wearing a white coat, it would label him as a doctor if it is a man, while it would label her a nurse if it was a women. [52]

The problematic discussion, however, is not whether discrimination is wrong and should be avoided. Instead, it involves the question of how to stop algorithms from reproducing and augmenting the patterns of discriminatory treatment that exist in the society in which they are created and used. As mentioned above, this can occur when structural discrimination is ingrained in the data used for training, or when developers' stereotypes or biases are represented in the labelling process and in the framing of the problem to be answered by the algorithm. These blind spots can also originate from wrongful choices made in the design and deployment of the algorithms. If historical structures of inequality and discrimination are entrenched in the datasets used to train algorithms, then these will rely on such biased data and reproduce the discriminatory human decisions from the past in their decisions.

2.3.3 Right to Freedom of Expression

Last, but not least, it is possible to mention another set of rights that can be equally enhanced as much as restricted by algorithmic profiling. As mentioned above, the advent of AI-based technology applicable in the digital markets has facilitated the possibility for users to communicate with each other and collect information across various channels. Rights based on the exchange of information as protected by Article 10-12 Charter—such as freedom of thought, conscience and religion; freedom of expression and information; freedom of assembly and of association; freedom to conduct a business—can be exercised freely by users online like never before. More specifically, Article 11 Charter protects freedom of expression and information in the EU. It includes 'freedom to hold opinions and to receive and impart information and ideas without interference by public authority and regardless of frontiers'.

Nevertheless, the use of algorithms can also negatively impact users' right to freedom of expression. By using algorithms for moderation of content online, online platforms have the ability to shape the public discourse around important topics by influencing users' opinions, ideas and information that they receive and are allowed to impart. This also means that freedom and pluralism of the media could be impacted. Through algorithmic profiling, online platforms are able to scrutinise in the smallest details the opinions and ideas expressed by users across channels and infer from proxies data even the ones that have not been expressed explicitly. Consequently, online platforms remain the only self-appointed supervisor of freedom of expression online, who can cleanse the Internet from deep fakes, disinformation content, fake news or antagonise fundamental rights and limit the transmission of certain information and monitor individuals and the content they create and share online. The separatory line between the two is very thin...

---

[52] Kay et al. (2015).

A case study from a German court concerning the ban of a user from a chat forum is explanatory of these concerns.[53] This case involves a private forum, moderated by some users of a private platform, and the instance of a single user who was denied access to the forum on the basis of arbitrary decision taken by the moderators. This instance can be interpreted as potential restriction of the individual right to freedom of expression. Although the court invoked only the general principle of good faith established by the German civil code (ordering the reintegration of the user because the owner of the platform had not previously established certain rules on the use of the chat), one could imagine that this case could have been solved also with reference to the values of rule of law and the German direct/indirect application of fundamental rights to private actors (so-called 'Drittwirkung').[54]

Similar case law from the CJEU has interpreted strictly any case that might concretely restrict the right to freedom of expression, freedom to hold opinions and to receive and impart information and ideas, due to interference of private entities (e.g. online platforms) or private individuals (e.g. other users).[55]

In conclusion, it has been shown how algorithmic profiling can be a source of threats to users' fundamental rights and freedoms. Data used to train algorithms and the outcomes of algorithms' decision-making processes can negatively impact users' fundamental rights. It is worth reiterating how, algorithms that are poorly built, trained on incorrect data, or data collected via poorly designed processes end up causing the algorithms to yield unexpected or wrong outcomes. It is necessary to make conscious efforts in the (de)selection and labelling of data, in the framing of the problem as well as in the development and supervision of the deployment of the algorithms in order to guarantee full protection of fundamental rights.

In order to ensure the protection of these rights, developers and data engineers shall use as guidance the boundaries set by the law, starting from the EU Treaties and the Charter. [56] It is necessary to ensure that all human choices concerning the algorithms' design, development, and deployment throughout the entire lifecycle are consciously trying to avoid potentially illegal outcomes from the automated profiling process (even unexpected ones).

[53] Landgericht Bonn, LG Bonn, judgment of November 16, 1999 - 10 O 457/99, openJur 2011, 77972.

[54] Karavas (2010).

[55] CJEU Case C-314/12, EU:C:2014:317.

[56] Other relevant international sources of fundamental rights are the International Covenant on Civil and Political Rights (1966) and the UN Guiding Principles on Business and Human rights (2011).

3 The Solution: The Function of the Rule of Law to Secure the Respect of Fundamental Rights in the Context of Algorithmic Profiling of Online Users

This paper adopts the concept of the rule of law as proposed by Suzor, which is grounded on the core idea developed by Raz.[57] For the scope of the following theoretical discussions, this principle is understood as a well-established concept in western liberal theory that anchors the legitimacy of governance in legality.[58] The rule of law requires those who are in charge of making decisions to do so without arbitrariness or capricious discretion, respecting the requirements provided by the law and following the liberal values of good governance. This last concept is central to the paper's discussions on the legitimacy of platform governance and provide a useful guide to understanding the role that private online platforms play in governing social life of users, both online and in the off line world. It argues that the concept of the rule of law should be made applicable also to private relationships and that self-regulation of online platforms/user relationships should be based on the values of the rule of law, nonetheless to guarantee users' consent, predictability of the platform's decisions and procedural fairness that respect of fundamental rights.[59]

Having introduced above the challenges for fundamental rights associated with algorithmic profiling of users and the concurrent existence of two regimes of regulation of this technological phenomenon, this section now moves on to present the rule of law as a possible solution for the aforementioned challenges to fundamental rights. The following section starts out with a general overview of the rule of law as an EU value and a short literature review, to help the readers better follow the ensuing discussion. Subsequently, it discusses the relevance of the rule of law for the creation of legal guardrails around private self-regulations of online platforms and draws on existing parallelism between the function of the rule of law and the function of private law. In the end, the section concludes with a discussion in concrete terms on the role of the rule of law in securing the respect of fundamental rights of users from algorithmic profiling.

---

[57] Raz (1977).

[58] Suzor (2018).

[59] This concept includes principles that are relevant within the Union and the author is aware that the latter can diverge from the conception of the rule of law from an international perspective. For this reason, the paper refers mainly to Union principles and values. However, at times reference is made to the concept of the rule of law under the ECHR in order to offer a comparative understanding of this concept for a more comprehensive analysis. It is understood that the ECHT is not directly enforceable by private parties in their relations. Nevertheless, the author believes that citing these principles can help explain the fundamental rights that can be 'protected' under the rule of law. As a consequence, this introduction is relevant for the subsequent discussion under the Sect. 3.1.

3.1 *The Rule of Law in the EU: A Stronghold for the Protection of Fundamental Rights*

The rule of law is one of the founding values of the European Union, alongside democratic values and fundamental rights. This principle is common to all Member States and a bedrock of the Union's identity, stemming from the common constitutional traditions of all the Member States. [60] In recent years, these founding values have come under attack around the world, testing the resilience of the rule of law also in Europe. With specific reference to the research matter of this paper, the extended use of algorithms and AI-based technology to shape the beliefs of online users, dominate their access to information and control the way they network with each other is just one of the many examples of attack that threaten the rule of law. As the other side to the same coin, algorithms.

Before going more in-depth into the discussion of how algorithms threaten fundamental rights and what the role of the rule of law is as a stronghold for their protection, it is necessary to present a brief overview of the origin of this principle and its interpretation in the EU. Since this paper is not a treaty on the rule of law, the readers should be mindful that the following is an introductory overview of this principle in Europe, necessary to set the stage for the following discussions (see Sects. 4.2 and 4.3).

3.1.1 The Rule of Law in the EU

The rule of law is enshrined in Article 2 TEU and its relevance is endorsed also by the Preambles to the Treaty and the Charter. The EU recognises the importance to guarantee the rights originating from the constitutional traditions common to the Member States as general principles of the Union's law (Article 6(3) TEU). The Treaties also recognise the accession to the Charter as well as to the ECHR pursuant to Article 6(1)-6(2) TEU as mandatory in order to conform Union's legislation and policies with fundamental rights and firmly anchor the EU and its Member States to the protection of fundamental rights.

As a consequence, it is worth noticing for now how Article 51 Charter limits its application primarily only to the EU institutions, its bodies and the Member States in compliance with the principle of subsidiarity. This provision aligns with Article 6(1) TEU and refers to all authorities set up by the Treaties or by secondary legislation, when they act to implement EU law (e.g. Articles 15 & 16 TFEU).

In the EU, the European Commission is responsible for guaranteeing the respect of the rule of law as a fundamental value, and for making sure that EU law, values and principles are respected. In 2014 the Commission launched an EU framework to

[60] This is also why, under Article 49 TEU, respect for the rule of law is a precondition for EU membership. Communication from the Commission to the European Parliament and the Council 'A new EU Framework to strengthen the rule of law' of 11.3.2014, COM (2014) 158 final.

strengthen the rule of law and in 2019 launched a 'Rule of Law Annual Review Report', based on the monitoring of the respect of this value in each Member States, ensure effective and coherent protection of fundamental rights and democracy across the Union.[61]

Moreover, the EU has also other instruments at its disposal aimed at protecting the value of the rule of law. Pursuant to Article 7 TEU, the EU can make use of an early-warning mechanism to evaluate the existence of, and possibly sanction, 'a serious and persistent breach' of EU values (thus also threats to the rule of law) by a Member State.[62] Furthermore, Member States hold a role in shaping the rule of law in the EU. In fact, the Commission has set up a network where Member States can provide their input and assist in the drafting of the annual rule of law reports.

Moreover, the Council of Europe provides recommendations and opinions to the Commission as a frame of reference for relevant standards and best practices in the protection of the rule of law. Since 2014, it also holds an annual dialogue among all Member States to promote and safeguard the rule of law.

Despite its importance, the rule of law still remains an elusive concept and its fluidity lends itself to multiple interpretations under EU law. The existing literature and jurisprudential discussion do not offer a unitary picture of the concept of rule of law in the EU as a well-established principle in its core meaning.[63] Given the significance of this concept, it can be perplexing that the precise content of the principles stemming from this concept is not clearly enunciated but vary depending on different national identities, constitutions, legal systems and traditions that the Union is bound to respect.

Recent rulings of the CJEU have highlighted the relevance of the rule of law in EU legal order stating that this value is central to the EU legal order not only as formal and procedural requirement, but also as substantive value to which the EU institutions are subjected.[64]

Another clarification is in order. The definition of the rule of law has evolved over time and different accounts connect various core elements or '*desiderata*' under this

[61] Communications from the Commission to the European Parliament, the European Council and the Council, The European Economic And Social Committee And The Committee Of The Regions 'Further strengthening the rule of law within the Union – State of play and possible next steps' COM(2019)163 final and 'Strengthening The Rule Of Law Within The Union A Blueprint For Action' COM (2019) 343 Final; Communication from the Commission to the European Parliament, the Council, the European Economic and Social Committee and the Committee of the Regions, 2023 Rule of Law Report. The Rule of Law situation in the European Union, COM/2023/800.

[62] This mechanism was recently activated for the first time against Poland and Hungary.

[63] This led the CJEU to affirm through its case law the principle of respect for fundamental rights, by stating that fundamental rights are enshrined in the general principles of Union law protected by the CJEU: among others, CJEU Case C-1/58, ECLI:EU:C:1959:4; CJEU Joined Cases C-36/59, 37/59, 38/59, 40/59, ECLI:EU:C:1960:36, CJEU Case C-11/70 ECR 01125; CJEU Case 29/69, ECLI:EU:C:1969:57. Italian Constitutional Court Case No. 183/73, Frontini v. Ministero Delle Finanze, 27 December 1973.

[64] For example, pursuant to CJEU Case C-64/16, ECLI:EU:C:2017:395; CJEU Case C-216/18; CJEU Case C-619/18, ECLI:EU:C:2019:531.

universally recognised concept. What can be found in common between all accounts of the rule of law in the EU is the principle that caters for everyone being equally subjected to the law, under the control of independent and impartial courts and free from arbitrary power. Furthermore, a non-exhaustive list of principles that compose the core meaning of the rule of law has been recognised by the case law of the CJEU, as well as by the Council of Europe. [65] These principles include legality and supremacy of the law, which implies a transparent, accountable, democratic and pluralistic process for enacting laws; separation of powers and prohibition of arbitrariness, thus accountability to the law; effective judicial protection by independent and impartial courts; respects of fundamental rights; non-discrimination, legal certainty and equality before the law. [66] Furthermore, it can be included with near consensus also a collection of institutional, formal, and procedural requirements such as e.g. separation of powers, publicity of the law, non-retroactivity, access to justice, due process and natural justice. [67]

As a consequence of this alignment in the Treaties (now including the Charter), it is possible to shortly conclude that EU and its Member States are in principle equipped to—and have to mandatorily—protect the fundamental rights of individuals against any threat to the rule of law. With particular reference to Member States, it follows unambiguously from the case-law of the CJEU that they are bind to respect fundamental rights recognised by the EU they act in the scope of Union law.[68]

3.1.2 The 'Public Law Presumption'

As mentioned, different accounts of the rule of law connect various core principles under this universally recognised concept entrenched in many legal systems. Under this term, it is possible to include with near consensus also a collection of institutional, formal, and procedural requirements such as, for example, separation of powers, publicity of the law, non-retroactivity, access to justice, due process and natural justice. [69]

[65] CJEU Joined Cases C-402/05P and C-415/05P ECLI:EU:C:2008:461, para 81; 281; CJEU Case C-274/12 P, ECLI:EU:C:2013:852, para 56; CJEU Case C-362/14, ECLI:EU:C:2015:650, para 60; 95. See also Council of Europe, Commissioner for Human Rights, The rule of law on the Internet and in the Wider Digital World (December 2014) 8.

[66] Annex to the Communication from the Commission to the European Parliament and the Council 'A new EU Framework to strengthen the rule of law' COM (2014) 158 final.

[67] For a broader analysis, Austin and Klimchuk (2014), p. 2f.

[68] The CJEU stated that 'it should be remembered that the requirements flowing from the protection of fundamental rights in the Community legal order are also binding on Member States when they implement Community rules'. CJEU Case C-292/97 ECLI:EU:C:2000:202, para 37; CJEU Case C-5/88 ECLI:EU:C:1989:321; CJEU Case C-260/89, ECLI:EU:C:1991:254; CJEU Case C-309/96, ECLI:EU:C:1997:631.

[69] For a broader analysis, Austin and Klimchuk (2014), p. 2f.

Consequently, the rule of law appears hardly at all in scholarly works concerned with private law. [70] On the contrary, there is a consensus (albeit largely implicit) that the rule of law is essentially a public law concept, of only marginal concern to private law scholars. Austin and Klimchuk dub this the ‘public law presumption’. [71] The impression is that the rule of law involves pre-eminently the role of lawmakers and the State, as well as the obligations of individuals subjected to the formers’ powers.

However, the perception that the rule of law is essentially part of the public law doctrine can be seen as a misperception. The rule of law does not concern only the conditions under which relationships between individuals and the State become subject to the law. Instead, it concerns also conditions under which the relationship between individuals takes shape, under the insignia of the law. In other words, there is also a private law relevance to the rule of law. It consists of securing values such as non-arbitrariness and guidance of the law, which constitutes the major substance of the rule of law while regulating the interaction of individuals—regarded as equal and autonomous—and their reciprocal rights. [72] This framework is enriched by a system of private law rules which allow private parties to plan their undertakings within set limits of the law, and, at the same time, prevent them from using their power arbitrarily or advancing one’s particular set of interests over another.

In addition, both the rule of law and private law carry out the important role of guaranteeing individuals’ freedom to pursue their ends, free from conscription by the State or abuse from other individuals, while also seeing their fundamental rights protected by the State, in case of infringement. This train of thought is supported by various scholars. For instance, Lucy contests the primacy of public law in the context of the rule of law and argues that also private law has the function of protecting individuals against arbitrariness in the context of relations between individuals. [73] Another scholar, Allan, goes as far as stating that: ‘private law is precisely the operation of the rule of law – the provision and enforcement of standards of legality in the context of civil society’. [74]

In short, here it suffices to summarise how the rule of law has relevance also for private law. In the specific context of this paper, we will see below how the rule of law plays a fundamental role in guaranteeing the respect of fundamental rights event

[70] For a broader analysis, Austin and Klimchuk (2014), p. 2f.; Dicey (1964), p. 193; Dworkin (1985), p. 11; Hayek (1944), p. 84; Allan (2014), p. 86.

[71] Austin and Klimchuk (2014), p. 2.

[72] Therefore, the ability of judiciary power (via its courts) to revise the content of agreement subjected to private law, by reference to abstract concepts—such as fundamental right or general principles of the law—may create an undesirable degree of uncertainty that purist private law scholars believe should be avoided at all cost. For a broader analysis, see Collins (2018), p. 4.

[73] Lucy (2014), p. 46. For example, Martin Krygier recently argued that ‘[w]hether or not the rule of law has claimed in a society is a matter found in the extent and quality of its reach and effects there: in interactions between individuals and the State, of course, but of equal or more importance, between individuals themselves’ (Krygier 2011).

[74] Allan (2014), p. 86.

in private contractual relationships and acts as a legal guardrail around the use of algorithm for profiling online users.

3.1.3 The Rule of Law and Private Parties

The previous sections highlighted the mandatory alignment of the EU, its institutions and Member States to the value of the rule of law and its relevance for private law relationships. Nonetheless, what is of relevance for this paper is the specific situation where private contractual relationships are established between online platforms and users, who are subjected to algorithmic profiling. Alongside, online platforms tend to issue self-regulation to govern the contractual relationships with the users of their services or goods.

In this specific case, the questions that arise are twofold: whether and how private parties might be bounded to the recognition and protection of fundamental rights accessed by the TEU and the Charter; at the same time, whether the rule of law is applicable to private contractual relationships in the context of algorithmic profiling.

So far, the paper has dealt with the formal and procedural aspects of the rule of law, as recognised under Union law.[75] Yet, the notion of the rule of law is more complex and includes also substantive aspects. This latter aspect implies that also private individuals and entities are endowed with rights and obligations pursuant to positive, Union and national law (thus the relevance of the rule of law for private law—Sect. 3.1.3 above). These rights and obligations originate in the relationship of private parties vis-à-vis another and vis-à-vis the State.

If we accept that the rule of law comprises the protection of fundamental rights within its scope, especially those rights recognised in the Charter and adopted within the EU *acquis*, then the substantive concept of the rule of law expands beyond the EU and its institutions, which are bound by the rule of law under both formal and procedural understanding. Consequently, this principle also includes the rights dimension which provides a substantive understanding of the rule of law within private relationships.[76] This substantive conception, in connection with the aforementioned twofold questions, will be answered hereafter (see Sects. 3.2 and 3.3).

On this note, another clarification is in order first when discussing the advent of AI technology in the EU digital markets. In the past years, the EU institutions have weighed in on the role that the rule of law has in the EU digital markets. More specifically, of relevance for the current matter at hand, they debated the growing concerns connected to the extensive use of algorithms on online users to shape their

[75] Tamanaha (2004).

[76] Although there are some legal theorists, such as Joseph Raz, who insist that the Rule of Law cannot be confused with human rights or social justice, it is possible to suppose that the substantive dimension of the Rule of Law embraces the preservation of property as a fundamental right and related aspects such as dignity and social welfare.

opinions, track the content they create and their interests, limit the transmission of certain information or monitor individuals and the content transmitted.

Most prominently, the EU Council has set up an Ad hoc Committee on Artificial Intelligence (CAHAI), which is responsible for examining the feasibility of a legal framework for the design, development, and deployment of algorithms, which should be based on Council of Europe standards on human rights, democracy and the rule of law.[77] After mapping the relevant international and national legal frameworks, algorithmic principles and ethical guidelines, the CAHAI prepared a report on global perspectives on the development of a legal framework on AI which analyses risks and opportunities originating from algorithms and impacting these three fundamental concepts.[78] In this regard, the question of the role and accountability of all relevant stakeholders (e.g. data engineers or developers, online platforms, business enterprises, nations, research institutions and civil society and users) in designing, developing and deploying algorithms technologies which respect to the rule of law remains to be further explored in another place.

As seen in Sect. 2.3, the impact of algorithms on fundamental rights cannot be ignored, thus, having received more attention lately also by EU institutions. Recent events have demonstrated that a lack of respect for the rule of law has negative consequences on fundamental rights thus becoming a reason of serious concern for the EU institutions as well as for the Member States. [79] On the other hand—of main relevance here—the use of algorithms to profile users online might clash with fundamental rights, by directly hindering the applicability of one or more Union core values. [80]

As a consequence, algorithmic profiling threatens the rule of law and challenges the legal, political and economic basis of the whole union, with a direct impact on the life of every individual that operates within the EU digital market. As some scholars wrote, 'the informational asymmetries, flawed epistemology of data-driven inferences together with the bias inherent in machine learning [...] bring about the concern that the "rule of law" might be exchanged for the "rule of technology"—accompanied by Kafkaesque, Huxleyan and Orwellian discourses of dystopia'.[81]

In conclusion, with reference to the two questions above from where we started, we can anticipate that in light of the horizontal effect of fundamental rights and the recent tendency of constitutionalisation of private law, private parties are bound to the recognition and protection of fundamental rights accessed by the TEU and the Charter (see Sect. 3.2 below). At the same time, in the context of algorithmic profiling, the rule of law might be deemed applicable to private contractual

[77] Council of Europe, Commissioner for Human Rights, The rule of law on the Internet and in the Wider Digital World, Issue Paper (December 2014).

[78] Council of Europe, Ad hoc Committee on Artificial Intelligence (CAHAI) (Resolution CM/Res (2011)24, 1353rd meeting 11 September 2019).

[79] For example, op. cit. CJEU Case C-619/18.

[80] Leslie et al. (2021).

[81] Bayamlıoğlu and Leenes (2018).

relationships. In essence, the role of this principle is that of offering guidance between the autonomy of the private law system and its interaction with the constitutional fundamental rights of the Union. The rule of law also sets boundaries to the self-appointed power of private parties to self-regulate their use of algorithms in their relationships with users, and the impact that these have on fundamental rights.

In light of the above, we can sum up the following. Considering that the protection of these rights as a fundamental right is conceived as forming the substantive dimension of the rule of law, any violation of these rights by the use of algorithmic profiling procedures may be contested by virtue of the argument of its incompatibility with the rule of law.

3.2 The Relevance of the Rule of Law to Create Legal Guardrails Around Private Self-Regulation of Online Platforms

While discussing the various dimensions of the rule of law—formal, procedural and substantive—two questions were posed. The first one asked whether and how private parties might be bound to the recognition and protection of fundamental rights accessed by the TEU and the Charter. We can affirm that the answer to this question is positive.

Taking into account the tendency of constitutionalisation of private law and the horizontal effect of fundamental rights, private parties are bound to the recognition and protection of fundamental rights in the Union.[82] The next paragraphs discuss each of these two factors.

Firstly, there has been a tendency to interpret private law in light of constitutional principles in recent years. In broader terms, constitutional law strives to limit public powers—more precisely in the form of State government and public entities—in order to protect citizens against arbitrariness and State abuse. In a text on this topic, Pollicino and De Gregorio highlight how the shift of power from public entities to private parties requires rethinking some well-established assumptions.[83] In fact, private parties are not required to comply with constitutional principles and safeguards, thus at times developing self-regulations that contradict the rule of law and clash with public values. Pollicino and De Gregorio define this shift as ‘a form of economic freedoms turning into forms of power [. . .] In the lack of any regulation,

[82] In 2018, the CJEU definitively established the direct effect of the Charter in the adjudication of litigations between private parties. See CJEU Case C-414/16, ECLI:EU:C:2018:257; CJEU Case C-68/17, ECLI:EU:C:2018:696; CJEU Joined Cases C-569/16 and C-570/16, ECLI:EU:C:2018:871; CJEU Case C-684/16, ECLI:EU:C:2018:874.

[83] Pollicino and De Gregorio (2021), p. 3.

the global activity of online platforms contributes to producing a para-legal environment on a global scale competing with States' authorities'.[84]

In particular, with reference to this constitutionalisation tendency, some authors such as Berman, Fitzgerald and Suzor have started using the term of 'digital constitutionalism'.[85] Suzor in particular has theorised the existence of so-called virtual communities, which are governed by a mixture of public and private power alike. What is of relevance here of Suzor's theory that denies the existence of a precise hierarchy between private self-regulation and national law. Instead, he considers these two sources as melding together in a 'mesh' of public and private governance schemes.[86] What can be agreed upon is the crucial role assigned to the State and constitutional law to delimit self-governance in virtual communities and power abuse based on self-regulations of few, stronger, big tech online platforms.

As Suzor argues, constitutional law can be used to determine the extent to which self-regulation issues by private parties need to comply with the values established by the State.[87] This has brought forth a limitation of private power. In fact, constitutional rights—as provided by constitutional law and its principles—have the role to inform private contract law and prompt it to conform with constitutional principles. As a consequence, principles like the rule of law tend to be transferred into private contractual relationships, via constitutionally informed self-regulation. To guarantee the democratic representation of users in the choices of this self-regulation, it is thus necessary to make use of constitutional principles to restore a balance of powers in the algorithmic society.[88]

Secondly, the effect of the rule of law on private parties is shaped by the horizontal effect of fundamental rights. This effect in return shapes private law.[89] Private law discipline does not protect individuals from acting arbitrarily and does not give them absolute liberty from State interference. Instead, it provides individuals with the legal power to protect their interests, and with redress mechanisms against actions from other individuals—or the State itself—which delimit the scope of their liberty. In the words of Austin, 'the law must be able to guide, but not so that individuals can plan their activities to avoid legal sanctions; law guides so that individuals can follow the instructions necessary to exercise their property powers'.[90]

---

[84] Cit. Pollicino and De Gregorio (2021).

[85] Fitzgerald entrusts a constitutionalising role to private law, Berman to constitutional law, Suzor to a private law informed by the principles of constitutional law, Karavas to norms produced by private actors, and finally Redeker, Gill and Gasser to the documents of Internet bill of rights. For a broad discussion around the literature on this topic, see Celeste (2019), p. 9.

[86] Suzor (2018).

[87] Op. cit. Suzor (2018).

[88] Frank Pasquale, Secret Algorithms Threaten the Rule of Law MIT Tech Review (June 1 2017). Available at: www.technologyreview.com/s/608011/secret-algorithms-threaten-the-rule-of-law/; Pasquale (2015).

[89] Karavas and Teubner (2005).

[90] Austin and Klimchuk (2014), p. 13.

Therefore, it becomes evident how algorithms shall not be allowed to ever undermine legality or limit access to justice in case of infringement of fundamental rights. Thus, users have the right to receive clear, transparent explanations of the way algorithms use their data and how they infer a decision, especially in the case users claim protection against decisions made by the algorithms in front of a court of law and need to produce evidence on data or functioning of the algorithms. Here it suffices to summarise how, in some contexts, algorithms are able to reduce users to 'meta profiles' and subject them to automated decision-making, potentially reducing their complexity as individuals and affecting their rights and economic opportunities online. At times, algorithms can expand users' rights and be a set of tools to protect them from unfair profiling. But, at most other times, algorithms can be a means to reproduce stereotypes, generalisations and discriminatory outcomes ingrained within the data. The risk is that the algorithms convey human biases and exponentially reinforce social hierarchies and material inequalities.[91]

Moving on to the second question, it speculated whether the rule of law is applicable to private contractual relationships in the context of algorithmic profiling and how it shapes these relationships. The answer to this question is discussed hereinafter.

In recent years there has been a flare-up in algorithmic principles and ethical guidelines issued by private parties, to self-regulate their deployment of algorithms. These privately promulgated, voluntary self-regulations act as a sort of 'soft law' and have the effect of diminishing the primary role of the law. They allow online platforms to exploit the contractual power self-appointed by these private regulations to bestow on themselves the authority of the legislator and the role of judges. This has two negative side effects: first, they eviscerate the State's power to issue legislation and weaken the rule of law; second, they exacerbate private interests and threaten public interests as well as fundamental rights.[92]

A further clarification is in order. The rule of law comes into play in parallel with private law as both have a complementary role in supporting the respect of the principle of legality and the protection of users against the risks arising from algorithms (to which they are subjected with or without their knowledge).

One way to counterbalance these negative consequences is making sure that algorithmic profiling always respects the function of the rule of law, even within private relationships, especially when fundamental rights could be deeply impacted. As explained, the rule of law plays a paramount substantive role within private contractual relationships between users and online platforms to ensure the protection of fundamental rights (Sect. 3.1). Under the discipline of private law, the autonomy of the individual and freedom of will to enter into an agreement is the first instance. However, even in these private law relations, private parties shall not interfere with

[91] Researchers have repeatedly demanded that AI research and development move away from behind closed-door industry settings, since most companies' self-governance commitments are failing to ensure accountability for AI systems (Whittaker et al. 2018, p. 32).

[92] Bakant (2015), p. 281.

fundamental rights and individuals' autonomy to self-determinate. In our specific case, the rule of law influences the contractual freedom of online platforms, and by reflection the algorithms they develop and deploy to profile users.[93]

In light of this, the power of private online platforms to substitute themselves to the States' power, reversing the value of the rule of law, must be limited. With reference to algorithms used for profiling users, it can be affirmed that the relationship between users and online platforms is primarily governed by the contractual terms included in the documents referred to as 'terms of service' or 'terms and conditions', as redacted by the online platforms. Consequently, the protection fully warded to users by the law as well as the procedural protections that public courts guarantee under the law, it strongly limited by a semblance of will of the parties to supersede certain rights. [94]

This is even more problematic if one considers that users cannot negotiate the contractual terms nor the use of their data but are instead somehow coerced to accept the 'terms of service' or 'terms and conditions' if they want to access the platforms or use the services offered by the online platforms. A wider implication to keep in mind is the risking for users of being cut out from the vast majority of social interactions, information sharing under a false sense of contractual freedom.

For this reason, the rule of law has a central meaning for private law due to its function of constraining arbitrary exercise of power, especially when one party develops and deploys algorithms to profile users online and restrict their fundamental rights. [95] Any violation of fundamental rights by the use of algorithmic profiling procedures use by private parties may be contested by virtue of its incompatibility with the rule of law.

In conclusion, it is possible to conclude how it is necessary to change the point of view in the conception of the relationship between rule of law and private law. The latter must keep the primary role of guiding private individuals in their endeavours, by allowing them to plan for the future and to create meaningful values for their businesses, and society. The rule of law, instead, has to maintain its primary role of guaranteeing the supremacy of the law, the non-arbitrariness, and the effectiveness of existing legislations to regulate new technological phenomena (such as AI and its algorithms) and respond adequately to current digital challenges to fundamental rights by guaranteeing their protection.

---

[93] The CJEU has recognized direct effects between private parties of e.g. freedom of movement, the right not to be discriminated against on grounds of sex, the principle of equal pay for equal work and the right to collective action. See, e.g. CJEU Case 43/75, ECLI:EU:C:1976:56; CJEU Case 36/74, ECLI:EU: C:1974:140; CJEU Case 13/76, ECLI:EU:C:1976:115; CJEU Case C-415/93, ECLI:EU:C:1995:463; CJEU Joined Cases C-51/96 and C-191/97, ECLI:EU:C:2000:199; CJEU Case C-281/98, ECLI:EU:C:2000:296; CJEU Case C-309/99, ECLI:EU:C:2002:98; CJEU Case C-438/05, ECLI:EU:C:2007:772; CJEU Case 149/77, ECLI:EU:C:1978:130; CJEU Case C-281/97, ECLI:EU:C:1999:396; CJEU Case C-333/97, ECLI:EU:C:1999:512; CJEU Case C-341/05, ECLI:EU: C:2007:809.

[94] A broad discussion can be found in Susskind (2018).

[95] Austin (2014), p. 273.

3.3 The Function of the Rule of Law to Secure the Respect of Fundamental Rights of Users from Algorithmic Profiling by Online Platforms

The previous sections have shown how, currently there is a number of existing legislations within the EU legal framework that are relevant and applicable to challenges raised by algorithmic profiling. Furthermore, we have shown how algorithms can also erode the procedural legitimacy of, and trust in, democratic institutions and the authority of the law, by clashing with existing the fundamental rights paradigm.

Given these concrete risks, we have seen above how the rule of law has a relevance also for private law relationships. This principle answers the need to set legal guardrails on the self-regulatory power of online platforms and it secures the protection of fundamental rights in the digital markets.

Before drawing conclusions, this section discusses certain parallelisms between the rule of law and those of private law, to showcase counteractions vis-à-vis the legal challenges generated by algorithmic profiling of users online, and its impact on fundamental rights.

3.3.1 Non-Arbitrariness v. Freedom to Pursue One's Own Ends

One main rule of law's principle emphasises the role of securing individuals from the arbitrary exercise of power, both from the State and from other individuals. [96] It has been shown how this function is carried on also by private law in the context of relations between private individuals. Its main role is to guarantee individuals' freedom to pursue their own ends, free from conscription, and secure the law's predictability.

When putting this reasoning in the context of algorithms, it is imperative to first identify who, across the network actors (natural or juridical persons) is accountable in each stage of the algorithms' life cycle. Then, it is imperative to identify whether these actors have acted within their rights or if they have exercised excessive arbitrariness in the choices of design, development, and deployment of the algorithm. Establishing levels of human discretion during the use of the algorithm means introducing human agency, autonomy and oversight in the decisional process. For instance, developers could decide not to use an algorithm in a particular situation, or not to use a particular function of the algorithms in connection with a specific group of users (such as minorities or protected categories). Human autonomy goes as far as allowing developers to override a decision made by an algorithm or to base the decision not solely on it.

[96] An exercise of power is arbitrary in the sense relevant to the rule of law when 'the agent answers only to his or her own arbitrium'. See Postema (2014), p. 17.

In light of this, it can be argued that private parties' contractual freedom and non-arbitrariness are two sides of the same coin. Private parties are free to decide how to satisfy their private interests and, accordingly, design, develop, and deploy algorithms. However, they are not free to act arbitrarily, and do not have absolute liberty to decide and act on their interests, if the latter have a negative impact on the private sphere of other online platforms or users. In conjunction with this, both online platforms and users have the right to resort to redress mechanisms against decision or actions taken by others which delimit the scope of their individual liberties, for instance by being biased or discriminatory.

3.3.2 The "Indeterminacy of the Law" Debate v. Self-Regulation of Private Parties

As mentioned, private actors play an important role in significantly shaping the field of algorithmic ethics through the adoption of voluntary codes of conduct and ethical guidelines. These privately promulgated, self-regulations act a sort of 'soft law' and have the effect of diminishing the primary rule of the law and the legal protection of human rights. For instance, whereas previously courts of law were the only ones with the power to determine what illegal hate speech is and protect the fundamental right of non-discrimination, today there are privately-owned algorithms that determine whether content online is to be tagged as hate speech and taken down. [97]

Since these algorithms de facto compete for judicial authority with the State's judges and for legislative power with the legislator, it can be argued the need of a regulatory framework that enhances legal certainty around algorithms. An effective regulatory framework for algorithms will require close cooperation between all stakeholders, including States, public sector bodies, civil society, and businesses in order to reflect diverse interests and perspectives. Thus, it is vital to maintain a balanced division of powers and to return the legislative and judiciary powers in the hands of their legitimate holders. Nevertheless, it will also be important to complement and support the implementation of hard law in context-specific manners. In this case, it will land mainly on private actors' responsibility to make sure to implement sector-specific guidelines or standards for the design and development of algorithms which respect human rights across the whole AI life cycle. [98]

3.3.3 Predictability v. Opacity

On the other side, another core element of the rule of law is predictability. Citizens' rights are secured under public, clear and accessible legal rules, which are to be applied predictably and not be subject to the whims of the State or particular

[97] Cohen (2019).

[98] UN Guiding Principles on Business and Human Rights (2011).

individuals.[99] However, the technological complexity associated with the algorithms' decision-making process does not make its decisions suitable to full predictability and human comprehension.

The opacity connected to how algorithms draw inferences from data makes it difficult for the average users to understand how algorithms work and claim (or prove) infringement of their rights (especially, if one considers the proprietary nature of algorithms, lack of disclosure, or the unequal access to data). At times it can be difficult even for those who have developed the algorithm to understand the decision-making process, let alone the users.

Thus, lack of transparency (due to opacity) and predictability of the AI decisions are two big issues that need to be tackled if one wants to guarantee the respect of the rule of law. As argued by Greenstein: 'the threat to the rule of law lies in the fact that most of these decision-making systems are "black boxes" because they incorporate extremely complex technology that is essentially beyond the cognitive capacities of humans and the law too inhibits transparency to a certain degree'.[100] A possible solution would be to require platforms to introduce explanatory tools (e.g. in the form of pop-ups) or ad hoc redress mechanisms where users can raise questions on how things work, or ask to get more information or clarifications within a reasonable time.[101]

3.3.4 Equality v. Digital Power Concentration

Lastly, as mentioned above, the principle of equality of the parties is challenged since algorithms are developed by a handful of large private actors (sometimes referred to as the Big Tech or Big Five). The influence of non-State actors on fundamental rights has steadily grown in the digital market. Tech companies have a huge capability to impact fundamental rights through their algorithm. Exorbitant digital power is concentrated in the hands of a few tech companies which dominate both the design and development of algorithms as well as the (eco)systems algorithms operate in and on.

Online platforms have obtained a super-dominant position, by owning personal and mass data used to train the algorithms that make autonomous decisions. On top of this, through the issuing of self-regulation—via privately issued principles of AI and ethical guidelines—online platforms self-regulate the development and deployment of algorithms used to profile users, allowing them to prioritise shareholders' interests over the protection of users' rights.

[99] Waldron (2016).

[100] Greenstein (2021).

[101] It is shocking for instance to mention the number of cases received by Meta Independent Oversight per year (1 million) and the number of decisions take (20!). Oversight Board first Annual Report (2022).

However, if too much political power is concentrated in the hands of a few private parties, it can alter the societal equilibrium and threaten democratic values. [102] Therefore, to protect the rule of law, it is indispensable that humans involved in the loop always make a diligent effort to design and develop only transparent and lawful algorithms, even if their autonomy and contractual freedom might allow them to pursue their own ends and commercial profits. As Austin argues, private ownership (of platforms) does not protect a sphere of individual liberty from State interference so that private parties can plan their activities in order to avoid legal sanctions. Instead, it provides individuals (users) with legal powers to secure legal consequences not otherwise possible and 'enlarge the scope of individual liberty through making future-oriented planning possible in a number of ways'. [103]

3.3.5 Protection of Fundamental Rights v. Relinquishing of Unwaivable Rights via Unilateral, 'Mass-Market Boilerplate' Provisions

Another element that has primary relevance is the fact that the use of algorithms on users is often hidden or unknown, making it difficult or impossible to know whether there is an impact on their fundamental rights. Users and society at large are subjected to algorithms when navigating on online platforms, at times even without their full acknowledgement or approval. For instance, algorithms are increasingly being incorporated into content moderation system that are intended to assist online platforms in their decision-making responsibilities: the algorithms are in charge of profiling users and deciding which content to show and to whom, but users are unaware of this work behind the scenes.

Borrowing the concept from Hayek again, it can be stated that the rule of law is not just about protection against the abuses of law, or the securing of predictability, but involves securing 'a sphere of freedom as independence' where individuals can pursue their own ends free from conscription from the State but also from the ends of others.

These algorithms can have wide societal implications in terms of limiting freedom of expression and opinion of users, as well as impacting the right not to be discriminated or the right to privacy (Sect. 3.1). Therefore, it can be argued that a priority of the EU institutions as well as Member States should be to enforce the rule of law and guarantee the protection of individuals' rights in the public sphere, but even of users on privately owned platforms. [104]

Furthermore, as it is often the case, users are subjected to terms and conditions to access the services of a platform. These terms have been unilaterally written by the

[102] Nemitz (2018); Webb (2019).

[103] Austin (2014).

[104] In fact, these platforms have grown in influence to a point where they have been considered equivalent to a 'modern day town square'. United States Supreme Court, Packingham v. North Carolina, 582 U.S. (2017).

online platforms and, more importantly, users do not have the bargaining power to negotiate the contractual obligations, nor the power to oppose the terms contained therein. If they want to access the platform, they are forced to accept these terms (often without even understanding them). In a very interesting paper, Radin argues that the rule of law requires that some rights are 'permanently in the care of the polity' and nonwaivable by individuals, since using fine print (i.e. boilerplate) in these terms and conditions to delete basic background rights 'may undermine the rule of law when the deletions are used against wide swaths of the public, especially when they result in loss of the right of redress'. [105]

In light of this, to respect the rule of law and guarantee non-arbitrariness and equality before the law, it is imperative that certain fundamental rights—that risk being erased by mass-market boilerplate—are secured through democratic processes and not subjected to waiving through contractual agreements. Especially if they refer to access to justice and judicial remedies.

4 Conclusions

This paper showed the explicit relevance of the rule of law for private law relationships. When discussing the specific case of algorithms used for profiling online users for matching purposes, we saw how the deployment of these algorithms can have deep impacts on the fundamental rights of users. By way of example, it has been presented how algorithmic profiling clashes with users' right to privacy, right not to be discriminated or right to free expression, among others and might erode the authority of the law and give arbitrary, self-regulatory power to online platforms.

In the context of algorithmic profiling, the rule of law plays an important role within any private law as it offers guidance to online platforms on how to plan their undertakings within set limits of the law and exercise their contractual autonomy (which private law system affords them), while, at the same time, it sets boundaries to the private parties self-regulatory power to profile users online, creating legal guardrails under the insignia of the law against the violation of fundamental rights of any individual impacted by said relationship.

The trade-off to keep in mind is the risk that algorithms reproduce stereotypes, generalisations and discriminatory outcomes ingrained within the data, conveying human biases and reinforcing social hierarchies and material inequalities. One way to counterbalance these negative consequences is to respect the function of the rule of law within private relationships, making it necessary to re-evaluate the State's power to limit private freedom and to interfere in private parties' autonomy to guarantee the supremacy of the law, to secure the respect of the rule of law and the protection of fundamental rights, thus, delimiting the discretion that online platforms impose on users and society alike through their self-regulations.

[105] Radin (2014).

Legislation and Legal Acts

Annex to the Communication from the Commission to the European Parliament and the Council A new EU Framework to strengthen the rule of law COM (2014) 158 final

Charter of Fundamental Rights of the European Union, (2016/C 202/02) OJ C 326, 26.20.2012

Communication from the Commission to the European Parliament and the Council A new EU Framework to strengthen the rule of law of 11.3.2014, COM (2014) 158 final

Communication from the Commission to the European Parliament, the Council, the European Economic and Social Committee and the Committee of the Regions A European agenda for the collaborative economy COM (2016) 0356 final, p. 3

Communication from the Commission to the European Parliament, the Council, the European Economic and Social Committee and the Committee of the Regions, 2023 Rule of Law Report. The Rule of Law situation in the European Union, COM (2023) 800. https://commission.europa.eu/publications/2023-rule-law-report-input-member-states_en

Communications from the Commission to the European Parliament, the European Council and the Council, The European Economic And Social Committee And The Committee Of The Regions Further strengthening the rule of law within the Union – State of play and possible next steps COM(2019)163 final

Communications from the Commission to the European Parliament, the European Council and the Council, The European Economic And Social Committee And The Committee Of The Regions Strengthening The Rule Of Law Within The Union A Blueprint For Action COM (2019) 343

Consolidated versions of the Treaty on European Union and the Treaty on the Functioning of the European Union (2016/C 202/01) 7.6.2016

Council of Europe, Ad hoc Committee on Artificial Intelligence (CAHAI) (Resolution CM/Res(2011)24, 1353rd meeting 11 September 2019)

Council of Europe, Commissioner for Human Rights, The rule of law on the Internet and in the Wider Digital World (December 2014)

Directive (EU) 2019/770 of the European Parliament and of the Council of 20 May 2019 on certain aspects concerning contracts for the supply of digital content and digital services, OJ L 136, 22.5.2019

Directive 2002/58/EC of the European Parliament and of the Council of 12 July 2002 concerning the processing of personal data and the protection of privacy in the electronic communications sector (e-Privacy Directive), OJ L 201, 31.7.2002

European Convention for the Protection of Human Rights and Fundamental Freedoms, 1950

International Covenant on Civil and Political Rights (1966)

Proposal for a Regulation of the European Parliament and of the Council laying down harmonised rules on artificial intelligence (artificial intelligence act) and amending certain union legislative acts, COM/2021/206 final

Protocol 12 of the European Convention on Human Rights (1950)
Regulation (EU) 2016/679 of the European Parliament and of the Council of 27 April 2016 on the protection of natural persons with regard to the processing of personal data and on the free movement of such data, and repealing Directive 95/46/EC
Regulation (EU) 2017/2394 of the European Parliament and of the Council of 12 December 2017 on cooperation between national authorities responsible for the enforcement of consumer protection laws and repealing Regulation (EC) No 2006/2004
Regulation (EU) 2022/1925 of the European Parliament and of the Council on contestable and fair markets in the digital sector and amending Directives (EU) 2019/1937 and (EU) 2020/1828 (Digital Markets Act) OJ L 265, 12.10.2022, p. 1–66
Regulation (EU) 2022/2065 of the European Parliament and of the Council of 19 October 2022 on a Single Market For Digital Services and amending Directive 2000/31/EC
UN Guiding Principles on Business and Human Rights (2011)
Working Party 29, Guidelines on Automated individual decision-making and Profiling for the purposes of Regulation 2016/679, 17/EN WP251 rev. 01, 6 February 2018

Case Law (in Antichronological Order)

CJEU Case C-252/21, Meta Platforms and Others (Conditions générales d'utilisation d'un réseau social), ECLI:EU:C:2023:537
CJEU Case C-930/19, X v État belge, ECLI:EU:C:2021:657
CJEU Case C-914/19, Ministero della Giustizia v GN, ECLI:EU:C:2021:430
CJEU Case C-597/19, Mircom International Content Management & Consulting (M.I.C.M.) Limited v Telenet BVBA, ECLI:EU:C:2021:492
CJEU, case C-645/19, Facebook Ireland Ltd and Others v Gegevensbeschermingsautoriteit, ECLI:EU:C:2021:483
CJEU Case C-216/18 PPU v. LM, Judgment of the Court (Grand Chamber) of 25 July 2018
CJEU Case C-619/18, European Commission v. Republic of Poland, ECLI:EU:C:2019:531
CJEU Case C-68/17, IR v JQ, ECLI:EU:C:2018:696
CJEU Joined Cases C-569/16 and C-570/16, Stadt Wuppertal and Volker Willmeroth als Inhaber der TWI Technische Wartung und Instandsetzung Volker Willmeroth e.K. v Maria Elisabeth Bauer and Martina Broßonn, ECLI:EU:C:2018:871
CJEU Case C-414/16, Vera Egenberger v Evangelisches Werk für Diakonie und Entwicklung e.V., ECLI:EU:C:2018:257

CJEU Case C-684/16, Max-Planck-Gesellschaft zur Förderung der Wissenschaften e.V. v Tetsuji Shimizu, ECLI:EU:C:2018:874
CJEU Case C-64/16, Associação Sindical dos Juízes Portugueses v Tribunal de Contas, ECLI:EU:C:2017:395
CJEU Case C-362/14, Maximillian Schrems v Data Protection Commissioner, ECLI:EU:C:2015:650
CJEU Case C-582/14, Patrick Breyer v Bundesrepublik Deutschland, ECLI:EU: C:2016:779
CJEU Case C-131/12, Google Spain, EU:C:2014:317
CJEU Case C-274/12 P, Telefónica SA v European Commission, ECLI:EU:C:2013: 852
CJEU Case C-314/12, UPC Telekabel Wien, EU:C:2014:192
CJEU Case C-70/10, Scarlet Extended SA v Société belge des auteurs, compositeurs et éditeurs SCRL (SABAM), ECLI:EU:C:2011:771
CJEU Joined Cases C-92/09 and C-93/09, Volker und Markus Schecke and Eifert, EU:C:2010:662
CJEU Joined Cases C-402/05P and C-415/05P Kadi and Al Barakaat International Foundation v Council and Commission, ECLI:EU:C:2008:461
CJEU Case C-438/05, International Transport Workers' Federation and Finnish Seamen's Union v Viking Line ABP and OÜ Viking Line Eesti, ECLI:EU: C:2007:772
CJEU Case C-341/05, Laval un Partneri Ltd v Svenska Byggnadsarbetareförbundet, Svenska Byggnadsarbetareförbundets avdelning 1, Byggettan and Svenska Elektrikerförbundet, ECLI:EU: C:2007:809
CJEU Case C-309/99, J. C. J. Wouters, J. W. Savelbergh and Price Waterhouse Belastingadviseurs BV v Algemene Raad van de Nederlandse Orde van Advocaten, intervener: Raad van de Balies van de Europese Gemeenschap, ECLI:EU:C:2002:98
CJEU Case C-281/98, Roman Angonese v Cassa di Risparmio di Bolzano SpA, ECLI:EU:C:2000:296
CJEU Case C-292/97 Kjell Karlsson and Others, ECLI:EU:C:2000:202
CJEU Case C-281/97, Andrea Krüger *v* Kreiskrankenhaus Ebersberg, ECLI:EU: C:1999:396
CJEU Case C-333/97, Susanne Lewen v Lothar Denda, ECLI:EU:C:1999:512
CJEU Joined Cases C-51/96 and C-191/97, Christelle Deliège v Ligue francophone de judo et disciplines associées ASBL, Ligue belge de judo ASBL, Union européenne de judo; and François Pacquée, ECLI:EU:C:2000:199
CJEU Case C-415/93, Union royale belge des sociétés de football association ASBL v Jean-Marc Bosman, Royal club liégeois SA v Jean-Marc Bosman and others and Union des associations européennes de football (UEFA) v Jean-Marc Bosman., ECLI:EU:C:1995:463
CJEU Case C-309/96, Daniele Annibaldi v Sindaco del Comune di Guidonia and Presidente Regione Lazio ECLI:EU:C:1997:631

CJEU Case C-260/89, Elliniki Radiophonia Tiléorassi AE and Panellinia Omospondia Syllogon Prossopikou v Dimotiki Etairia Pliroforissis and Sotirios Kouvelas and Nicolaos Avdellas and others, ECLI:EU:C:1991:254
CJEU Case C-5/88 Hubert Wachauf v Bundesamt für Ernährung und Forstwirtschaft, ECLI:EU:C:1989:321
CJEU Case 149/77, Gabrielle Defrenne v Société anonyme belge de navigation aérienne Sabena, ECLI:EU:C:1978:130
CJEU Case 13/76, Gaetano Donà v Mario Mantero, ECLI:EU:C:1976:115
CJEU Case 43/75, Gabrielle Defrenne v Société anonyme belge de navigation aérienne Sabena, ECLI:EU:C:1976:56
CJEU Case 36/74, B.N.O. Walrave and L.J.N. Koch v Association Union cycliste internationale, Koninklijke Nederlandsche Wielren Unie and Federación Española Ciclismo, ECLI:EU: C:1974:140
CJEU Case C-29/69, Erich Stauder v City of Ulm – Sozialamt, ECLI:EU:C:1969:57
Joined Cases C-36/59, 37/59, 38/59, 40/59 Präsident Ruhrkolen-Verkaufsgesellschaft mbH, Geitling Ruhrkohlen-Verkaufsgesellschaft mbH, Mausegatt Ruhrkohlen-Verkaufsgesellschaft mbH and I. Nold KG v High Authority of the European Coal and Steel Community, ECLI:EU:C:1960:36
CJEU Case C-1/58 Friedrich Stork & Cie v High Authority of the European Coal and Steel Community, ECLI:EU:C:1959:4
United States Supreme Court, case Packingham v. North Carolina, 582 U.S. (2017)
Italian Constitutional Court, case 11/70 Internationale Handelsgesellschaft (Solange I) [1970] ECR 01125; case No. 183/73, Frontini v. Ministero Delle Finanze, 27 December 1973
Landgericht Bonn, LG Bonn, judgment of November 16, 1999 - 10 O 457/99, openJur 2011, 77972

Online Resources

Alistair Barr Follow, Google Mistakenly Tags Black People as 'Gorillas,' Showing Limits of Algorithms, The Wall Street Journal, 1 July 2015 https://www.wsj.com/articles/BL-DGB-42522
Antoine Allen, The 'three black teenagers' search shows it is society, not Google, that is racist, The Guardian, 10 June 2016 https://www.theguardian.com/commentisfree/2016/jun/10/three-black-teenagers-google-racist-tweet
Elle Hunt, Tay, Microsoft's AI chatbot, gets a crash course in racism from Twitter, The Guardian, 24 March 2016 https://www.theguardian.com/technology/2016/mar/24/tay-microsofts-AI-chatbot-gets-a-crash-course-in-racism-from-twitter
Frank Pasquale, Secret Algorithms Threaten the Rule of Law MIT Tech Review, 1 June 2017 www.technologyreview.com/s/608011/secret-algorithms-threaten-the-rule-of-law/

Frank Pasquale, Secret Algorithms Threaten the Rule of Law, MIT Technology Review, June 1, 2017, https://www.technologyreview.com/2017/06/01/151447/secret-algorithms-threaten-the-rule-of-law/

Gartner Online Glossary https://www.gartner.com/en/information-technology/glossary/big-data

IEEE Ethically Aligned Design: A Vision for Prioritizing Human Well-being with Autonomous and Intelligent Systems (2017) https://iapp.org/resources/article/ethically-aligned-design-a-vision-for-prioritizing-human-wellbeing-with-artificial-intelligence-and-autonomous-systems/

Jessica Fjeld, Nele Achten et al. Principled Artificial Intelligence: Mapping Consensus in Ethical and Rights-Based Approaches to Principles for AI (2020) Berkman Klein Center Research Publication No. 2020-1 https://cyber.harvard.edu/publication/2020/principled-ai>

Jeremy Waldron, The Rule of law , Stanford Encyclopaedia of Philosophy, 2016 https://plato.stanford.edu/entries/rule-of-law/#ValuUndeRuleLaw

Kashmir Hill, 'God View': Uber Allegedly Stalked Users For Party-Goers' Viewing Pleasure, Forbes, 10 March 2014 https://www.forbes.com/sites/kashmirhill/2014/10/03/god-view-uber-allegedly-stalked-users-for-party-goers-viewing-pleasure/

Nicholas Confessore, Cambridge Analytica and Facebook: The Scandal and the Fallout So Far The New York Times, 4 April 2018 https://www.nytimes.com/2018/04/04/us/politics/cambridge-analytica-scandal-fallout.html

Oversight Board first Annual Report 2022, June 2023 https://www.oversightboard.com/news/560960906211177-2022-annual-report-oversight-board-reviews-meta-s-changes-to-bring-fairness-and-transparency-to-its-platforms/

References

Books and Papers

Ali M et al (2021) Ad delivery algorithms: the hidden arbiters of political messaging. In: Proceedings of the 14th ACM International Conference on Web Search and Data Mining (WSDM '21). Association for Computing Machinery, New York, NY, USA, pp 13–21

Allan TRS (2014) The rule of law as the rule of private law. In: Austin LM, Klimchuk D (eds) Private law and the rule of law. Oxford University Press

Austin (2014) The Power of the Rule of Law, in: Austin L., Klimchuk D. (eds.) Private law and the rule of law. Oxford University Press

Austin LM, Klimchuk D (2014) Private law and the rule of law. Oxford University Press

Bakant J (2015) The invisible hand of law: private regulation and the rule of law. Cornell Int Law J:279

Bayamlıoğlu E, Leenes R (2018) The 'rule of law' implications of data-driven decision-making: a techno-regulatory perspective. Law Innov Technol 10(2):295–313

Benkler Y (2019) Don't let industry write the rules for AI. Nature 16(1):569

Bodei R (2019) Dominio e sottomissione. Schiavi, animali, macchine, Intelligenza Artificiale [eng. Domination and submission. Slaves, animals, machines, Artificial Intelligence], il Mulino

Buolamwini J, Gebru T (2018) Gender shades: intersectional accuracy disparities in commercial gender classification. Proc Mach Learn Res Conf Fairness Account Transpar 81:1–15
Celeste E (2019) Digital constitutionalism: a new systematic theorisation. Int Rev Law Comput Technol 33(1):76–99
Coeckelbergh M (2019) Artificial intelligence: some ethical issues and regulatory challenges. Technol Regul:31–34
Cohen JE (2019) Between truth and power: the legal constructions of informational capitalism. Oxford University Press
Collins H (2018) Private law, fundamental rights, and the rule of law. West Va Law Rev 121(1)
Danaher J (2016) The threat of algocracy: reality, resistance and accommodation. Philos Technol 29:245
Dicey AV (1964) Introduction to the study of the law of the constitution, 10th edn. Macmillan
Dourish P (2016) Algorithms and their others: algorithmic culture in context. Big Data Soc 3:1
Dworkin R (1985) A matter of principle. Harvard University Press
Frantziou E (2015) The horizontal effect of the charter of fundamental rights of the EU: rediscovering the reasons for horizontality. Eur Law J:657–679
Gillespie T (2014) The relevance of algorithms. In: Gillespie T et al (eds) Media technologies: essays on communication, materiality, and society. MIT Press, p 167
Greenstein S (2021) Preserving the rule of law in the era of artificial intelligence. Artif Intell Law
Hayek FA (1944) The road to serfdom. University of Chicago Press
Imana B et al (2021) Auditing for discrimination in algorithms delivering job ads. In: Proceedings of the Web Conference 2021 (WWW '21). Association for Computing Machinery, New York, NY, USA, pp 3767–3778
Karavas V (2010) Governance of virtual worlds and the quest for a digital constitution. In: Graber CB, Burri-Nenova M (eds) Governance of digital game environments and cultural diversity: transdisciplinary enquiries, pp 153–169
Karavas V, Teubner G (2005) Www.CompanyNameSucks.Com: the horizontal effect of fundamental rights on private parties within autonomous internet law. Constellations 12(2):262–282
Kay M et al (2015) Unequal representation and gender stereotypes in image search results for occupations. In: Proceedings of the 33rd Annual ACM Conference on Human Factors in Computing Systems (CHI'15)
Krygier M (2011) Four puzzles about the rule of law: why, what, where? and who cares? In: Fleming JE (ed) Getting to the rule of law. NYU Press
Leslie D et al (2021) Artificial intelligence, human rights, democracy, and the rule of law: a primer. The Council of Europe
Lucy W (2014) The rule of law and private law. In: Austin LM, Klimchuk D (eds) Private law and the rule of law. Oxford University Press
Lyon D (2001) Surveillance society: monitoring everyday life. Open University Press
Mayer-Schoenberger V, Cukier K (2013) Big data: a revolution that will transform how we live, work, and think. Houghton Mifflin Harcourt
Mittlestadt B et al (2016) The ethics of algorithms: mapping the debate. Big Data Soc 3
Nemitz P (2018) Constitutional democracy and technology in the age of artificial intelligence. Philos Trans R Soc 376(2133)
Neumann N (2016) The power of big data and algorithms for advertising and customer communication. In: 2016 International Workshop on Big Data and Information Security (IWBIS), Jakarta, Indonesia
Newell S, Marabelli M (2015) Strategic opportunities (and challenges) of algorithmic decision-making: a call for action on the long-term societal effects of datification. J Strateg Inf Syst 24
O'Neil C (2016) Weapons of math destruction: how big data increases inequality and threatens democracy. Crown, New York
Pagallo U (2018) Algo-rhythms and the beat of the legal drum. Philos Technol 31:507
Pasquale F (2015) Black box society: the secret algorithms that control money and information. Harvard University Press

Pasquale F (2016) Two narratives of platform capitalism. Yale Law Policy Rev 35:309
Pollicino O, De Gregorio G (2021) Constitutional law in the algorithmic society. In: Micklitz H, Pollicino O, Reichman A, Simoncini A, Sartor G, De Gregorio G (eds) Constitutional challenges in the algorithmic society. Cambridge University Press, Cambridge
Postema GJ (2014) Fidelity in law's commonwealth. In: Austin LM, Klimchuk D (eds) Private law and the rule of law. Oxford University Press
Radin MJ (2014) Boilerplate: a threat to the rule of law? In: Austin LM, Klimchuk D (eds) Private law and the rule of law. Oxford University Press
Raz J (1977) The rule of law and its virtue. Law Q Rev 93:195–211
Sartor G (2017) Human rights and information technologies. In: Brownsword R et al (eds) The Oxford handbook of law, regulation and technology. Oxford University Press, pp 424–450
Simoncini A, Longo E (2021) Fundamental rights and the rule of law in the algorithmic society. In: Micklitz H et al (eds) Constitutional challenges in the algorithmic society. Cambridge University Press
Susskind J (2018) Future politics: living together in a world transformed by tech. Oxford University Press
Suzor N (2018) Digital constitutionalism: using the rule of law to evaluate the legitimacy of governance by platforms. Social Media+Society 4(3):1–11
Tamanaha B (2004) On the rule of law: history, politics, theory. Cambridge University Press, Cambridge
Tene O, Polonetsky J (2013) Big data for all: privacy and user control in the age of analytics. Northwest J Technol Intellect Property 11:239
Webb A (2019) The big nine: how the tech titans and their thinking machines could warp humanity. Public Affairs U.S
Whittaker M et al (2018) AI Now 2018 Report 4
Wiedemann K (2022) Profiling and (automated) decision-making under the GDPR: a two-step approach. Comput Law Secur Rev 45

AI-Based Decision-Making and the Human Oversight Requirement Under the AI Act

Claes G. Granmar

Contents

Abstract In the EU, software classified as artificial intelligence (AI) is considered to categorically pose a high risk to human health, safety and fundamental rights if it is applied in relation to products covered by the system for public surveillance and enforcement known as the "new legal framework", and when implemented in certain areas beyond the general product safety regime. Whereas private parties carry the enforcement costs regarding low- or no-risk AI, the EU Member States must, according to the AI Act, have a dialogue with those who provide and apply high-risk AI professionally to ensure compliance prior to marketing and as long as the system is in use. Since the AI system learns and adapts, Article 14 of the AI Act provides that a natural person shall be designated by the professional user to oversee the high-risk AI system continuously. However, the AI Act does not define the rights and interests that it is intended to safeguard. A case in point is the right to data

C. G. Granmar (✉)
Faculty of Law, Stockholm University, Stockholm, Sweden
e-mail: claes.granmar@juridicum.su.se

E. Gill-Pedro, A. Moberg (eds.), *YSEC Yearbook of Socio-Economic Constitutions 2023*, YSEC Yearbook of Socio-Economic Constitutions (2024) 2023: 181–210,
https://doi.org/10.1007/16495_2024_68, Published online: 20 February 2024

protection, which is mainly particularised in the General Data Protection Regulation (GDPR). Measures typically need to be taken ex ante to ensure that data processing by a high-risk AI system complies with the data subject's right under Article 22 of the GDPR "not to be subject to a decision based solely on automated processing, including profiling, which produces legal effects concerning him or her or similarly significantly affects him or her". In that context, the relationship between the system for impact assessment established primarily by Article 35 of the GDPR and the compliance regime introduced by the AI Act is explored.

1 Introduction

In the near future, software that performs tasks that have traditionally required human cognitive ability, commonly referred to as artificial intelligence (AI), will fundamentally change the human condition.[1] AI challenges the notion of a "thing" that can be "used" when writing, speaking, painting, sculpturing, composing or inventing on par with skilled humans or even beyond human capacity.[2] When combined with advances in physics, materials, medicine, mechanics and robotics, AI could create a brave new world that escapes human control.[3] In a society where "productivity" is the guiding star, humans will soon find themselves at a disadvantage to AI both as labourers and as decision-makers in many instances.[4] Paradoxically, unrestrained market liberalisation that promotes technological development may turn out to be "the road to serfdom".[5] However, law in terms of a social construct can provide a normative framework that shape reality even if it

[1]See Communication from the European Commission, *Artificial Intelligence for Europe*, COM (2018) 237 final, 25.4.2018. See also, Boden (2018).

[2]See e.g., Diakopoulos (2019). See as to generative AI e.g., Miller (2020). See decisions of the European Patent Office ("EPO") of 27 January 2020 on application 18 275 163 and 18 275 174. See also in UK law, Thaler (Appellant) v. Comptroller-General of Patents Designs and Trademarks (Defendant) UKSC 2021/0201 [2021] EWCA Civ. 1829. See also [2022] Bus LR 375, [2021] EWCA Civ. 1374, [2021] RPC 19.

[3]See e.g. Boström (2016); Tegmark (2018); Future of Life Institute Open Letter 2023 https://futureoflife.org/open-letter/pause-giant-ai-experiments/ last visited 2023-12-05; UK Government AI Safety Institute www.gov.uk/government/news/prime-minister-launches-new-ai-safety-institute, last visited 2023-12-05; and President Bidens Executive Order on Safe, Secure and Trustworthy AI, www.whitehouse.gov/briefing-room/presidential-actions/2023/10/30/executive-order-on-the-safe-secure-and-trustworthy-development-and-use-of-artificial-intelligence/ last visited 2023-12-05.

[4]See as to labour law e.g. De Stefano, V. (2018), International Labour Organisation Working Paper No. 246, Negotiating the algorithm: Artificial Intelligence and labour protection; and Aloisi and De Stefano (2022).

[5]Compare with Hayek (2007) advocating unrestrained liberalism as a way out of central planning to freedom.

needs to be implemented through machine code. Indeed, in a democracy that recognises the rule of law, algorithmic decision-making can only be accepted within the limits of legal norms as we know them, and the law cannot be overridden by algorithms.[6]

Within the substantive and territorial scope of competences conferred upon the European Union (EU), the "rule of law" implies that all normative measures need to be in accordance with the Treaty on European Union (TEU) and the Treaty on the Functioning of the European Union (TFEU), as complemented by the Charter of Fundamental Rights of the European Union (EU Charter).[7] In addition, the European Commission, the European Parliament and the Council of Ministers have adopted a declaration on digital rights and principles (EU Declaration on Digital Rights).[8] In order to safeguard a human-centric transition to AI dependency, the EU has decided to introduce a specific Regulation on AI (AI Act).[9] Whereas some AI applications are strictly prohibited, and others escape the scope of the Regulation, transparency requirements apply to all general purpose AI systems, and powerful foundation models such as ChatGPT are subject to additional rules, including ongoing risk assessments and reporting.[10] However, most of the rules and procedures enshrined in the AI Act concern AI applications that are considered to pose a *high risk* to human health, safety and fundamental rights. As regulation by design is crucial, and the AI developer becomes a *de facto* regulator, a framework for cooperation between the industry and public powers regarding high-risk AI is needed. Hence, the AI Act requires public investments in systems to approve high-risk AI prior to marketing and to ensure continuous compliance by those who professionally apply high-risk AI in the Union. Conversely, private parties must largely bear the costs of enforcing fundamental rights and interests reconciled in EU law regarding the provision and application of low- or no-risk AI.

---

[6] See the European citizen's proposals 35(3), 35(8) and 37(3) in the report from the conference on the future of Europe https://conference-delegation.europarl.europa.eu/cmsdata/267078/Report_EN.pdf, last visited 2023-12-05.

[7] Consolidated version of the Treaty on European Union and Consolidated version of the Treaty on the functioning of European Union, Official Journal ("OJ") C 326/1, 26.10.2012; and Charter of the Fundamental Rights of the European Union, OJ C 326/391, 26.10.2012.

[8] European Declaration on Digital Rights and Principles for the Digital Decade, 2022 Users/Admin/Downloads/European_Declaration_on_Digital_Rights_and_Principles_signed_002_sPqb0eme38-LoyyLQatnQJjkCZGU_94370.pdf, last visited 2023-12-05.

[9] A provisional agreement on the text of the AI Act was reached on the 8th of December 2023. See for the time being Commission's Proposal for a Regulation of the European Parliament and the Council laying down harmonised rules on artificial intelligence and amending certain Union legislative acts, COM(2021) 206 final, 2021/0106 (COD), 2021.04.21. See the European Parliament proposed amendments to the European Commission's proposal, P9_TA(2023)0236, 14.06.2023.

[10] See as to prohibited AI applications, Article 5 of the Commission proposal for an AI Act, supra note 9, and as to transparency requirements in Article 52 of the AI Act.

According to Article 14(1) of the AI Act, a high-risk AI system shall be designed and developed in such a way, including with appropriate human-machine interface tools, that it can be effectively overseen at some level by natural persons during the period in which it is employed.[11] A case in point of the oversight requirement is the duty to ensure that the AI system complies with the right to privacy and data protection under Articles 7 and 8 of the EU Charter.[12] Indeed, whether or not the AI system poses a high risk to humans, it must respect the rights of each identified or identifiable natural person in the EU (data subject) as particularised primarily in the provisions of the General Data Protection Regulation (GDPR).[13] An aspect of data protection that is becoming increasingly important in the light of the implementation of AI systems is the right of the data subject under Article 22 of the GDPR "not to be subject to a decision based solely on automated processing, including profiling, which produces legal effects concerning him or her or similarly significantly affects him or her" unless it can be justified.[14] In Case C-634/21, SCHUFA Holding I, handed down in December 2023, the European Court of Justice (ECJ) explains that the concept of "decision" shall be broadly defined.[15] An impact assessment is required under Article 35 of the GDPR if the type of processing of personal data is likely to result in a high risk to the basic rights and freedoms of the data subject.

Whereas both Article 35 of the GDPR and Article 14 of the AI Act provide public bodies with tools to *ex ante* monitor and prevent high-risk processing of personal data, data processing in violation of Article 22 of the GDPR can lead to *ex post facto* action by data subjects and their representatives.[16] Articles 22 and 35 of the GDPR are broader in scope than Article 14 of the AI Act insofar as the former provisions cover processing beyond the application of high-risk AI. However, Article 14 of the AI Act has a broader scope than Articles 22 and 35 of the GDPR insofar as the duty of human oversight applies also to the processing of non-personal data and to ensure health, safety and fundamental rights beyond data protection. Although the legal

---

[11] See also recitals 33, 43, 48, 71 and 72 in the preamble of the Commission Proposal for an AI Act, supra note 9.

[12] Article 16 of the TFEU on the right to data protection is highlighted as the legal basis for the AI Act in the preamble of the Commission's Proposal for an AI Act, supra note 9.

[13] Regulation (EU) 2016/697, General Data Protection Regulation, OJ L 119/1, 04.05.2016. See also Regulation (EU) 2018/1725, EU Institutions and Data Protection Regulation, OJ L 295/39, 21.11.2018; and Directive (EU) 2016/680, on data protection and law enforcement, OJ L 119/89, 04.05.2016.

[14] Bygrave (2020), pp. 522–542.

[15] Judgement of 7 December 2023, OQ v Land Hessen ("SCHUFA Holding I"), Case C-634/21, EU:C:2023:957.

[16] See as to the possibility for national authorities to interpret and apply the GDPR when enforcing legal regimes other than the GDPR, judgement of 4 July 2023, Meta Platforms and Others, C-252/21, EU:C:2023:537. See as to the data subject's status as a "consumer", Judgement of 25 January 2018, Maximillian Schrems v Facebook Ireland Limited, Case C-498/16, EU:C:2018:37. See as to the possibility for consumer organisations to invoke the GDPR on behalf of the data subjects under Article 80 of the GDPR, Judgement of 28 April 2022, Meta Platforms Germany, Case C-319/20, EU:C:2022:322.

frameworks are different in nature and are applied in different ways, they need to be coordinated when high-risk AI systems make decisions concerning data subjects. As AI systems are developed by commercial companies, data protection and human oversight requirements need to be seen in the light of the right to conduct business under Article 16 of the EU Charter to foster a value-based competitive European AI industry.

In this chapter, the interrelations between Article 14(1) of the AI Act and Articles 22 and 35 of the GDPR are explored. Given the abundance of situations where decisions are based on automated data processing, only a systematic overview of the protection of personal data in the Union through continuous control of high-risk decision-making AI systems can be provided.

2 Regulation of High-Risk AI and Human Oversight

Obviously, the difficulty of defining "AI" in just a few words has hampered work on the AI Act. However, the text of the AI Act agreed on 8 December 2023 embraces the definition of AI proposed by the Organisation for Economic Co-operation and Development (OECD): "An AI system is a machine-based system that, for explicit or implicit objectives, infers, from the input it receives, how to generate outputs such as predictions, content, recommendations, or decisions that can influence physical or virtual environments."[17] On that note, the learning approaches currently listed in Annex I of the AI Act must be understood as examples and may be amended through a simplified legislative procedure.[18] It may often be clear whether an algorithm learns, adapts and influences its environment. Nonetheless, industry associations and similar organisations will need to specify in dialogue with public authorities and bodies what technologies constitute AI in a given sector.

Although it is key for the industry to define AI, the applicability of the AI Act is not determined so much by learning approaches or technology standards as it depends on the actual or indended deployement of the AI system.[19] Like most computer programs, a data processing system classified as AI can solve different

[17] Compare Article 3(1) in the Commission's Proposal for an AI Act, and the amendments proposed by the Parliament, supra note 9. See section 1 of the OECD, *Recommendation of the Council on Artificial Intelligence*, OECD/LEGAL/0449.

[18] See as to the legislative procedure Articles 4, 7(1), 11(3), 43(5) and (6), 48(5), 73 and 74 of the Commission's Proposal for an AI Act, supra note 9. See also Article 291 in the TFEU, and Regulation (EU) No. 182/2011 on the possibility for the Member States to control the Commission's exercise of its implementing powers, OJ L 55/13, 28.02.2011.

[19] A "general purpose AI system" such as ChatGTP4 does not in itself entail a high risk, but as it may easily become a systematic threat these systems are subject to transparency requirements under Article 52 of the AI Act. See the Future of Life Institute, General Purpose AI and the AI Act, https://artificialintelligenceact.eu/wp-content/uploads/2022/05/General-Purpose-AI-and-the-AI-Act.pdf, last visited 2023-12-14. See also Lucci (2023), pp. 1–23. See also the AI Act the amendments proposed by the Parliament regarding Article 52 of the proposed AI Act, supra note 9.

tasks, and whether the system poses an unacceptable risk, high risk or low risk to health, safety and fundamental rights depends on its interaction with the physical or virtual environment. An AI system that is harmless in one context can be catastrophic when applied in another which is particularly problematic when it comes to general purpose AI models such as ChatGPT. Beyond general purpose AI, an AI system poses, according to Article 6(1) of the AI Act, a high risk if it is intended to be used as a safety component of a product, or is itself a product, which must undergo a conformity assessment within the scope of Union measures listed in Annex II of the Act.[20] These legal acts concern, for instance, robotics, aviation, cars, toys, lifts and medical devices.[21] As the AI Act lays down a legal and administrative framework to ensure compliance with rules and procedures across several sectors, it fits like a piece into the puzzle of the so-called new legislative framework (NLF) that establishes a Union-wide system for surveillance, conformity assessment, accreditation of assessment bodies and the use of CE marking.[22] Indeed, only certified and registered high-risk AI will be accepted on the internal market.[23] However, clarification is needed regarding the criteria for distinguishing between an embedded AI system and AI as a product in itself and on the meaning of a "safety component".[24] Is, for instance, a lane keeping system built into a motor vehicle a safety component, and what about AI embedded in a toy car to personalise its interaction with the child?

In addition to the application of AI in relation to products covered by the NLF, AI intended to be used for a purpose listed in Annex III of the AI Act is a high-risk system, unless the output is purely incidental to such an activity.[25] It follows from Annex III that an AI system poses a high risk when applied in the areas of biometric identification and categorisation of natural persons; management and operation of

---

[20] According to Article 30 of the Commission's Proposal for an AI Act, supra note 9, each Member State shall designate or establish a notifying authority responsible for organising the work of the AI conformity assessment bodies pursuant to Articles 31 - 39 of the proposed Act. See also Regulation (EC) No 765/2008 in accordance with EN-ISO/IEC 17065/2012, as to the NLF supra note 3.

[21] See e.g., Directive 2006/42/EC, on machinery, OJ L 157/24, 09.06.2006, and European Commission, Proposal for a Regulation of the European Parliament and the Council on machinery products, COM/2021/202 final, 21.04.21.

[22] See as to horizontal NLF framework applying to several specific acts listed in Annex II, Regulation (EC) 765/2008 on market surveillance, OJ L 218/30, 13.08.2008; Decision 768/2008/EC on market surveillance and compliance of products and amending several legislative acts, OJ L 218/82, 13.08.2008; and Regulation (EU) 2019/1020, on market surveillance and compliance of products amending several legislative acts, OJ L 169/1, 25.06.2019.

[23] See as to conformity assessment, CE marking, documentation, and registration of high-risk AI systems, Articles 43 - 50 of the Commission's Proposal for an AI Act, supra note 9. See as to monitoring and compliance, Articles 61 - 68 of the proposed AI Act including the provisions in Articles 63 and 65 thereof complementing Regulation (EU) 2019/1020, supra note 22.

[24] For instance, the EU database for stand-alone high-risk AI systems established by Article 60 of the AI Act requires a definition of "safety component".

[25] See Article 6(1) and Appendix II of the Commission's Proposal for an AI Act, supra note 9 Appendix III of the Commission's Proposal for an AI Act, supra note 9, specifies the areas of activities referred to in Article 6(2) of the proposed AI Act.

critical infrastructure; educational and vocational training; employment, worker management and access to self-employment; access to and enjoyment of essential private or public services and benefits; law enforcement; migration, asylum and border control management; as well as administration of justice and democratic processes.

All activities within the substantive and territorial scope of EU law, including data processing by high-risk AI systems, must be aligned with the values and objectives of the Union as set out in the TEU, TFEU and the EU Charter (primary law), which is transposed into the domestic legal systems mainly through legislation adopted on the basis of primary law, (secondary legislation).[26] Article 7 of the TFEU unequivocally establishes that, the Union shall "ensure consistency between its policies and activities, taking all of its objectives into account". Furthermore, it follows from the principle of sincere cooperation enshrined in Article 4(3) of the TEU that the Member States need to abide by this "normative source code".[27] Shortly after the EU Charter became primary law in 2009, the ECJ made it abundantly clear in its ruling in Case C-617/10, Åklagaren v. H. Å. F., that "situations cannot exist which are covered by European Union law without those fundamental rights being applicable".[28] In order to ensure a system-coherent legal development, conflicting rights and interests are reconciled through proportionate limitations often particularised in secondary legislation.[29] Whereas secondary legislation is valid only to the extent that it ensures vertical consistency by specifying, as opposed to extending, limiting or altering primary law, all secondary legislation must be horizontally consistent, and whereas internal and external EU actions must correlate, legal developments must be consistent over time to ensure the rule of law.[30] It cannot be emphasised enough that those who provide or apply AI systems in the Union, irrespective of whether the systems are posing a high risk or not, are already subject to legal requirements.[31]

[26] See primarily Articles 5(2), 3, 2, 6(1) of the TEU in that order and Articles 51 and 52 of the EU Charter, supra note 7. See recently e.g., the European Commission's Proposal for a Directive on Corporate Sustainability Due Diligence amending Directive (EU) 2019/1937, COM/2022/71 Final 2022/0051(COD) 2023.02.2022.

[27] See as to the concept of a "methodological source code" of EU law in Granmar (2021), pp. 225–244, at 227 et seq. See as to the implication of the duty of sincere cooperation, judgement in Meta Platforms and Others, C-252/21, supra note 16, paras. 53 and 54. See also judgement of 7 November 2013, UPC Netherlands, C-518/11, EU:C:2013:709, para. 59 and judgement of 1 August 2022, Sea Watch, C-14/21 and 15/21, EU:C:2022:604, para. 156.

[28] Judgement of 26 February 2013, Åklagaren v H. Å. F., C-617/10, EU:C:2013:105, para. 21.

[29] See as to proportionality Article 52 of the EU Charter, supra note 7.

[30] See Article 263 of the TFEU and e.g., Judgement of 21 December 2016, Tele2 Sverige AB and Secretary of State for the Home Department, joined Cases C-203/15 and C-298/15, EU:C:2016:970.

[31] See for instance the interrelation between data protection and freedom of expression that applies also to AI systems, Judgement of 6 November 2003, Lindquist, C-101/01, EU:C:2003:596, paras. 89–90.

Hence, some kind of soft law approach requiring "ethical" AI would be a normative anomaly.[32]

It is a common misunderstanding that the AI Act imposes an "undue regulatory burden" on the industry by introducing new legal duties that restrict some kind of utopian state of economic freedom. AI-related trade and competition is covered by Treaty provisions regarding the internal market, and secondary legislation particularising the protection of health, safety and fundamental rights. Consequently the judiciary could have explained the requirements regarding AI under existing EU law in the absence of an AI Act.[33] However, secondary legislation is preferable to reactive and time-consuming court proceedings as it increases predictability and "efficiency" by reducing the costs for access to justice. Indeed, the *telos* to safeguard and reconcile fundamental rights and interests requires an EU-wide system for the assessment of compliance and public enforcement regarding high-risk AI. In contrast, product standards and fundamental rights are mainly defined by other legal frameworks.

As to consistency between the AI Act and the NFL, many products that will soon be running on high-risk AI are covered by international, regional and national safety and interoperability standards.[34] Since the products become interactive by means of AI and their performance change over time, these product standards may need to be amended to ensure continuous compliance. When the "product standards" have been published in the Official Journal of the EU, they are considered to have the same binding effect as secondary legislation.[35] In order to ensure horizontal consistency with the product standards, Article 40 of the AI Act clarifies that a high-risk AI system is presumed to be in conformity with the legal requirements under chapter 2, Title III, of the Act "to the extent those standards cover those requirements".[36] In case there are no EU standards, the Commission may adopt an implementing act with specifications as to the requirements set out in chapter 2, Title III, of the Act.[37] In addition to the relations with sector specific rules and regulations, the AI Act must be read in conjunction with horizontally applicable EU regimes on, for instance, cybersecurity, environmental protection and strategic autonomy.[38] Evidently, the AI

[32] Compare with Commission report by Crémer, J., de Montjoye, Y-A, and Schweitzer, H., *Competition Policy for the Digital Era,* (2019) https://ec.europa.eu/competition/publications/reports/kd0419345enn.pdf, last visited 2023-12-13.

[33] Hence, Article 114 of the TFEU on the internal market is highlighted as the legal basis for the AI Act in the preamble of the Commission's Proposal for an AI Act, supra note 9.

[34] See the World Forum for the harmonisation of vehicle regulations (UNECE WP 29) unece.org/transport/vehicle-regulations, last visited 2023-12-13. See also Mc Fadden et al. (2021); and Ryck et al. (2020), p. 152.

[35] See judgement of 27 October 2016, James Elliot Limited, C-613/14, EU:C:2016:821. It may be considered problematic that legal acts with the same effect as legislation are adopted without a legislative process.

[36] See also Article 42 of the Commission's Proposal for an AI Act, supra note 9.

[37] Article 41 of the Commission's Proposal for an AI Act, supra note 9.

[38] See, the GDPR, supra note 13. See as to cybersecurity Article 15 of the Commission's Proposal for an AI Act, supra note 9, and Directive (EU) 2022/2555 on measures for a high common level of

Act must also sit well with the Union's data protection regime and it's centrepiece; the GDPR. Recital 4 in the preamble of the GDPR clarifies that the processing of personal data shall be designed to serve mankind, and that the protection of personal data shall be considered in relation to its overall function in society and be balanced against other fundamental rights in accordance with the principle of proportionality.[39] Hence, the protection of personal data may, insofar as it is necessary, be limited by the respect for private and family life, home and communication; freedom of thought, conscience and religion; freedom of expression and information; freedom to conduct business; and the right to an effective remedy and to a fair trial.[40]

According to Article 59 of the AI Act, national competent authorities shall be established or designated by the Member States for the purpose of the application and implementation of the Regulation. It is necessary to coordinate the designation of national supervisory authorities among the Member States as well as to coordinate the implementation of the AI Act with the work of public bodies that already monitor markets and set standards for products relating to AI.[41] In that connection, the administrative framework established by the AI Act must be reconciled with the system of national data protection agencies (DPAs) set up by the GDPR.[42] Although in theory there is nothing to prevent a DPA from being a national market surveillance authority and *vice versa*, the difference in tasks is likely to militate against such a solution. Whereas the DPA deals with the enforcement of the GDPR, the market surveillance authority controls compliance with a wide range of legal requirements regarding high-risk AI systems.

Since legislators and courts can rarely assess the risk of AI systems and expert authorities are normally not involved in the programming and training of AI, the AI Act imposes self-assessment and reporting obligations on natural and legal persons, public authorities, agencies and other bodies developing high-risk AI systems or applying such systems in a professional activity.[43] As the deontic modalities of human language need to be translated into machine language, the providers of high-risk AI are required to ensure compliance with legal duties by design. Undeniably, the liability of legal entities supplying high-risk AI systems or applying them

cybersecurity across the Union amending Regulation (EU) 910/2014 and Directive (EU) 2018/1972, OJ L 333/80, 27/12/2022 ("NIS 2 Directive"). See also Regulation (EU) 2019/881 on ENISA and on information and communication technology cybersecurity certification, OJ L 151/15, 07/06/2019 ("Cyber Security Act").

[39] See also the European Commission's White Paper on Artificial Intelligence, supra note 1.

[40] See as to the data minimisation requirement under Article 5(1)(c) of the GDPR in Opinion by AG Pikamäe of 16 March 2023, UF and AB v Land Hessen ("SCHUFA Holding II"), joined Cases C-26/22 and C-64/22, EU:C:2023:222, para. 87.

[41] See Article 59 of the Commission's Proposal for an AI Act, and amendments proposed by the Parliament, supra note 9.

[42] See Articles 51–66 of the GDPR, supra note 13, and the duty of national competition authorities to cooperate with DPA:s, judgement in Meta Platforms and Others, C-252/21, supra note 16, paras. 56 to 61.

[43] See Articles 3(1)(4) and 16-29 of the Commission's Proposal for an AI Act, supra note 9.

professionally is extended as AI processes data in an autonomous way and the output changes over time. Considering the need to continuously protect human health, safety and fundamental rights some microeconomic theories based on "price equilibrium" as the sole yardstick suggest that the AI Act creates "allocative inefficiencies" that reduce European competitiveness.[44] However, from a "rule of law" point of view, there are no good reasons why people should not have the same rights in a society that depends on AI as in the world we know. As only natural and legal persons can be held responsible for the performance of a high-risk AI system, Article 14 of the AI Act establishes a human oversight regime.

According to Article 14(3) of the AI Act, human oversight shall be ensured by measures identified and built into the high-risk AI system before it is placed on the market or put into service when technically feasible, and/or by measures that are appropriate to be implemented by the user. Article 14(3) of the AI Act shall be read in conjuntion with Article 13(1) of thereof, establishing that a high-risk AI system must be designed and developed in such a way that it is sufficiently transparent to allow users to understand how it works at some level.[45] Moreover, Article 13(2) of the AI Act establishes that the AI system must be accompanied by intelligible instructions regarding its use in a digital format or in a durable medium.[46] Hence, the natural person responsible for overseeing the high-risk AI system shall, pursuant to Article 14(4) of the AI Act, be enabled to do the following, as appropriate to the circumstances:

(a) understand the capacities and limitations of the high-risk AI system and be able to duly monitor its operation, so that signs of anomalies, dysfunctions and unexpected performance can be detected and addressed as soon as possible;
(b) remain aware of the possible tendency of automatically relying or over-relying on the output produced by a high-risk AI system ("automation bias"), in particular for high-risk AI systems used to provide information or recommendations for decisions to be taken by natural persons;
(c) be able to correctly interpret the high-risk AI system's output, taking into account in particular the characteristics of the system and the interpretation tools and methods available;
(d) be able to decide, in any particular situation, not to use the high-risk AI system or otherwise disregard, override or reverse the output of the high-risk AI-system;
(e) be able to intervene on the operation of the high-risk AI system or interrupt the system through a "stop" button or a similar procedure.[47]

---

[44] See e.g., Perloff (2018). It cannot be ruled out that product development can constitute a legitimate interest that needs to be reconciled with other legitimate interests such as data protection, see judgement in Meta Platforms and Others, C-252/21, supra note 16, para. 122. See Articles 53 - 55 of the Commission's Proposal for an AI Act.

[45] See Article 52 of the Commission's Proposal for an AI Act, and amendments proposed by the Parliament, supra note 9.

[46] Compare with Article 12 of the GDPR, supra note 13.

[47] See the Commission's Proposal for an AI Act, and amendments proposed by the Parliament, supra note 9.

3 Use of High-Risk AI, Automated Decisions and the GDPR

Considering the "black box problem" already at the current stage of AI development, and the speed of automated data processing, it seems unrealistic that a person overseeing a high-risk AI system would be able to intervene and override a processing activity in real time to ensure compliance. If a problem is detected, probably by software monitoring the AI system, the person overseeing the system can at best interrupt it through a "stop" button or a similar procedure. In that connection, the reference to the "user" of AI in the AI Act may be called into question. Is a thing that learns and makes decisions that humans cannot control or even understand the reasons for a tool in the hands of man? True, a thing can be "used" even if it controls human behaviour, perhaps in accordance with basic computer scripts, such as traffic lights or elevators. And arguably, anything that performs tasks on behalf of natural or legal persons or lifts responsibilities from people's shoulders can be "used".[48] But there is a point where generative or general purpose AI makes the idea of using a thing illusory long before a singularity occurs where humans no longer fit into the equation.[49]

Another aspect of the concept of "use" is the question of who is considered to be "using" the AI system. Since the AI Act only applies to "professional use", it does not apply to high-risk AI systems embedded in, for instance, motor vehicles used for private purposes.[50] Perhaps, the notion of "use" in the AI Act could refer to the application of high-risk AI in the same way as mechanical solutions can be "used" by the producer of a thing. In parity with the "use" of a servomechanism, an AI system can be "used" as a safety component in a vehicle. Although the private owner of the motor vehicle is not subject to the AI Act, a manufacturer, distributor or post-sale service provider may have an obligation to comply with the human oversight requirement under Article 14 of the AI Act if they somehow use the device for a specific purpose. However, a legal entity that does not retain control over, or even access to, the AI system cannot possibly designate a person that shall continuously minimise the risk of the system. Even if the provider "makes use of" a high-risk AI system in terms of determining the means and purposes of data processing, the legal entity is not "using" the system under Article 14 of the AI Act unless it can continuously monitor and modify the system.[51]

Far from all output of a high-risk AI system, can be considered to be an automted "decision". In many instances, high-risk AI systems merely collect, organise and present data sets that can support human decision-making without determining how

[48] Software will soon be integrated with humans, https://www.neuralink.com, last visited 2023-12-05. See as to the concept of being "human" European resolution of 16 February 2017 with recommendations to the Commission on Civil Law Rules on Robotics (2015/2103/(INL)), P8_TA (2017)0051.

[49] See as to generic AI that invents and creates new things, supra note 2.

[50] See also the limitations in Article 2(2) of the Commission's Proposal for an AI Act, supra note 9.

[51] Compare with the notion of "controller" in Article 4(7) of the GDPR, supra note 13.

conflicting rights and interests are to be reconciled in a given situation. However, output data labelled "prediction" or "recommendation" may in fact be a "decision" if people involved in the decision-making process rely on the output data without critically evaluating the information. In this connection, a distinction needs to be made between automated decisions based on the processing of personal data and non-personal data. Because if the processing activity involves personal data the data subject is *prima facie* entitled not to be subject to a decision based solely on automated processing, including profiling, which produces legal effects concerning him or her or similarly significantly affects him or her pursuant to Articles 22(1) of the GDPR.[52]

When shifting the perspectives from the obligations under the AI Act for those who supply and professionally apply high-risk AI systems to the obligations under the GDPR, it is necessary to establish who the "controller" and "processor". Without an in-depth analysis of these Union concepts, the legal entities professionally applying high-risk AI systems can, in most instances, determine the purposes and means of the processing of personal data and, hence, be the "controller" of the processing.[53] It could also happen that the provider of a high-risk AI system remains the controller, because, in contrast to the definition of "user" under Article 14 of the AI Act, a legal entity that determines the means and purposes of data processing can be the "controller" of a processing activity without being able to continuously monitor and modify the system's operations.[54] As to the "processor", it may be tempting to consider the possibility of holding AI responsible for data processing on behalf of the controller considering the system's level of autonomy. Then again, only a natural or legal person applying the AI system can be classified among processors, as an AI system has no more legal personhood than a conventional car or a toothbrush.[55]

In Case C-634/21, SCHUFA Holding I, the ECJ was for the first time asked to clarify the meaning of a "decision based solely on automated data processing" under Article 22 of the GDPR.[56] In brief, the German administrative court of first instance, which turned to the ECJ for clarification, had to decide in the main proceedings whether Article 22(1) of the GDPR is applicable in a systematic analysis with regard to "scores" that a credit information agency provides to its contractual partners, such as banks, regarding the creditworthiness of their customers. As mentioned, Article 22 of the GDPR applies to automated decision-making irrespective of whether the software is classified as high-risk AI. However, if the software employed by the

[52] See Judgement in SCHUFA Holding I, Case C-634/21, supra note 15, paras. 52 and 64; and Opinion of Advocate General Pikamäe of 16 March 2023 on the SCHUFA Holding I, Case C-634/21, EU:C:2023:220, para. 31.

[53] See further as to the notion of controller, Judgement of 13 May 2014, *Google Spain SL and Google Inc. v Agencia España Proteccion de datos (AEPD) and Mario Costejo González*, Case C-131/12, EU:C:2014:317.

[54] Ibid.

[55] See Kingwell (2020).

[56] Opinion of Advocate General Pikamäe of 16 March 2023, Case C-634/21, supra note 52.

credit information agency belonged to the AI technology family, it was a high-risk system pursuant to Article 5(b), Annex III, of the AI Act. When the AI Act enters into force, the person overseeing the system should, therefore, be aware of the risk of automation bias under Article 14(4)(b) of the AI Act. In any event the question was whether Article 22(1) of the GDPR can apply to a legal entity such as SCHUFA Holding AG (SCHUFA), which provided the probability values, without formally determining how the scores are to be used. Because the scores may *de facto* determine whether, for instance, a contracting bank grants a mortgage loan to one of its clients.

In the main proceedings, the data subject had been refused a mortgage loan by a bank which based its decision on the creditworthiness scores that had been provided by SCHUFA. Therefore, the data subject requested SCHUFA to grant it access to data collected about her and information about the predictive model. Moreover, she asked SHUFA to erase some data that were allegedly incorrect. On that note, Article 8 of the EU Charter establishes that everyone "has the right of access to data which has been collected concerning him or her, and the right to have it rectified". However, SCHUFA rejected the request, arguing that the disclosure of the methods for calculating creditworthiness scores would infringe the company's proprietary rights to trade secrets.[57] Furthermore, SCHUFA maintained that it was the contractual bank that had made the decision. As SCHUFA merely provided the data subject with credit ratings and some general information on the applied computing principles, she lodged a complaint with the competent DPA. Following the rejection of the complaint, she appealed the decision to the administrative court.

In its preliminary ruling, the ECJ construes Article 22(1) of the GDPR lexically and states that the provision applies if three cumulative criteria are met, namely, that there is a "decision"; that the decision is based "solely on automated processing, including profiling"; and that the decision produces "legal effects" for a data subject or "similarly significantly" affects him or her.[58] Turning first to the concept of "decision", the ECJ establishes that it shall, pursuant to recital 71 in the preamble of the GDPR, be broadly defined and encompass, for instance, the automatic refusal of an online credit application or e-recruiting practices without human intervention.[59] However, the court seems to confuse the first and third criteria written into Article 22(1) of the GDPR when it finds support for a broad construction of "decision" in the fact that the provision applies not only to the processing of personal data that produce "legal effects" for the data subject but also to acts that "similarly significantly affect him or her".[60] Whereas the wording of the provision makes it

[57] See Articles 17 and 11 of the EU Charter.

[58] See Judgement in SCHUFA Holding I, Case C-634/21, supra note 15, para. 43.

[59] See Judgement in SCHUFA Holding I, Case C-634/21, supra note 15, para. 45. See the requirement to use appropriate mathematical or statistical procedures for profiling in recital 71 of the preamble to the GDPR, supra note 13. See also Opinion of the Advocate General in SCHUFA Holding I, Case C-634/21, supra note 52, paras. 37, 38, and 43.

[60] See Judgement in SCHUFA Holding I, Case C-634/21, supra note 15, para. 44.

possible to take economic and social effects beyond legal effects into account, not all processing having such effects constitutes a "decision". By contrast, the reference to Advocate General Pikamäe's Opinion on the case is convincing.[61] In paragraph 38 of the Opinion, the Advocate General elaborates on the purpose of Article 22(1) of the GDPR and finds that for the purpose of protecting natural persons against "the potentially discriminatory and unfair effects of automated processing of data, it seems that particular vigilance is required and must also be reflected in the interpretation of that provision".

When it comes to the second criterion that the decision must be "based solely on automated processing, including profiling", the ECJ pays much heed to the fact that the assessment of creditworthiness is caught by the definition of "profiling" enshrined in Article 4(4) of the GDPR.[62] In that connection, the ECJ refers to point 33 in the Opinion on the case where the Advocate General gives a more comprehensive explanation to why the processing constitutes profiling. However, it remains unclear why the ECJ emphasises the classification of the processing as profiling when Article 22(1) of the GDPR applies as soon as the decision is based solely on automated processing irrespective of whether it belongs to the sub-category of profiling. Indisputably, the probability value established by SCHUFA is based on automated processing. Indeed, the relevant questions are instead whether it is SCHUFA or the contracting bank that decides whether to grant a mortgage loan to a customer of the contracting bank and whether this decision is *based* on automated processing within the meaning of Article 22(1) of the GDPR.

Finally, the ECJ recognises that according to the factual findings in the main proceedings, an insufficient probability value provided to a contracting bank by a credit rating agency such as SCHUFA "leads in almost all cases, to the refusal of that bank to grant the loan applied for".[63] Hence, the court finds that a probability value such as that at issue in the case, affects the data subject significantly within the meaning of Article 22(1) of the GDPR.[64] A restrictive construction of the right akin to a prohibition against automated data processing, would result in a lacuna in the intended legal protection. Consequently, the establishment of a probability value regarding the ability to meet payment commitments shall constitute "automated individual decision-making" where a third party "draws strongly on that probability value to establish, implement or terminate a contractual relationship with that person".[65]

If looking at the Advocate General's Opinion beyond the points explicitly referred to by the ECJ in the preliminary ruling, he advises against a formalistic

---

[61] See Judgement in SCHUFA Holding I, Case C-634/21, supra note 15, para. 46.

[62] See Judgement in SCHUFA Holding I, Case C-634/21, supra note 15, para. 47.

[63] See Judgement in SCHUFA Holding I, Case C-634/21, supra note 15, para. 48.

[64] See Judgement in SCHUFA Holding I, Case C-634/21, supra note 15, para. 49. See also Opinion of the Advocate General in SCHUFA Holding I, Case C-634/21, supra note 52, para. 35.

[65] Judgement in SCHUFA Holding I, Case C-634/21, supra note 15, paras. 61 and 73.

approach to the definition of a "decision". Although it is difficult to provide a definition in the abstract, the Advocate General acknowledges that the "binding character" of the scores provided by a credit rating agency should be taken into account. In contrast to the court, he explains that the probability value provided by a credit rating agency such as SCHUFA is a *de facto* decision if the contractual partner has no latitude to apply the probability value resulting from the data processing pursuant to internal rules and practices.[66] In that connection, the Advocate General recognises that "the score established by a credit information agency and transmitted to a financial institution *generally tends to predetermine* the financial institution's decision to grant or refuse to grant credit to the data subject".[67] Furthermore, "the credit information agency should, in general, be the only entity capable of responding to requests from the data subject based on rights guaranteed by the GDPR".[68] Since the contractual partner does not have any information about the computing model, it would be too easy to circumvent the rights akin to a prohibition under Article 22(1) of the GDPR by confining the provision's applicability to the contractual partner's formal decision. Such a formal approach to determine when a decision is made would effectively deprive the data subject of her or his right to access the collected data, the right to rectification and the right to be forgotten as particularised in Articles 15, 16 and 17 of the GDPR, respectively. As the credit rating agency was considered to be the controller, the Advocate General expanded on the balance between these data protection rights and the protection of a trade secret and concluded that the complexity of an algorithm tells against the disclosure of a trade secret and that the information should be presented in a more accessible way pursuant to Article 12 of the GDPR.[69]

This author is convinced by the Advocate General's Opinion on the meaning of an automated "decision". However, clarifications regarding the notion of a decision "based" solely on automated processing in Article 22(1) of the GDPR are conspicuously absent also in the Opinion. It stands to reason that the provision encompasses more than "automated decisions" since a decision is "based" on automated data processing also when humans rely on the output data without a latitiude to decide how to use the information. Conversely, the provision can apply to different steps in a decision-making procedure. In a blockchain where every step is crucial, the final output is based on several "decisions".[70]

[66] Opinion of the Advocate General in SCHUFA Holding I, supra note 52, para. 44.

[67] Opinion of the Advocate General in SCHUFA Holding I, supra note 52, para. 54. See also Article 15(1)(h) of the GDPR, and recitals 58 and 63 in the preamble to the GDPR, supra note 13.

[68] Opinion of the Advocate General in SCHUFA Holding I, supra note 52, para. 50. In fact, this line of reasoning is based on observations submitted by the referring court referred to by the ECJ, see Judgement in SCHUFA Holding I, Case C-634/21, supra note 15, para. 23.

[69] Recital 58 in the preamble to the GDPR, supra note 13. See also judgement in Meta Platforms and Others, C-252/21, supra note 16, para. 122 where the ECJ recognises that product development can justify limitation in data protection.

[70] Compare with judgement of 10 July 2018, Tietosuojavaltuutettu, Case C-25/17, EU:C:2018:551.

4 Justification of Automated Decisions and High-Risk AI

Even if the processing of personal data amounts to a decision, it does not trigger Article 22(1) of the GDPR if the processing can be justified on one of the bases set out in Article 22(2) thereof. Article 22(2)(a) of the GDPR justifies an automated decision insofar as it "is necessary for entering into, or performance of, a contract between the data subject and the data controller". When references are made to the controller, the same applies *mutatis mutandis* to processors. Article 22(2)(b) of the GDPR establishes that a decision can also be "authorised by Union or Member State law to which the controller is subject and which also lays down suitable measures to safeguard the data subject's rights and freedoms and legitimate interests". Finally, Article 22(2)(c) of the GDPR provides that an exemption from Article 22(1) of the GDPR is made insofar as the automated decision "is based on the data subject's explicit consent".

According to Article 22(3) of the GDPR, exemptions from the prohibition under Article 22(1) of the GDPR can be made pursuant to Articles 22(2)(a) and (c) thereof only if suitable measures are implemented "to safeguard the data subject's rights and freedoms and legitimate interests". As mentioned, this qualification is written immediately into Article 22(2)(b) of the GDPR. However, in contrast to the letter of Article 22(2)(b) of the GDPR, the data subject has, pursuant to Article 22(3) of the GDPR, "at least the right to obtain human intervention on the part of the controller to express his or her point of view and to contest the decision" when applying Articles 22(2)(a) and (c) thereof. Having said that, also the *Union or Member State law* referred to in Article 22(2)(b) of the GDPR must be aligned with all provisions in the EU Charter, as particularised in the GDPR. As explained by the ECJ in Joined Cases C-26/22 and 64/22, SCHUFA Holding II, concerning the early discharge of remaining debts in the context of insolvency proceedings, the national legislation must ensure that the personal data are lawfully processed pursuant to Articles 5 and 6 of the GDPR.[71] As national law that does not meet these requirements infringes the GDPR approximates national law beyond its immediate scope of applicability.[72] Within the substantive and territorial scope of competences conferred upon the EU, the Member States must, as mentioned, cooperate sincerely to ensure a consistent legal development.

When it comes to *consent* as the basis for the justification of automated decision-making, the "express consent" criterion in Article 22(2)(c) of the GDPR is qualified by the "informed consent" criterion in Article 6(1)(a) thereof since a decision would violate the latter provision if it cannot be shown that the data subject understood what he or she was expressly consenting to. In Case C-252/21, Meta Platforms Inc. and Others, concerning the competence of national competition authorities to interpret the GDPR, the ECJ clarified that a valid "consent" must be given for a specific

---

[71] Judgement of 7 December 2023, UF and AB v Land Hessen (SCHUFA Holding II), Joined Cases C-26/22 and C-64/22, EU:C:2023:958.

[72] See also Opinion of the Advocate General in SCHUFA Holding I, supra note 52, para. 61.

purpose and be freely given as opposed to being required to access a service.[73] Hence, Article 22(2)(c) of the GDPR does rarely apply to the "click and wrap" contracts commonly used by big tech companies to provide individuals with access to digital services.

When applicable, the possibility to justify automated decisions for *contractual reasons* under Article 22(2)(a) of the GDPR corresponds to the legal basis for data processing under Articles 6(1)(b) and (c) of the Regulation. On that note, the ECJ clarifies in the Meta Platforms Inc. and Others case that only the processing of personal data that are "objectively indispensable" for the entering into, or performance of, a contract between the data subject and the data controller can be considered "necessary".[74] As a result of digitalisation, the reference point for what can objectively be considered indispensable is likely to shift towards more acceptance as there are simply no alternatives. When the whole business hinges on AI, automated contracting may be the only option. However, there are limits beyond data protection to how much decision-making power can be assigned to machines. For instance, automated decisions for contractual reasons in the health care sector are acceptable only to the extent that human dignity and integrity are respected.

Article 22(4) of the GDPR establishes that no exemptions from paragraph 1 are allowed if a decision is based on sensitive data covered by Article 9(1) of the GDPR. Hence, Article 22 of the GDPR does not *per se* justify automated decisions based on data regarding racial or ethnical origin, political opinion, religious belief or sexual orientation.[75] However, exemptions from this far-reaching restriction can be made if the criteria in Article 9(2)(a) and (g) of the GDPR are met and suitable measures to safeguard the data subject's rights, freedoms and legitimate interests are in place. In that connection, the onus is on the controller or processor to prove that an automated decision based on sensitive data is justified.

In most instances, Article 22(2)(b) of the GDPR provides the most solid basis for automated decisions. Indeed, as the SCHUFA Holding I and II cases show, a decision based on automated processing can be made without prior contact between the controller and the data subject, which excludes consent or contractual necessities as a basis for justifying an automated decision.[76] Furthermore, information asymmetries and power imbalances between data subjects and controllers suggest that automated decisions should be prohibited as a rule of thumb unless they are permitted by Union or Member State law to which the controller or processor is subject.[77] However, also the possibility to justify automated decisions under Article 22(2)(b) of the GDPR is limited for an abundance of reasons beyond the rights

[73] judgement in Meta Platforms and Others, C-252/21, supra note 16, paras. 140–154 addressing the definition of consent enshrined in Article 4(11) of the GDPR, supra note 13.

[74] Judgement in Meta Platforms and Others, C-252/21, supra note 16, paras 97–98.

[75] See Judgement in SCHUFA Holding I, Case C-634/21, supra note 15, para. 55.

[76] Opinion of the Advocate General in SCHUFA Holding I, supra note 52, para 49.

[77] See recital 43 in the preamble to the GDPR, supra note 13, and judgement in Meta Platforms and Others, C-252/21, supra note 16, para. 149.

enshrined in Article 6 thereof. In the public sector, the State has an obligation to provide public services to everyone, including those who are computer illiterate. In the absence of a general duty to accept software updates and new man/machine interfaces, there is also little room for automated decisions in the context of democratic processes.[78] Moreover, courts should be careful with automated decisions, albeit the judiciary may benefit from AI support, and AI may solve petty disputes, for instance in the course of e-commerce.[79] Arguably, the reliance on automated decision-making is in many instances less problematic when it comes to services of general economic interests (SGEI) and the private sector.

5 Impact Assessments and High-Risk AI

Obviously, data subjects and their representatives, such as consumer organisations, may invoke Article 22 of the GDPR against legal entities that provide or apply high-risk AI systems professionally.[80] As the person who is designated to oversee such a system under Article 14 of the AI Act will rarely be able to intervene casuistically to ensure compliance with, for instance, the GDPR, high-risk AI systems must be designed to prevent violations of the data subject's rights.[81] When a type of data processing by an AI system is likely to result in a decision that poses a high risk to the data subject's rights and freedoms, an *ex ante* assessment of compliance with Article 22 of the GDPR is required.

According to Article 35(1) of the GDPR, the "controller" shall, prior to the processing of personal data, carry out an assessment of the impact of the envisaged processing operations on the protection of personal data (impact assessment), where "a type of processing in particular using new technologies, and taking into account the nature, scope, context and purpose of the processing, is likely to result in a high risk to the rights and freedoms of natural persons". Consequently, an impact assessment concerns a category of data processing as opposed to a casuistic assessment. Article 35(3)(a) of the GDPR provides that an impact assessment is required, in particular, in the case of "a systematic and extensive evaluation of personal aspects relating to natural persons which is based on automated processing, including profiling, and on which decisions are based that produce legal effects concerning the natural person or similarly significantly affect the natural person". An impact

[78] Compare Article 2(2) of the Commission's Proposal for an AI Act with Annex III, p. 8, thereof, supra note 9.

[79] Ibid. Compare with Susskind (2019).

[80] Article 80 of the GDPR, supra note 13. See also Judgement in Maximillian Schrems v Facebook Ireland Limited, Case C-498/16, supra note 16; and Judgement in Meta Platforms, Case C-319/20, supra note 16. See also, Jain (2022).

[81] If the software concerned in the SCHUFA Holding I Case belonged to the AI technology family, it was a high-risk AI system pursuant to point 5(b), Annex III, of the Commission's Proposal for an AI Act, supra note 9.

assessment is, therefore, required if the processing of personal data is likely to infringe the rights akin to a prohibition against automated decision-making in Article 22 of the GDPR. In many instances, controllers and processors must designate a data controller officer.[82] According to Article 37 of the GDPR such an officer shall be appointed when the envisaged data processing activity is carried out by a public authority, where the core activities of the controller require regular and systematic monitoring of data subjects on a large scale, or where the core activities concern processing of certain categories of sensitive data.

As a first step when assessing the impact of a type of processing, the controller shall, pursuant to Article 35(2) of the GDPR, seek advice from the data protection officer. In cases where an impact assessment indicates that the type of processing "would result in a high-risk in the absence of measures taken by the controller to mitigate the risk", the controller shall, according to Article 36(1) of the GDPR, consult the competent DPA prior to the processing activity. If the DPA finds that the intended processing would infringe the GDPR, "in particular where the controller has insufficiently identified or mitigated the risk", the authority shall, within a period of up to 8 weeks of receipt of the request for consultation, or a longer period, if necessary, issue a written advice. Moreover, the DPA "may use any of its powers referred to in Article 58". According to that provision, the authority can request additional information and consultations, obtain access to premises and carry out reviews and data protection audits *ex officio*. Article 58(2) of the GDPR establishes that a supervisory authority may take corrective measures such as issuing warnings, reprimands, and orders, and it may ultimately suspend the processing.

According to Article 42 of the GDPR, a data protection certification mechanism as well as seals and marks demonstrating compliance with the GDPR shall be introduced preferably on the EU level. Certification bodies shall be accredited by DPAs or specific national accreditation bodies.[83] In that respect, the GDPR, like the AI Act, is docked with the NLF enforcement system. Certification shall be issued to a controller or processor for a maximum period of 3 years and may be repeatedly renewed as long as all the relevant requirements continue to be met.[84] However, even if a controller or processor has been certified, a DPA may, pursuant to Article 58(1)(c) of the GDPR, carry out a review during an impact assessment and withdraw the certification, or order the certification body to withdraw it under Article 58(2)(h) thereof.

Along the lines of the normative source code of EU law, the notion of "high-risk to the rights and freedoms of natural persons" used in Article 35(1) of the GDPR should correlate with the notion of "high-risk system" under Article 6 of the AI Act and Appendices II and III thereto. Furthermore, the reference in Article 35(1) of the

---

[82] Article 37 of the GDPR, supra note 13.

[83] Article 43 and point 5(b), Annex III, of the Commission's Proposal for an AI Act, supra note 9, and Regulation (EC) No 765/2008 in accordance with EN-ISO/IEC 17065/2012, see further as to the NLF supra note 22.

[84] Article 43(7) of the Commission's Proposal for an AI Act, supra note 9.

GDPR to "new technologies" when determining whether an *ex ante* impact assessment is required can be seen as a "bridge" to the AI Act. Indeed, it is difficult to imagine a situation where the processing of personal data by an AI system classified as "high-risk" under the AI Act is not caught by Article 35(1) of the GDPR. Article 29(6) of the AI Act, therefore, establishes that those who professionally apply high-risk AI systems shall "use the information provided under Article 13 to comply with their obligation to carry out a data protection impact assessment under Article 35 [of the GDPR and the corresponding EU directive approximating national law on data processing for the purpose of prevention, investigation, detection, prosecution of criminal offences] where applicable." As mentioned, Article 13 of the AI Act requires the functioning of a high-risk AI system to be transparent at some level and be accompanied by instructions on how to use the system. Indeed, the natural or legal person using the high-risk AI system professionally must routinely ensure compliance with Article 35(1) of the GDPR pursuant to Article 14 of the AI Act. It seems to be a good idea to designate the natural person who oversees the high-risk AI system according to Article 14 of the GDPR and as the data controller officer pursuant to Article 37 of the GDPR.

If the software is classified as high-risk AI, and the controller or processor is not complying with the impact assessment requirements, the AI system is, according to Article 65 of the AI Act, a "product presenting a high risk" pursuant to the NLF. In that case, the national market surveillance body designated in accordance with the AI Act shall carry out an evaluation of compliance with that Act.[85] Hence, an infringement of the GDPR may result in an infringement also of the AI Act. A legal entity that applies the high-risk AI system professionally without complying wit the GDPR shall, according to Article 71 of the AI Act, be subject to effective, proportionate and dissuasive penalties determined by the EU Member State having jurisdiction over the processing activity concerned.[86]

In addition to investigating compliance with the AI Act in connection with an impact assessment, the market surveillance authority may take compliance with the GDPR into account by its own initiative if there are sufficient grounds to consider that the system poses a risk to the data subjects' rights and freedoms.[87] Hence, a market surveillance authority can interpret the GDPR when enforcing the AI Act. However, the authority must comply with previous decisions of a competent DPA regarding the relevant provisions, and in the absence of such clarifications, it must consult the competent DPA.[88] As the ECJ explained in the Meta Platforms Inc. and

[85] See as to the definition of market surveillance authority Article 3(28) of the Commission's Proposal for an AI Act, supra note 9, and Articles 63–68 thereof, aligning the system for market surveillance and enforcement under Regulation (EU) 2019/1020, supra note 22.

[86] See also Article 61 of the Commission's Proposal for an AI Act, supra note 9, requiring providers to establish a post-market monitor system that is proportionate to the nature of the technology and the duty to report serious incidents under Article 62 thereof.

[87] Article 65(1) of the Commission's Proposal for an AI Act, supra note 9.

[88] Compare with the duty of national competition authorities to cooperate with DPA:s, judgement in Meta Platforms and Others, C-252/21, supra note 16, paras. 37–63.

Others case mentioned above, the fact that national authorities have different tasks does not preclude authorities other than DPAs from interpreting and applying the provisions of the GDPR in order to perform their respective duties.[89] Although the Meta Platforms Inc. and Others case concerned competition authorities, the same should apply *mutatis mutandis* to market surveillance authorities under the AI Act. In the name of consistency, it may be necessary for the market surveillance authority to examine whether an undertaking's conduct is in compliance with rules other than those enshrined in the AI Act, "such as the rules on the protection of personal data laid down in the GDPR".[90]

Indisputably, the duty to cooperate *ex ante* with public authorities to justify processing activities limits the economic freedom of those who provide and professionally apply high-risk AI. Having said that, the Union has in no way set out to categorically hamper industrial development. It is stressed in the preparatory works of the AI Act that it aims at preserving the "EU's technological leadership and to ensure that Europeans can benefit from new technologies developed and functioning according to Union values, fundamental rights and principles".[91] Along those lines, the AI Act promotes research and development (R&D) by establishing "regulatory sandboxes" that give more leeway for data processing prior to marketing of the system.[92] Under certain conditions set out in Article 54 of the AI Act, personal data collected for other purposes may be processed when developing and testing innovative AI systems.

It is old news that "the fruits of the Tree of Knowledge" should be handled with much care because when "eating" them, "good and evil are mixed", resulting in increased disorder for humanity.[93] Evidently, measures that are "effective" in getting black figures in the quarterly report may be very ineffective if the chosen objective is a human-centric socio-economic development.[94] As we are now paying for the environmental "externalities" of increased productivity during the twentieth century, the assumption that industrial development creates jobs and generates "consumer welfare" must be called into question in view of the productivity of AI. It has been stressed that an "AI world order" may result in "tremendous social disorder and political collapse stemming from widespread unemployment and gaping inequality".[95] It is probably wiser to safeguard democracy, the rule of law and fundamental rights in line with the EU Declaration on Digital Rights than to rely on Mammon to

[89] Judgement in Meta Platforms and Others, C-252/21, supra note 16, paras. 43–44.

[90] Judgement in Meta Platforms and Others, C-252/21, supra note 16, para. 48.

[91] See Commission's Proposal for an AI Act, supra note 9, chapter 1.1.

[92] See Article 53 in the Commission's Proposal for an AI Act, supra note 9.

[93] For those who are interested in theology, the story in the Jewish Christian tradition is found in Genesis 2–3.

[94] See as to the error in the logic of making "efficiency" an objective, Dworkin (1980). p. 1 *et seq.*

[95] Quote from Lee (2019), p. 5. See, for an overview, also Lee (2018); Zuboff (1989); Winner (1986); Russel and Norvig (2016); M. Tegmark, Life 3.0, supra note 3; and N. Bostrom, Superintelligence, supra note 3.

shape the future. At the end of the day, "the dance around the golden calf" leads astray. Hence, broader perspectives are needed to channel the current industrial revolution toward improved human conditions.[96]

6 Automated Decision-Making and Low-Risk AI

Perhaps the right not to be subject to a decision based solely on automated processing, was once upon a time introduced to limit the ability of public authorities to rely on such decisions in order to protect the individual against the State.[97] Also, the use of AI by banks and in the financial sector, more broadly speaking, attracted attention early on. However, along with the development of the Internet of Things (IoT), many everyday objects will become interactive and start making decisions that have historically been reserved for humans. In that connection, Article 22 of the GDPR, as mentioned, applies the same irrespective of whether the category of data processing is considered to pose a high risk to the rights and freedoms of natural persons or not. Contrary to the high-risk processing of personal data, automated decisions based on low-risk data processing do not require an impact assessment under Articles 35, 36 and 58 of the GDPR. More to the point, society does not provide an administrative framework for the public enforcement of individual rights unless the type of data processing is considered to pose a high risk to humans. However, the reliance on low-risk AI systems makes Article 22 of the GDPR increasingly topical as most AI based decisions will be made by computer systems of that kind.

When it comes to SGEI, for instance, the purchase of a train ticket from a low-risk AI device will have legal effects and must, therefore, be justified pursuant to Article 22(2) of the GDPR. In the private sector, it is conceivable that for instance household equipment will be running on AI systems. A refrigerator with an embedded AI system can automatically order edibles in the name of the owner from an AI system applied by the seller. In that connection, the seller's AI system must process data regarding the individual who owns the AI refrigerator in accordance with Article 22(2) of the GDPR.

From a human-centric point of view, it would be inappropriate to require humans to be constantly ready to react to the whims of AI requesting consent under Article 22(2)(c) of the GDPR. Furthermore, it is questionable to what extent the fulfilment of a contract can justify decisions. If the owner of the AI refrigerator has concluded an agreement with a vendor allowing the low-risk AI to purchase edibles within certain limits and the AI system enters into purchasing contracts beyond those limits, to what extent must the data subject pursuant to Article 22(2)(a) of the GDPR accept

[96] Holy Bible, Exodus 32.

[97] See for an overview of the development of the provision in Bygrave (2020), supra note 14; and the EU Declaration on Digital Rights, supra note 8.

the automated decisions? Since the AI system is not a legal entity, the owner of such an IoT device may, in the near future, be subject to contractual obligations that he or she would not have freely chosen to undertake. Hence, low-risk AI will pose challenges that need to be addressed in civil law. As AI systems may also cause non-contractual liability because of emissions, property damage or personal injury, the EU has proposed a directive approximating AI liability.[98] Probably there will be an insurance solution based on strict liability, like the one for pets.

Given, on the one hand, the broadly defined scope of Article 22(1) of the GDPR and, on the other hand, the narrowly defined exceptions in Articles 22(2)(a) and (c) of the GDPR, the right to rely on decision-making low-risk AI probably needs to be particularised in sector-specific legislation. Arguably, any low-risk AI decision based on the automated processing of personal data should, in parity with what was said about the grounds of justification in case the type of processing is considered to pose a high risk to humans, normally be warranted under Article 22(2)(b) of the GDPR. However, contrary to the constraints on automated decisions by high-risk AI systems in the public sector under Article 22(2)(b) of the GDPR, a more permissive approach to the application of low-risk AI systems would be possible under Union and Member State laws. Ultimately, the frameworks must be aligned with the normative source code of EU law.

7 Conclusions

Since the EU Charter has the same legal value as the EU Treaties, the ECJ has clarified that situations cannot exist under EU law where the fundamental rights set out in the Charter do not apply. This remains true as European societies become increasingly reliant on software classified as AI. In response to the challenges to democracy, the rule of law and the fundamental rights posed by new technologies, the Union seeks to seize the opportunity to safeguard a human-centric digital transition by means of the social construct called law. An important piece in the normative puzzle is the AI Act. Whereas some AI applications are strictly prohibited, and many AI applications escape its scope, the AI Act establishes a legal and administrative framework with regard to high-risk AI applications.

Instead of laying down detailed rules on data processing, the AI Act establishes rules and procedures for cooperation between public bodies and the industry to ensure regulation by design. It complements the NLF by *ex ante* conformity assessments and *ex post facto* enforcement without defining the product standards required to protect human health, safety and fundamental rights. Indeed, the supply and professional application of high-risk AI would have been subject to the same standards even without the introduction of the AI Act. Hence, it is a

[98] See European Commission's Proposal for a Directive on adapting non-contractual civil liability rules to artificial intelligence, COM/2022/496 final (AI Liability Directive).

misunderstanding that the AI Act would impose new regulatory burdens on businesses. Although a high knowledge threshold and new administrative procedures entail costs for the industry, the purpose of the AI Act is rather to clarify existing legal obligations under primary EU law and to promote the effective enforcement of individual rights and public interests. According to Article 14 of the AI Act, high-risk AI shall be designed and developed in such a way that it can be continuously overseen by natural persons who can control its performance. Given the degree of autonomy of high-risk AI, the concept of "use" needs to be clarified in order to allocate the duty to comply with the human oversight requirement in some instances. As always with EU law, understanding the AI Act requires a systematic approach, and disparate analyses of the Regulation's provisions in isolation tend to lead to anomalous results.

When it comes to AI-based decision making the right for data subjects under Article 22 of the GDPR moves into the limelight. A provider or professional user of the high-risk AI system, which is considered to be the controller or processor of a high-risk processing operation, shall, according to Article 35 of the GDPR, typically carry out an *ex ante* impact assessment. In case the assessment shows that the processing is likely to infringe on the data subjects' rights, it would be an infringement also of the AI Act to pursue the data processing activity. If the market surveillance authority considers that the processing of personal data is incompatible with Article 14 of the AI Act, the Member State concerned shall provide for effective and dissuasive sanctions. A market surveillance authority will also be able to interpret and apply the GDPR on its own initiative under the AI Act as long as the actions are coordinated with the competent DPA. In contrast, society does not provide an administrative system for data protection when the type of processing does not involve a high risk for the infringement of the data subjects' rights and freedoms. Nonetheless, the day-to-day reliance on automated decisions by low- or no-risk AI is likely to raise more questions about the scope of Article 22 of the GDPR than high-risk AI systems.

As explained by the ECJ in the SCHUFA Holding I case, the notion of "automated decision" in Article 22(1) of the GDPR should be broadly defined and can encompass also decisive steps in the decision-making process. Moreover, the notions of "legal effect" for the data subject or "similarly significantly affects him or her" in that provision are broad in scope. In contrast, the exceptions in Article 22(2) of the GDPR are narrowly defined. When it comes to the necessity for the conclusion or performance of a contract under Article 22(2)(a) of the GDPR, the ECJ has clarified, with regard to the corresponding notion in Article 6 of the GDPR, that only the processing of personal data that are "objectively indispensable" for that purpose can be "necessary". In addition, information asymmetries and power imbalances make consent a questionable basis for automated decisions under Article 22(2)(c) of the GDPR. Indeed, the ECJ has clarified that a valid "consent" must be given for a specific purpose and be freely given as opposed to being required to access a service. In case an automated decision is made without any prior contact between the controller and the data subject, consent and contractual necessity can of course not justify exemptions from the rights amounting to a prohibition against automated decision-making laid down in Article 22(1) of the GDPR. Conclusively, automated decisions captured by Article 22(1) of the GDPR must, as a rule of thumb, be authorised by Union or national law under Article 22(2)(b) of the GDPR. This legislation, in turn, must transpose the basic rights to data protection under Article 6(1) thereof. There are also basic rights and interests beyond data protection that may limit the freedom of national and supranational legislators to allow automated decisions under Article 22(2)(b) of the GDPR. Whereas the implementation of decision-making AI should be carefully circumscribed in the public sector, less strict requirements may apply in the private sector and regarding SGEI.

As access to personal data is essential for the development and training of AI systems, the right to data protection as particularised primarily in the GDPR may translate into short-term social costs. In particular, the system of public enforcement of the rights regarding high-risk data processing laid down primarily in Article 35 of the GDPR as well as the broader human oversight requirements under Article 14 of the AI Act impose an administrative burden on the industry. However, in the long-term perspective, data protection and the human oversight of high-risk AI are likely to be effective means for sustainable development and human-centred social development. Since there is nothing inherently good in AI, self-learning algorithms can only serve people in Europe well insofar as they incorporate the normative source code of EU law. Indeed, a socio-economic development based on democracy, the rule of law and fundamental rights is inherently good for mankind.

EU Legislative Acts

Directive (EU) 2022/2555 on measures for a high common level of cybersecurity across the Union amending Regulation (EU) 910/2014 and Directive (EU) 2018/1972, OJ L 333/80, 27/12/2022

Regulation (EU) 2019/1020, on market surveillance and compliance of products amending several legislative acts, OJ L 169/1, 25.06.2019

Regulation (EU) 2019/881 on ENISA and on information and communication technology cybersecurity certification, OJ L 151/15, 07/06/2019

Regulation (EU) 2018/1725, EU Institutions Data Protection Regulation, OJ L 295/39, 21.11.2018

Regulation (EU) 2016/697, General Data Protection Regulation, OJ L 119/1, 04.05.2016

Directive (EU) 2016/680, on data protection and law enforcement, OJ L 119/89, 04.05.2016

Regulation (EU) No. 182/2011 on the possibility for the Member States to control the Commission's exercise of its implementing powers, OJ L 55/13, 28.02.2011

Decision 768/2008/EC, on market surveillance and compliance of products and amending several legislative acts, OJ L 218/82, 13.08.2008

Regulation (EC) 765/2008 on market surveillance, OJ L 218/30, 13.08.2008

Directive 2006/42/EC, on machinery, OJ L 157/24, 09.06.2006

EU Proposals

European Parliament, Proposed amendments to the European Commission's proposal for rules on artificial intelligence, P9_TA(2023)0236, 14.06.2023
European Commission's Proposal for a Directive on adapting non-contractual civil liability rules to artificial intelligence, COM/2022/496, 28.09.2022
European Commission's Proposal for a Directive on Corporate Sustainability Due Diligence amending Directive (EU) 2019/1937, COM/2022/71 Final 2022/0051 (COD) 2023.02.2022
European Commission, Proposal for a Regulation of the European Parliament and the Council laying down harmonised rules on artificial intelligence and amending certain Union legislative acts, COM(2021) 206 final, 2021/0106 (COD), 2021.04.21
European Commission, Proposal for a Regulation of the European Parliament and the Council on machinery products, COM/2021/202 final, 21.04.21

Other Public Print

Consolidated version of the Treaty on European Union and Consolidated version of the Treaty on the functioning of European Union, OJ C 326/1, 26.10.2012
Charter of the Fundamental Rights of the European Union, OJ C 326/391, 26.10.2012
European resolution of 16 February 2017 with recommendations to the Commission on Civil Law Rules on Robotics (2015/2103/(INL)), P8_TA(2017)0051.
Commission report by J. Crémer, Y-A de Montjoye, and H. Schweitzer, *Competition Policy for the Digital Era,* (2019) https://ec.europa.eu/competition/publications/reports/kd0419345enn.pdf
Commission Communication, *Artificial Intelligence for Europe*, COM(2018) 237 final, 25.4.2018
De Stefano, V. (2018) International Labour Organisation Working Paper No. 246, Negotiating the algorithm: Artificial Intelligence and labour protection
OECD, Recommendation of the Council on Artificial Intelligence, OECD/LEGAL/0449

Case Law of the European Court of Justice

Judgement of 7 December 2023, OQ v Land Hessen ("SCHUFA Holding I"), Case C-634/21, EU:C:2023:957
Judgement of 7 December 2023, UF and AB v Land Hessen (SCHUFA Holding II), Joined Cases C-26/22 and C-64/22, EU:C:2023:958
Judgement of 4 July 2023, Meta Platforms and Others, C-252/21, EU:C:2023:537

Judgement of 1 August 2022, Sea Watch, C-14/21 and 15/21, EU:C:2022:604
Judgement of 28 April 2022, Case C-319/20, Meta Platforms, EU:C:2022:322
judgement of 10 July 2018, Tietosuojavaltuutettu, Case C-25/17, EU:C:2018:551
Judgement of 25 January 2018, Case C-498/16, Maximillian Schrems v Facebook Ireland Limited, EU:C:2018:37
Judgement of the ECJ, 27 October 2016, James Elliot Limited, C-613/14, EU: C:2016:821
Judgement of 13 May 2014, *Google Spain SL and Google Inc. v Agencia España Proteccion de datos (AEPD) and Mario Costejo González*, Case C-131/12, EU: C:2014:317.
Judgement of 7 November 2013, UPC Netherlands, C-518/11, EU:C:2013:709
Judgement of 26 February 2013, Åklagaren v H. Å. F., C-617/10, EU:C:2013:105
Judgement of 21 December 2016, Tele2 Sverige AB and Secretary of State for the Home Department, joined Cases C-203/15 and C-298/15, EU:C:2016:970
Judgement of 6 November 2003, Lindquist, C-101/01, EU:C:2003:596, paras. 89-90

Opinions European Court of Justice

Opinion by Advocate General Pikamäe of 16 March 2023, OQ v Land Hessen (SCHUFA Holding I), Case C-634/21, EU:C:2023:222
Opinion by Advocate General Pikamäe of 16 March 2023, UF and AB v Land Hessen (SCHUFA Holding II), joined Cases C-26/22 and C-64/22, EU:C:2014: 317

UK Case Law

Thaler (Appellant) v. Comptroller-General of Patents Designs and Trademarks (Defendant) UKSC 2021/0201 [2021] EWCA Civ. 1829.
[2022] Bus LR 375, [2021] EWCA Civ. 1374, [2021] RPC 19.

European Patent Office Case Law

27 January 2020, EP 18 275 163
27 January 2020, EP 18 275 174

Online Resources

European citizen's proposals 35(3), 35(8) and 37(3) in the report from the conference on the future of Europe https://conference-delegation.europarl.europa.eu/cmsdata/267078/Report_EN.pdf

European Declaration on Digital Rights and Principles for the Digital Decade, 2022 Users/Admin/ Downloads/European_Declaration_on_Digital_Rights_and_Principles_signed_002_sPqb0eme38LoyyLQatnQJjkCZGU_94370.pdf

Future of Life Institute Open Letter 2023 https://futureoflife.org/open-letter/pause-giant-ai-experiments/

Future Life Institute, General Purpose AI and the AI Act, https://artificialintelligenceact.eu/wp-content/uploads/2022/05/General-Purpose-AI-and-the-AI-Act.pdf

President Bidens Executive Order on Safe, Secure and Trustworthy AI, www.whitehouse.gov/briefing-room/presidential-actions/2023/10/30/executive-order-on-the-safe-secure-and-trustworthy-development-and-use-of-artificial-intelligence/

UK Government AI Safety Institute www.gov.uk/government/news/prime-minister-launches-new-ai-safety-institute

World Forum for the harmonisation of vehicle regulations (UNECE WP 29) unece.org/transport/vehicle-regulations

References

Monographs

Aloisi A, De Stefano V (2022) Your boss is an algorithm. Hart Publishing

Boden MA (2018) Artificial intelligence: a very short introduction. Oxford University Press

Boström N (2016) Superintelligence. Oxford University Press

Diakopoulos N (2019) Automating the news: how algorithms are rewriting the media. Harvard University Press

Hayek FA (reprint 2007) The road to serfdom. University of Chicago Press (originally 1944 Routledge Press)

Kingwell MA (2020) In: Dubber MD et al (eds) Sentient AIs Persons? in the Oxford Handbook on Ethics of AI. Oxford Academic

Lee K-F (2018) AI Superpowers, China, Silicon Valley, and the New World Order. Houghton Mifflin Harcourt

Miller AI (2020) The artist in the machine: the world of AI powered creativity. Massachusetts Institute of Technology Press

Perloff, J. M. (2018) Microeconomics, Global edition, 8th edn. Pearson

Russel S, Norvig P (2016) Artificial intelligence: a modern approach, 3rd edn. Pearson

Tegmark M (2018) Life – being human in age of artificial intelligence. Penguin Books

Winner L (1986) The whale and the reactor. University of Chicago Press

Zuboff S (1989) In the age of the smart machines: the future of work and power. Basic Books

Chapters in Anthologies

Bygrave LA (2020) Article 22 Automated individual decision making, including profiling. In: Kuner C, Bygrave LA, Docksay CD, L. (eds) The EU general data protection regulation (GDPR): a commentary. Oxford University Press, pp 522–542

Articles

Dworkin R (1980) Why efficiency? – a response to professors Calabresi and Posner. Hofstra Law Rev 8(5), article 5:1

Granmar CG (2021) Global applicability of the GDPR in context. Int Data Priv Law 11(3):225–244

Jain P (2022) Standing for Non-Profit Associations or Consumer Associations to File Collective Actions without a Data-Subjects Mandate: Case C-319/20 Meta Platforms. European Law Blog, 16 May 2022

Lee K-F (2019) Youth Law Journal (YJL), 2nd edn. Oxford

Lucci N (2023) ChatGTP, a case study on copyright challenges for generative artificial intelligence systems. Eur J Risk Regul 1–23

Mc Fadden M, Jones K, Taylor E, Osborn G (2021) Harmonising artificial intelligence: the role of standards in the EU AI regulation. Oxford Commission on AI & Good Governance

Ryck MD, Verstayhe M, Debrouwere D (2020) Automated guided vehicle systems, state-of-the-art control algorithms and techniques. J Manuf Syst 54:152

Part III

Algorithmic Hiring Systems: Implications and Recommendations for Organisations and Policymakers

Jason D. Schloetzer and Kyoko Yoshinaga

Contents

J. D. Schloetzer
McDonough School of Business, Georgetown University, Washington, DC, USA
e-mail: jds99@georgetown.edu

K. Yoshinaga (✉)
Graduate School of Media and Governance, Keio University, Kanagawa, Japan
e-mail: kyokoy@sfc.keio.ac.jp

E. Gill-Pedro, A. Moberg (eds.), *YSEC Yearbook of Socio-Economic Constitutions 2023*, YSEC Yearbook of Socio-Economic Constitutions (2024) 2023: 213–246,
https://doi.org/10.1007/16495_2023_61, Published online: 3 November 2023

Abstract Algorithms are becoming increasingly prevalent in the hiring process, as they are used to source, screen, interview, and select job applicants. This chapter examines the perspective of both organisations and policymakers about algorithmic hiring systems, drawing examples from Japan and the United States. The focus is on discussing the drivers underlying the rising demand for algorithmic hiring systems and four risks associated with their implementation: the privacy of job candidate data; the privacy of current and former employees' workplace data; the potential for algorithmic hiring bias; and concerns surrounding ongoing oversight of algorithmically-assisted decision-making throughout the hiring process. These risks serve as the foundation for developing a risk management framework based on management control principles to facilitate dialogue within organisations to address the governance and management of such risks. The framework also identifies areas policymakers can focus on to help balance (1) granting organisations unfettered access to the personal and potentially sensitive data of job applicants and employees to develop hiring algorithms and (2) implementing strict data protection laws that safeguard individuals' rights yet may impede innovation, and emphasises the need to establish an intra-governmental AI oversight and coordination function that tracks, analyses, and reports on adverse algorithmic incidents. The chapter concludes by highlighting seven recommendations to mitigate the risks organisations and policymakers face in the development, use, and oversight of algorithmic hiring.

1 Introduction

Concerns about the responsible use of artificial intelligence (AI) are growing worldwide as its use becomes more sophisticated and ingrained across society. The COVID-19 pandemic and the seismic shift to remote working arrangements continue to accelerate digital transformation and AI adoption. For instance, a 2021 survey of nearly 1000 business leaders with knowledge of AI in the workplace indicates that AI is at least moderately functional in 61–93% of surveyed organisations, depending on the industry, an increase of up to 37 percentage points since the 2020 survey.[1] These implementations include integrating algorithmic hiring systems in human resource management (HRM) activities, particularly in sourcing, screening, interviewing, and selecting employees[2] across organisations of all types.[3]

[1]KPMG Homepage, available at: https://info.kpmg.us/news-perspectives/technology-innovation/thriving-in-an-ai-world/ai-adoption-accelerated-during-pandemic.html.

[2]DIGIDAY Homepage, available at: https://digiday.com/marketing/ai-is-being-used-to-recruit-and-onboard-talent/.

[3]The Markup Homepage, available at: https://themarkup.org/news/2021/12/23/public-agencies-are-buying-up-ai-driven-hiring-tools-and-bossware.

As the integration of algorithmic hiring systems proliferates, questionable applications of the technology continue to bring attention to the potential for significant negative consequences. For instance, in 2019, a U.S.-based recruiting technology firm began using facial recognition to help organisations screen job applicants based on their facial movements and tone of voice during AI-driven interviews. The organisation counts nearly 700 clients and reports screening over six million job applicant videos in 2020 alone. However, in 2021, the firm discontinued its facial recognition feature amid concerns that it failed to accurately assess the traits it intended to evaluate.[4] In 2019, Recruit Career Company, a job data provider in Japan, sold clients algorithmically-generated data of nearly 8000 job seekers on the probability that they would decline job offers based on their web-browsing histories of jobs posted by other prospective employers. The sale was made without the knowledge or consent of the job applicants, thereby infringing on existing laws in Japan, such as the Act on the Protection of Personal Information[5] and the Employment Security Act.[6] The revelation of this situation spurred a debate on the appropriateness of collecting, analysing, and monetising predictive data that can adversely impact job applicants' careers.[7]

Academic and practitioner studies have taken notice of the potential benefits and risks associated with the rise of algorithms in the hiring context, primarily highlighting the concerns such tools raise for notions of fairness, equity, and bias. For instance, De Stefano and Doellgast note the importance of employee voice during the early stages of AI system development, particularly in the HRM domain.[8] Bogen and Rieke discuss how algorithms are being introduced into the hiring process, focusing on their implications for equity.[9] Garr surveys several platforms designed to promote diversity and inclusion in hiring.[10] Sanchez-Monedero et al. analyse vendors that offer algorithmic hiring tools from the perspective of UK law, addressing concerns over discrimination and data protection.[11] Broadly considering the use of data science in the human resource function, Cappelli et al. identify practical challenges to implementing algorithmic systems in hiring and propose a

---

[4] Details provided by various news articles compiled by Lutz, Roman. (2019-11-06) Incident Number 95. In McGregor, S. (ed.) Artificial Intelligence Incident Database. Partnership on AI from incidentdatabase.ai/cite/95.

[5] Act on the Protection of Personal Information, available at: https://elaws.e-gov.go.jp/document?lawid=415AC0000000057.

[6] Employment Security Act, available at: https://elaws.e-gov.go.jp/document?lawid=322AC0000000141.

[7] The Japan Times articles available at: https://www.japantimes.co.jp/news/2019/09/06/business/corporate-business/ministry-says-recruit-career-acted-illegally-rikunabi-data-scandal-demands-corrective-steps/, https://www.japantimes.co.jp/news/2019/08/27/business/corporate-business/recruit-career-job-data-scandal/.

[8] De Stefano and Doellgast (2023), pp. 9–20.

[9] Bogen and Rieke (2018).

[10] Garr and Jackson (2019).

[11] Sanchez-Monedero et al. (2020).

framework to help address them.[12] Ajunwa provides a legal framework to consider the problems algorithmic tools introduce, arguing against using subjective evaluative measures such as "cultural fit" to assess job candidates.[13] Kim also raises legal concerns over hiring algorithms in sourcing and screening contexts.[14] Raghavan et al. conduct an in-depth review of the de-biasing-related practices of a sample of vendors of algorithmic hiring systems, with a particular focus on de-biasing the screening process, while Chamorro-Prezumic et al. argue that academic research has been unable to keep pace with rapidly evolving technology, allowing vendors to develop tools lacking rigorous independent research.[15,16]

Despite high-profile instances of questionable technology use and concerns about fairness, equity, and bias, organisations continue to pursue emerging technologies that can provide business understanding on enduring HRM questions about improving hiring and employee evaluation processes. Respondents to a 2021 survey indicate that they soon expect technology-enabled solutions will contact job applicants (55% of respondents), schedule interviews (51%), and conduct interviews (44%).[17] The speed and scale at which emerging technologies offer perceived answers to HRM questions and society's increasing acceptance of AI push organisations and policymakers into uncharted territory with the potential for higher rewards and risks that may become difficult to reverse. To address such issues, organisations and policymakers need to consider actions that manage the emerging risks associated with algorithmic hiring systems.

Our interdisciplinary approach in this chapter is intended to integrate the perspectives of organisations and policymakers. Business practitioner-oriented commentators often highlight the benefits of AI with fragmented discussions of its potential risks and little depth on the regulatory implications of using AI in the hiring process. Policy-oriented and legal discussions provide rigorous depth of the evolving regulatory frameworks governing AI in the workplace but with a somewhat narrow view of the dynamic nature of organisations' intentions of using AI-based tools to overhaul the hiring process. By combining both fields' perspectives, illustrated with examples from organisations and policymakers in Japan and the U.S., we hope to foster dialogue among and within organisations and policymakers around governing, measuring, and managing algorithmic hiring system risk.

---

[12] Peter Cappelli, Prasanna Tambe, and Valery Yakubovich, Artificial intelligence in human resources management: Challenges and a path forward. Available at SSRN 3263878, 2018.

[13] Ajunwa (2020).

[14] Kim (2018), p. 313; Kim (2020).

[15] Manish Raghavan, Solon Barocas, Jon Kleinberg, Karen Levy: Mitigating Bias in Algorithmic Hiring: Evaluating Claims and Practices, available at: https://arxiv.org/pdf/1906.09208.pdf.

[16] Tomas Chamorro-Premuzic, Dave Winsborough, Ryne A Sherman, and Robert Hogan, New talent signals: Shiny new objects or a brave new world? Industrial and Organisational Psychology, 9(3):621–640, 2016.

[17] Business Wire Homepage, available at: https://www.businesswire.com/news/home/20211018005055/en/Nine-in-10-Americans-Believe-Bots-Will-Be-Important-for-the-Future-of-Work.

The following section summarises the potential benefits organisations believe will arise from implementing algorithmic hiring systems. We then illustrate emerging risks for organisations and policymakers to consider regarding such implementations. Next, we discuss how organisations and policymakers can balance these potential benefits and risks by identifying seven broad recommendations on responsible development, use, and oversight of algorithmic hiring.[18]

2 Organisations' Views on the Potential Benefits of Using Algorithmic Hiring Systems

Hiring decisions are among the most consequential for organisations, which face financial pressure to make high-quality hires quickly and at low cost.[19,20] As a result, organisations are searching for ways to improve their hiring process, which, broadly speaking, has four stages: sourcing, screening, interviewing, and selecting candidates.[21] Sourcing involves building a candidate pool, which is then screened to identify candidates to interview. After candidates are interviewed, selected candidates receive offers. Our discussion primarily centers on using algorithms to screen, interview, and select candidates, which occurs after the job applicant applies (i.e., sourcing).

There is demand for using algorithmic tools to screen, interview, and select job applicants; surveys reveal that 55%[22] of U.S. HRM leaders and 83%[23] of U.-S. organisations use predictive algorithms in hiring. Multiple drivers fuel this demand. There is the promise of cost savings and scalability commensurate with automating the arguably repetitive process of reviewing resumes, conducting interviews, and collecting additional information that can enhance the hiring decision.[24] There is the practical expectation that algorithmic tools can reduce HR costs because they can process vast numbers of resumes at little incremental cost, reducing the

[18] While we focus on the hiring process, the discussion is germane to other HRM contexts, including using algorithmic tools to predict which employees to terminate, which employees may depart the organisation voluntarily, and which employees might experience emotional issues on the job.

[19] This section summarises the views expressed during monthly roundtables of 20–50 Chief Data Officers convened by a global consulting firm. From time to time, discussions of algorithmic hiring tools arise, focusing on their development and implementation challenges.

[20] Mariotti (2017).

[21] Bogen and Rieke (2018).

[22] Mercer Homepage, available at: https://www.mercer.com/content/dam/mercer/attachments/private/global-talent-trends-2020-report.pdf.

[23] Government Matters Homepage, available at: https://govmatters.tv/eeoc-working-to-stop-artificial-intelligence-from-perpetuating-bias-in-hir-ing/#:~:text=With%2083%25%20of%20U.S.%20employers,assistance%20to%20employers%2C%20Burrows%20said.

[24] Manish Raghavan, Solon Barocas, Jon Kleinberg, Karen Levy: Mitigating Bias in Algorithmic Hiring: Evaluating Claims and Practices, available at: https://arxiv.org/pdf/1906.09208.pdf.

amount of human work necessary to review an ever-increasing number of resumes. For instance, in Japan, where the "shukatsu" recruitment process begins around the same time each year and requires a lengthy resume called an "entry sheet," organisations can use AI-based hiring systems to review entry sheets to identify candidates that best match their needs. Such automation allows HR functions to focus on interviewing candidates instead of reviewing resumes. Such potential efficiencies may become even more beneficial as job candidates leverage text-generative AI to prepare cover letters and resumes tailored to specific job openings with less time commitment.

Beyond cost savings and scalability, algorithmic hiring systems can strengthen the consistency of outcomes by standardising the decisions and actions of multiple individuals across an organisation who screen and interview candidates. There is concern among organisations that human recruiters miss relevant job applicant experience, fail to ask the "right" questions during job interviews, and perform inconsistently due to individual biases. The belief is that AI-based hiring tools promote consistency across job applications, particularly in the screening process by, for instance, reducing the likelihood that different HR employees use different bright lines (e.g., elite university, a minimum number of years of work experience) to screen out otherwise suitable candidates. Consistency via algorithmic hiring systems can help organisations identify job applicants who may be overlooked because of persistent biases in the human-led screening and interviewing processes. The idea here is that consistent job applicant processing allows organisations to reduce human judgment in hiring, potentially enhancing transparency and fairness and increasing workplace diversity by limiting human bias.[25]

3 Four Emerging Risks in the Algorithmic Hiring System Context

As discussed in the prior section, organisations adopt algorithmic hiring systems for multiple interconnected reasons—efficiently screening, interviewing, and selecting job applicants at scale and bringing consistency to this process, which can enhance transparency, fairness, and diversity in hiring and mitigate bias. This section examines four emerging risks resulting from integrating algorithmic tools in the hiring process that both organisations and policymakers should consider, given their probability of occurring and the magnitude of their consequences for individuals, groups, and society—risks regarding the privacy of job candidate data, risks regarding the privacy of current and former employees' workplace data, the potential for algorithmic hiring bias, and risks regarding ongoing oversight of algorithmically-

[25] Upturn Homepage, available at: https://www.upturn.org/static/reports/2018/hiring-algorithms/files/Upturn%20%2D%2D%20Help%20Wanted%20-%20An%20Exploration%20of%20Hiring%20Algorithms,%20Equity%20and%20Bias.pdf.

assisted decision-making in hiring. From an organisational viewpoint, these risks can negatively impact reputations, trigger regulatory scrutiny, and result in legal action and penalties; they also have implications for the type of job applicants an organisation attracts and the work life of current and, potentially, prior employees.

3.1 Data Privacy Concerns Resulting from Collecting Job Applicant Data

A straightforward algorithmic hiring tool could score each job applicant based on keywords in job application materials, with a higher score suggesting a candidate is a better fit for the job. Using such tools to screen job applicants then becomes an effort to train an algorithm to learn which job applicants are predicted to perform better on the job based on resume keywords associated with current employees and past applicants who were not hired. In practice, algorithmic hiring tools have developed into more sophisticated systems.

Organisations can either rely on vendor-developed tools or develop their algorithms in-house. Raghavan et al. note that most vendors offer custom or customisable screening tools adapted to the organisation's data or job requirements.[26] In practice, decisions about what organisations want to predict (e.g., employee performance reviews or retention time) and training data needs are jointly determined based on where the data originate. Multiple vendors build screening tools using data from the organisation's past and current employees. Broadly speaking, vendors ask organisations to determine what outcomes they want to predict. Vendors offering customisable tools without using organisational data either use the vendor's job role analysis or an organisation's knowledge of employee skill requirements to determine data needs.[27] In some cases, the vendor's algorithmic hiring system is designed to score job applicant traits for a particular job role or score various cognitive or behavioural characteristics, such as leadership ability or teamwork. These tools differ from traditional approaches that rely on a few questions, focusing instead on building psychographic profiles that may even incorporate AI to analyse video interviews.

Whether relying on a vendor or developing in-house algorithmic tools, important data privacy risks arise from collecting job applicant data. While privacy issues when developing the "best" training data are common across machine learning applications, building an algorithmic screening tool on multiple years of past and current employee data and then using that tool to evaluate future job applicants raises unique privacy concerns. For instance, when an applicant applies for an open position and provides their resume and other requested application materials, it

[26] Manish Raghavan, Solon Barocas, Jon Kleinberg, Karen Levy: Mitigating Bias in Algorithmic Hiring: Evaluating Claims and Practices, available at: https://arxiv.org/pdf/1906.09208.pdf.

[27] Ibid.

may or may not be appropriate for the organisation to assume that the applicant has given implied consent in the collection, storage, and use of this data for an undetermined length of time and in ways that may have been unforeseen when the data was initially collected. When an applicant is unaware that their data will be stored for future use to create unknown algorithmic hiring tools—or, perhaps, other algorithms implemented outside of the hiring process (e.g., targeted advertising)—the risk of data privacy comes into question. Especially in Japan, where organisations need to obtain consent from or at least notify the data owner that personal data collection is occurring under the Act on the Protection of Personal Information (a comprehensive personal data protection law), it may violate the law if the organisation fails to notify the job applicant that it may or intends to use their personal data for future use.

Beyond job application materials, organisations increasingly collect data from social media such as LinkedIn, Twitter, Facebook, Instagram, and TikTok to develop a broader view of the job candidate. For instance, a recent survey commissioned by Express Employment Professionals notes that 71% of over 1000 hiring managers report using social media sites to research job candidates, with 55% reporting they have found content that has caused them not to hire an applicant.[28] While a human may currently complete this process, algorithmic hiring systems can automate the collection and integration of social media data with job applicants' submitted materials. This situation extends privacy concerns around the collection of job applicant data because it crosses into the personal domain, such as the intentional or unintentional collection of posts, images, and names of friends and family in the applicant's non-work-related social network. As was the case in Japan with Recruit Career Company, there is also the risk that a third party would sell data, such as job applicants' web-browsing histories of jobs posted by other employers, to help organisations assemble information about the likelihood of applicants' declining a job offer. While the Recruit Career Company situation violated Japan's Personal Data Protection Law, in jurisdictions that lack a provision limiting the use and transfer of personal data to third parties, such as at the federal level in the U.S., this issue could arise.

Moreover, organisations are exploring algorithmic tools beyond simple resume keyword screening by turning to facial recognition, speech recognition, and language processing tools to collect rich data during different stages of the hiring process. Thus, algorithmic hiring tools could eventually construct extensive profiles of numerous job applicants—combining job applicant materials with social media data, applicant psychographic and behavioural profiles, the results of knowledge assessments developed by organisations, data generated from job interview-specific gameplay, algorithmic-predicted employee performance reviews and retention

[28] "71% of Hiring Decision-Makers Agree Social Media is Effective for Screening Applicants" news provided by Express Employment Professionals, available at: https://www.prweb.com/releases/71_of_hiring_decision_makers_agree_social_media_is_effective_for_screening_applicants/prweb17467312.htm.

times, cultural "fit" scores, and the deconstruction of rich data sources such as facial expressions, tone, and language characteristics collected from video interviews. The potential for data privacy concerns around job applicant data abounds, touching on a range of sensitive areas from applicant race, ethnicity, gender identity, socioeconomic background, and age to traits such as candidate's political views, social circle, and mental and physical health.[29,30]

3.2 Data Privacy Concerns Resulting from Integrating Employee Surveillance Data with Algorithmic Hiring Systems

Similar arguments on data privacy concerns for job applicants can be constructed regarding an organisation's employees. Once a job applicant is hired, they create data while completing tasks. As data-driven organisations increasingly implement extensive workforce surveillance and people analytics, it will become increasingly common for organisations to collect and build vast repositories of data about how employees carry out their work. Organisations are already collecting data regarding the emotion and tone of internal emails and their recipients, screenshots of employees' computers, data logs of the applications used and websites visited on organisation-provided computers and mobile phones, and scans of employees' meeting calendars.[31] Organisations are also analysing employees' social media posts, collecting biometrics data from company-issued wearables, and digitalising offline behaviours (e.g., video surveillance) to create detailed profiles of workplace activities.[32]

Organisations not only can leverage data about their current employees' work practices but also integrate this data with employee performance reviews, compensation data, and other HR data (e.g., internal promotion outcomes). The collection and integration of numerous data sources about current employees can yield unprecedented insights into the features of a "good" employee. For instance, a large U.S.-based organisation is experimenting with using people analytics to estimate the probability that a current employee will depart within the next year, integrating this probability into HRM decisions about the number of job candidates to hire for specific positions and general workforce planning.[33] This example illustrates how algorithmic hiring systems could eventually use rich workplace surveillance data

[29] Kramer and Ward (2010), pp. 2273–2287.

[30] Zhou et al. (2015).

[31] Examples collected in 2022 from private conversations with executives as part of a monthly roundtable of Chief Data Officers convened by a global consulting firm.

[32] See, for example, Leidner et al. (2021).

[33] Example collected in May 2022 from private conversations with executives as part of a monthly roundtable of Chief Data Officers convened by a global consulting firm.

from current and past employees to develop new predicted outcomes, going well beyond those used in current systems.

As such, the data privacy risks around collecting and using current and past employee data and, more broadly, workplace surveillance might enter the risk calculus for algorithmic hiring rather than remain a distinct issue. As organisations seek to broaden the data they integrate into the hiring process, there is a risk of going too far.[34] For instance, if an organisation allows employees to work remotely, collecting location data may violate privacy if the employee does not want the organisation to gain access to their work location. This type of sensitive data may be treated differently in various legal jurisdictions. For instance, in Israel, the Privacy Protection Authority ("PPA") published an opinion emphasising that collecting and processing a person's location data is a significant violation of privacy, even during work hours.[35]

Other examples of the data privacy risks associated with integrating workforce surveillance with algorithmic hiring systems are apparent. Collecting data logs of the applications used and websites visited on organisation-provided computers and mobile phones, combined with employee location data, can allow organisations to infer employees' working habits and daily private life routines. For instance, if an employee logs out of their workplace-provided computer and then begins to post on social media with their personal mobile phone, an organisation can start to develop profiles of their employees' personal lives (e.g., meeting family and friends at a restaurant after work) that go beyond what is necessary to assess job performance. Organisations that are analysing the tone of employee emails are determining which employees and departments are communicating with negative tones, using this data to assess the organisation's culture in more nuanced ways than annual employee surveys.[36] Combining such data with the tone of employees' social media posts or keywords used in their posts could reveal private information about employees' mental states that could be used as inputs into hiring algorithms via refinements of the features of a "good" employee. In essence, there is the risk that employees and job applicants will lose control over their data contributions to the organisations they work for, previously worked for, and apply for employment opportunities.

In the extreme, one can envision private data on current and past employees and job applicants migrating onto a technological platform (e.g., blockchain), enabling intricate details of employees' work history and job applicant activity to follow them

---

[34] Meribeth Banaschik, How location tracking is raising the stakes on privacy protection, EY, available at: https://www.ey.com/en_gl/forensic-integrity-services/how-location-tracking-is-raising-the-stakes-on-privacy-protection.

[35] Beverley Zabow, Tracking of Employee Location Data is a significant violation of privacy according to the Israeli Privacy Protection Authority, INPLP, available at: https://inplp.com/latest-news/article/tracking-of-employee-location-data-is-a-significant-violation-of-privacy-according-to-the-israeli-privacy-protection-authority/.

[36] Example collected in September 2021 from a private research study with a start-up developing algorithms that use the tone of employee emails to predict a measure of "corporate culture" that senior executives and boards of directors can routinely monitor and intervene if necessary.

throughout their careers—a "know your employee" situation much like how financial services firms conduct a "know your client" investigation when determining whether to provide financial services to a specific client. And organisations may seek to monetise this private data when personal data protection laws do not exist (e.g., at the U.S. federal level). For instance, organisations could sell what they know about current and previous employees' work practices or performance outcomes to benchmark providers and consulting firms that evaluate industry performance.[37]

3.3 Algorithmic Hiring Bias Concerns Resulting from Job Applicant and Employee Data Collection

Sections 3.1 and 3.2 highlight the type of job applicant and employee data organisations are collecting (or will soon be capable of collecting), processing, and storing and the data privacy risks associated with integrating this data into algorithmic hiring systems. This section discusses the potential for poor-quality training data to create biases that become ingrained in algorithmic hiring systems.

Data quality reflects an organisation's ability to collect, combine, transform, and organise data from disparate internal and third-party sources. Characteristics of high-quality data include its accuracy, consistency, integrity, timeliness, validity, and completeness.[38] As organisations are increasingly aware, assembling quality data free from embedded biases is challenging. To illustrate, in 2017, Amazon abandoned the development and use of a hiring algorithm that scanned resumes for 50,000 keywords that were included on job applicants' resumes over the prior decade. An important goal for the algorithm was to assign job applicants a score from one to five; applicants who scored a five would be elevated to the top of the applicant pool. However, Amazon observed that its algorithm systematically filtered out women candidates. Scrutiny of the training data revealed that the resumes were predominately male applicants, reflecting the male dominance in the tech industry. In essence, Amazon's system learned that men were preferable to women, penalising resumes that included the word "women's," as in "women's chess club captain," and downgraded graduates of two all-women's colleges. While Amazon adjusted the algorithm to render it neutral to these particular terms, the lack of insight into the algorithm's job applicant scoring predictions raised concerns that it would eventually learn other difficult-to-detect discriminatory practices.[39]

[37] Example collected in December 2022 from private conversations with executives as part of a monthly roundtable of Chief Data Officers convened by a prominent global consulting firm.

[38] IBM Homepage, ibm.com/analytics/data-quality.

[39] All details about the Amazon situation are provided by various news articles compiled by Anonymous. (2016-08-10) Incident Number 37. In McGregor, S. (ed.) Artificial Intelligence Incident Database. Partnership on AI from incidentdatabase.ai/cite/37.

Algorithmic hiring systems are often viewed as a process by which an algorithm predicts a predetermined output (e.g., predicted employee performance rating of a job applicant) from a given set of inputs (e.g., keywords from the resumes of current employees with high performance ratings). In reality, neither the inputs nor outputs are fixed, creating opportunities for bias to creep into the algorithmic development process.

Algorithms often rely in whole or in part on organisations to determine the appropriate predicted outcome given constraints on data availability. Many organisations fail to maintain comprehensive and accessible data about employee performance, and thus, a vendor or in-house data scientist may need to improvise using the limited available data.[40] Quality data sources may be distributed across numerous legacy technology platforms that the data scientist cannot readily integrate. The access rights to the data may reside with multiple employees across the organisation—not just in human resources—and the necessary data may reside in legal jurisdictions that complicate data access. Moreover, desirable data sources may be stale, missing, or omitted, creating situations that jeopardise the quality of data used to develop algorithmic hiring systems. Relying on the organisation's data has already forced the vendor or in-house data scientist to only learn from the organisation's current and, perhaps, past employees; hence, there is limited data available about the potential performance of those job applicants who were not hired, an essential yet missing opportunity for model training. That is, the organisation may choose not to hire an applicant who goes on to have a highly successful career, and the hiring algorithm would be unable to learn from this situation.

To illustrate the risks of bias entering the algorithm development process, consider the example of a large U.S.-based organisation that wanted to assess the extent of bias in its hiring process.[41] The third-party data scientist struggled to access quality data on current employees' age, race, ethnicity, gender identity, and sexual orientation. To compensate, the organisation surveyed current employees, asking them to provide this information voluntarily, and sought to develop an algorithm that predicts the gender, race, and ethnicity of a current employee or prior job applicant based on their name if these details were missing. Such efforts are problematic—for instance, current employees may hesitate to provide sensitive personal data voluntarily, and those who do provide it may give false information to comply with the request. This situation raises several issues, including potential bias in the set of employees who respond to the survey and the accuracy of their responses. Moreover, algorithms that use names to predict employee and applicant gender, race, and ethnicity can be fraught with errors and their own biases (e.g., attempting to infer gender based on international names, failing to reflect gender identity). Therefore, data quality issues create significant risks that can erode the ability of organisations

[40] Peter Cappelli, Prasanna Tambe, and Valery Yakubovich, Artificial intelligence in human resources management: Challenges and a path forward. Available at SSRN 3263878, 2018.

[41] Example collected in June 2021 from private conversations with executives as part of a monthly roundtable of Chief Data Officers convened by a prominent global consulting firm.

to implement algorithmic hiring systems that support notions of transparency, fairness, and de-biased hiring decisions.

Even when a large, population-representative training dataset is available, the target outcome of interest to the organisation may have inherent biases. As Raghavan et al. note, target outcomes such as employee performance evaluations can exhibit historical biases against minority groups because the performance rating itself can include bias.[42,43,44] Moreover, as the Amazon example highlights, predicting the success of future employees based on current employees' characteristics inherently skews the algorithm toward identifying job applicants based on the extent to which they resemble those who have already been hired, which may be a biased set of employees when compared with the original pool of job applicants.

This leads to an inherently challenging technical problem: on the one hand, more data is typically beneficial in creating and validating an algorithm; on the other hand, using data from related but somewhat different sources can lead to inaccurate conclusions. Pooling data from multiple organisations or geographic locations may reduce variance due to small sample sizes at a particular organisation, but it comes at the cost of skewing the outcomes away from the organisation's specific needs. There is no obvious answer or clear best practice here. Larger organisations may be better able to rely solely on their data; smaller organisations might turn to off-the-shelf, vendor-developed algorithms, thereby assuming that the job candidate pool and job role on which the tool was developed are sufficiently similar to warrant generalising its outcomes. The potential ability of algorithms to de-bias hiring likely remains elusive and could unintentionally become ingrained in the hiring process.

3.4 *Concerns Regarding Ongoing Oversight of Algorithmic Hiring Systems*

Artificial intelligence governance commentators have written about the need to monitor the use of AI-powered algorithms in hiring. One frequent viewpoint is the need to develop organisational standards and public policymaking around algorithmic auditing, particularly the need for organisations to audit hiring algorithms for evidence of discriminatory hiring practices.[45] While such a focus is undoubtedly warranted, algorithmic audits need to adopt a broader view of the risks associated

[42] Sidanius and Crane (1989), pp. 174–197.

[43] Neumark et al. (1996), pp. 915–941.

[44] Riach and Rich (2002), pp. F480–F518.

[45] See, for example, https://www.brookings.edu/research/auditing-employment-algorithms-for-discrimination/ and https://hbr.org/2018/11/why-we-need-to-audit-algorithms and https://www.technologyreview.com/2021/02/11/1017955/auditors-testing-ai-hiring-algorithms-bias-big-questions-remain/.

with the ongoing use of algorithmic hiring systems to enhance their risk management capabilities.

As with many systems, a robust performance measurement and monitoring process needs to assess all aspects of the system, not only its outcomes. If the monitoring and assessment process focuses only on hiring outcomes, there is a risk that organisations will fail to recognise the risks present throughout the entire hiring process across the lifecycle of the algorithmic tool. From ensuring data privacy to monitoring changes in applicable laws and regulations, from modifications to critical data sources that adversely impact data quality, to a shift in the demographics or geographies of job applicants, from human-computer interactions and the need to track and evaluate human overrides of the algorithmic tools to strategic decisions by the organisation to add entirely new employee skillsets that the model has not been trained to accommodate, there are numerous concerns resulting from the on-going use of algorithmic hiring systems that extend beyond focusing on the potential for discriminatory hiring outcomes. Highly secure, privacy-enhanced but biased systems, unbiased but opaque and uninterpretable systems, and unbiased algorithms that infringe on employee privacy are all undesirable. Hence, there is the risk that organisations and policymakers will fail to treat hiring algorithms as a system of interconnected features that require comprehensive performance monitoring and auditing/assessment activities extending beyond outcome-focused determinations of whether algorithms yield biased, discriminatory hiring.

4 How Organisations Can Support the Responsible Development and Use of Algorithmic Hiring Systems

The extensive use of algorithms in HRM can impact society as a whole, and organisations have a social responsibility to mitigate the risks of using algorithmic hiring systems. This section draws from management control system frameworks to characterise how organisations can responsibly develop and use algorithmic hiring systems to achieve their potential benefits while mitigating the risks outlined in Sect. 3.[46] Particularly, Sect. 4.1 discusses the importance of developing a culture of control on the use of AI-based tools in general and AI-based hiring systems specifically. Section 4.2 emphasises the importance of an "Algorithmic Hiring Ethics Committee" to oversee the end-to-end hiring process, thereby enabling strong action controls over the ongoing use of these hiring systems. Finally, Sect. 4.3 highlights the importance of performance measurement and monitoring, fostering a results-control-focused mindset along every step of an AI-enabled hiring process. The propositions are interrelated, such that guidelines may not be followed without an oversight committee, performance measurement and monitoring cannot be

[46] See Merchant and Van der Stede (2017), for an excellent treatment of management control system theory.

developed without guidelines, and an oversight committee might struggle to make informed, consistent decisions without performance measurement across the entire hiring process.

4.1 Develop a Culture of Control in the Development and Use of Algorithms in the Hiring Process

A critical means for organisations to manage algorithmic hiring system risk is to develop a culture of control and accountability over AI by focusing on two broad areas: (1) an internal code of conduct and (2) publicly-accessible documents on how the organisation develops, acquires via vendors, and implements AI-based hiring systems. Strong governance requires an interdisciplinary oversight committee that can drive and enhance internal practices and norms to foster an awareness of risk—the often-termed "AI Ethics Committee" or IBM's "Privacy and AI Ethics Oversight Body."[47,48] While the vision for this oversight function is to determine the overarching principles and policies that direct an organisation's mission, goals, values, culture, and risk tolerance toward AI-based implementations in general, part of this effort should focus specifically on AI-based implementations in the hiring process. The oversight committee that develops and communicates the code of conduct should include the developers of the algorithmic hiring tools (e.g., vendors, in-house developers), operators of the system (e.g., those who perform system maintenance), users of the AI-based hiring tool (e.g., recruiters, hiring managers), data providers, risk management personnel, and legal and compliance experts who can ensure that hiring algorithms comply with appropriate employment laws and regulations. It is also important for the committee to include the voice of current employees who may not have direct involvement in the hiring process but will eventually interact with future employees hired via the AI-based hiring process.

The code of conduct should cover, in reasonable detail, the research and development (R&D) guidelines around AI and principles regarding AI utilisation at each stage of the hiring process—sourcing, screening, interviewing, and selecting—to increase awareness of the risks that can arise from utilising algorithms in hiring. The code of conduct should consider the risks outlined in the previous section to ensure a broad understanding of the importance of data privacy for job applicants, data privacy for past and current employees (including drafting policies about workplace surveillance and people analytics), and characterising the algorithmic auditing/assessment process to ensure a holistic approach to ongoing performance

---

[47] Reid Blackman, Why you need an AI ethics committee, Harvard Business Review, July-August 2002, available at: https://hbr.org/2022/07/why-you-need-an-ai-ethics-committee.

[48] For more on IBM's AI ethics practices, see https://newsroom.ibm.com/The-Davos-Agenda-Fostering-Responsible-AI-Leadership and https://www.weforum.org/agenda/2021/09/case-study-on-ibm-ethical-use-of-artificial-intelligence-technology/.

measurement, management, compliance, and accountability. Moreover, the guidelines should consider the interconnectivity and interoperability of algorithmic hiring systems with other AI systems, their security and transparency, and reinforce that humans use these systems and are ultimately responsible for algorithmic-assisted decisions.[49]

Once established, a summary of these internal R&D guidelines and utilisation principles should be made publicly available and positioned within an organisation's environmental, social, and governance (ESG) responsibilities, given the impact of hiring for society.

4.2 *Ensure Robust, Centralised Control Over Algorithmic Hiring Systems*

Extending the above discussion, organisations using algorithmic hiring systems should have a global view of their development and use and the rapidly evolving global regulatory environment around the use of AI in hiring. A centralised, interdisciplinary team, perhaps comprised of individuals who establish the organisational-level code of conduct discussed in Sect. 4.1, should have the authority to review proposed implementations and modifications to hiring algorithms and maintain responsibility for monitoring their ongoing performance. This "Algorithmic Hiring Ethics Committee," which focuses specifically on the risks of AI in the hiring process, should, at a minimum:

- Establish a clear "owner" responsible for algorithmic hiring systems and all associated activities,
- Be responsible for maintaining all established governance documents,
- Ensure mechanisms are in place to inventory algorithmic hiring systems,
- Be aware of all updates, customisation, phasing out, and decommissioning of algorithmic hiring systems, requesting scrutiny where appropriate,
- Maintain job applicant and employee data catalogues and awareness of data access rights to control data privacy and preserve human dignity and autonomy,
- Maintain open communications with the direct and indirect internal users of such systems,
- Have responsibility for the routine performance monitoring of algorithmic hiring systems, including the resources needed to conduct routine and ad hoc algorithmic audits,
- Ensure contingency processes are in place to handle undesirable algorithmic-only and human-algorithmic incidents,
- Understand and track relevant legal and regulatory trends,

[49]The EU's General Data Protection Regulation emphasises the importance of human intervention in automatic decision-making, as does the Japanese Ministry of Internal Affairs and Communication's AI R&D guidelines.

- Possess the power to request information and compel action from parties across the organisation and, if relevant, third-party vendors involved in algorithm development, and
- Provide periodic updates to the organisation's risk management function, executive team, and, if appropriate, the board of directors on evolving risks, failures, and incidents.

In addition, organisations that utilise algorithmic hiring systems must take responsibility for educating internal and external end users on how the systems operate (i.e., the principles of proper utilisation and accountability). To this end, the Algorithmic Hiring Ethics Committee should be responsible for designing processes that allow job applicants and employees—current and past—to inquire about collecting, processing, and storing their data in the hiring process and voice their concerns about the organisation's system.

4.3 Ensure Ongoing Performance Monitoring of Algorithmic Hiring Systems and Accountability for Results

As noted in Sect. 4.2, the "Algorithmic Hiring Ethics Committee" should collect performance information and ensure appropriate ongoing monitoring, perhaps through a robust algorithmic audit[50] and/or continual performance reporting process, to ensure the system continues functioning as intended across time. This algorithmic audit and/or performance reporting must consider the entire hiring process—sourcing, screening, interviewing, and selecting—and view algorithmic hiring as a system of interconnected tools requiring broad-based performance monitoring and assessment activities across an algorithm's lifecycle, going beyond focusing on whether algorithms generate discriminatory hiring outcomes.

This broader algorithmic review should include managing the risks discussed in Sect. 3 regarding the quality, privacy, and security of job applicant and employee data, the potential for algorithmic bias, and mitigating the risk of a narrow focus of assessing hiring outcomes to ensure that assessments are broad-based and encompassing. Ideally, an independent party would have a role in the monitoring process to bring independence and professional skepticism to the evaluation and possess the expertise and perspective to identify issues and suggest improvements or alternatives to the organisation's developers and internal users. The guiding principle is that algorithmic hiring system developers and internal users should remain accountable to internal and external stakeholders for the system's overall

[50] See, for example, https://www.brookings.edu/research/auditing-employment-algorithms-for-discrimination/ and https://hbr.org/2018/11/why-we-need-to-audit-algorithms and https://www.technologyreview.com/2021/02/11/1017955/auditors-testing-ai-hiring-algorithms-bias-big-questions-remain/.

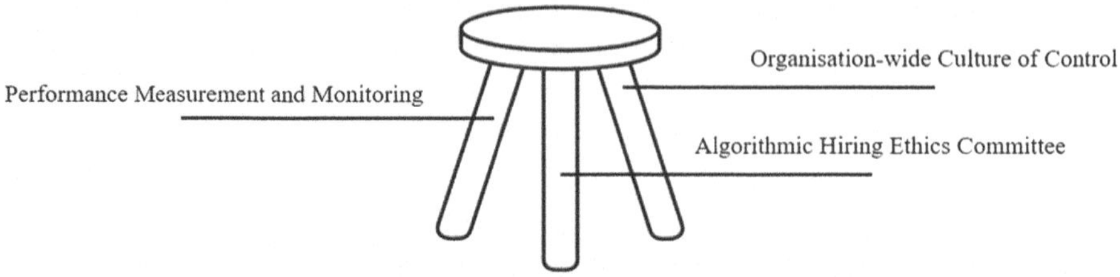

Fig. 1 Management control framework for supporting the development and use of algorithmic hiring systems

performance beyond assessing whether the algorithm generates discriminatory hiring outcomes long after system implementation (Fig. 1).

5 How Policymakers Can Support the Responsible Development and Use of Algorithmic Hiring Systems Within Organisations

Policymakers undoubtedly have an essential role in supporting the responsible development and use of algorithmic hiring systems. This section discusses how policymakers can balance regulation that protects society from harm while fostering innovation and promoting rigorous industry self-regulation.

5.1 Create AI Governance Frameworks that Foster Responsible Development and Utilisation of Algorithmic Hiring Systems Within Organisations

Policymakers globally are actively exploring the creation of broad AI governance frameworks to foster the responsible development and use of AI in society. For instance, the general approach in the EU is to create legally binding "hard law," such as the proposed Artificial Intelligence Act.[51] Alternatively, policymakers in other countries, including Japan and the U.S., are taking a non-binding "soft law" approach by developing guidelines, sets of principles, private standards, and partnership programs to regulate the development and use of AI.

Japan provides a fruitful example of adopting a "soft law" approach to regulating the development and use of AI in society. For instance, in 2016, Japan took the lead in introducing principles for AI research and development designed to guide related G7 and OECD discussions. Former Internal Affairs Minister Takaichi proposed that

[51] The EU's proposed AI Act, available at: https://artificialintelligenceact.eu/the-act/.

G7 countries take the lead in international discussions and formulate "AI R&D Guidelines," which consisted of eight "AI R&D Principles"—transparency, controllability, safety, security, privacy, ethics, user assistance, and accountability—as a non-binding international framework; the participating G7 and OECD countries agreed to the proposal. In 2017, the Ministry of Internal Affairs and Communications (MIC) released guidelines for developers—the "AI R&D Guidelines for International Discussions"[52] adding "collaboration" to the previously articulated eight principles, reflecting the critical principle of the interconnectivity and interoperability of AI systems.

Japan has actively continued to issue guidance in these areas. For instance, in 2019, the Cabinet Office's Council published "Social Principles of Human-Centric AI," focusing on factors society (especially state legislative and administrative bodies) should consider regarding AI. This complements and extends the "R&D and Utilization Principles of AI," which is intended to guide the developers and operators engaged in AI R&D and social implementation. The Social Principles provides seven principles for implementing AI in society—(1) human-centric, (2) education/literacy, (3) privacy, (4) ensuring security, (5) fair competition, (6) fairness, accountability, and transparency, and (7) innovation under the three basic philosophies: dignity, diversity and inclusion, and sustainability. Also in 2019, MIC issued "AI Utilization Guidelines," which consisted of ten principles to address the risks associated with AI systems.[53] These non-regulatory, non-binding soft laws are used by prominent Japanese companies, including SONY, Fujitsu, NEC, and NTT Data, to develop their AI policies and communicate them to external parties to enhance transparency and bolster accountability to all stakeholders.[54]

More recently, in July 2021, the Ministry of Economy, Trade, and Industry (METI) published "AI Governance in Japan Ver.1.1"[55] report in which it stated that AI governance should be designed mainly with soft laws in Japan at least at this moment from the perspective of balancing respect for AI principles and promotion of innovation. Also, it released "GOVERNANCE INNOVATION Ver. 2: A Guide to Designing and Implementing Agile Governance" which introduced the concept of "Agile Governance," which is a multi-stakeholder governance model to encourage the continual assessment of current conditions and risks, enhancing the agility and

---

[52] The Conference toward AI Network Society, Draft AI R&D Guidelines for International Discussions, 28 July 2017, available at: https://www.soumu.go.jp/main_content/000507517.pdf.

[53] The ten principles are: proper utilization, data quality, collaboration, safety, security, privacy, human dignity and individual autonomy, fairness, transparency, and accountability. The Conference toward AI Network Society, AI Utilization Guidelines - Practical Reference for AI Utilization, 9 August 2019, available at: https://www.soumu.go.jp/main_content/000658284.pdf.

[54] See, for example, NTT's "Our Approach to the Use and R&D of AI," available at: https://www.rd.ntt/e/ai/0005.html.

[55] "AI Governance in Japan" Ver.1.1, available at: https://www.meti.go.jp/shingikai/mono_info_service/ai_shakai_jisso/pdf/20210709_8.pdf.

flexibility of the desired end goal or system.[56] And in 2022, METI published "Governance Guidelines for Implementation of AI Principles Ver. 1.1," which guides how to analyse the risks associated with AI system implementations, among other topics, and offers illustrative examples to help organisations adopt the suggested principles.[57]

Japan is also amending sector-specific hard laws such as the Act on Improving Transparency and Fairness of Digital Platforms (TFDPA)[58] and the Financial Instruments and Exchange Act.[59] The TFDPA requires designated digital platform providers to ensure transparency and fairness in the digital market, intending to prevent violations of the Antimonopoly Act,[60] and the Financial Instruments and Exchange Act requires investors conducting high-speed algorithmic trading to register with the government and establish a risk management system, among other regulatory requirements.[61]

The evolving rulemaking in the U.S. also offers relevant examples. For instance, in late 2022, the White House Office of Science and Technology Policy issued "The Blueprint for an AI Bill of Rights: Making Automated Systems Work for the American People," which provides five non-binding principles that should guide the design, use, and deployment of automated systems—safe and effective systems, discrimination protections, data privacy, notice and explanation, and "human alternative, consideration, and fallback."[62] In July 2023, the White House secured voluntary commitments from Amazon, Anthropic, Google, Inflection, Meta, Microsoft, and OpenAI to move toward safe, secure, and transparent development of AI by (1) ensuring products are safe before introducing them to the public through internal and external security testing and sharing information across the industry and with governments, society, and academia on AI risks, (2) building systems that put security first by investing in cybersecurity and insider threat safeguards, and to facilitate third-party discovery and reporting of vulnerabilities in their AI systems, and (3) earning the public's trust by ensuring that the users know when content is AI generated, such as a watermarking system or publicly reporting their AI systems'

[56] Governance Innovation Ver. 2 - A Guide to Designing and Implementing Agile Governance, METI, available at: https://www.meti.go.jp/press/2021/07/20210730005/20210730005-2.pdf.

[57] Governance Guidelines for Implementation of AI Principles Ver. 1.1, available at: https://www.meti.go.jp/shingikai/mono_info_service/ai_shakai_jisso/pdf/20220128_2.pdf.

[58] https://elaws.e-gov.go.jp/document?lawid=502AC0000000038.

[59] https://www.japaneselawtranslation.go.jp/ja/laws/view/4405.

[60] https://www.meti.go.jp/english/mobile/2021/20210423001en.html.

[61] Amendments to Legislation on High Frequency Trading, Anderson Mori and Tomotsune, June 2017, available at: https://www.amt-law.com/asset/pdf/bulletins2_pdf/170614_00.pdf.

[62] The White House, "Blueprint For An AI Bill of Rights - Making Automated Systems Work For The American People," October 2022, available at: https://www.whitehouse.gov/wp-content/uploads/2022/10/Blueprint-for-an-AI-Bill-of-Rights.pdf.

capabilities, limitations, and areas of appropriate and inappropriate use.[63] Other federal-level actions on AI policy include the AI Accountability Policy led by NTIA/Department of Commerce[64] and ongoing efforts at the Equal Employment Opportunity Commission (EEOC)[65] and the National Institute of Standards and Technology (NIST).[66] For instance, in early 2023, NIST released the risk management framework "Artificial Intelligence Risk Management Framework (AI RMF 1.0),"[67] which is intended for voluntary use and aims to improve the ability to incorporate trustworthiness considerations into the design, development, use, and evaluation of AI products, services, and systems.[68]

As these examples illustrate, governments are beginning to issue guidance and frameworks to help support organisations' adherence to soft laws. The Japanese context provides some evidence that such an approach can provide at least some of the intended benefits. In 2005, METI created the "Information Security Governance" Policy Framework.[69] At the time, the Japanese government noticed the growing risk of information technology (IT) systems in organisations and society and recognised that organisations needed to ensure that appropriate information security measures were implemented proactively in consideration of organisations' social responsibilities. The government believed IT systems needed strong internal controls and helped establish an environment encouraging voluntary efforts by organisations to develop appropriate information security measures. In response, METI developed three tools for establishing information security governance: (1) an information security benchmark to help organisations rigorously and comprehensively self-assess the gap between their organisations current condition and a desirable level of information security, (2) a model for information security reporting to encourage organisations to disclose their information security efforts, thereby promoting security measures to customers, investors, and other stakeholders, and motivating third-party assessments of the reports, and (3) guidelines for business continuity planning to encourage organisations to develop such plans. This initiative has led many

[63] The White House, "Fact Sheet: Biden - Harris Administration Secures Voluntary Commitments from Leading Artificial Intelligence Companies to Manage the Risks Posed by AI," available at: https://www.whitehouse.gov/briefing-room/statements-releases/2023/07/21/fact-sheet-biden-harris-administration-secures-voluntary-commitments-from-leading-artificial-intelligence-companies-to-manage-the-risks-posed-by-ai/#:~:text=As%20part%20of%20this%20commitment,help%20move%20toward%20safe%2C%20secure%2C.

[64] NTIA website: https://ntia.gov/press-release/2023/ntia-receives-more-1400-comments-ai-accountability-policy.

[65] EEOC website: https://www.eeoc.gov/ai.

[66] AI Risk Management Framework (AI RMF 1.0), https://www.nist.gov/itl/ai-risk-management-framework.

[67] Ibid.

[68] AI RMF Development, NIST, available at: https://www.nist.gov/itl/ai-risk-management-framework/ai-rmf-development.

[69] Information Security Governance in Japan, OECD Homepage, available at: https://www.oecd.org/sti/ieconomy/35493201.pdf.

organisations to build robust information security governance. In the context of AI governance, creating informed frameworks may encourage management to establish robust AI governance within their organisations, perhaps functioning as part of their environmental, social, and governance (ESG) efforts.

While the examples highlighted from Japan and the U.S. are mainly soft-law approaches to policymaking, it is important to note that guidelines may be insufficient if organisations fail to adopt them due to their non-binding and voluntary nature.[70] In Japan, there is the belief that soft law works because of Japan's historical culture of government and business relations.[71] Japanese organisations often adopt government-issued non-binding guidelines, as the major organisations are often involved in the rulemaking process through membership in a government ministry's commission, and smaller organisations tend to follow larger organisations' lead. For example, this situation is believed to be why many Japanese organisations are already following MIC's guidelines on developing and using AI. More generally, for soft law to increase its credibility and effectiveness globally, it is fundamental for a soft-law program to include incentives so that stakeholders are motivated to implement and enforce them using a toolkit of organisational mechanisms. For instance, as Calo notes, organisational efforts to develop and publish high-minded principles in the context of AI are likely ineffective when those stated principles are unaccompanied by further action.[72] As the examples from Japan and the U.-S. demonstrate, governments can help this situation by providing frameworks and tools for organisations to follow and can become even more effective if combined with sector-specific hard law regulations.

Whether to take a hard law or soft law approach depends on each country's broader legal context of jurisdiction, including existing rules and regulations, legal culture, corporate culture—such as the level of business-government trust and adherence to soft laws—and the level of social sanctions organisations may face from non-adherence, among other factors. With AI's continual evolution, regulation requires flexibility to accommodate the uncertainty around its development in different contexts and across time. Flexibility is an advantage of soft law, and there is increasing awareness of the need for flexibility even within the hard law approach. For instance, in its feedback on the EU's proposed AI Act, the Leverhulme

---

[70] See Gary Marchant, "Why Soft Law is the Best Way to Approach the Pacing Problem in AI," Artificial Intelligence & Equality Initiative, September 29, 2021, available at: https://www.carnegiecouncil.org/media/article/why-soft-law-is-the-best-way-to-approach-the-pacing-problem-in-ai for an interesting discussion of this issue in the context of AI.

[71] See "Chapter 19 Government-Business Relations in Japan and Korea," Min Chen from "Understanding Business Environments," edited by Michael Lucas, Taylor & Francis Group, 2000. ProQuest Ebook Central, available at: http://ebookcentral.proquest.com/lib/georgetown/detail.action?docID=242233.

[72] Effective and Trustworthy Implementation of AI Soft Law Governance", IEEE TRANSACTIONS ON TECHNOLOGY AND SOCIETY, VOL. 2, NO. 4, DECEMBER 2021, https://par.nsf.gov/servlets/purl/10344125; Ryan Calo, Artificial Intelligence and the Carousel of Soft Law, IEEE Transactions on Technology and Society, Vol. 2, No. 4, December 2021, available at: https://ieeexplore.ieee.org/document/9539878 .

Centre for the Future of Intelligence and the Centre for the Study of Existential Risk suggested the Act allow for changes to the list of restricted and high-risk systems to be proposed, thereby increasing the proposed regulation's flexibility.[73]

5.2 *Protect Job Applicants and Employees from Risks Associated with Algorithmic Hiring Systems*

The previous section introduced how soft and hard law can have important roles in creating an AI governance framework that is both broadly applicable and can apply to the development and use of algorithmic hiring systems specifically. Yet, AI in the hiring process requires focused attention from policymakers, as employment-related issues can significantly impact individuals and society. Particularly, addressing the algorithmic hiring system risks discussed in Sect. 3 around collecting and using job applicant and employee data requires the (re)consideration of personal data protection laws and treatment of individuals' sensitive personal data.

In the U.S., at the federal level, while "The American Data Privacy Protection Act" is perhaps the closest the U.S. has come to passing federal legislation in the area, no comprehensive data protection law is currently in place, leaving a patchwork of multiple state-level data privacy laws. For instance, particularly on algorithmic hiring systems, the New York City Council enacted a law requiring organisations to notify employees and job candidates residing in NYC of the organisation's use of algorithms in the hiring process.[74] While such disclosure may prove beneficial in the short run, the use of algorithmic hiring tools is increasingly widespread, and job applicants will come to expect that they are interacting with such a system. Statements from the Federal Trade Commission indicate that it may take action if a recruitment system vendor informs clients that its algorithmic system provides "100% unbiased hiring decisions" while knowingly developing the algorithm using data that lacks racial or gender diversity, suggesting such statements would constitute deception.[75]

In Japan, the Act on the Protection of Personal Information (Act No. 57 of 2003; the "APPI"[76]) regulates the collection and use of personal data, which would apply to job applicants and employees. The basic rule is that when handling personal information, an organisation shall specify its purpose (Article 17) and obtain prior

[73] Feedback from: University of Cambridge (Leverhulme Centre for the Future of Intelligence and Centre for the Study of Existential Risk), https://ec.europa.eu/info/law/better-regulation/have-your-say/initiatives/12527-Artificial-intelligence-ethical-and-legal-requirements/F2665626_en.

[74] The New York City Council Homepage: https://legistar.council.nyc.gov/LegislationDetail.aspx?ID=4344524&GUID=B051915D-A9AC-451E-81F8-6596032FA3F9.

[75] U.S. FTC Homepage, Statement from a blog in April 2021, available at: https://www.ftc.gov/news-events/blogs/business-blog/2021/04/aiming-truth-fairness-equity-your-companys-use-ai.

[76] https://elaws.e-gov.go.jp/document?lawid=415AC0000000057.

consent beyond the scope of the initial purpose of use (Article 18). It also regulates the handling of personal data and forbids organisations from acquiring personal data by deception or other wrongful means (Article 20) and to promptly notify the individual or publicly announce the purpose of use when acquiring the personal data (Article 21). For sensitive personal data (referred to as "special care-required personal information"), prior consent is needed (Article 20, section 2) except in some instances where it is difficult to obtain consent. Here, sensitive personal data includes information relating to race, creed, social status, medical records, criminal records, criminal victimisation, and other data that need special care to prevent discrimination, prejudice, or disadvantage (Article 2, section 3).

Collecting data from job applicants during the recruitment process and from employees during workplace surveillance undoubtedly contains sensitive information such as enumerated above. While it may be the case that implied consent can be inferred by the data subject providing job application materials or working at the organisation, obtaining explicit consent from employees and job applicants when collecting and processing their personal data may be infeasible and impractical. It would appear that if organisations notify job applicants and employees that it is collecting their personal data for specific purposes such as developing algorithmic hiring systems, the data are pseudonymised and become unidentifiable at a glance, and measures are established that secure the identifiable personal data, organisations should be able to use the data without explicit consent.

However, in Japan, organisations are prohibited from providing data to third parties even with pseudonymisation (Article 41, section 6) due to the potential for reversing pseudonyms, thereby enabling the identification of individuals through malicious means and security breaches. In the EU, where the pseudonymised data is considered personal data, the EU General Court essentially ruled that if the recipient of information (e.g., third parties) cannot reidentify the individual after reidentification tests, the pseudonymised data will not constitute personal data.[77] The Court highlights that to assess whether reidentification is reasonably possible or not, this test of feasibility and effort shall be carried out from the perspective of the recipient of the information, opening the door to consider that in some cases, recipients of information not provided with the "key" to re-identify (and additional safeguards) may be out of the scope of the GDPR.[78] This ruling is well suited to the current status of data processing. As long as the data processor does not have access to the key to re-identify the individuals, it should be regarded as anonymised data to such a data processor, which would not constitute personal data and not require consent. Hence, the data would be available for algorithmic training data.

[77] Judgment of the General Court (Eighth Chamber, Extended Composition) of 26 April, 2023. Case T-557/20: https://eur-lex.europa.eu/legal-content/EN/TXT/?uri=CELEX%3A62020TJ0557.

[78] Santiago De Ampuero Castellanos, Gonzalo Gállego, Juan Ramón Robles, Hogan Lovells, Sending personal data, receiving non-personal data: Recent EU judgment reinforces the power of pseudonymization, https://www.jdsupra.com/legalnews/sending-personal-data-receiving-non-4948289/.

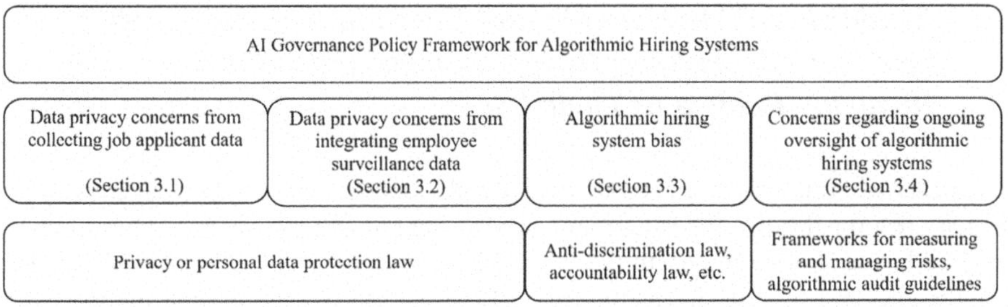

Fig. 2 Potential policy frameworks around algorithmic hiring system risks

To further address issues raised in Sect. 3 on data quality, algorithmic hiring bias, and the risks associated with performance monitoring and assessment, policymakers need to consider developing policies that enhance notions of equity, transparency, and accountability in hiring. Many but not all countries have anti-discrimination laws or equality acts. In the U.S., under laws enforced by EEOC,[79] it is illegal to discriminate against an individual (e.g., job applicant or employee) because of their race, color, religion, sex (including gender identity, sexual orientation, and pregnancy), national origin, age (40 or older), disability, or genetic information.[80] In contrast, Japan lacks comprehensive anti-discrimination laws, relying instead on several regulations in different sectors. For instance, the Labor Standards Act, Employment Security Act, and Equal Employment Opportunity Act require equal opportunity and treatment between men and women in employment. However, general anti-discrimination laws may be insufficient to address algorithmic biases. This situation has been recognised to some extent in the U.S., and several bills on algorithmic accountability being introduced. For example, Senators Ron Wyden and Cory Booker and Representative Yvette Clarke introduced the "Algorithmic Accountability Act of 2022"—an update of the 2019 Act—a bill which intended to increase transparency and accountability for automated decision systems.[81] The bill required organisations to conduct impact assessments for bias and assess algorithm effectiveness, among other factors, when using automated systems to make critical decisions; this would presumably apply to decisions made throughout the hiring process. However, the bill was rejected on 3 January 2023 after failing to pass before the 117th Congress adjourned (Fig. 2).[82]

[79] https://www.eeoc.gov/statutes/laws-enforced-eeoc.

[80] https://www.eeoc.gov/prohibited-employment-policiespractices.

[81] Ron Wyden Press release "Wyden, Booker and Clarke Introduce Algorithmic Accountability Act of 2022 To Require New Transparency And Accountability For Automated Decision Systems" (February 3, 2022) available at: https://www.wyden.senate.gov/news/press-releases/wyden-booker-and-clarke-introduce-algorithmic-accountability-act-of-2022-to-require-new-transparency-and-accountability-for-automated-decision-systems.

[82] Digital Policy Alert, "United States of America: Rejected Algorithmic Accountability Act of 2022," available at: https://digitalpolicyalert.org/event/8384-rejected-algorithmic-accountability-act-of-2022.

5.3 Establish an AI Oversight and Coordination Agency that Oversees Algorithmic Hiring Systems and Collects Incidents Related to Their Use

It appears reasonable for governments to embolden the government agency with primary responsibilities for labour and employment to actively oversee algorithmic-enabled hiring. For example, in the U.S., this agency is the EEOC. Title VII of the Civil Rights Act of 1964 forms the basis of regulatory oversight regarding discrimination in employment. It prohibits discrimination concerning several protected attributes ("race, color, religion, sex, and national origin"), establishing the EEOC to ensure compliance.[83] The EEOC, in turn, issued the Uniform Guidelines on Employment Selection Procedures (UGESP) in 1978 to set standards for how employers can choose their employees. The UGESP governs aspects of hiring discrimination pertinent to the algorithmic hiring system discussion.[84]

To this end, in late 2021, the EEOC launched the "Artificial Intelligence and Algorithmic Fairness Initiative" to guide organisations, vendors, employees, and job applicants to ensure that these tools are used fairly and consistently with U.S. federal equal employment opportunity laws.[85] As part of this initiative, the EEOC can investigate claims raised by job applicants of unfair algorithmic hiring practices and, if necessary, bring litigation against the organisation. The EEOC's efforts continue to be active and expanding, including the 2023 guidance "Assessing Adverse Impact in Software, Algorithms, and Artificial Intelligence Used in Employment Selection Procedures Under Title VII of the Civil Rights Act of 1964." [86] This guidance is part of the EEOC's 2021 agency-wide initiative to ensure that utilising AI, machine learning, and other emerging technologies in hiring and other employment decisions complies with federal civil rights laws.

This newly-issued guidance addresses the potential discriminatory impact of using algorithmic tools in the hiring process, highlighting examples of tools that organisations should be mindful of as potential sources of bias—resume scanners that prioritise applications using specific keywords, employee-monitoring software that rates employees based on their keystrokes or other factors, virtual assistants or chatbots that ask job candidates about their qualifications and reject those who do not meet predefined requirements, video interviewing software that evaluates candidates

---

[83] Title VII of the Civil rights Act of 1964, EEOC, available at: https://www.eeoc.gov/statutes/title-vii-civil-rights-act-1964.

[84] Equal Employment Opportunity Commission, Civil Service Commission et al., Uniform guidelines on employee selection procedures. Federal Register, 43(166):38290–38315, 1978.

[85] Artificial Intelligence and Algorithmic Fairness Initiative, EEOC, available at: https://www.eeoc.gov/ai.

[86] Select Issues: Assessing Adverse Impact in Software, Algorithms, and Artificial Intelligence Used in Employment Selection Procedures Under Title VII of the Civil Rights Act of 1964, EEOC, available at: https://www.eeoc.gov/select-issues-assessing-adverse-impact-software-algorithms-and-artificial-intelligence-used.

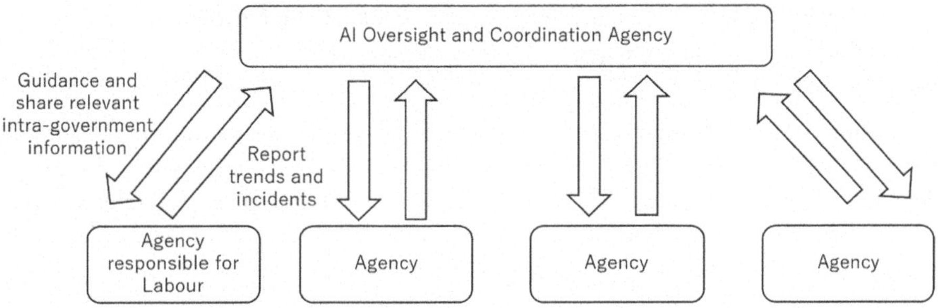

Fig. 3 AI Oversight and Coordination Agency

based on their facial expressions and speech patterns, and tests that yield "job fit" scores for applicants or employees regarding their personalities, aptitudes, cognitive skills or perceived "cultural fit" based on their performance on a game or traditional test. The guidance provides direction for evaluating the extent to which bias may permeate a process, states that organisations may still be liable for their vendors' violations of federal employment discrimination laws, and reminds organisations that AI systems are not wholly objective because humans develop them and are subject to biases that can create disparate hiring outcomes.

Although individual agencies (departments, ministries) can oversee the responsible development and use of AI in general and algorithmic hiring systems in particular, it may be the case that a single agency should possess the authority to coordinate intra-government collaboration and promote partnerships between industry, academia, and the public and private sectors. For instance, in the U.S., the Department of Commerce recently established a high-level committee to advise the President and other federal agencies on a range of AI-related issues.[87] Japan does not currently have an agency that oversees AI in general or AI hiring in particular. The National Center for Incident Readiness and Strategy of Cybersecurity (NISC) plays a leading role in cybersecurity as a focal point in coordinating intra-government collaboration and promoting partnerships between industry, academia, and the public and private sectors,[88] so it may be reasonable to expand NISC's role to include coordinating intra-government cooperation on the issues arising from the development and use of AI and also have Japan's Ministry of Health, Labour and Welfare examine the progress of the U.S.'s EEOC (Fig. 3).

[87] U.S. Department of Commerce Homepage, https://www.commerce.gov/news/press-releases/2021/09/department-commerce-establishes-national-artificial-intelligence.

[88] NISC website: https://www.nisc.go.jp/eng/index.html.

5.4 *Collect, Analyse, and Report Failures and Incidents Caused by Algorithmic Hiring Systems*

Algorithmic hiring system failures and incidents will occur at the organisational level. However, these failures and incidents have broad social implications, as hiring decisions impact job outcomes, with trickle-down consequences for families and even where individuals and families live. Given the local nature of failures and incidents and their broader social implications, policymakers can consider establishing a mechanism that collects and analyses AI failures and incidents, including those related to algorithmic hiring. For instance, governments can establish a third-party organisation or independent agency similar to the aviation (U.-S. Federal Aviation Administration,[89] Japan Transport Safety Board[90]), transportation (U.S. National Highway Traffic Safety Administration,[91] Japan's Institute for Traffic Accident Research and Data Analysis[92]), consumer products safety (U.S. Consumer Products Safety Commission,[93] Japan's Consumer Safety Investigation Commission[94]), pharmaceuticals (U.S. Food and Drug Administration[95]) and information security (Computer Security Incident Response Team,[96] JPCERT/CC[97]) areas that collects, analyses, and reports the seemingly unavoidable failures and incidents that will arise from the development and use of AI-based technologies, particularly incidents from algorithmic hiring systems that have broad societal outcomes (e.g., vendor-developed systems that are deployed across multiple organisations, which could impact tens of thousands of job applicants and employees).

6 Summary and Conclusion

The hiring process has long lacked transparency. While organisations must comply with existing laws prohibiting discrimination in employment, they nonetheless have the latitude to hire candidates they believe will perform well. Whether conscious or unconscious, human bias inevitably plays a role in hiring decisions. While creating algorithmic tools poses challenges, there is a promising way forward by raising

[89] Accident & Incident Data: https://www.faa.gov/data_research/accident_incident.

[90] JTSB: http://www.mlit.go.jp/jtsb/english.html.

[91] NHTSA: https://www.nhtsa.gov/recalls.

[92] Institute for Traffic Accident Research and Data Analysis (Japan): https://www.itarda.or.jp/.

[93] Consumer Product Safety Commission: https://www.cpsc.gov/Recalls.

[94] Consumer Safety Investigation Commission: https://www.caa.go.jp/policies/council/csic/.

[95] Recalls, Market Withdrawals, & Safety Alerts, FDA: https://www.fda.gov/safety/recalls-market-withdrawals-safety-alerts.

[96] CSIRT: https://www.csirt.org/index.html.

[97] JPCERT/CC: https://www.jpcert.or.jp/english/.

human awareness about human biases and data-related issues. Particularly, algorithmic hiring systems can promote transparency if individuals understand the reasoning behind the systems' outcomes. A concept known as "explainable AI" offers potential solutions, providing insights into how AI-based decisions are reached. By incorporating explainable AI, black-box AI hiring systems can become more transparent and accountable, enhancing the overall ability of AI hiring systems to deliver on their intended goals.[98]

Algorithmic hiring systems are trained on the personal data of job applicants and past and current employees. Some of this personal data may be viewed as sensitive personal data. While implementing strict data protection laws that safeguard individuals' rights may become the center of debate globally, personal data protection laws that are overly strict may come at the cost of hindering innovation, particularly in the algorithmic hiring context. We should never forget the legislative purpose of personal data protection law—individuals do not want their names to be revealed in public or used in a way that would bring personal harm. Obtaining consent is becoming a mere formality, as individuals lack the technical knowledge of what they may be consenting to, and organisations use data in ways that were unforeseeable when the data has been collected. It remains important to reconsider how organisations notify job applicants and employees of what data are being collected and the potential purposes for which their data may be utilised. To balance personal data protection with AI development, involving organisations in developing soft and hard laws is increasingly important.

This chapter has highlighted emerging risks in the use of algorithms in the hiring process, including risks associated with job applicant data privacy, past and current employee data privacy, algorithmic-enabled hiring biases, and the risk that organisations will adopt too narrow of a lens on the ongoing monitoring and assessment of algorithmic hiring system performance. In analysing these risks, we have discussed how organisations can implement management controls to engage in risk management, and policymakers can devise frameworks and regulations that balance the perceived benefits of algorithmic hiring systems with emerging risks.

An interesting inter-disciplinary interplay exists between organisations improving the governance and management controls around algorithmic hiring as part of their environmental, social, and governance (ESG) practices and policymaking that balances society's needs with organisations' desire to foster innovation. The following recommendations shed light on this interplay:

Organisations can consider the following:

[98] Examples of "Explainable AI" projects in the U.S. and Japan: DARPA (https://www.darpa.mil/program/explainable-artificial-intelligence), IBM (https://www.ibm.com/watson/explainable-ai?utm_content=SRCWW&p1=Search&p4=43700064515261154&p5=e&gclid=Cj0KCQiA_8OPBhDtARIsAKQu0gbpp4lCILcpxGx_StSlNqWc6plfR0R4HB3iXA0g8c4RUugk47gQi1IaAqzREALw_wcB&gclsrc=aw.ds), Google (https://cloud.google.com/explainable-ai), NEC (https://www.nec.com/en/global/solutions/ai/xai/index.html), Fujitsu and Hokkaido University (https://www.fujitsu.com/global/about/resources/news/press-releases/2021/0204-01.html).

1. Creating guidelines on the development and use of algorithms in the hiring process, including a code of conduct, internal R&D guidelines, and AI utilisation principles, and providing publicly-accessible documents on how the organisation develops and utilises algorithmic hiring systems.
2. Ensuring robust, centralised control over algorithmic hiring systems by forming an interdisciplinary team—an "Algorithmic Hiring Ethics Committee"—with broad authority to oversee algorithm use across the hiring process.
3. Establishing ongoing performance monitoring of algorithmic hiring systems and accountability for results.

Policymakers can consider the following:

1. Creating AI governance frameworks that foster organisations' responsible development and utilisation of algorithmic hiring systems.
2. Developing policies and regulations that protect job applicants and employees from data privacy risks, data quality, algorithmic bias, and the risks related to performance monitoring and assessment associated with algorithmic hiring systems.
3. Establishing an AI Oversight and Coordination Agency that oversees algorithmic hiring systems.
4. Collecting, analysing, and reporting failures and incidents caused by algorithmic hiring systems.

It appears inevitable that advancements in artificial intelligence will transform many aspects of the hiring process as recruitment system technologies evolve. We should always consider when and where it is appropriate to use algorithms in the hiring process and refrain from fully yielding our human ability to make hiring and employment-related decisions.

Acknowledgements I would like to thank Professor Jack Balkin, Professor Anupam Chander and my colleagues at Georgetown Institute for Technology Law & Policy and the Yale Information Society Project for their support and encouragement.

This work was supported by JST Moonshot R&D Grant Number JPMJMS2215.

References

Journals and Articles

Ajunwa I (2020) The paradox of automation as anti-bias intervention. Cardozo Law Rev 41

Garr SS, Jackson C (2019) Diversity & inclusion technology: the rise of a transformative market. Technical report, RedThread Research

Kim PT (2018) Big data and artificial intelligence: new challenges for workplace equality. Univ Louisville Law Rev 57:313

Kim PT (2020) Manipulating opportunity. Virginia Law Rev 106

Kramer RSS, Ward R (2010) Internal facial features are signals of personality and health. Q J Exp Psychol 63(11):2273–2287

Leidner D, Tona O, Wixom BH, Someh IA (2021) Putting dignity and the core of employee data use. MIT Sloan Manag Rev

Mariotti A (2017) Talent acquisition benchmarking report. Technical report, Society for Human Resource Management

Neumark D, Bank RJ, Van Nort KD (1996) Sex discrimination in restaurant hiring: an audit study. Q J Econ 111(3):915–941

Riach PA, Rich J (2002) Field experiments of discrimination in the marketplace. Econ J 112(483): F480–F518

Sidanius J, Crane M (1989) Job evaluation and gender: the case of university faculty. J Appl Soc Psychol 19(2):174–197

Books and Chapters

Bogen M, Rieke A (2018) Help wanted: an exploration of hiring algorithms, equity, and bias. Technical report, Upturn

De Stefano V, Doellgast V (2023) Regulating AI at work: labour relations, automation, and algorithmic management. Transfer 29(1):9–20

Merchant K, Van der Stede W (2017) Management control systems: performance measurement, evaluation and incentives, 4th edn

Proceedings and Conference Papers

Sanchez-Monedero J, Dencik L, Edwards L (2020) What does it mean to solve the problem of discrimination in hiring? Social, technical and legal perspectives from the UK on automated hiring systems. In Proceedings of the conference on fairness, accountability, and transparency. ACM, 2020

Zhou D, Luo J, Silenzio VMB, Zhou Y, Hu J, Currier G, Kautz H (2015) Tackling mental health by integrating unobtrusive multimodal sensing. In 29th AAAI conference on artificial intelligence, 2015

Online Publications

Banaschik M How location tracking is raising the stakes on privacy protection. EY. Available at https://www.ey.com/en_gl/forensic-integrity-services/how-location-tracking-is-raising-the-stakes-on-privacy-protection

Blackman R Why you need an AI ethics committee. Harvard Business Review, July-August 2002. https://hbr.org/2022/07/why-you-need-an-ai-ethics-committee

Business Wire Homepage. https://www.businesswire.com/news/home/20211018005055/en/Nine-in-10-Americans-Believe-Bots-Will-Be-Important-for-the-Future-of-Work

Calo R Artificial Intelligence and the Carousel of Soft Law, IEEE Transactions on Technology and Society, 2, 4, December 2021. Available at https://ieeexplore.ieee.org/document/9539878

Cappelli P, Tambe P, Yakubovich V (2018) Artificial intelligence in human resources management: challenges and a path forward. Available at SSRN 3263878

Chamorro-Premuzic T, Winsborough D, Sherman RA, Hogan R (2016) New talent signals: Shiny new objects or a brave new world? Industrial and Organisational Psychology 9(3):621–640. https://www.weforum.org/agenda/2021/09/case-study-on-ibm-ethical-use-of-artificial-intelligence-technology/

Chen M (2000) Chapter 19, Government-business relations in Japan and Korea. In: Lucas M (ed) Understanding business environments. Taylor & Francis Group, ProQuest Ebook Central, Hoboken. http://ebookcentral.proquest.com/lib/georgetown/detail.action?docID=242233

De Castellanos SA, Gállego G, Robles JR, Lovells H Sending personal data, receiving non-personal data: recent EU judgment reinforces the power of pseudonymization. https://www.jdsupra.com/legalnews/sending-personal-data-receiving-non-4948289/

DIGIDAY Homepage. https://digiday.com/marketing/ai-is-being-used-to-recruit-and-onboard-talent/

Digital Policy Alert. United States of America: Rejected Algorithmic Accountability Act of 2022. Available at https://digitalpolicyalert.org/event/8384-rejected-algorithmic-accountability-act-of-2022

Engler A Auditing employment algorithms for discrimination, Brookings, 12 March 2021. Available at https://www.brookings.edu/research/auditing-employment-algorithms-for-discrimination//

Government Matters Homepage. https://govmatters.tv/eeoc-working-to-stop-artificial-intelligence-from-perpetuating-bias-in-hir-ing/#:~:text=With%2083%25%20of%20U.S.%20employers,assistance%20to%20employers%2C%20Burrows%20said

Guszcza J, Rahwan I, Bible W, Cebrian M, Katyal V (2018) Why we need to audit algorithms, Harvard Business Review, 28 November 2018. https://hbr.org/2018/11/why-we-need-to-audit-algorithms/

IBM Homepage. ibm.com/analytics/data-quality (last accessed 24 November 2021). https://newsroom.ibm.com/The-Davos-Agenda-Fostering-Responsible-AI-Leadership

KPMG Homepage. https://info.kpmg.us/news-perspectives/technology-innovation/thriving-in-an-ai-world/ai-adoption-accelerated-during-pandemic.html. Accessed 18 July 2023

Marchant G Why soft law is the best way to approach the pacing problem in AI. Artificial Intelligence & Equality Initiative, September 29, 2021., https://www.carnegiecouncil.org/media/article/why-soft-law-is-the-best-way-to-approach-the-pacing-problem-in-ai

Mercer Homepage. https://www.mercer.com/content/dam/mercer/attachments/private/global-talent-trends-2020-report.pdf

PRWeb 71% of hiring decision-makers agree social media is effective for screening applicants. https://www.prweb.com/releases/71_of_hiring_decision_makers_agree_social_media_is_effective_for_screening_applicants/prweb17467312.htm

Raghavan M, Barocas S, Kleinberg J, Levy K. Mitigating bias in algorithmic hiring: evaluating claims and practices. https://arxiv.org/pdf/1906.09208.pdf. Accessed 12 January 2022

Schellmann H Auditors are testing hiring algorithms for bias, but there's no easy fix, 11 February 2021. MIT Technology Review. Available at https://www.technologyreview.com/2021/02/11/1017955/auditors-testing-ai-hiring-algorithms-bias-big-questions-remain/

The Markup Homepage. https://themarkup.org/news/2021/12/23/public-agencies-are-buying-up-ai-driven-hiring-tools-and-bossware

Zabow B Tracking of employee location data is a significant violation of privacy according to the Israeli Privacy Protection Authority, INPLP. Available at https://inplp.com/latest-news/article/tracking-of-employee-location-data-is-a-significant-violation-of-privacy-according-to-the-israeli-privacy-protection-authority/

Laws, Guidelines, Cases of International Institutions, Countries/ Areas

EU

The proposed Artificial Intelligence Act. https://artificialintelligenceact.eu/the-act/
Feedback from: University of Cambridge (Leverhulme Centre for the Future of Intelligence and Centre for the Study of Existential Risk). (2021). https://ec.europa.eu/info/law/better-regulation/have-your-say/initiatives/12527-Artificial-intelligence-ethical-and-legal-requirements/F2665626_en

Cases

Judgment of the General Court (Eighth Chamber, Extended Composition) of 26 April 2023. Case T-557/20: https://eur-lex.europa.eu/legal-content/EN/TXT/?uri=CELEX%3A62020TJ0557. Accessed 27 July 2023.

Japan

Act on the Protection of Personal Information. https://elaws.e-gov.go.jp/document?lawid=415AC0000000057
AI R&D Guidelines for International Discussions. MIC. 28 July 2017., https://www.soumu.go.jp/main_content/000507517.pdf
AI utilization guidelines - Practical reference for AI utilization. MIC. 9 August 2019., https://www.soumu.go.jp/main_content/000658284.pdf
AI Governance in Japan Ver.1.1, METI, 9 July 2021. https://www.meti.go.jp/shingikai/mono_info_service/ai_shakai_jisso/pdf/20210709_8.pdf
Amendments to Legislation on High Frequency Trading, Anderson Mori and Tomotsune, June 2017. https://www.amt-law.com/asset/pdf/bulletins2_pdf/170614_00.pdf
Consumer Safety Investigation Commission. https://www.caa.go.jp/policies/council/csic/
Employment Security Act. https://elaws.e-gov.go.jp/document?lawid=322AC0000000141
Governance Innovation Ver. 2 - A guide to designing and implementing agile governance,. METI. 30 July 2021. Available at https://www.meti.go.jp/press/2021/07/20210730005/20210730005-2.pdf
Governance Guidelines for Implementation of AI Principles Ver. 1.1. METI. 28 January 2022. https://www.meti.go.jp/shingikai/mono_info_service/ai_shakai_jisso/pdf/20220128_2.pdf
Information Security Governance in Japan. OECD Homepage. https://www.oecd.org/sti/ieconomy/35493201.pdf
Institute for Traffic Accident Research and Data Analysis (Japan). https://www.itarda.or.jp/
JPCERT/CC. https://www.jpcert.or.jp/english/
JTSB. http://www.mlit.go.jp/jtsb/english.html
Making the digital market easier to use: The act on improving transparency and fairness of digital platforms (TFDPA), METI. (2021). https://www.meti.go.jp/english/mobile/2021/20210423001en.html
NISC website. https://www.nisc.go.jp/eng/index.html
NTT "Our Approach to the Use and R&D of AI". https://www.rd.ntt/e/ai/0005.html

U.S.A.

Consumer Product Safety Commission. https://www.cpsc.gov/Recalls

CSIRT. https://www.csirt.org/index.html

Department of Commerce. https://www.commerce.gov/news/press-releases/2021/09/department-commerce-establishes-national-artificial-intelligence

EEOC. https://www.eeoc.gov/ai; https://www.eeoc.gov/statutes/laws-enforced-eeoc; https://www.eeoc.gov/prohibited-employment-policiespractices; https://www.eeoc.gov/statutes/title-vii-civil-rights-act-1964; https://www.eeoc.gov/select-issues-assessing-adverse-impact-software-algorithms-and-artificial-intelligence-used

FAA. https://www.faa.gov/data_research/accident_incident

FTC. Statement from a blog in April 2021. https://www.ftc.gov/news-events/blogs/business-blog/2021/04/aiming-truth-fairness-equity-your-companys-use-ai

FDA. https://www.fda.gov/safety/recalls-market-withdrawals-safety-alerts

The New York City Council Homepage. https://legistar.council.nyc.gov/LegislationDetail.aspx?ID=4344524&GUID=B051915D-A9AC-451E-81F8-6596032FA3F9

NHTSA. https://www.nhtsa.gov/recalls

NIST. AI Risk Management Framework (AI RMF 1.0). https://www.nist.gov/itl/ai-risk-management-framework and https://www.nist.gov/itl/ai-risk-management-framework/ai-rmf-development

NTIA. https://ntia.gov/press-release/2023/ntia-receives-more-1400-comments-ai-accountability-policy

The White House. Blueprint for an AI bill of rights - making automated systems work for the American people. October 2022. https://www.whitehouse.gov/wp-content/uploads/2022/10/Blueprint-for-an-AI-Bill-of-Rights.pdf

The White House. Fact sheet: Biden - Harris administration secures voluntary commitments from leading artificial intelligence companies to manage the risks posed by AI. (2023). https://www.whitehouse.gov/briefing-room/statements-releases/2023/07/21/fact-sheet-biden-harris-administration-secures-voluntary-commitments-from-leading-artificial-intelligence-companies-to-manage-the-risks-posed-by-ai/#:~:text=As%20part%20of%20this%20commitment,help%20move%20toward%20safe%2C%20secure%2C

Newspapers and Press Releases

The Japan Times. https://www.japantimes.co.jp/news/2019/09/06/business/corporate-business/ministry-says-recruit-career-acted-illegally-rikunabi-data-scandal-demands-corrective-steps/ and https://www.japantimes.co.jp/news/2019/08/27/business/corporate-business/recruit-career-job-data-scandal/

Ron Wyden Press release. Wyden, Booker and Clarke Introduce Algorithmic Accountability Act of 2022 To Require New Transparency And Accountability For Automated Decision Systems (February 3, 2022). Available at https://www.wyden.senate.gov/news/press-releases/wyden-booker-and-clarke-introduce-algorithmic-accountability-act-of-2022-to-require-new-transparency-and-accountability-for-automated-decision-systems

Various news articles compiled by Anonymous. (2016-08-10) Incident Number 37. in McGregor, S. (ed.) Artificial Intelligence Incident Database. Partnership on AI from incidentdatabase.ai/cite/37

Various news articles compiled by Lutz, Roman. (2019-11-06) Incident Number 95. in McGregor, S. (ed.) Artificial Intelligence Incident Database. Partnership on AI from incidentdatabase.ai/cite/95

AI Gender Biases in Women's Healthcare: Perspectives from the United Kingdom and the European Legal Space

Pin Lean Lau

Contents

Abstract This paper engages with a key debate surrounding artificial intelligence in health and medicine, with an emphasis on women's healthcare. In particular, the paper seeks to capture the lack of gender parity where women's health is concerned, a consequence of systemic biases and discrimination in both historical and contemporary medical and health data. The existing literature review demonstrates that there is not only a gender data gap in AI technologies and data science fields—but there is also a gender data gap in women's healthcare that results in algorithmic gender bias, impacting negatively on women's healthcare experiences, treatment protocols, and finally, rights in health. On this basis, the article seeks to offer a concise exploration of the gender-related aspects of medicine and healthcare, shedding light on the biases encountered by women in the context of AI-driven

P. L. Lau (✉)
Brunel Law School, Brunel University London, London, UK
e-mail: PinLean.Lau@brunel.ac.uk

E. Gill-Pedro, A. Moberg (eds.), *YSEC Yearbook of Socio-Economic Constitutions 2023*, YSEC Yearbook of Socio-Economic Constitutions (2024) 2023: 247–274,
https://doi.org/10.1007/16495_2023_63, Published online: 8 December 2023

healthcare. Subsequently, it conducts a doctrinal comparative law examination of the existing legislative landscape to scrutinise whether current supranational AI regulations or legal frameworks explicitly encompass the protection of fundamental rights for female patients in the realm of health AI. The scope of this analysis encompasses the legal framework governing AI-driven technologies within the European Union (EU), the Council of Europe (CoE), and, to a limited extent, the United Kingdom (UK). Lastly, this paper explores the potential utility of data feminism (that draws on intersectionality theory) as an additional tool for advancing gender equity in healthcare.

1 Introduction

The use of artificial intelligence (AI) in the modern healthcare system and biomedicine has enabled the transformation of techniques, tools and methods of healthcare and medical delivery and treatment. For example, rehabilitative robotics are instrumental in helping patients re-acquire motor skills, through 'implementation of efficient robot strategies' that allows these AI systems to behave as 'trainers' for the human sensory motor systems.[1] Other uses of AI in biomedical health are also relevant for patient monitoring, genetic algorithms, optimisation techniques,[2] and other machine learning methodologies that would support the processing of large amounts of data for diagnostic purposes.

As healthcare tech companies enter the space of health data, either by acquiring or collaborating with small, health-focused companies, to help them 'manage' data, continued deep ethical solutions is necessary: to balance individuals' rights in biomedicine, against the 'paternalistic' non-opt out of health-search tools.[3] The establishment of the European Health Data Space (EHDS)[4] serves the core purpose of facilitating the secure and interoperable exchange of health data across European Union (EU) Member States to enhance healthcare outcomes, research, and system efficiency. It aims to promote cross-border health data sharing, support healthcare research and innovation, improve patient care quality, monitor public health, ensure data privacy and security, foster interoperability, empower patients in controlling their health data, address health inequalities, and create a robust ecosystem for health innovation. This move, for one, demonstrates that practical applications of AI in biomedicine, continue to serve in importance for a plethora of medical treatments, research, and diagnostics.[5]

[1] Colombo and Sanguineti (2018).

[2] Vlamos et al. (2013).

[3] Copeland et al. (2020).

[4] 'European Health Data Space' (12 May 2023) <https://health.ec.europa.eu/ehealth-digital-health-and-care/european-health-data-space_en> accessed on 16 September 2023.

[5] Lee and Yoon (2021).

Notwithstanding these positive developments, the use and deployment of AI in healthcare still does not adequately represent most communities. Unlike AI technologies in other industries, AI in healthcare warrants special consideration because of its implications on public and individual health and lives. For instance, big datasets of health data (including personal data) are usually used to train AI algorithms to be used in healthcare systems. High-quality health data is difficult to gather, as it is often unstructured, incorrect (due to measurement mistakes in self-reported health or medical records) and biased (due to absence of inclusive clinical data and underrepresentation of minorities). Inaccuracies in the large training datasets might cause outcomes that are prejudicial, and could result in personal harm, or even death. Racial and gender prejudice may result in inaccurate diagnosis and exacerbate existing socioeconomic disparity. The right of patients to have full knowledge and informed consent to medical treatment is threatened by a lack of openness and the capacity to explain algorithms, findings, and techniques resulting from algorithms, with vulnerable groups possibly being at increased risk of damage as a result.

In the context of women's general healthcare which is the subject of this chapter, the existing literature review demonstrates that there is clearly a gender data gap in AI technologies and data science fields.[6] Because traditional evaluations of women's healthcare, including prospective iterations of AI use in these fields, have rarely focused on biological differences between men and women (with the exception of gynaecological specifics and/or breast cancer)—even until today—most of the available data in women's healthcare also present the gender gap problem. This gender data gap in women's healthcare ultimately results in algorithmic gender bias when AI systems are used to evaluate the data,[7] especially impacting negatively on women's healthcare experiences, treatment protocols, and finally, their rights in health.[8]

On this basis, the main inquiries in this paper are three-fold. First, it provides a brief explanation of the gendered dimensions of medicine and healthcare, and how biases in women's healthcare vis-à-vis AI have been presented. Second, through a doctrinal analysis of the legislative landscape, it questions if existing supranational AI legislation or legal frameworks expressly provide for the fundamental rights protection of women patients in health AI. This paper seeks to analyse the legal framework for AI-driven technologies within the jurisdiction of the EU, the Council of Europe (CoE) and (limitedly) the United Kingdom (UK) by using a simple comparative law approach. Third, this paper enquires if data feminism,[9] may be suggested as an additional tool to increase health equality for women. For avoidance of doubt, references to gender or sex in this paper is intended to encompass women.

---

[6] Cleghorn (2021).

[7] Criado-Perez (2020).

[8] Danesi (2021).

[9] D'Ignazio and Klein (2020).

2 The Gender Gap in Medicine and Healthcare

The history of medicine, tracing back to 2600 BC, has not solely been a scientific exploration diseases, medicine, and medical treatment; it has also served as a reflection of societal and cultural norms[10] that have deeply entrenched the role of the man within its foundations. Despite the current presence of women in prominent positions within the field of medicine, the historical narrative reveals immense challenges faced by women as physicians and clinicians in their quest for gender equality. In May 2021, the Department of Health and Social Care in England released a report of an independent review by the British Medical Association (BMA)[11] shedding light on the gender pay gap in medicine. The report's findings underscored the persistence of a substantial wage disparity, with women general practitioners earning 15.3% less than men, and clinical academics earning 11.9% less than men.[12] Another BMA report, titled Sexism in Medicine,[13] uncovered deeply troubling and alarming shocking and concerning levels of sexism in the medical profession. This sexism manifested in various forms ways within the institutional structure of the National Health Service (NHS) and the medical field in the United Kingdom (UK).[14] Consequently, it comes as no surprise that the historical mistreatment of women as patients seeking medical treatment or interventions, mirrors the injustices faced by women within the medical profession.

In the United Nations' International Women's Day 2023 theme, DigitALL: Innovation and Technology for Gender Equality,[15] it was highlighted that women still experience digital inequalities, with only 22% of women making up the global percentage of work in AI, and at least 44% of 133 AI systems across industries found to demonstrate gender bias.[16]

Further governmental reports in the United Kingdom (UK) have highlighted the gender data gap in medicine, resulting in lower quality of healthcare for women. For example, the Cumberlege Report[17] was an independent review of specific medicines and medical devices—its main findings indicated that women who had been the subject of those specific interventions suffered harm the most. It also found that the healthcare system (including the UK NHS (National Health Service), private

[10] Kushner (2008).

[11] British Medical Association (2021).

[12] Ibid., 1.

[13] British Medical Association and Jewett (2021).

[14] Ibid., 3.

[15] United Nations, 'DigitALL: Innovation and Technology for Gender Equality - UN Observance of International Women's Day 2023 | UN Web TV' (*UN Web TV*, 8 March 2023) <https://media.un.org/en/asset/k1m/k1mpovmzy5> accessed on 12 March 2023.

[16] 'In Focus: International Women's Day' (*UN Women – Headquarters*, 1 March 2023) <https://www.unwomen.org/en/news-stories/in-focus/2023/03/in-focus-international-womens-day> accessed on 13 March 2023.

[17] Cumberlege (2020).

providers, professional organisations and regulators, and pharmaceutical and device manufacturers) is 'disjointed, siloed, unresponsive and defensive. It does not adequately recognize that patients are its *raison d'etre*'.[18] Another report issued by MBRRACE-UK (Mothers and Babies: Reducing Risks through Audits and Confidential Enquiries across the UK)[19] found that systemic biases concerning pregnancy and maternal health, amongst other issues, were deeply ingrained in women's healthcare, particularly affecting women of colour from lower income communities.[20]

3 Systemic Biases in Women's Healthcare and AI Algorithm Biases

3.1 Androcentricity in Medicine and Healthcare

Technoscience and techno-cultural studies have historically been dominated by men—not only from a scientific perspective, but also through cultural and sociological practices.[21] Technologies, as a whole, viewed through the lens of techno-cultural storytelling,[22] excluded women and their bodies from the advancement of technologies. The pervasiveness of androcentricity[23] in medicine contributes to this exclusion, highlighting the likelihood that 'ongoing discrepancies in the care of female patients'[24] do have a significant impact on patient care through the experience of female patients.

This is not to imply that the feminist techno-science field has been insignificant since the mid-1990s. For example, prominent scholars such as Donna Haraway in '*Modest_Witness@Second_Millennium. FemaleMan©_Meets_OncoMouse™. Feminism and Technoscience*',[25] explores how boundaries between technology and culture are shaped, constructed and situated in the sphere of feminist engagement with technoscience. Sandra Harding's work emphasises the importance of addressing gender bias and cultural values in scientific theory through Standpoint Theory,[26] the notion that perspectives of marginalised and/or oppressed individuals can help to create more objective accounts of the world. In Karen Barad's seminal

[18] Ibid.
[19] MBRRACE-UK et al. (2020).
[20] Ibid.
[21] Lan (2012), p. 166.
[22] Paxling (2019).
[23] Merone et al. (2022), p. 49.
[24] Merone (2022), p. 6.
[25] Haraway (1997).
[26] Harding (2009), p. 192.

work,[27] she challenges the notion that questions concerning the interaction and evolution of nature and culture are fundamentally flawed. Instead, she redefines our comprehension of scientific and political activities and their intricate interplay. Consequently, she places significant emphasis on the ethical conduct of science and underscores shifts in our comprehension of political actions, critically revising Judith Butler's influential performativity theory.[28] These examples, encompassing a trove of important feminist scholarship in techno-science, amongst other notables, represent an alternative view in the frontiers of technologies and law scholarship. Nevertheless, whilst these remain important and critical works that seek to pivot the manner and approaches for health and medicine, mostly through the employment of various feminist theories and methodologies, the pervasive androcentricity of hundreds of years of systemic in-graining tend to overshadow them.

This pervasive androcentricity in medicine and healthcare consequentially translates into medical and clinical data. According to Kate Young:

> Medicine defines the female and male bodies as distinct but not equal; analyses of medical texts throughout history reveals the male body to be constructed as superior and the template against which bodies are judged. Any aspect of the female body that differs from the male or that cannot be given a male comparative (exemplified by the uterus) is viewed as evidence of deviation or "fault".[29]

An illustration of this deeply systemic androcentricity is in clinical trials for drugs (medication). Studies have demonstrated that a gender gap in the drug trials have resulted in women experiencing adverse drug reactions (ADRs) twice as often as men.[30] This is particularly because a one-size-fits-all approach was often used, and based on male-dominated clinical trials, not considering the fundamental biological differences between men and women. Hence, whilst women were given the same dosage of a particular drug, they reacted differently to the same drug, metabolised the drugs in different ways and always almost had a higher concentration of the drugs in their system.[31] The exclusion of women from clinical trials which 'neglects sex differences in pharmacokinetics and dimorphisms in body weight, risks overmedication of women, and contributes to female-biased adverse drug reactions'.[32]

The gender data gap in medicine and healthcare also risks misdiagnosis in women. An example of this is the way women with acute myocardial infarction

---

[27] Barad (2007).

[28] Butler (2011).

[29] Young et al. (2019), p. 337.

[30] 'Lack of Females in Drug Dose Trials Leads to Overmedicated Women: Gender Gap Leaves Women Experiencing Adverse Drug Reactions Nearly Twice as Often as Men, Study Shows' (*ScienceDaily*) <https://www.sciencedaily.com/releases/2020/08/200812161318.htm> accessed on 13 March 2023.

[31] Zucker and Prendergast (2020), p. 32.

[32] Ibid.

(MI) present their symptoms (which are different from men).[33] Because women's symptoms are different from men's, they are less likely to be identified as suffering from MI during an angiogram, and therefore, does not leave space for the condition to be appropriately managed or monitored. In the long-term, women therefore were more likely to suffer adverse reactions, over-complications and even overall mortality, due to this oversight.[34]

3.2 Algorithm Gender Biases in AI

An emerging kind of bias and discrimination against women in healthcare (besides other under-represented population groups) is already rearing its ugly head vis-à-vis AI-driven technologies. AI systems are operated through methods of machine learning and algorithms used to train the systems, so that a certain function or task can be performed independently and on automation. When AI systems are first 'taught', not only is it vital that the relevant machine learning method used is appropriate; it is also crucial that the data sets (training data) that would allow the system to learn and diffuse patterns, is also of good quality, and is representative and inclusive. Otherwise, the real possibilities of gender bias undoubtedly manifest in the outcomes of the algorithms.

The kinds of gender biases that can occur due to a lack of reflection into algorithm deployments include, for example, unrepresentative data that might be 'tainted' with bias, built in with historical prejudices that translate into the inequalities in society. Data can also be inadequate and unrepresentative—for example, as illustrated above, where women are deliberately excluded from medical or clinical trials, resulting in a gender gap in medical data.[35] Gender biases resulting from algorithms also further contribute to harmful gender stereotypes in society,[36] where fixed norms regarding men and women continue to be perpetuated, inadvertently resulting in women's symptoms of pain and illness being treated less seriously than men's.[37] From the perspective of women surgeons working in health and medicine, gender biases are prevalent in workplace factors such as parental leave, epistemic injustices in terms of assessing women surgeons' capabilities and credibility, expectations relating to surgery care work, and objectification.[38] What is clear is that women in STEM

[33] Merone et al. (2022).

[34] Ibid.

[35] 'Lack of Females in Drug Dose Trials Leads to Overmedicated Women: Gender Gap Leaves Women Experiencing Adverse Drug Reactions Nearly Twice as Often as Men, Study Shows' (n 30).

[36] 'A Union of Equality: Gender Equality Strategy 2020-2025 | Communication from the Commission to the European Parliament, The Council, The European Economic and Social Committee and the Committee of the Regions' 5.

[37] Cleghorn (2021).

[38] Hutchison (2020), p. 236.

(science, technology, engineering and mathematics) fields continue to face gender discrimination, as studies have demonstrated that men evaluate the quality of research unveiling gender biases as less meritorious than women do.[39]

Algorithms, the means by which AI-driven technologies process data and arrive at outcomes, are the backbone of how these processes arrive at a particular decision or outcome.[40] Any machine learning system or algorithm that is trained with human-generated data will only be as effective and fair as the data it has been trained with. It is therefore important that AI product makers, developers and innovators are aware of the potential biases that they might face during each cycle of the development stage. They should also consider the various factors that they might use to train their systems, such as their quality and diversity.[41] For many years, too, men's bodies were regarded as the standard for any form of medical testing—and the exclusion of women from medical research and trials meant that women's health is and continues to be at risk[42]—no less so in AI-driven systems too due to inadequacy of data. Hence, the phrase 'rubbish in, rubbish out' has been used to describe this kind of phenomenon.

It is also worth considering algorithms from the viewpoint vis-à-vis Louise Amoore's critical work, *Cloud Ethics,*[43] which delves into 'algorithms as ethicopolitical entities that are entangled with the data attributes of people'.[44] Amoore's focal point on algorithmic logic is its impact on decision-making and human relations. She argues that algorithmic systems shape the possibilities of what one can and cannot do, based on the logics of probability, which are shaped by what is currently known, nameable, and measurable, and by datasets composed of past actions. Amoore critiques the ethicopolitics of algorithms as one that 'reduces the intractable difficulties and duress of living' into a single human-readable and actionable meaning, promising certainty but ultimately delivering a mirage. Instead, she defends uncertainty as an inescapable quality of human relations and decision-making, and questions the consequences of eliminating uncertainty through algorithmic logic. Amoore states:[45]

> The very essence of algorithms is that they afford greater degrees of recognition and value to some features of a scene than they do to others. In so doing, algorithms generate themselves as ethicopolitical beings in the world. If to have ethics is not merely to have a code prohibiting, for example, bias or assumptions, but to work on oneself via relations, then the ethicopolitics of algorithms involves investigations of how they learn to recognize and to act, how they extract assumptions from data relations, and how they learn what ought to be from relations with other humans and algorithms.

[39] Handley et al. (2015), p. 13201.

[40] Tomasz Müldner, 'An Algorithm for Explaining Algorithms', 30.

[41] Manyika (2019).

[42] Westervelt (2015).

[43] Amoore (2020).

[44] Ibid.

[45] Ibid., 8.

The main takeaway from *Cloud Ethics* is that algorithmic systems are not neutral, but rather 'ethicopolitical arrangements of values, assumptions, and propositions about the world'.[46] Therefore, we cannot hold out for the false promise of an unbiased algorithm that would overcome opacity with clarity and precision. Instead, we must consider the algorithmic ethicopolitics for what it brings into the world and for the world it creates.[47] Amoore argues that we need to be mindful of the technical meaning of computer science and artificial intelligence subfields, but not beholden to such definitions. We should also be open to cross-field borrowing, where other fields can 'play with the arrangements, thresholds, and assumptions of algorithms'.[48]

In a recent study on AI-driven technologies and women's healthcare, Lau et al conducted a systematic literature review to determine if AI-driven technologies adequately represented medical data and research of women's healthcare. One key finding from this research was that there was clearly a lack of representative data on women's healthcare conditions.[49] The authors divided the research inquiry into five thematic clusters,[50] comprising, amongst others, gender equality and health AI. It is unsurprising that the findings of this study point to the need for a much more significant body of required research for the improvement of AI risk prediction models for many aspects of women's healthcare.[51] In addition, the authors note that the representation of women's healthcare conditions are low and uneven in comparison to other available general health data,[52] and even if sparsely available, has been limited to disease-specific interventions. Hence, when AI-driven technologies or systems are deployed in medicine and healthcare, based on limited availability of good quality and representative data regarding women, any resulting outcomes thereof will clearly be skewed.

Besides the exclusion of women from many clinical trials,[53] resulting in incomplete data sets to train systems for disease and illness suffered by women—algorithmic bias can result in false diagnosis, and even useless, or wrong treatment protocols.[54] A lack of diversity in AI development teams can also contribute to gender bias, because perspectives from women and gender minorities may be under-represented, leading to oversights in algorithm design.[55] The latter may be a cumulative result of the under-representation of women, not only in AI,[56] but also related STEM education and industries. For example, whilst women represented

[46] Burrell (2020), p. 410.
[47] Ibid.
[48] Ibid., 411.
[49] Lau et al. (2023), p. 2.
[50] Ibid., 4.
[51] Ibid., 7.
[52] Ibid., 12.
[53] Deziel (2016).
[54] Gerke et al. (2020), p. 304.
[55] Fosch-Villaronga et al. (2022), p. 105735.
[56] Cerit et al. (2020), p. 100009.

52% employment in science and technology in Europe, women who are scientists and engineers account for only 41% of the field.[57] The European Commission Gender Equality Strategy 2020–2025[58] even recognises that women are under-represented in higher paid professions,[59] even though there are just as many women graduates than men. In terms of digital transition, women only represent 17% of people in ICT studies and careers in the EU, and only 36% of STEM graduates.[60]

Hence, what is clear is that even 'good' algorithms can become sexist in their outcomes, based upon the kind and quality of data that is used to train the AI systems.[61] There is, therefore, urgent need for actions that can be taken by and with various organisations, policy makers, inventors, creators, consumers and patients so that a holistic and concerted effort can be deployed to combat AI biases.[62]

4 The Regulatory Framework for AI in Healthcare

In the evolving technological landscape that encompasses AI and other new and emerging technologies, so, too began the urgency for global organisations, legislators, and policy makers, (amongst other stakeholders), to consider an AI-related regulatory or legislative framework that would, at the very least, enable a form of democratic governance. For this chapter, focus is levied on the current regulatory efforts of the European Union (EU), Council of Europe (CoE) and the UK, and analysing the extent to which these efforts expressly address the interests and rights of patients in health AI, particularly women. Whilst it is recognised that there are myriad international and regional human rights instruments that currently do seek to advance and champion the human rights of women, such as the United Nations Convention on the Elimination of All Forms of Discrimination against Women (CEDAW),[63] a nuanced focus is sought through interrogating existing AI-related regulatory efforts, and whether the concerns raised in this chapter thus far, may be adequately addressed vis-à-vis legislation.

---

[57] 'Science and Technology Workforce: Women in Majority - Products Eurostat News - Eurostat' <https://ec.europa.eu/eurostat/web/products-eurostat-news/w/ddn-20230602-1> accessed on 16 September 2023.

[58] 'A Union of Equality: Gender Equality Strategy 2020-2025 | Communication from the Commission to the European Parliament, The Council, The European Economic and Social Committee and the Committee of the Regions' (n 37).

[59] Ibid., 9.

[60] Ibid., 10.

[61] Smith and Rustagi (2021).

[62] Alake (2020).

[63] UN General Assembly, 'Convention on the Elimination of All Forms of Discrimination against Women' (1979) 20, retrieved in April 2006 <https://www.files.ethz.ch/isn/125360/8009_UN_Convention_Discrimination_Women.pdf> accessed on 31 May 2017.

4.1 The European Union Artificial Intelligence Act (EU AI Act)

For those working in the field of AI, law, and governance, as well as industry where AI systems are implemented, deployed, or manufactured, the EU AI Act[64] is likely to be regarded as one of the most comprehensive proposals for a governance framework for AI. It is possible that the EU AI Act will be regarded as the first global law enacted by a major regulator. The key feature of the EU AI Act is its risk-based approaches to assess AI applications, divided into risk categories.[65]

The risk-based approaches in the Act correspond with the relevant compliance and conformity assessments imposed on primarily AI 'providers'[66] (which may include various AI developers, manufacturers, processors, those who put the AI systems on to the market), and 'importers' and 'distributors'.[67] Obligations are also imposed on 'users', although the clarity on what amounts to 'users' would be better made apparent (not having the same meaning of 'users' used in the General Data Protection Regulation[68] (GDPR)). Each of the risk categories would be subject to different requirements, such as codes of conduct, transparency obligations, or conformity assessments. For example, under the EU AI Act, an AI system could be assessed as high risk if it falls within one of the standalone AI systems listed in Annex III and poses a significant risk of harm to the health, safety or fundamental rights of natural persons, or if, pursuant to Article 6(1) of the Act, it is a safety component of an AI system or it is itself an AI system regulated by the harmonised legislation set out in Annex II(A). High-risk AI systems may include medical devices, biometric systems, AI for critical infrastructure management, and AI for essential services access (e.g. immigration services), amongst others.

Because the EU AI Act is very much focused on risks as its main object and justification, thereby establishing rules that are proportionate and seek to be effective,[69] it is easy to question how its scope would be effective in protecting the interests of the 'end users' of AI systems and technologies. Experts that have evaluated the EU AI Act also wonder, that even though 'this scheme has worked

---

[64] Proposal for a REGULATION OF THE EUROPEAN PARLIAMENT AND OF THE COUNCIL LAYING DOWN HARMONISED RULES ON ARTIFICIAL INTELLIGENCE (ARTIFICIAL INTELLIGENCE ACT) AND AMENDING CERTAIN UNION LEGISLATIVE ACTS 2021 ({SEC(2021) 167 final} - {SWD(2021) 84 final} - {SWD(2021) 85 final}).

[65] 'Regulatory Framework Proposal on Artificial Intelligence | Shaping Europe's Digital Future' (6 February 2023) <https://digital-strategy.ec.europa.eu/en/policies/regulatory-framework-ai> accessed on 16 March 2023.

[66] Article 3, EU AI Act.

[67] Articles 26 to 28, EU AI Act.

[68] 'REGULATION (EU) 2016/ 679 OF THE EUROPEAN PARLIAMENT AND OF THE COUNCIL - of 27 April 2016 - on the Protection of Natural Persons with Regard to the Processing of Personal Data and on the Free Movement of Such Data, and Repealing Directive 95/ 46/ EC (General Data Protection Regulation)' 88.

[69] Mahler (2021).

relatively well for tangible products, where the manufacturer of a product is the analogue of the provider in the Act, this top-down allocation of duties will be more challenged in a world of "upstream" AI services, which can be re-used downstream in a wide variety of unforeseeable contexts'.[70] Further evaluation is needed on these issues, including the transparency and risk management approaches that have been recently voted upon, and how AI systems that may be used for a number of different purposes may be categorised.

Although Article 37 of the EU AI Act provides that some AI systems deserve special consideration, particularly because of 'the access to and enjoyment of certain essential private and public services and benefits necessary for people to fully participate in society or to improve one's standard of living', health or medical AI was initially not addressed as part of this special consideration. The article goes on to denote that AI systems should not lead to 'discrimination of persons or groups and perpetuate historical patterns of discrimination... or create new forms of discriminatory impacts'. The use of AI in specific areas such as critical infrastructure (Article 34), education or vocational training (Article 35), employment (Article 36) and law enforcement (Article 38), are expressly identified—whereas health or medicine, was markedly missing. In a later version of the Act, Article 37 was amended to include 'healthcare services, and essential services, including but not limited to housing, electricity, heating/cooling and internet'.

The little mention of health or medical AI in the EU AI Act also appears limitedly by reference to the Medical Devices Regulation[71] and the In-Vitro Diagnostic Medical Devices Regulation.[72] There is concern, therefore, that the scope of the EU AI Act does not particularly value the implications ensuing from the use of health or medical AI systems. As correctly identified by Palmieri and Goffin:[73]

> Although the AI Act is not intended to be applied specifically to the health sector but is intended to be applied horizontally, it aims to solve *ab origine*, risks that could seriously impact the health of the patient who comes into contact with an AI. Health, as is often said, is wealth and represents the necessary precondition for the enjoyment of all other rights recognised in the European Union. Therefore, while exploring the suitability of the AI Act to, *lato sensu*, protect fundamental rights, the health sector deserves special attention.

Whilst the EU AI Act was seen as a pre-eminent in setting out (to a certain extent) harmonised rules for market placement and use of AI in the EU, critics are of the opinion that its scope is too broad and does not adequately factor in fundamental rights protections. For those who work within the field of health or medical AI, the

[70] Edwards (2022).

[71] REGULATION (EU) 2017/ 745 OF THE EUROPEAN PARLIAMENT AND OF THE COUNCIL - of 5 April 2017 - on medical devices, amending Directive 2001/ 83/ EC, Regulation (EC) No 178/ 2002 and Regulation (EC) No 1223/ 2009 and repealing Council Directives 90/ 385/ EEC and 93/ 42/ EEC 175.

[72] REGULATION (EU) 2017/746 OF THE EUROPEAN PARLIAMENT AND OF THE COUNCIL of 5 April 2017 on in vitro diagnostic medical devices and repealing Directive 98/79/EC and Commission Decision 2010/227/EU 2016.

[73] Palmieri and Goffin (2023).

EU AI Act does not necessarily provide the clarity it sought to do. Whilst it is necessary for the EU AI Act to be read in conjunction with other horizontal EU-level regulations or legislation, the particularities of health or medical AI need to be considered to protect patient interests, which include women's healthcare interests too. This is sorely poorly articulated in the Act.

For individuals operating within the health or medical AI sector, the EU AI Act has the potential to offer increased clarity, although it currently provides only limited recognition of the unique challenges posed by AI in healthcare services. Achieving gender equality should be an essential objective within the EU AI Act and could arguably be treated as a 'special consideration'. However, the specific mechanisms for implementing these special considerations in practice still require thorough deliberation. While it is imperative for the EU AI Act to be interpreted alongside other overarching EU regulations and legislation, it is equally crucial to address the distinct nuances of health and medical AI to safeguard patient interests, including those related to women's healthcare. The extent to which gender considerations and vulnerabilities are integrated into appropriate legislation remains to be seen, particularly in light of the EU's internal market demands and technical harmonisation measures.

It is unsurprising that the EU AI Act has faced criticisms from prominent corporations in Europe (including companies such as Renault, Siemens, and Heineken). The concerns voiced by these corporations in an open letter[74] was that the overly cautious approaches in the EU AI Act, for example, relating to generative AI systems (as an example) that fall under 'foundation models', are overly burdensome, and carries disproportionate compliance and conformity costs. These companies warn that burdensome regulations in the EU AI Act may cause AI providers to withdraw from the European market. It may even cause providers to make their way to other regional hubs with pro-innovation approaches to regulating AI[75] (for example, in the UK), or even in China, with its liberal governance approaches to AI.[76]

As the trilogues (between the European Commission, Council and Parliament) loom in the horizon, there are still key issues under the EU AI Act that require urgent deliberation and attention. One of these is implementation and enforcement mechanisms of the Act, differing significantly across the board in the proposals by the Commission, Council and Parliament. Whilst an AI auditing ecosystem is also envisaged, until now, there is a lack of detail as to how this will be achieved. Other contentious debates that remain under the EU AI Act include the list of

---

[74] Butcher (2023).

[75] 'A Pro-Innovation Approach to AI Regulation' (*GOV.UK*) <https://www.gov.uk/government/publications/ai-regulation-a-pro-innovation-approach/white-paper> accessed on 15 September 2023.

[76] 'Translation: Measures for the Management of Generative Artificial Intelligence Services (Draft for Comment) – April 2023' (*DigiChina*) <https://digichina.stanford.edu/work/translation-measures-for-the-management-of-generative-artificial-intelligence-services-draft-for-comment-april-2023/> accessed on 15 September 2023.

high-risk AI systems, definitions of AI, and questions regarding the ban of real time biometrics.

Ultimately, the question is whether the EU AI Act may have a negative impact on Europe's competitiveness, technological advancement, and ability to foster robust innovations in the AI sector.[77]

4.2 The Council of Europe Consolidated Working Draft Framework Convention on Artificial Intelligence, Human Rights, Democracy and the Rule of Law (CoE AI Convention)

In an exciting unfolding of events, the Council of Europe (CoE), in January 2023, published its Zero Draft Framework Convention on Artificial Intelligence, Human Rights, Democracy and the Rule of Law (CoE AI Convention).[78] Although it cannot be said that this was not foreseeable, scholars in the field were optimistic regarding this new framework from the CoE, believing that this framework may become a critical companion to the EU AI Act. Some key fundamental rights protection in the CoE AI Convention include rights to privacy, data protection, respect for human dignity, and most importantly, prohibition against discrimination, as contained in Article 3.[79]

The CoE AI Convention, however, is an extremely new instrument currently being negotiated (at the current time of writing this chapter), involving the CoE members, and observer countries, stakeholders from civil society and the private sector. The Zero Draft version[80] provides some optimism where health or medical AI is concerned. Chapter III (application of AI systems in provision of goods, facilities and services), Article 8, Section A, for example, provides obligations for public and private actors to ensure compatibility with national and international laws 'in provision of goods, facilities and services in essential areas, such as but not restricted to, *health* [emphasis own], family care, housing, energy consumption, transport, food supply, education, employment, finance, environmental protection, digital information, media and communication…'. Further, Chapter IV of the Zero Draft

[77] Raposo (2022).

[78] Revised Zero Draft Framework Convention on Artificial Intelligence, Human Rights, Democracy, and the Rule of Law 2023 (CAI (2023) 01).

[79] Article 3 of the CoE AI Convention reads: *'The implementation of the provisions of this Convention by the Parties shall be secured without discrimination on any ground such as sex, gender, sexual orientation, race, colour, language, age, religion, political or any other opinion, national or social origin, association with a national minority, property, birth, state of health, disability or other status, or based on a combination of one or more of these grounds'.*

[80] Revised Zero Draft Framework Convention on Artificial Intelligence, Human Rights, Democracy, and the Rule of Law.

CoE AI Convention encompasses fundamental principles of AI systems. These include principles relate to equality and anti-discrimination (Article 12); privacy and personal data protection (Article 13); accountability, responsibility and legal liability (Article 14); transparency and oversight (Article 15); safety (Article 16); safe innovation (Article 17), and public consultation and additional measures (Article 18).

The Zero Draft version has now been superseded by the Consolidated Working Draft,[81] which comes after the initial review of the revised Zero Draft and has been assembled by the Chair of the Committee for Artificial Intelligence (CAI), with support from the Secretariat. Designed to serve as a foundation for upcoming deliberations, the draft incorporates elements that were provisionally accepted during the initial review of the revised Zero Draft, along with recommendations formulated by the Chair in collaboration with the Secretariat. Similar to the EU AI Act, Article 2 of the CoE AI Convention emphasises a risk-based strategy, necessitating each Party to establish and implement a tailored set of measures within its domestic legal framework. These measures should align with the potential severity and likelihood of negative impacts on human rights, fundamental freedoms, democracy, and the rule of law throughout the entire lifecycle of artificial intelligence systems, from design and development to usage and decommissioning. In essence, this approach mandates parties to evaluate the risks associated with AI system usage and then implement corresponding actions to guarantee the full adherence to the convention's principles and obligations.

Interestingly, there is an express reference to gender equality in the Preamble of the CoE AI Convention. Paragraph 3 of the Preamble recognises the potential of AI systems to promote 'gender equality and the empowerment of all women and [children/girls], and other important goals and interests, by enhancing progress and innovation'. Additionally, in Paragraph 6 of the Preamble, it expresses concern that discrimination in digital contexts, particularly those involving artificial intelligence systems, prevent women, [girls/children], and members of other groups from fully enjoying their human rights and fundamental freedoms, which hinders their full, equal and effective participation in economic, social, cultural and political affairs.

However, AI systems for application of health and medicine is not expressly identified. It may be argued, however, that the CoE AI Convention applies to the design, development, use and decommissioning of AI systems that have the potential to interfere with the respect for human rights and fundamental freedoms, the functioning of democracy and the observance of rule of law. Therefore, by this interpretation, if health or medical AI systems have the potential to interfere with human rights and fundamental freedoms, democracy and the rule of law, the CoE AI Convention would *lato sensu* apply to them.

Another broad interpretation might be made in respect of the definition of 'AI system' in Article 3, which broadly includes any algorithmic system or combination

[81] Committee on Artificial Intelligence, 'CAI(2023)18 - Consolidated Working Draft Framework Convention on AI, Human Rights, Democracy and the Rule of Law'.

of such systems that uses computational methods derived from statistics or other mathematical techniques and that generates text, sound, image or other content or either assists or replaces human decision-making. This broad definition could potentially include AI systems used in health and medicine that have the potential to interfere with the rights of women.

Whilst it may be too early to speculate and interpret the provisions of the CoE AI Convention, at this infant stage, it may placate those who have been concerned about the human rights implications of AI. It is possible to interpret that the combination of Articles 3, the specific mention of health in Article 8, Section A, and the fundamental principles in Articles 12 to 18, are likely to provide a measure of comfort regarding the use of AI and protective human rights mechanisms that are available to individuals. Conversely, the CoE AI Convention is also likely to address and counter the existing issues faced in women's healthcare and medical treatment in a more dignified manner.

4.3 The UK's Pro-Innovation Approach to Artificial Intelligence Regulation

On 29 March 2023, the Department for Science, Innovation, and Technology unveiled a white paper titled 'AI Regulation: A Pro-Innovation Approach'.[82] This document outlines the UK government's strategy for regulating AI in a manner that fosters innovation while acknowledging the potential benefits and challenges associated with this technology. The proposed regulatory framework has been carefully crafted to prioritise proportionality, trustworthiness, adaptability, and clarity. Five core principles underpin this framework, guiding how regulators address AI-related risks: encompassing (1) safety, security, and robustness; (2) appropriate transparency and explainability; (3) fairness; (4) accountability and governance; and (5) contestability and redress.

The UK government's approach is deliberately designed to avoid burdensome legislation that could stifle innovation. Instead, it champions adaptability in AI regulation, allowing regulators to tailor the implementation of these principles to the specific context of AI within their respective sectors. Continuous evaluation will ensure effective application of these principles and identify any impediments. This regulatory framework aims to achieve three key objectives: promoting responsible AI innovation, bolstering public trust through effective risk management, and positioning the UK as a global leader in AI governance.

To further facilitate implementation, key regulators will issue additional guidance and resources over the coming year, specifying how these principles apply within their respective domains. However, variations in regulatory approaches may lead to

[82] 'A Pro-Innovation Approach to AI Regulation' (n 76).

potential gaps, potentially necessitating legislation to ensure consistent adherence to these principles.

From the standpoint of gender equality, it is heartening to note that the White Paper does, indeed, expressly recognise gender equality.[83] The interpretation of fairness by regulators is expected to include consideration of compliance with relevant laws and regulations in the UK, including those which contravene the Equality Act 2010, or the Human Rights Acy 1998. These Acts prohibit discrimination of the basis of gender, amongst other protected characteristics.

In contrast to the EU's approach, the UK's strategy places a stronger emphasis on promoting innovation and experimentation, maintaining a lighter regulatory touch. The EU, on the other hand, appears to adopt a more cautious stance, relying on extensive regulation in the EU AI Act, to ensure ethical AI use aligned with the public interest. This juxtaposition highlights differing regulatory philosophies between the two entities in addressing the challenges and opportunities posed by AI technologies.

Notwithstanding, in the public consultation put forward by the UK government regarding the White Paper, some key concerns have been raised by various parties. The Ada Lovelace Institute provides its recommendations in order to reflect effective AI regulation vis-à-vis coverage, capability and urgency.[84] In each of these categories, it was recognised that the UK's diffused legal and regulatory framework for AI has significant gaps and that safer guard rails, clarity in rights, and possibly, the establishment of new institutions, may be necessitated.[85] The UK Law Society also made several recommendations in their response to the public consultation, including, amongst others: the provision of precise definitions for key terms, such as 'high-risk context', 'dangerous capabilities', and 'meaningful human intervention' within the AI domain; the establishment of regulator-guided appeal mechanisms and the appointment of an AI officer in legal entities of a specific size or those operating in high-risk sectors; and mitigation of divergence, duplication, and fragmentation by ensuring alignment across sectors and on an international scale.[86]

The dimensions of health or medicine is markedly absent from the White Paper. However, the UK has adopted a unique approach to this. Ahead of the release of the White Paper, the Medicines and Healthcare products Regulatory Agency (MHRA) has proactively initiated measures to facilitate the integration of AI. In 2022, it unveiled a roadmap outlining the prerequisites for AI and software used in medical devices. Presently, the MHRA is in the process of revising its regulatory framework to safeguard patient interests and uphold the UK's global reputation for responsible

[83] Ibid., 9.

[84] 'Regulating AI in the UK' <https://www.adalovelaceinstitute.org/report/regulating-ai-in-the-uk/> accessed on 15 September 2023.

[85] Ibid.

[86] 'A Pro-Innovation Approach to AI Regulation – Law Society Response' (*The Law Society*, 27 June 2023) <https://www.lawsociety.org.uk/campaigns/consultation-responses/a-pro-innovation-approach-to-ai-regulation> accessed on 15 September 2023.

innovation. A forthcoming directive from the MHRA will focus on enhancing the transparency and interpretability of AI components within medical devices. This guidance will encompass the unique challenges posed by AI within the health and social care sectors, aligning with legal product safety requirements. The MHRA also indicated its intention to collaborate with the Information Commissioner's Office (ICO) and the National Data Guardian to address concerns related to patient data protection and trust concerning medical devices. The ultimate goal is to provide manufacturers with a well-defined set of criteria for responsible innovation moving forward.[87]

5 Incorporating Data Feminism as a Reflective Tool for Gender Equality

In situating experiences and narratives of privilege and oppression within healthcare, this chapter recommends for deeper reflections and insights into data feminism,[88] which employs intersectionality narratives to influence, embed, and allow for an expansion of the insularity regarding AI in women's healthcare. Whilst this may be easier said than done, this necessitates us to consciously, holistically, and ethically employing the use of AI-driven technologies in every aspect; fabricating a comprehensive ecosystem of women's health that no longer look towards men's biological bodies as the standard in medicine and healthcare.

The word 'intersectionality' is often credited to Kimberle Crenshaw, who coined the term in 1989, although it should be acknowledged that claims about the interconnectedness of race, class, gender, sexuality, and other social identities have always functioned as part of the everyday life experiences of many marginalised groups' activities. According to Crenshaw, intersectionality is 'a metaphor for understanding the ways that multiple forms of inequality or disadvantage sometimes compound themselves and create obstacles that often are not understood among conventional ways of thinking'.[89] Nonetheless, although Crenshaw is credited as the originator of the term 'intersectionality', it is important to note that this concept was not a novel mode of thought. Preceding Crenshaw's introduction of the term, Black feminist literature had already illuminated instances of inequality that Black women experienced due to the intertwining forces of sexism and racism. An illustrative example can be found in the work of the Combahee River Collective, an organisation rooted in Black lesbian socialist feminism, which authored 'A Black Feminist Statement' in 1977.[90] This statement is frequently recognised as one of the earliest articulations of the intersectionality concept. Nevertheless, it is, and remains, a

[87] Foster and Badger (2023).

[88] D'Ignazio and Klein (2020).

[89] Crenshaw (1989).

[90] Cole (2009).

powerful analytical framework and tool for academic scholarship, and a compelling driver for societal, policy, and legislative movement, change and development.

5.1 Intersectionality in Data Feminism

An acute awareness of how intersectionality affects women in oppression is necessitated when considering women's healthcare as part of the qualitative nature of medical data and medical treatment. As stated by feminist Zoe Samudzi, 'intersectionality is such a vital framework for understanding systems of power, because 'woman' is not a catch-all category that alone defines all our relationships to power'. This situates oppression on the opposite spectrum from 'privilege' (where even 'privilege' for women does not equate to the same kind of 'privilege' for men).

What does this mean for women's healthcare more broadly? A very insightful direction is provided by scholars Catherine D'Ignazio and Lauren F. Klein, who proffer intersectionality in a concept they term 'data feminism'.[91] Data feminism, according to D'Ignazio and Klein, is one of the approaches employing feminist theory, that may overcome the 'overwhelming white, male, techno-heroic' in big data, data science and AI. In essence, data feminism emphasises the employment of black feminism (including that of Kimberle Crenshaw) as a lens by which to view how power structures operate in society, especially in relation to women. In an interview with Nightingale, The Journal of Visualization Society, D'Ignazio offers this food for thought:[92]

> We try to ask questions like: How do these structural inequalities permeate the data science process? How did they infect every stage of the pipeline? What kind of questions even get asked? Right on down to what kinds of colors you choose to represent different things in your chart. So that's kind of the intentionally broad focus on power while still being focused on gender throughout, but like, power writ large.

Hence, power differentials between men and women; as well as between white women and Black women, academic researchers and indigenous communities, and people in the Global North and the Global South—these are all intersecting systems of power in a society.

In an idealised world, intersectionality and data feminism may be one of the solutions to address algorithm biases in women's healthcare in a mindful way—with the core of the theory providing specific strategies to data scientists in working towards attaining ethical, equitable, equal data justice. Embracing the 7 principles of data feminism (examine power; challenge power; elevate emotion and embodiment; rethink binaries and hierarchies; embrace pluralism; consider context; and make labour visible) is also a starting point when considering how AI is used in women's healthcare and how better data can be gathered. This can also extend to machine

[91] D'Ignazio and Klein (2020).

[92] Forrest (2019).

learning methods in AI, and designing experiments and research for data, whilst simultaneously working towards intentionality to improve women's healthcare and AI in holistic ways.

5.2 *Using Data Feminism to Enhance Gender Health Equality*

Data feminism can be a powerful framework for enhancing gender equality in health and medicine by challenging existing data practices, biases, and inequalities. This paper identifies several ways in which data feminism can be applied to this context.

In the realm of data feminism, there is a fundamental call for a critical approach to data collection and analysis.[93] This movement urges us to scrutinise the methods by which data is gathered, particularly in the context of health and medicine. It prompts us to question the procedures for gathering data, ensuring a diverse representation in clinical trials, and taking into account the complex web of social and cultural factors that shape health outcomes. One potent tool at the disposal of researchers is intersectional analysis,[94] which helps us delve deeper into how gender intersects with other factors such as race, socioeconomic status, and age in determining health disparities.

Amidst this, data feminism also shines a spotlight on the pervasive presence of bias within data, especially within algorithmic systems. In the domain of healthcare, this manifests as a need to closely inspect AI algorithms for any gender bias that may affect diagnosis and treatment recommendations.[95] The identification and rectification of these biases is seen as a vital pathway towards fostering more equitable healthcare outcomes. Furthermore, data feminism champions the empowerment of individuals, with a special focus on women, in taking control over their own health data.[96] This translates to a call for informed consent, transparency in data usage, and the concept of data sovereignty. In essence, it emphasises that women should have the autonomy to decide how their health data is employed and shared.

Crucially, the data feminism framework incorporates an intersectional lens, acknowledging that individuals have multiple identities that intersect to shape their unique experiences and vulnerabilities. This inclusive approach is instrumental in health and medicine as it helps uncover and address disparities that disproportionately affect marginalised women, such as transgender women, women of colour, and women with disabilities.[97]

---

[93] Dórea and Revie (2021).

[94] Rascouet-Paz (2020).

[95] Alake (2020).

[96] Welten et al. (2022).

[97] Baah et al. (2019), p. 12268.

Moreover, data feminism encourages a transformation in the narratives surrounding healthcare. This entails challenging and redefining the dominant narratives that often reinforce gender stereotypes. In the context of healthcare, it might involve reimagining how medical conditions are framed and discussed, diminishing the stigma surrounding them, and acknowledging the intricate interplay of gender identity in health narratives.

A key pillar of this movement involves fostering inclusivity in research and leadership within the healthcare sector. Encouraging more women to pursue careers in data science, health informatics, and medical research is essential for cultivating research practices that are inherently inclusive and gender-aware.[98] Data feminism also finds a place in policy advocacy. It serves as a valuable guide for efforts aimed at improving gender equality in health and medicine.[99] These efforts encompass policies that address crucial areas such as data privacy, gender-based violence, reproductive rights, and healthcare access, especially for marginalised women. Promoting data literacy, particularly among women and underserved communities, is deemed a critical step in this journey. When individuals possess an understanding of how data is utilised in healthcare decision-making, they can emerge as informed advocates for their own health.

Finally, data feminism underscores the importance of community engagement. Listening to the experiences of communities, particularly those who have historically been underserved, is an indispensable aspect of this movement. These communities offer invaluable insights into healthcare needs and concerns that may not find representation in traditional healthcare data.[100]

Given the ways in which data feminism can be applied, one possible avenue of incorporation of these concepts is to look towards a legal framework, applied through regulations and guidelines. Applying bottom-up regulation and incorporating data feminism principles into regulatory frameworks is a dynamic approach to ensure more equitable and inclusive governance of emerging technologies.[101] Bottom-up regulation empowers grassroots movements, marginalised communities, and individuals to actively participate in shaping policies that affect them. When combined with data feminism, which focuses on addressing gender disparities and promoting intersectional inclusivity, this approach fosters a collaborative and diverse regulatory process. It encourages data-driven decision-making that is sensitive to gender and social inequalities, ensuring that the voices of women, especially those from underrepresented backgrounds, are heard and their unique needs are considered. By intertwining bottom-up regulation and data feminism, regulatory frameworks become more responsive to the concerns of the most vulnerable, leading to more just and balanced technological advancements.

---

[98] Lau et al. (2023).

[99] Darian et al. (2023).

[100] Kelly et al. (2021).

[101] Meslin (2010).

5.3 *Beyond Data Feminism: Health Ecosystems, Bottom-Up Regulatory Approaches, and Gender Medicine for AI and Women's Healthcare*

In conjunction with the ways data feminism can be used to enhance gender health equality above, another further measure proposed in this chapter is the creation and advancement of a women's health ecosystem. An ecosystem in the healthcare setting, or of health systems are not new ideas, but their success has rarely been documented due to low implementation of ecosystem models.[102] This chapter recommends that a specific women's health ecosystem, and embracing fundamental rights values, intersectionality, and data feminism, can be built on a smaller scale with an identified number of vested stakeholders. A women's health ecosystem is 'the optimal governance model when a high level of modularity (offerings of different players can be flexibly combined) meets a significant need for coordination in order to align stakeholder activities'.[103] Besides the clear stakeholders such as healthcare providers, insurers, pharmaceutical companies, policy makers, suppliers, regulators—the added dimensions of intersectionality and data feminism mean that this women's health ecosystem can also incorporate civil society representative groups, patient groups for under-represented women, feminist data scientists and data engineers, bioethicists, and more. A women's health ecosystem could likely advance the proliferation of AI to reduce women's health inequalities, whilst advancing equality, no longer looking towards men's biological bodies as the standard in medicine and healthcare, but consciously and intentionally investing in health or medical AI design, research, technology, deployment, ethics, and use that is fair, unbiased, representative, and equitable.

Governance vis-à-vis regulatory frameworks can look to fostering bottom-up regulation where several crucial actions and strategies can be put into motion. The foundation of this approach is community engagement, where open forums and public consultations are organised to facilitate meaningful dialogues between the public and regulatory bodies. Inclusivity is paramount, with various stakeholders, including civil society organisations, industry representatives, academic experts, and marginalised communities, being invited to contribute their perspectives. Other potential actions may include participatory decision-making mechanisms, such as citizen juries and public referendums, which can empower individuals to directly influence regulatory decisions; capacity building initiatives (including education on data privacy, digital literacy, and technology governance); advocacy networks and coalitions serving as intermediaries between communities and regulatory bodies; and mandating of impact assessments to comprehensively evaluate the social, economic, and environmental consequences of emerging technologies, with results made available for public scrutiny and input. In this manner, flexibility in regulation

[102] Pidun et al. (2021).

[103] Ibid.

is maintained, allowing for adaptability to changing circumstances and new knowledge, thus preventing rigidity that could hinder innovation or community-driven solutions. These actions collectively create a regulatory environment that is more democratic, inclusive, and responsive to the needs and concerns of the wider community, particularly in the realm of emerging technologies.

Beyond this, recognising and acknowledging that the simplest ways to begin striving for gender equality in medicine and healthcare only requires (at the beginning) education and reorientation. These might include, the inclusion of a higher percentage of women in healthcare and STEM decision making, from research to policy making, to leadership.[104] Including critical modules of gender, including new disciplines such as gender medicine,[105] and studies of other intersectional and historical inequalities as part of healthcare and medical curriculum is equally impactful. Finally, practising a more dynamic form of informed consent[106] in women's healthcare, listening to their voices and needs to eradicate the barriers that cause their societal invisibility, allows co-creation and cooperation that may fully leverage the benefits of AI-driven technologies.

6 Conclusion

In essence, systemic biases in women's healthcare will continue to permeate, unless specific, concentrated, and intentional measures are taken to dismantle the patriarchal model of medicine and healthcare. Acknowledging the complexities of algorithms, and the intricate ethicopolitical dimensions highlighted by Amoore, challenges us to think critically about the role of algorithmic systems in shaping our lives and to consider the ethical implications of their use. Data and algorithms are far from neutral entities; they inherently carry the biases, values, and perspectives of their creators and the historical contexts in which they were developed. Data, often drawn from real-world sources, can reflect existing societal prejudices and inequalities. Algorithms, designed by humans, make decisions based on this data and may inadvertently perpetuate or even exacerbate these biases. Whether in employment, criminal justice, or healthcare, these technologies can reinforce and perpetuate inequalities, leading to decisions that disproportionately affect marginalised groups. Recognising the non-neutrality of data and algorithms is the first step in addressing and mitigating these biases, and it underscores the importance of ethical and responsible development and deployment of technology.

Furthermore, whilst the examination of relevant existing legislation demonstrates, to a certain extent, the express intentions for gender equality based on principles of non-discrimination and equality, the assessment nevertheless underscores greater

[104] Hillman (2020).

[105] Shai et al. (2021).

[106] Rao (2016).

need for comprehensive and explicit actions to protect women's health rights in the face of rapidly advancing AI technologies. In addition to the strategies outlined to enhance gender health equality, this chapter had proposed the establishment of a women's health ecosystem that aligns with fundamental rights values, intersectionality, and data feminism. This ecosystem involves various stakeholders, including healthcare providers, insurers, pharmaceutical companies, and policymakers, but also integrates civil society groups, underrepresented patient associations, feminist data scientists, and bioethicists. This approach aims to advance AI technologies in reducing women's health inequalities and promote equitable healthcare, breaking away from the traditional male-centric medical standards. Simultaneously, the governance of regulatory frameworks can embrace bottom-up regulation through community engagement, participatory decision-making, and capacity-building initiatives. Moreover, the chapter underscores the importance of education, increased representation of women in healthcare leadership and decision-making, integration of gender and intersectional studies in medical curricula, and the practice of dynamic informed consent to eliminate barriers and harness the potential of AI-driven healthcare technologies.

Finally, in attempting to raise the intriguing prospect of leveraging data feminism as an additional tool to advance gender equality in healthcare, a critical approach to data collection and analysis is championed. This approach encourages the examination of data gathering methods in health and medicine, with a focus on diversity in clinical trials and the influence of social and cultural factors on health outcomes. Intersectional analysis is a powerful tool to understand how gender intersects with factors such as race and socioeconomic status. Data feminism also highlights the presence of bias in data, especially in healthcare algorithms, emphasising the need to address and rectify such biases for more equitable outcomes. It calls for empowering individuals, especially women, in controlling their health data through informed consent and transparency. The movement promotes inclusive research, challenges dominant healthcare narratives, and advocates for policies that enhance gender equality, while also stressing the importance of data literacy and community engagement.

In essence, the pursuit of AI gender equality in medicine and healthcare begins with education, reshaping leadership, and expanding curricula to include gender-focused disciplines. It extends to the dynamic practice of informed consent and actively listening to women's voices and needs to dismantle the societal barriers that have rendered them invisible in healthcare decisions. By fostering cooperation and co-creation, these fundamental changes will unlock the full potential of AI-driven technologies to create a healthcare system that truly serves the needs of all, upholding the principles of equality, inclusivity, and fairness. Together, the integrated approach of a women's health ecosystem, a responsive regulatory framework, and a commitment to gender awareness in healthcare will drive us closer to the goal of equitable, accessible, and effective medical and healthcare services for all.

Ultimately, this paper augments a promising avenue for future research and policy development in this domain, with the potentiality to offer valuable insights for further exploration and action in achieving gender health equality. Indeed, this paper lays the foundation for a promising trajectory in the field of research and policy development, offering a wealth of valuable insights and opportunities for continued exploration and decisive action aimed at achieving gender health equality. The multifaceted approach presented, encompassing data feminism, regulatory frameworks, educational reforms, and informed consent practices, underscores the need for comprehensive and collaborative efforts to transform healthcare and medical AI into instruments of gender equity. This forward-looking perspective not only informs current discussions but also serves as a catalyst for future initiatives that will reshape the landscape of healthcare, ensuring that it truly meets the diverse and evolving health needs of all individuals.

References

A Pro-Innovation Approach to AI Regulation – Law Society Response (The Law Society, 27 June 2023). <https://www.lawsociety.org.uk/campaigns/consultation-responses/a-pro-innovation-approach-to-ai-regulation>

A Pro-Innovation Approach to AI Regulation (GOV.UK). <https://www.gov.uk/government/publications/ai-regulation-a-pro-innovation-approach/white-paper>

A Union of Equality: Gender Equality Strategy 2020-2025 | Communication from the Commission to the European Parliament, The Council, The European Economic and Social Committee and the Committee of the Regions

Alake R (2020) Algorithm bias in artificial intelligence needs to be discussed (and addressed). Medium, 28 April 2020. <https://towardsdatascience.com/algorithm-bias-in-artificial-intelligence-needs-to-be-discussed-and-addressed-8d369d675a70> a

Amoore L (2020) Cloud ethics: algorithms and the attributes of ourselves and others. Duke University Press

Assembly UG, 'Convention on the Elimination of All Forms of Discrimination against Women' (1979) 20, retrieved in April 2006 <https://www.files.ethz.ch/isn/125360/8009_UN_Convention_Discrimination_Women.pdf>

Baah FO, Teitelman AM, Riegel B (2019) Marginalization: conceptualizing patient vulnerabilities in the framework of social determinants of health – an integrative review. Nurs Inq 26:e12268. <https://www.ncbi.nlm.nih.gov/pmc/articles/PMC6342665/>

Barad K (2007) Meeting the universe halfway: quantum physics and the entanglement of matter and meaning. Duke University Press

British Medical Association (2021) BMA commentary on mend the gap: the independent review into gender pay gaps in medicine in England. Department of Health and Social Care

British Medical Association, Jewett C (2021) Sexism in medicine. British Medical Association

Burrell J (2020) The ethics of uncertainty - Louise Amoore, cloud ethics: algorithms and the attributes of ourselves and others (Durham, NC, Duke University Press, 2020, 232 p.). Eur J Sociol 61:409. <https://www.cambridge.org/core/product/identifier/S0003975620000193/type/journal_article>

Butcher M (2023) European VCs and tech firms sign open letter warning against over-regulation of AI in draft EU laws. TechCrunch, 30 June 2023. <https://techcrunch.com/2023/06/30/european-vcs-tech-firms-sign-open-letter-warning-against-over-regulation-of-ai-in-draft-eu-laws/>

Butler J (2011) Bodies that matter: on the discursive limits of 'sex'. Routledge

Cerit J, Dindarian A, Cilo-van Norel N (2020) Women, AI, and the power of supporting communities: a digital gender-support partnership. Patterns 1:100009. <https://www.ncbi.nlm.nih.gov/pmc/articles/PMC7660405/>

Cleghorn E (2021) Unwell women: misdiagnosis and myth in a man-made world. Dutton, Penguin Random House LLC

Cole ER (2009) Intersectionality and research in psychology. Am Psychol 64:170

Colombo R, Sanguineti V (eds) (2018) Rehabilitation robotics, 1st edn. Academic Press. <https://www.elsevier.com/books/rehabilitation-robotics/colombo/978-0-12-811995-2>

Committee on Artificial Intelligence, 'CAI(2023)18 - Consolidated Working Draft Framework Convention on AI, Human Rights, Democracy and the Rule of Law'

Copeland R, Mattioli D, Evans M (2020) Inside Google's quest for millions of medical records. The Wall Street Journal (11 January 2020). <https://www.wsj.com/articles/paging-dr-google-how-the-tech-giant-is-laying-claim-to-health-data-11578719700>

Crenshaw K (1989) Demarginalizing the intersection of race and sex: a black feminist critique of antidiscrimination doctrine, feminist theory and antiracist politics. Univ Chic Leg Forum 1989

Criado-Perez C (2020) Invisible women: exposing data bias in a world designed for men, 1st edn. Vintage Books, Random House

Cumberlege J (2020) First do no harm - the report of the independent medicines and medical devices safety review. <https://www.webarchive.org.uk/wayback/archive/20200721101148mp_/https:/www.immdsreview.org.uk/downloads/IMMDSReview_Web.pdf>

D'Ignazio C, Klein LF (2020) Data feminism. The MIT Press

Danesi CC (2021) The impact of artificial intelligence on women's rights: a legal point of view. In: Miller K, Wendt K (eds) The fourth industrial revolution and its impact on ethics. Springer International Publishing. <http://link.springer.com/10.1007/978-3-030-57020-0_20>

Darian S et al (2023) Enacting data feminism in advocacy data work. Proc ACM on Hum-Comput Interact 7:1. <https://dl.acm.org/doi/10.1145/3579480>

Deziel S (2016) How medical research has failed women. Chatelaine, 31 May 2016. <https://www.chatelaine.com/health/women-medical-research-bias/>

Dórea FC, Revie CW (2021) Data-driven surveillance: effective collection, integration, and interpretation of data to support decision making. Front Vet Sci 8. <https://www.frontiersin.org/articles/10.3389/fvets.2021.633977>

Edwards L (2022) Expert explainer- the EU AI Act: a summary of its significance and scope. <https://www.adalovelaceinstitute.org/wp-content/uploads/2022/04/Expert-explainer-The-EU-AI-Act-11-April-2022.pdf>

European Health Data Space (12 May 2023). <https://health.ec.europa.eu/ehealth-digital-health-and-care/european-health-data-space_en>

Forrest J (2019) None of us are free if some of us are not: Catherine D'Ignazio on Data Feminism. Nightingale, 18 November 2019. <https://medium.com/nightingale/catherine-dignazio-on-data-feminism-ce3b3c65f04a>

Fosch-Villaronga E et al (2022) Accounting for diversity in AI for medicine. Comput Law Secur Rev 47:105735. <https://www.sciencedirect.com/science/article/pii/S0267364922000784>

Foster J, Badger G (2023) AI white paper published – signalling a "pro-innovation approach" to AI regulation. Hill Dickinson, April 2023. <https://www.hilldickinson.com/insights/articles/ai-white-paper-published-signalling-pro-innovation-approach-ai-regulation>

Gerke S, Minssen T, Cohen G (2020) Ethical and legal challenges of artificial intelligence-driven healthcare. Artificial Intelligence in Healthcare. Elsevier. <https://linkinghub.elsevier.com/retrieve/pii/B9780128184387000125>

Handley IM et al (2015) Quality of evidence revealing subtle gender biases in science is in the eye of the beholder. Proc Natl Acad Sci 112:13201. <https://www.pnas.org/doi/abs/10.1073/pnas.1510649112>

Haraway DJ (1997) Modest_Witness@Second_Millennium. FemaleMan_Meets_Oncomouse: feminism and technoscience. Routledge

Harding S (2009) Standpoint theories: productively controversial. Hypatia 24:192. <https://www.cambridge.org/core/journals/hypatia/article/abs/standpoint-theories-productively-controversial/3AECE924A2BFC03CFDC9CB27BAC75BCE>

Hillman S (2020) Why women are still "the other" in medicine. Warwick Knowledge Centre, 6 March 2020. <https://warwick.ac.uk/newsandevents/knowledgecentre/health/patient-care/women_in_medicine/>

Hutchison K (2020) Four types of gender bias affecting women surgeons and their cumulative impact. J Med Ethics 46:236. <https://jme.bmj.com/content/46/4/236>

In Focus: International Women's Day (UN Women – Headquarters, 1 March 2023). <https://www.unwomen.org/en/news-stories/in-focus/2023/03/in-focus-international-womens-day>

Kelly C et al (2021) "Doing" or "using" intersectionality? Opportunities and challenges in incorporating intersectionality into knowledge translation theory and practice. Int J Equity Health 20: 187. <https://equityhealthj.biomedcentral.com/articles/10.1186/s12939-021-01509-z>

Kushner H (2008) The art of medicine. Medical historians and the history of medicine. Lancet 372: 710

Lack of Females in Drug Dose Trials Leads to Overmedicated Women: Gender Gap Leaves Women Experiencing Adverse Drug Reactions Nearly Twice as Often as Men, Study Shows (ScienceDaily). <https://www.sciencedaily.com/releases/2020/08/200812161318.htm>

Lan KW (2012) Technofetishism of posthuman bodies: representations of cyborgs, ghosts, and monsters in contemporary Japanese science fiction film and animation. University of Sussex

Lau PL, Nandy M, Chakraborty S (2023) Accelerating UN sustainable development goals with AI-driven technologies: a systematic literature review of women's healthcare. Healthcare 11: 401. <https://www.mdpi.com/2227-9032/11/3/401>

Lee D, Yoon SN (2021) Application of artificial intelligence-based technologies in the healthcare industry: opportunities and challenges. Int J Environ Res Public Health 18:271. <https://www.mdpi.com/1660-4601/18/1/271>

Mahler T (2021) Between risk management and proportionality: the risk-based approach in the EU's artificial intelligence act proposal. 30 September 2021. <https://papers.ssrn.com/abstract=4001444>

Manyika J, Silberg J, Presten B (2019) What do we do about the biases in AI? Harv Bus Rev. <https://hbr.org/2019/10/what-do-we-do-about-the-biases-in-ai>

MBRRACE-UK et al (2020) Saving lives, improving mothers' care - lessons learned to inform maternity care from the UK and Ireland confidential enquiries into maternal deaths and morbidity 2016-18. National Perinatal Epidemiology Unit, University of Oxford

Merone L (2022) Exploring androcentricity in medicine, medical research and education, and the impacts on the experiences of female patients. James Cook University

Merone L et al (2022) Sex inequalities in medical research: a systematic scoping review of the literature. Women's Health Reports 3:49. <https://www.ncbi.nlm.nih.gov/pmc/articles/PMC8812498/>

Meslin EM (2010) The value of using top-down and bottom-up approaches for building trust and transparency in biobanking. Public Health Genomics 13:207. <https://www.ncbi.nlm.nih.gov/pmc/articles/PMC2865393/>

Müldner T, An algorithm for explaining algorithms. 30

Palmieri S, Goffin T (2023) A blanket that leaves the feet cold: exploring the AI act safety framework for medical AI. Eur J Health Law 1:1. <https://brill.com/view/journals/ejhl/aop/article-10.1163-15718093-bja10104/article-10.1163-15718093-bja10104.xml>

Paxling L (2019) Transforming technocultures: feminist technoscience, critical design practices and caring imaginaries

Pidun U et al (2021) The untapped potential of ecosystems in health care. BCG Global, 29 March 2021. <https://www.bcg.com/publications/2021/five-principles-of-highly-successful-health-care-ecosystems>

Proposal for a REGULATION OF THE EUROPEAN PARLIAMENT AND OF THE COUNCIL LAYING DOWN HARMONISED RULES ON ARTIFICIAL INTELLIGENCE (ARTIFICIAL INTELLIGENCE ACT) AND AMENDING CERTAIN UNION LEGISLATIVE ACTS 2021 ({SEC(2021) 167 final} - {SWD(2021) 84 final} - {SWD(2021) 85 final})

Rao R (2016) Informed consent, body property, and self-sovereignty. J Law Med Ethics 44:437. <https://www.cambridge.org/core/product/identifier/S1073110500020568/type/journal_article>

Raposo VL (2022) Ex Machina: preliminary critical assessment of the European Draft Act on Artificial Intelligence. Int J Law Inf Technol 30:88. <https://doi.org/10.1093/ijlit/eaac007>

Rascouet-Paz (2020) The indispensable work of understanding intersectionality. Annual Reviews, 11 March 2020. <https://www.annualreviews.org/shot-of-science/story/indispensable-work-understanding-intersectionality>

Regulating AI in the UK. <https://www.adalovelaceinstitute.org/report/regulating-ai-in-the-uk/>

REGULATION (EU) 2016/ 679 OF THE EUROPEAN PARLIAMENT AND OF THE COUNCIL - of 27 April 2016 - on the Protection of Natural Persons with Regard to the Processing of Personal Data and on the Free Movement of Such Data, and Repealing Directive 95/ 46/ EC (General Data Protection Regulation) 88

REGULATION (EU) 2017/ 745 OF THE EUROPEAN PARLIAMENT AND OF THE COUNCIL - of 5 April 2017 - on medical devices, amending Directive 2001/ 83/ EC, Regulation (EC) No 178/ 2002 and Regulation (EC) No 1223/ 2009 and repealing Council Directives 90/ 385/ EEC and 93/ 42/ EEC 175

REGULATION (EU) 2017/746 OF THE EUROPEAN PARLIAMENT AND OF THE COUNCIL of 5 April 2017 on in vitro diagnostic medical devices and repealing Directive 98/79/EC and Commission Decision 2010/227/EU 2016

Regulatory Framework Proposal on Artificial Intelligence | Shaping Europe's Digital Future (6 February 2023) <https://digital-strategy.ec.europa.eu/en/policies/regulatory-framework-ai>

Revised Zero Draft Framework Convention on Artificial Intelligence, Human Rights, Democracy, and the Rule of Law 2023 (CAI (2023) 01)

Science and Technology Workforce: Women in Majority - Products Eurostat News - Eurostat. <https://ec.europa.eu/eurostat/web/products-eurostat-news/w/ddn-20230602-1>

Shai A, Koffler S, Hashiloni-Dolev Y (2021) Feminism, gender medicine and beyond: a feminist analysis of "gender medicine". Int J Equity Health 20:177. <https://equityhealthj.biomedcentral.com/articles/10.1186/s12939-021-01511-5>

Smith G, Rustagi I (2021) When good algorithms go sexist: why and how to advance AI gender equity (SSIR). Stanford Social Innovation Review, 31 March 2021. <https://ssir.org/articles/entry/when_good_algorithms_go_sexist_why_and_how_to_advance_ai_gender_equity>

Translation: Measures for the Management of Generative Artificial Intelligence Services (Draft for Comment) – April 2023 (DigiChina). <https://digichina.stanford.edu/work/translation-measures-for-the-management-of-generative-artificial-intelligence-services-draft-for-comment-april-2023/>

United Nations (2023) DigitALL: innovation and technology for gender equality - UN Observance of International Women's Day 2023 | UN Web TV. UN Web TV, 8 March 2023. <https://media.un.org/en/asset/k1m/k1mpovmzy5>

Vlamos P et al (2013) Artificial intelligence applications in biomedicine. Adv Artif Intell 2013: 1. <https://www.hindawi.com/archive/2013/219137/>

Welten S et al (2022) A privacy-preserving distributed analytics platform for health care data. Methods Inf Med 61:e1. <http://www.thieme-connect.de/DOI/DOI?10.1055/s-0041-1740564>

Westervelt A (2015) The medical research gender gap: how excluding women from clinical trials is hurting our health. The Guardian (30 April 2015). <https://www.theguardian.com/lifeandstyle/2015/apr/30/fda-clinical-trials-gender-gap-epa-nih-institute-of-medicine-cardiovascular-disease>

Young K, Fisher J, Kirkman M (2019) "Do mad people get endo or does endo make you mad?": Clinicians' discursive constructions of medicine and women with endometriosis. Fem Psychol 29:337. <https://doi.org/10.1177/0959353518815704>

Zucker I, Prendergast BJ (2020) Sex differences in pharmacokinetics predict adverse drug reactions in women. Biol Sex Differ 11:32. <https://doi.org/10.1186/s13293-020-00308-5>

The Role of AI in Mental Health Applications and Liability

Petra Müllerová

Contents

Abstract The COVID-19 pandemic has affected the entire area of health care, including care provided to patients with mental health problems. Due to the stressful nature of the pandemic, the number of patients experiencing mental health problems, especially depression or anxiety, has increased. Even well-before the pandemic, Europe struggled with a lack of mental health care, which was especially caused by the long waiting times. The problem seems to have been solved by the plethora of mental health applications that are freely available on the market. Given the user's

P. Müllerová (✉)
Lund University, Lund, Sweden
e-mail: petra.mullerova@jur.lu.se

E. Gill-Pedro, A. Moberg (eds.), *YSEC Yearbook of Socio-Economic Constitutions 2023*, YSEC Yearbook of Socio-Economic Constitutions (2024) 2023: 275–310,
https://doi.org/10.1007/16495_2023_60, Published online: 10 November 2023

accessibility to these applications, I decided to scrutinise the safety of using AI in these health apps, with a particular focus on chatbots. I examined whether existing European legislation may protect users from possible harm to their health and require these mental health applications to be certified as medical devices.

After analysing the Product Liability Directive and the upcoming legislation focused on liability associated with AI, I must state that there is insufficient transparency and protection for users of these applications. Based on experience from the user's perspective, I have identified the lack of (1) scheduling an appointment with a healthcare professional, (2) human oversight, and (3) transparency as regards the type of AI used. Due to the 'black box problem', it is likely that the user who was harmed will not be able to get compensation because of the difficulty of proving causality between the defect and the damage.

1 Introduction

The COVID-19 pandemic represented a significant global health challenge. Developed states with public healthcare had a great advantage in dealing with this crisis, which affected not only patients with COVID-19 but also patients suffering from other diseases. They thus caused new diseases, especially in the field of mental health. More than 678 million people suffered from the disease, but the measures imposed to restrict the spread of the coronavirus limited the availability of health services for hundreds of millions of people suffering from other diseases.[1] The attention of all European Union (EU) Member States focused on developing a vaccine and stopping the spread of the virus. All patients suffering from non-life-threatening illnesses were placed in the adjacent dormitory. Many Member States cancelled preventive care, postponed most operations, and tried to keep as many places in the hospital as possible for patients with COVID-19. At this moment, Member States that have already introduced telemedicine services—in at least certain fields of the healthcare sector—could provide consultations to patients via video call and prescribe e-prescriptions. Those Member States that did not have such a developed eHealth sector had to improvise to ensure the continuation of health care. Their efforts were mainly focussed at the level of hospitals or even healthcare professionals. One of the ways to achieve affordable and effective health care in these dire times is through the use of mobile health apps.

[1] Worldometer (2020).

In some European countries, such as Germany,[2] France,[3] or the UK,[4] some of these applications were part of the healthcare system and therefore established medical means. This in contrast to other countries, especially from Central and Eastern Europe, that had no extensive experience using these applications.[5] However, the market for mobile health applications, which already contained more than 300,000 applications in 2017, provided a helping hand. Due to the easy availability and simplicity of the use of these health apps, which are used by means of smartphones and the Internet, as well as the low costs—or even no costs—attached to them, health professionals from various fields began to use health applications for diagnosis, treatment, and monitoring of their patients. The benefit was evident: no longer was there a need to schedule a physical appointment with their patients, thereby halting the spread of the coronavirus. Particularly, the use of mobile applications in three fields began to increase, namely (1) applications enabling video calls between doctor and patient, (2) applications aimed at specialists in dermatology, ophthalmology, and laryngology that allow sending imaginary of the symptoms, and (3) applications that are monitoring the condition of chronically ill patients, for example, the glucose levels of people with diabetes. The COVID-19 pandemic was a big boom for developing these applications. More than 90,000 mobile health applications were launched in 2020 alone, which translates to an average of 250 new health apps being launched every day in 2020.[6]

Healthcare professionals were not the only actors looking for ways to stabilise the health of citizens. The citizens themselves became the main actors. Thanks to every citizen with a smartphone connected to the Internet, citizens have access to health apps irrespective of their doctor's decision.[7] Especially, psychological help has become a highly sought-after area. Naturally, long-term patients who could not visit any therapists, psychologists, or psychiatrists began to seek the help of these easily retrievable healthcare applications. Research conducted by The Organization for the Review of Care and Health Apps (ORCHA) within the UK shows that the number of downloads of digital mental apps has increased by almost 200% from the summer of 2019 to the summer of 2020. [8] The second large group seeking these apps

[2]Germany disposes of a special system called DIGA, which is controlled by the German Federal Institute for Drugs and Medical Devices. Based on this system, the manufacturers can register the Digital Health Applications as medical devices. More information can be found at this link: https://www.bfarm.de/EN/Medical-devices/Tasks/DiGA-and-DiPA/Digital-Health-Applications/_node.html.

[3]Müllerová (2020), p. 139.

[4]The UK has a special organisation that checks the security of digital health applications.

The Organization for the Review of Care and Health Apps (ORCHA) provides the core infrastructure to overcome these barriers and introduce digital health safely. More information can be found at this link: https://orchahealth.com/.

[5]Nahy and Williams (2021), p. 11.

[6]IQVIA (2021), p. 4.

[7]Ming et al. (2020).

[8]ORCHA (2021), p. 3.

was new patients, who often developed mental health problems caused by the COVID-19 pandemic. Due to the strict measures in most European countries, such as restricting all aspects of social life and—often—multiple lockdowns, a significant part of the population began to suffer from social isolation, anxiety, and even depression. A particular group was teenagers and children who could not attend school for several months in many countries. The lack of contact with peers at such a sensitive age could lead to turbulence in their mental development and significantly affect their mental health. For these reasons, mobile applications focusing on mental health became the most numerous groups of health applications in 2020, accounting for up to 22%.[9] Although the COVID-19 pandemic was not the cause of the emergence of mental health applications (MHA), it catalysed these applications' massive growth and further development.

This article's central research focus is an examination of the safety of MHAs, with a specific emphasis on the under-regulated category encompassing those not categorised as medical devices and lacking prescription by healthcare professionals. The primary research pertains to freely accessible MHAs tailored for the diagnosis or treatment of depression or anxiety, with a particular emphasis on the integration of AI technology, notably in the form of chatbots, as a potential source of risk. Considering that users of these MHAs may belong to a vulnerable demographic grappling with mental health challenges, this article places paramount importance not only on scrutinising their safe usage but mostly on delving into the potential harms stemming from the use of AI within MHAs, as well as the mechanisms available for addressing liability in the context of these issues. The overarching research question driving this study is as follows: To what extent does the existing European legislative framework adequately protect users of AI-based MHAs in the event of harm? To address this question comprehensively, the research encompasses a doctrinal analysis of both existing and forthcoming European legislation. Additionally, the study incorporates an original qualitative inquiry conducted on a sample of MHAs, thereby providing valuable insights into the practical implementation and implications of these regulations within the sphere of AI-based MHAs. To address the aforementioned research question effectively, it is imperative to first identify the motivations driving both society and individuals towards the use of these applications. This includes an assessment of societal and technological readiness, as well as individuals' willingness to incorporate MHAs into their mental health treatment. By evaluating these factors, it becomes possible to ascertain whether the utilisation of MHAs represents a pertinent issue of contemporary significance. Subsequently, a comprehensive examination of the existing European legislation governing MHAs will be conducted. Within the framework of these identified concerns, the study will endeavour to provide insights that align with the provisions of existing and forthcoming European legislation, ultimately contributing to a more robust understanding of safeguarding AI-based MHAs and their users.

---

[9]IQVIA (2021), p. 8.

1.1 Why Are Mobile Health Applications a Vital Topic for European Healthcare Systems?

Miller and Polson point out that, especially in the field of mental health, we have already crossed the border of utopia and set up a new epoque of digital health, which is, however, accompanied by many unanswered ethical and legal questions.[10] These applications already exist and play a vital role in the lives of 22–44% of European citizens throughout the EU.[11] Every day we are confronted with up to 370,000 health applications that are just a simple click away through, for instance, Google Play and the Apple Store. With the COVID-19 pandemic, the supply and demand of these applications has substantially grown.[12] Within Germany, 35% of the population used health applications in 2020, while in 2021, this number has risen to 42%.[13] Member States are aware of this vast, uncontrollable market, which—I argue—should not be made tame by regulatory means. On the contrary, governments should promote the use of mobile applications for the benefit of their healthcare systems and increase the quality of their healthcare services provided to citizens. Some Member States understood this opportunity and started working on integrating various elements of health. Sweden declared in 2025 Visas for eHealth 2025:

> In 2025, Sweden will be the best in the world at using the opportunities offered by digitisation and eHealth to make it easier for people to achieve good and equal health and welfare [. . .][14]

The market forecast of the Health Mobile Apps for 2026 is around $4230 million. This is an extreme increase compared to 2018, when the market value was only $609 million.[15] There are two factors that have promoted the use of these applications in the European healthcare systems. The *first* factor is the ageing European population. The population in Member States is ageing at different rates. Nevertheless, there is a common denominator, namely the working population is decreasing, and the older people (over 65 years old) and very old citizens (over 85 years old) are increasing. The EU's median age is projected to increase by 4.5 years during the next three decades, which means it will reach 48.2 years by 2050.[16] These statistics indicate that our ageing population will require more intensive and, due to the lengthening life expectancy, more extended health care than is the case nowadays. Wildenbos' research has confirmed the theory that these apps represent a promising future for older adults in the treatment of chronic diseases. However, the research also points out that cognitive and physical ability barriers of older adults are

---

[10] Miller and Polson (2019), p. 213.

[11] Buchholz (2020).

[12] ORCHA (2021).

[13] Statista (2022).

[14] Ministry of Health and Social Affairs (2016), p. 3.

[15] Statista (2021).

[16] Eurostat (2020).

currently not applied to the fullest in mobile health interfaces.[17] Zooming specifically in on the issue of mental health, already today, more than 20% of people over 60 years old suffer from mental illnesses, which account for more than 6% of all diseases in this segment of the population. We cannot forget that among these illnesses, neurological diseases—such as dementia—affect mainly older people. The World Health Organization predicts that the number of people with dementia will triple in the next 30 years.[18] Moving on to the *second* factor, which goes hand in hand with the first factor, is the lack of healthcare professionals, specifically psychologists. Studies show that, with some exceptions, such as Denmark or Sweden, most Member States still need to meet the recommended limit of 20 psychologists per 100,000 inhabitants. Particularly, Spain appears to have the most significant shortage and has only 5.14 psychologists per 100,000 inhabitants.[19] This ratio will most likely not improve, seeing the decrease in the number of the working population and the increase of life expectancy. Bohr and Memarzadeh convincingly argue that the shortage of healthcare professionals is creating a need for AI as a tool used to fill this gap in demand.[20] In addition to the aforementioned two factors, two causes support the implementation of MHA, namely (1) long waiting times, and (2) life in rural or isolated areas. The waiting time is often a reason that discourages patients from seeking treatment. In most cases, the waiting period varies from 1 month to 8 months, depending on the Member State and the severity of the diagnosis. It is also important to mention the last factor, which is the physical availability of health care. In 2019, more than 22% of people over 65 were living in rural areas and 38% in intermediate regions.[21] These areas usually require travelling to a larger city for treatment which can be a complicated factor for older people, thereby making it unavailable for them.

MHA seems the perfect solution to all the complications, as defined above. Older people are the first generation that could master the use of modern technologies to a greater extent for the benefit of their health. In 2020, more than 60% of this part of the population stated that they regularly use the Internet. In some countries such as Denmark, Sweden, and Netherlands, more than 90% of this age group is able to use the Internet for the purpose of their health. Although applications cannot fully replace face-to-face therapy with a psychologist, they can monitor the patient, provide important information to the psychologist about the patient, and be the last resort in an emergency that may also call for help. Psychologists can save time and devote themselves to new patients on the waiting list. An important factor, especially for older people or people living in isolated areas, is the possibility of connecting with their doctor without needing to travel to bigger cities. However, according to

[17] Ernsting et al. (2017); Wildenbos et al. (2019), p. 76.

[18] World Health Organisation (2017).

[19] Bernardo et al. (2021).

[20] Bohr and Memarzadeh (2020), p. 34.

[21] Eurostat (2020).

Statens medicinsk-etiska råd (SMER),[22] these applications can also contribute to providing better health care to patients through faster diagnosis, greater awareness and control of their body and behaviour or better cooperation with their doctor. On a broader scale, these applications can benefit the healthcare system, especially since they may result in significant financial savings.[23]

1.2 Preparedness of Society for Mental Health Apps as the Standard Device in Healthcare

If we talk about the preparedness of society, there are two questions to be answered. First, from the position of the user, the question is raised whether European citizens are ready to transform themselves from application users to patients who listen to the advice of their 'online therapist'? Due to the advanced development of health applications in the UK, I will start with the report of the company ORCHA, which is active in the industry of Digital Mental Health. Research on 2000 subjects confirmed that 36% of adults are interested in getting a referral to an MHA to help them address their problems with anxiety, stress, depression, panic attacks, eating disorders or self-harm. The percentage of positive answers decreases with age. Concretely, amongst the age group of 18 and 24, up to 55% indicated they would like a referral for an MHA. Based on this survey, young people prefer to use mental health applications over physical contact with a doctor. On the other hand, a study by the University of Edinburgh marked the interest of young people between 17 and 25 years as only moderate and recommended application developers to increase awareness of the usefulness of these applications.[24] Therefore, the ORCHA report should be taken with a grain of salt. Even more, the ORCHA survey only offered the interviewees a choice of closed alternatives, namely whether they would prefer either a physical meeting with a therapist or the use of MHA. Focussing again on the first report, it seems no surprise that the interviewees would rather seek the advice of a physician than that of a freely available application, especially when considering the seriousness of the specified problems.

To properly set up the methods of discovering people's intentions to use these applications is also essential. As many as 37% of respondents said convenience is the most crucial criterion. Although patients can always call the emergency line, they cannot expect their doctor to be always available. In these situations, the application can provide a certain sense of security and stability. Two other reasons in the study are connected to flexibility and immediacy. The application enables frequent therapy in the comfort of your home, without the need to travel or hire a babysitter for

---

[22] The organ named by the Swedish government has the task of analysing medical-ethical issues from an overall societal perspective and stimulating the public debate on medical-ethical issues.

[23] SMER (2017), p. 4.

[24] Sawrikar and Mote (2022), p. 5.

children, or during a lunch break without the need to leave work. Thus, these apps provide people who cannot secure enough time to visit a doctor for therapy. Another issue, especially vocalised by people in the prime of productive age, is the costs. If they are unwilling or simply cannot wait for a timeslot for therapy that is reimbursed by the State, there are no valid options left than the use of an application, seeing that they often cannot financially afford private therapy. Young people between the ages of 18 and 24 also consider applications to be trustworthy. This group overall marks digital healthcare as more private, probably because they do not have to share sensitive personal data face-to-face with another person.[25] Generally, it is necessary to expand awareness among people about the usefulness of these applications. This holds even more true, as people do not have a negative attitude towards them and would like to use them.

The second point of view is the overall preparedness of the healthcare system to implement health applications. Here, not only the applications themself will play a role, but especially the ecosystem in which these applications are situated, which is either an accelerator or a brake to their implementation. This ecosystem can be divided into four fields, namely (1) the technological background, (2) the awareness of technologies, (3) the availability of data, and (4) the maturity of the business model. The first area is the technological background, which offers a robust infrastructure in the form of fast Internet, high-quality smart devices, and developing AI. These three elements can play an even more significant role in application management. Turning to the second field: the awareness of technologies, which is not only limited to people owning devices for the use of these applications but also that they are used to working with these apps. Nowadays, every smartphone or smartwatch has a pre-installed fitness app and some well-being or MHA, which means that the technology enables the use of these apps. The OECD report for the years 2019 and 2020 claims that personal consultations fell by almost 20% on average in Member States. On the other hand, teleconsultations have doubled from 11% to 22% in 12 of them.[26] According to Davenport the third area is the availability of data, practically any data necessary for the operation of the application. Due to Big data, it is relatively easy to get to all the required data flows. The last area is the maturity of the business model. Due to the use of some types of AI, applications can also learn and thus determine a model that will sell the given application well. Some apps are more successful at this than others. Given that already established business models exist in other branches of industry, they can also be applied in the healthcare sector.[27]

---

[25] ORCHA (2022), p. 3.

[26] Orăştean et al. (2022), p. 68.

[27] Davenport et al. (2022), p. 4.

1.3 Concerns in Using Mental Health Applications for Diagnosis, Treatment and Monitoring of Patients

According to the ORCHA report, people identify three problems related to MHAs, which negatively affect their use. The indicated problems are (1) protection of personal data and their privacy, (2) scientifically based treatment and (3) its effectiveness and reimbursement of these services.[28] In part, these concerns are intertwined with the concerns of healthcare professionals, which are particularly: (1) the safety and usability of the applications, and (2) liability, especially in the case of using AI.[29]

Mental health is a sensitive and personal issue; for this reason, patients often take longer and are more prudent when choosing their therapist than their general practitioner. Entrusted health data are generally considered sensitive data. As many as 35% of people are concerned about the security of their personal data that they entrust to MHAs.[30] At first glance, the issue of personal data protection is solved by the European General Data Protection Regulation 2016/679 (GDPR).[31] Article 9 regulates the processing of special categories of data, which also includes health data. This data may be collected, processed, or provided to third parties only if the conditions defined in Article 9 are met. Paragraph 2, letter a) of Article 9 seems to be problematic since it requires the data subject to give explicit consent to processing their health data. This formulation gives the data subjects room to decide to whom and for what purpose they entrust their health data. However, this provision does not consider the practical functioning of MHAs. In reality, the user grants consent to the specified purposes of personal data processing within the 'terms and conditions' of the MHA. A large Deloitte study from 2017 showed that an average of 87% of users do not read the terms and conditions to which they consent for the purpose of applications.[32] These facts offer the possibility of using the user's personal health data for further sharing with third parties (especially for profit) and using their data by the application manufacturer. Although the manufacturer's main interest may be selling the user's data and thereby creating a financial profit, it may be vital for the manufacturer to use the user's data. Particularly, the users' data may play a role in maintaining and improving the quality of the application. However, applications using AI based on machine learning also need this data to train the AI. The question remains whether users would still be willing to use MHA if they read all the terms and conditions for processing their data. In conclusion, these applications pose a danger to the user's health data. However, the danger is not rooted in the misuse of

[28] ORCHA (2022), p. 6.

[29] Byambasuren et al. (2019).

[30] ORCHA (2021).

[31] Regulation (EU) 2016/679. The protection of natural persons with regard to the processing of personal data and on the free movement of such data. European Parliament and Council. http://data.europa.eu/eli/reg/2016/679/oj.

[32] Deloitte (2017), p. 8.

the user's data, but rather stems from taking advantage of the incapacity or impossibility of the user to become familiar with the precise terms and conditions of the processing of their data. Although this may seem like a fraudulent technique to obtain user data, the responsibility regarding the data is also on the user's side. For this reason, the concern expressed in the survey is whether it is valid.

The biggest concern is shared by both users and healthcare providers and revolves around whether the MHAs provide scientific evidence-based treatment. Almost half of the users expressed concern that AI in the form of a chatbot in an MHA cannot provide them with scientifically based treatment that is equivalent to the treatment provided by a doctor. This concern was also expressed by healthcare providers, who argue that before they start providing applications to their patients, the applications should be objectively assessed as to whether they are of high quality and useful.[33] These concerns were also expressed by SMER in their publication 'The Quantified Human: Ethical Aspects on Self-monitoring by Wearables and Health Apps', where they state:

> However, only a few of the health apps currently available have been developed on the basis of scientific evidence and ethics.[34]

The Swedish authorities only confirmed the concerns of Swedish physicians that already in 2015 indicated the lack of evidence-based content as the most substantial weakness of health apps.[35] If we look at health apps in general, according to a BBC study of 5000 health apps, more than 80% do not meet the standards set by UK legislation.[36] The shortcomings stem not only from the failure to meet the standards from the creation phase but also from a lack of regular updates in the scientific and security fields. And out of 83% of health applications, only 1% of all downloaded health apps make up.[37] This means that most of these applications are unsuccessful and do not provide further updates although they continue to be used by hundreds of thousands of people. Users often never find out that their applications are no longer up-to-date and secure. A study in the UK examined MHAs, and of the 676 applications reviewed, only 32% met the minimum standards for safety. Even a Karolinska Institute study confirmed that mental applications could be harmful to users:

> [...] some apps developed for the purpose of suicide prevention included some potentially harmful content, such as featuring descriptions of suicide, and could in fact be used as a source of ideas by highly vulnerable people. This wasn't the apps' intended use, but because they hadn't been adequately tested, this significant safety issue hadn't been addressed.[38]

[33] E-hälsomyndigheten (2022), p. 21.

[34] SMER (2017), p. 2.

[35] Zhang and Koch (2015).

[36] Kleinman (2021).

[37] IQVIA (2021), p. 10.

[38] ORCHA (2022), p. 6.

Baskar and Rao underline that users, healthcare professionals, experts and authorities agree on the need to sufficiently clinically test health applications as regards their scientific basis and the available updates.[39]

The last concern revolves around liability in case of harm to the patient's health. Considering MHAs, the user's disease can worsen due to incorrect treatment, insufficient monitoring, or incorrect diagnosis. Suppose it is an application that only connects patients with healthcare professionals—who remain responsible for the diagnoses and treatments, the fault lies with the healthcare professionals, and their liability is defined by national law. The problem is present in applications where diagnoses and treatments are performed in whole or in part by AI, mainly in the form of chatbots. For a closer definition of this problem, we must realise that for the successful introduction of these applications in the healthcare sector, there is one more factor that plays a pivotal role—the legal infrastructure. In the next chapter, I will describe the existing legal regulations that regulate MHAs and the shortcomings that complicate determining the liability for AI decisions in the context of MHAs.

2 Legal Basis for Using Mental Health Applications

Before delving on the regulation governing MHAs, it is necessary first to discuss what MHAs entail. Both European law and the national law of Member States do not define MHAs. Even if European law does not have a health applications definition, it works with the concept of health apps. Thus, I considered the definition proposed by two national authorities: (1) the Swedish authority *eHälsomyndigheten* and (2) the French authority *Haute autorité de santé* (HAS). The approach of these authorities shows the different existing views on the issue of health applications without a specific focus on mental health. The Swedish report *'Hälsoappar förutsättningar och användning'* broadly defines health applications to also include certain social services. According to eHälsomyndigheten, a health app is used by individuals or staff in healthcare and social services to maintain or improve the individual's health.[40] HAS specifies that—according to literature—health apps are medical devices. However, according to HAS, this usage is not yet routine practice:

> Each app generally targets a very specific objective, but the sector as a whole claims to enhance the quality of care in general, increase efficiency, and improve clinical research.... This empowerment does not replace healthcare professionals but helps supplement treatment. This should help optimise referrals to healthcare professionals.[41]

---

[39] Bhaskar and Rao (2022), p. 51.

[40] Hälsoappar förutsättningar och användning (2022), p. 4.

[41] Haute Autorité de Santé (2021), p. 9.

Given that this contribution specifically focuses on the MHAs—as defined above and classified by the INQVIA—I will not discuss MHAs falling outside this scope.[42] Consequently, I have excluded apps of the wellness and disease prevention category, although such apps may be aimed at mental health, which includes those dedicated to meditation, stress management, or better sleep. Additionally, I excluded applications dealing with treatment because these apps prescribe medicine. However, MHAs fulfil the category of diagnostic and monitoring applications. For the purposes of this article, I will discuss MHAs that diagnose or monitor the user's mental problems, which require therapy, possibly medication treatment. Thus, this contribution covers, for example, diseases like depression and anxiety.

The EU has adopted regulation dealing with defective products that has been affecting the user's health for several decades. In the 1990s, diagnostic, monitoring or treatment devices were placed in the limelight. Since these products are believed to cause harm to the patient's health, Directive 93/42/EEC of 14 June 1993 concerning medical devices[43] has been amended to increase patient safety. This Directive had to be modified to better correspond to new technologies—also in the field of AI. Consequently, the EU adopted two new directives to regulate all types of medical devices: Medical Devices Regulation 2017/745/EU (MDR)[44] and In Vitro Diagnostic Medical Devices Regulation 2017/746/EU (IVDR).[45] These directives were supposed to come into effect in May 2020. Due to the COVID-19 pandemic, their entry into force was postponed by 1 year. Although it may seem clear that MHAs will fall under this European regulation, this is not the case in the vast majority of cases. Therefore, I must not only define what a medical device is but also what other possibilities of regulation, if any, exist for MHAs. The following section will explain how two similar applications can be subject to different European regulations.

2.1 What Happens if the Mental Health Application Is Considered a Medical Device?

In the context of MHAs falling under the regulation of the MDR, we will start from the definition of the medical device given in Article 2, para 1:

---

[42] Haute Autorité de Santé (2021), p. 10.

[43] Directive 93/42/EEC of 14 June 1993 concerning medical devices. Council of the European Communities. http://data.europa.eu/eli/dir/1993/42/oj.

[44] Regulation (EU) 2017/745 of the European Parliament and of the Council of 5 April 2017 on medical devices, amending Directive 2001/83/EC, Regulation (EC) No 178/2002 and Regulation (EC) No 1223/2009 and repealing Council Directives 90/385/EEC and 93/42/EEC. European Parliament and Council. http://data.europa.eu/eli/reg/2017/745/oj.

[45] Regulation (EU) 2017/746 of the European Parliament and of the Council of 5 April 2017 on in vitro diagnostic medical devices and repealing Directive 98/79/EC and Commission Decision 2010/227/EU. European Parliament and Council. http://data.europa.eu/eli/reg/2017/746/oj.

> 'medical device' means any instrument, apparatus, appliance, software, implant, reagent, material or other article intended by the manufacturer to be used, alone or in combination, for human beings for one or more of the following specific medical purposes:
> - diagnosis, prevention, monitoring, prediction, prognosis, treatment or alleviation of disease,
> - diagnosis, monitoring, treatment, alleviation of, or compensation for, an injury or disability,
> - investigation, replacement or modification of the anatomy or of a physiological or pathological process or state,
> - providing information by means of in vitro examination of specimens derived from the human body, including organ, blood and tissue donations.

Based on the definition, MHAs meet the conditions to be considered a medical device, given that it is software that diagnoses or monitors a disease. Article 1, which discusses the MDR's scope, does not exclude MHAs from its field of application. The fundamental question is why MHAs are deemed medical device? Due to the risks that medical devices pose to the patient's health, they are covered by stricter safety rules intended to protect the patient from death or severe harm caused by such medical devices. Concisely, all medical devices must comply with the general safety and performance requirements set out in Annex I and the evaluation of undesirable side effects. Depending on the classification that ranges from one to four, medical devices are subjected to additional conditions within the framework of clinical testing. However, medical devices have one evaluation criterion in common, namely they must all undergo clinical testing based on the latest scientific evidence. Thus, the use of a medical device represents a much greater guarantee for patients and healthcare professionals. On this basis, Gordon and the collective recommended that MHAs be classified as medical devices.[46]

Due to the safety requirements imposed on medical devices—which differ in accordance to their classification, it is necessary to identify which type of medical device the MHAs entail. According to the MDR, medical devices are classified into four categories: I, IIa, IIb and III. As there is only a small risk associated with devices in class I, their conformity assessment procedure is carried out under the sole responsibility of the manufacturer. The notified body's involvement is only mandatory for medical devices placed in classes IIa, IIb and III. Annex VIII lays down further rules to determine to which class a medical device belongs. It is impossible to assess in which class all MHAs are placed, given that they have different purposes, methods, and the severity of the disease they target. However, some characteristics can help us to judge to which classes these applications may belong.

The MHA should be considered an 'active device'—as defined by Article 2, para 4—as the device depends on a source of energy other than that generated by the human body. The definition in the MDR mentions that software shall also be deemed an active device. Annex VIII was introduced to bring a new definition of the so-called 'Active device intended for diagnosis and monitoring', which is an active device that supplies information for detecting, diagnosing, monitoring, or treating

[46] Gordon et al. (2020).

physiological conditions, states of health, illnesses, or congenital deformities. The most MHAs should be regarded as 'Active device intended for diagnosis and monitoring'. Exceptions to this statement are possible based on the differences among MHAs. Under rules 11 and 13 of Annex VIII, MHAs are software as defined in the MDR, namely as active device intended for diagnosis and monitoring. However, there are further no common denominators as regards the applicability of the other rules in Annex VIII to medical devices. Put differently, these rules of Annex VIII are 'class-specific'. Generally speaking, as the class increases, restrictions increase, especially these applicable to clinical testing. This comes as no surprise since the higher the class, the bigger the risk posed by the medical device. Zooming in on the specific rules of Annex VIII, if the given MHA is used to collect information for the diagnosis, it will be classified as class IIa. However, if it can cause death, MHA becomes the highest class—class III. In case of the possibility of severe deterioration of a person's state of health, the MHA is classified in class IIb.

There is a possibility that MHA will cause death or severe injury to the user. For this reason, I chose exclusively applications dealing with serious mental illnesses, such as depression and anxiety.[47] When using an AI chatbot, we may theoretically end up in a situation where the AI fails to diagnose the user's condition correctly. The user may receive the wrong treatment based on the chatbot's incorrect diagnosis. Theoretically, this error can worsen the disease, i.e. severe deterioration of a person's health and—in extreme cases where the user has suicidal tendencies—the patient's death. However, obtaining data about such an event is practically impossible, thus, no records of such an incident occurring. The missing statistical data are caused by several cumulative factors, such as the anonymity of the MHA user, the possibility of ceasing the use of the application at any time without giving a reason, and the lack of involvement of a medical professional. For this reason, the inclusion of MHA in class IIb or III is only speculative and would have to be assessed by the supervisory authority. All MHAs not worsening the patient's disease will be classified as class I. Even if MHAs fall into the lowest risk group and only undergo clinical testing by the manufacturer, the user's protection is significantly increased. This is mainly because clinical testing must take place, which means that manufacturers of MHA must demonstrate that the application includes the latest scientific evidence and safety requirements. This European legislation currently provides the best guarantee for manufacturers using AI who do not know if their MHA is safe.

2.2 *Mental Health Applications Do Not Have To Be Certified as a Medical Device*

In its report from 2022 on the use of health applications, the Swedish authority eHälsomyndigheten admits that MHAs may not always be considered medical

[47] Parmar (2022), p. 8.

devices and, therefore, may not need to adhere to the MDR.[48] The doctors can also prescribe a health application that is not certified at the EU level as a medical device, but they must carry out a risk assessment for the patient themself. Does this practice comply with European law?

The Court of Justice of the European Union (CJEU) decided in the Brain Products GMBH case of November 15, 2017, that:

> The concept of the medical device does not cover an object designed by its manufacturer for use in human beings to study a physiological process only if it is intended for a medical purpose.[49]

This decision gives a vast space for health apps without a medical purpose. Given the lack of a legislative framework, private companies prefer to invest in developing health apps that can be put on the market without meeting the demanding medical device conditions. In addition, the CJEU expressly declared that sports wearable devices (for example, wellness and fitness applications) make it possible to measure the functioning of the human body, such as blood pressure and the heartbeat. Consequently, these sports wearable devices are not subject to a certification procedure for medical devices. De Grove Valdeyron notes that it is in the developer's interest to minimise the beneficial aspect of health used to measure physiological parameters. In case they are successful in applying the exception for sporting goods, they avoid the strict obligations linked to medical devices.[50] A good example is the Apple company, which never presents the Apple Watch as a medical device. However, under the definition in the MDR, the Apple Watch is software that monitors physiological processes in the human body, such as heart rate or blood pressure, which entails that the Apple Watch is a medical device. Not all manufacturers of smart watches market their application to be excluded from the MDR's scope. An example is the Empatica Embrace, which is specifically designed to monitor these patients.[51]

I have to add that developers also benefit from the CJEU's decision entailing that '*[g]eneral-purpose software used in a medical environment is not a medical device*'.[52] This line of case law not only eliminates connected fitness and well-being wearable devices but also those that do not clearly fall within the scope of a medical device. This can be the case with MHAs, which may be regarded as a medical device tailored to treat the patient's anxiety by providing breathing exercises or monitoring their panic attacks. However, the using of MHA needs to be completed through the expertise of therapists, or at least the therapist's access to patient data. MHAs that entirely treat the patient—without any intervention of therapists—may adversely affect the patient. Thus, these MHAs will be placed in a higher risk

---

[48] E-hälsomyndigheten (2022), p. 19.

[49] CJEU, Case C-219/115, Brain Products GmbH contre BioSemi VOF e.a, ECLI :EU : C :2012 :742. point 11.

[50] De Grove-Valdeyron (2019).

[51] Davenport et al. (2022), p. 51.

[52] Point 5.

class by the MDR. Some medical devices, after the adoption of the MDR, met the new conditions to be classified as high-risk medical devices. Due to technological progress and increased security protection, they were pushed to a higher risk class. Martelli pointed out that, these devices will have to meet stricter conditions for clinical studies, and this means a significant increase in cost for manufacturers.[53] Consequently, it is not worthwhile for some manufacturers to register their products as medical devices. Even if most MHAs should be classified as class I, i.e. the class with the lowest security requirements, the manufacturers must conduct a clinical study. Due to their intention to generate profits, they are trying to take advantage of the decision of the CJEU by claiming that their MHAs pursue other purposes than medical one. This explains why manufacturers prefer to label MHA as a wellness or mood application, which aims to improve the user's well-being or healthy lifestyle. Based on this legislative analysis, I state that user protection is significantly reduced due to the possibility of freely introducing MHA to the market as a wellness app, thereby falling outside the regulatory framework of the MDR.

3 Users' Perspectives of AI in Mental Health Applications

AI used in applications is often seen as the manufacturer's know-how—or even the manufacturer's corporate secrets. However, when looking at an MHA, the operation is based on chatbots driven by AI. Thus, the application becomes an opaque and impregnable castle behind whose walls not only ordinary users, but also experienced programmers cannot see. If the manufacturer does not want to show how the AI works, the user cannot determine when and how it affects him. This lack of transparency innate to AI algorithms is often referred to as the 'black box problem'. Zednik confirms that machine learning is opaque; it is difficult to know why they do what they do or how they work, therefore it is necessary to create a framework paying particular attention to users.[54]

If we want to examine what harm the user may incur and who is responsible for the harm caused, we need to consider the MHAs from the user's perspective. Put differently, we are to examine the MHA from a position that regards the AI as a transparent mechanism due to the fact that it does not know the input or output data, the biases it contains, or the purpose for which the AI was programmed. Thus, in this section, I only use data that can be found by the user. Based on this assessment, I have identified possible criteria pivotal to classify MHA, which will aid to identify the risks of individual applications and subsequently examine the responsibility of individual actors.

---

[53] Martelli et al. (2019).

[54] Zednik (2021), p. 265.

3.1 *Determination of Relevant Factors to Identify the Riskiness of MHAs*

As already mentioned, the user does not know what kind of AI is used in each application. Given that the issue of safe use of AI in MHAs is closely related to the point of liability when harm occurs to the user's health, there is a need to identify the actors providing these MHAs. I have identified three factors—based on ethical[55] and legal criteria—that could help to determine liability: (1) the presence of human oversight, (2) the presence of a healthcare professional, and (3) the use of AI based on machine learning. The source was the MHAs analysis data of the project *'Best for you app library'*, which scrutinised several thousand MHAs. Their assessment is based on ORCHA's research, according to the Evidence Standards Framework for Digital Health Technologies. This project assessed 20 applications focusing on the treatment of depression. Based on this data, I have identified three likely models that are used. However, since the project could not confirm the inclusion of the three factors determining liability, the following is based on probability. The method of using AI or the involvement of human oversight can only be precisely identified with access to the manufacturer's data. For this reason, I modulated theoretical models, which are most likely reflected in real MHAs.

The first factor I examined was the involvement of a healthcare professional. I have classified four possible variants, some of which may overlap. I evaluated whether the healthcare professional (a) participated in the creation of the application; (b) can be involved during the use of the application; (c) cannot influence the content of the application during the time of use of the app; (d) did not participate in any way either in the creation or during the use of the application. I started with 20 applications, all rated 65% or higher as part of the project. Any score below 65% would indicate that an App has some issues that users should investigate further before using this app.[56] A total of eight applications fulfil the requirement entailing that a professional is present during the creation of the application and the use of the app. However, eleven applications showed either the inability to connect with a professional while using the application or content that did not correspond to the participation of a healthcare professional. Only one application demonstrated the non-involvement of a professional. Since I used a database with preselected applications that are all deemed to be safe, I maintain that the statistics would be different in the case of randomly selected MHAs. In the next chapter, where I will talk about the involvement of AI and the subsequent risks reflected in the liability for injury, I will evaluate applications that are unsupervised by healthcare professionals at the time the application is used by the user.

As part of human oversight, I can assess the relevance of individual functions and the availability of technical support. Only one application provided support and

[55] Morley et al. (2020).

[56] The search in the library Best for you is available at this link: https://bestforyou.orcha.co.uk/defaultsearch/?search=Depression.

control of all areas of the application and indicated the time period before soliciting help from healthcare professionals. Most of the applications, 16, provided support and managed all parts of the application but did not specify a (recommended) maximum time of using the app before seeking professional help. Only three applications did not provide support or did not control certain parts of the application at all. All of the applications showed the presence of human oversight.

Given that ORCHA examines MHAs only from the user's perspective, it is practically impossible to detect whether the application uses deep machine learning (DML) or another type of AI. On the other hand, according to some experts, it is necessary to develop and reveal the theoretical possibilities of the functioning of the AI algorithm to bring greater transparency.[57] For this reason, I did not assess individual applications within the framework of missing data from the manufacturer and divided MHA into theoretical models of AI use. First, MHAs that use AI but without a deep learning machine system often use chatbots, which are mainly based on so-called language models. These chatbots chat with the user without the potential to improve their abilities based on the user's response. The second group is represented by MHA, which uses DML. This group can be divided into supervised and unsupervised systems. It is necessary to clarify that when I describe supervised DML, I do not mean control by healthcare professionals. I mean rather developers or other AI experts who control the 'behaviour of AI' but not the actual recommendation it gives. In all cases of DML, I am talking about applications without the presence of healthcare professionals.

Every AI system has pitfalls and can be dangerous for users under certain circumstances. In any case, from the point of view of responsibility for causing harm to the user's health, I find AI DML potentially more complex. DML differs from machine learning in that it 'thinks' in a more complex and nonlinear manner, i.e. processes input to output in several layers. The algorithm applies a nonlinear transformation to its input and uses what it learns to produce an output. The process continues until the output reaches an acceptable level of accuracy. The training of this AI is based on having inputs and outputs

> Supervised machine learning is the construction of algorithms that are able to produce general patterns and hypotheses by using externally supplied instances to predict the fate of future instances.[58]

Unsupervised machine learning is trained only on input data, and the algorithms bring their outputs without human intervention. The additional value of this method consists of innovation and the discovery of new connections.

---

[57] Turk (2018).

[58] Singh et al. (2016).

3.2 *Classification of Mental Health Applications According to the Level of Risk for Users*

Based on the familiarity with how 20 MHAs work, I have divided them into three theoretical models according to the three essential identified criteria, as defined in Sect. 3.1. Given the lack of data and resources, I could not create these categories based solely on user experience of MHAs. I started from the ORCHA library, which does not recommend the use of MHA that may be harmful to the user's health. Thus, such applications are already filtered out. From this point of view, my research—which only includes 20 applications—is merely indicative of demonstrating the diversity of individual MHAs, even within one group.

The first group of MHA represents a low risk to the user's health. AI is used as a predefined model for evaluating users' inputs, and, when there seems a need for professional advice, AI enables the intervention of a healthcare professional. The healthcare professional is present in the creation process of MHA and represents a part of human oversight in the case of emergency, but also as an optional service add-on available for users. In this case, the MHA minimises the possible negative impact of AI on users and I have not considered further analysis of these applications due to their high level of security.

The second group may pose a medium risk to users. The healthcare professional is absent and does—thus—provide human oversight. In some MHAs, presence during the development procedure is only ensured, which means that human oversight sees solely upon AI technical support without implementing new scientific evidence with the assistance of healthcare professionals. All services are built on users' communication with AI that does not work on DML.

The third group is classified as high-risk applications. These MHAs completely lack any involvement of healthcare professionals. Some of the applications do not even have any form of human oversight. The application is based on using an unsupervised DML system. Given the unpredictability of the patient's mental health condition and without human oversight of AI decision-making, I find it ethically problematic to allow unsupervised DML to train on data of the patients with mental health problems.

3.3 *Bias as a Possible Cause of Damage to the Health of Mental Health Apps Users*

One of the dangers identified by many healthcare experts when using DML AI is bias. According to the literature, bias can be useful to compensate for human shortcomings, which means that it may reduce human prejudice. Thus, having

DML AI bias may actually contribute to achieving a balanced system.[59,60] As part of the literature review, these DML AI prejudices have been demonstrated to reduce human error[61] or reduce bias that may be present within medical research and public health databases.[62] The European Union Agency for Fundamental Rights (FRA) points out that the development of these disruptive technologies is only possible provided fundamental rights are respected. However, AI bias, the algorithm's bias, is a danger that needs to be addressed. FRA specifies it as follows:

> [...] the tendency of the algorithm to evaluate big data in such a way that it leads to a disadvantage for certain groups, such as women, ethnic minorities or people with disabilities.[63]

In the medical environment, Shusted, in their research on an AI used for preventive control for lung cancer, has shown that AI used produced biased results based on race. The study showed that men of colour are more likely to develop and die from lung cancer than a man from any other different racial or ethnic group. This is compounded by the fact that men of colour are diagnosed with late-stage lung cancer. Given that AI has limited imputations, the researchers investigated whether the input data creates this bias. They found that the guidelines recommend starting preventive screening at 50 years. However, black men have different physiological predispositions, and cancer appears at an earlier age. Thus, AI-based diagnostics could not be functional for this specific group of patients without considering these specifications.[64]

In assessing bias, I will not proceed from the position of discrimination they can create but rather from the definition provided by the Dictionary of Public Health, which defines it as:

> Systematic distortion of results or findings from the true state of affairs, or any of several varieties of processes leading to systematic distortion.[65]

Bias in health care needs to be identified, mainly due to the possible exclusion of a particular part of the population, which is not accurately represented in the general data set. This may result in inaccurate predictions, diagnoses or even treatments, which can have unfair and—more worrisome—damaging consequences for the health of the patients that are part of this inaccurately represented segment of society. The MHA, without subsequent control of a healthcare professional, can base the whole diagnosis or treatment based on bias.

---

[59] Wachter et al. (2018).

[60] Murphy (2021).

[61] Markowetz et al. (2014).

[62] Crawford and Whittaker (2016).

[63] European Union Agency for Fundamental Rights (2022), p. 17.

[64] Shusted et al. (2021).

[65] Last (2007).

In the field of healthcare as a professional field with significant implications, Rajkomar detected four types of bias:[66]

1. Bias stemming from defining the problem and the model used; algorithms are only the results of those who define the problem that must be solved and determine which code to use. For the algorithm to work, it is necessary to correctly establish what a 'successful solution' entails.[67] In MHAs, especially if a healthcare professional is not involved in developing the application, we risk creating an incorrect model that will create bias.
2. Bias arising from training data; data is the second component for creating accurate algorithms. To achieve this goal, machine learning AI is tracked using input data. However, every set of data used for the creation of machine learning AI is—in fact—incomplete; there is a shortage of data from some sections or even a complete lack thereof. Thus, the AI will be trained to create accurate results based on the data that was provided and biased results based on the data that was not provided. A good example is Tat's research that systematically reviewed data from 207 American studies on acute coronary syndrome, which confirmed the underreporting of data from women and patients of colour. Due to the lack of data from these groups, men suffering from chest pain are 2.5 times more likely to be referred to a cardiologist. Further, patients of colour are 40% less likely to receive pain medication than other patients. Concisely, these inaccurate predictions were the result of the lack of data in these groups of society.[68]
3. Bias caused by the interaction with healthcare professionals; healthcare professionals create inputs during the development of the application—but also in the later training process—which can be subjective or do not evaluate the latest scientific findings. MHAs that use this type of information from healthcare professionals, especially various databases of healthcare data, need to overcome this kind of bias. Not only do the databases often contain errors, but also the impossibility of explaining the specific facts of the case. This type of bias is, of course, lacking in MHAs that do not have a healthcare professional present. These MHAs are even more prone to the fourth type of bias.
4. Bias arising from the interaction with the user, namely the patient; the field of mental health is extremely subjective; therefore, users of MHA may not be able to describe all symptoms sufficiently objectively, or they simply downplay, forget or wrongly appraise them.

The existence of bias in the framework of MHAs may lead to incorrect diagnoses, wrong treatments or disregarding urgent cases. Unsupervised DML significantly increases the risk of bias, the training data contains only input data, and the algorithm itself selects examples from them. As a result, the DML AI can identify possible undiscovered connections, but it lacks supervision that would evaluate the

[66] Rajkomar et al. (2018).

[67] Brault and Saxena (2021).

[68] Tat et al. (2020).

correctness of its conclusion. Mental health provides an extremely broad spectrum of deviations within the emotional, communicative, and cognitive field of the user, which may result in AI discovering connections based on wrong premises. Without subsequent control, the user's health may be damaged. Closely related, is how AI often trains or 'learns' on new data provided by users. In the case of unsupervised DML, the so-called 'Artificial Stupidity' can occur, which entails that the AI evaluates certain circumstances as significant, which—in fact—are unimportant to humans, such as unidentifiable noise or a minor change in writing, as significant. In this case, there is a complete reinterpretation of the object, which, as stated by SMER, can have significant consequences in healthcare.[69] Thus, the author agrees with Brault and Saxena that evaluating the validity of the correlation and of the causality can only be executed by humans.[70]

At the same time, there is an assumption that the majority of MHAs will not use unsupervised DML, since a human is involved in the training of DML. This effect manifests itself in two aspects, which are fallibility and reluctance. Both are associated with using the user's data as training data for the algorithm. Fallibility means that users may make mistakes or input data that their memory has distorted. Reluctance is more focused on knowingly providing incorrect data. Put differently, the users are unwilling to share complete or accurate data. In the case of mental health, which deals with the individual's private feelings and thoughts, both fallibility and reluctance may very well manifest—at least to some extent. Tegen, in her study, shows that both aspects independently lead to a decrease in the accuracy of DML systems.[71] Seeing the subjectivity of mental health, the manufacturer of MHA takes a significant risk when using this technology if the manufacturer issues unsupervised AI, it will lead to a significant distortion based on the user's data. Their AI model will 'learn' behaviour that will not display an objective attitude towards the given problem. Perhaps the least famous example outside the healthcare industry is the chatbot 'Tay', which Microsoft created on March 23, 2016. Based on the data provided by a Twitter user (only two tweets), she accepted anti-Semitic attitudes. Due to the hateful content Tay generated, she was taken down within 24 h. Even if this example is extreme, it shows how easy it is to change the output of a DML system based on consciously or unconsciously faulty data from the user.[72]

---

[69] SMER (2020), p. 5.

[70] Brault and Saxena (2021).

[71] Tegen (2022).

[72] Paul Mason (2016).

4 Liability Concerning the Mental Health Applications

As part of the use of AI in applications, many ethical and legal questions arise, which are often unclear, and European society is in the process of answering them. Of course, the law is significantly delayed because these technologies progress daily. The problem is mainly the complexity of this area and its rapid development. OurWold data provided a comparison: in 2018, 2019 and 2022, several hundred experts were asked in which year there would be a 50% chance that 'Human-Artificial Intelligence' would exist. Whereas in 2018, only 75% of experts marked the date in the nearest 100 years, in 2022, this number has risen to 90%. Legislation is not able to keep up with this rapid development.[73] Therefore, we should at least focus on areas where the use of AI can pose harm to the user's health or even result in the user's death. Thus, in this part, I focused on liability when using AI in MHAs.

Liability is regulated in European law through the harmonisation of national law through the Product Liability Directive (PLD) and the non-harmonised national level of the Member States. As regards the former: given that the PLD is a directive, it must be transposed into national law. Consequently, the PLD may be adapted to fit the national legal order, which, thus, also brings the possibility of differences at the level of the Member States. Concerning the latter: particularly, the framework of civil law plays a role. The national civil law is particularly related to the liability associated with the provision of healthcare services and the presence of a healthcare professional. However, the EU is in the process of also harmonising this field with its Regulation on Artificial Intelligence (AI Act), which means a new dimension to product liability in the health fields. Further, there is a need to consider future European regulation, which, like the revised Directive on liability for defective products and the AI Liability Directive, should take note of the specific issues brought by AI.

4.1 Application of the Product Liability Directive on the Mental Health Applications

PLD establishes in Article 1 a basic rule that recognises a producer's liability for damage caused by a defect in their product. This general rule certainly contains exceptions, but—in principle—it applies to all types of products, including medical devices. Given that this is a directive, which is subsequently transposed by Member States, there is solely a harmonised framework as regards principles. The compensation process is determined by national law, and may thus differ from Member State to Member State. An important factor to examine in MHAs is whether a healthcare professional is present while using the MHA. The question of whether the MHA is

[73] Roser (2023).

regarded as a medical device or rather merely a medium that connects the user to the healthcare professional is of vital importance since the obligations stemming from the PLD will differ. Generally, the healthcare provider is responsible for providing treatment and providing medical devices. Their responsibility is mainly determined by a special law that deals with providing health services. In most cases, the healthcare professional is not responsible for the result of the treatment, as this cannot be guaranteed. Their liability lies in providing treatment within the standard of care, which means that they are to provide treatment in accordance with current medical and scientific knowledge. Within the Member States, we may encounter the term 'lege artis', 'Best Practices' or 'Best Guidelines'. Healthcare professionals and providers of medical services are insured for possible malpractice, which allows that compensation can be paid to the concerned patient. The presence of a healthcare professional will therefore bring specific rules for using MHA.

Whether MHA using AI falls within the purview of the PLD, the MHA must be covered by the definition of a product under Article 2 of the PLD:

> Product means all movables, with the exception of primary agricultural products and game, even though incorporated into another movable or into an immovable. 'Primary agricultural products' means the products of the soil, of stock-farming and of fisheries, excluding products which have undergone initial processing. 'Product' includes electricity.

The software can therefore be considered a thing incorporated into another movable thing. Examples include smartphones and smartwatches. However, Schneeberger argues that the definition of product liability primarily addresses 'tangible' products (e.g. embedded software as part of a composite product), not 'intangibles' like non-embedded standalone software.[74] On the other hand, Wagner claims that this shortcoming arises only from the circumstances of the adoption of the Directive in 1985. The legislators had no reason to include media-free, merely downloadable software, but clearly would have done so if the PLD had been adopted today. For these reasons, the Product Liability Directive, as it stands, would already cover non-embedded software and even computer programs loaded via the cloud.[75] Schönberger, on the other hand, argues that software is much more rewarded for services than for products. As he specifies:

> Services are clearly beyond the scope of the Product Liability Directive, and any suggestions that 'intangibles' and non-embedded software, in particular, would fall within its scope are misconceived.[76]

Despite the lack of clarity of legislators' intentions and different legal opinions, it is necessary for the article to take a position on whether MHAs fall within the scope of PLD and, if appropriate, under what circumstances. Although MHA is software installed in a movable object, it is not necessarily dependent on its location in that specific movable object. In that case, software within a medical device is directly

[74] Schneeberger et al. (2020), p. 220.

[75] Wagner (2017), p. 59.

[76] Schönberger (2019), p. 199.

programmed for that single device and is, therefore, its component. If we accept this hypothesis, MHA with an AI system will not fall under the scope of PLD.

Even if MHA is considered as a product in the sense of PLD, further unresolved legal issues arise. The manufacturer will be liable for the harmful effects MHA will cause to the users, including injury or even death. The PLD does not specify more precisely whether it also covers damage in the context of mental health, which will most often occur when using MHA. However, this type of harm may be regulated in national law, but this does not provide the same protection within the framework of the EU.

Another complication is the so-called causality. The injured person shall be required to prove not only the damage caused by the MHA and the defect of the MHA but also the causal relationship between the defect and the damage. Even if they mimic human brain neural networks, AI devices 'think' differently than humans—potentially more quickly and accurately.[77] However, we are unable to predict what they will decide in a given case. The European Commission (Commission), in its White Paper on Artificial Intelligence, notes that it may not be fair to require the injured party to prove this causal relationship that may not even be verifiable by the manufacturer themselves.

> Injured persons may not have effective access to the evidence necessary to bring a case to trial and may have less effective remedies available to them compared to situations where the harm is caused by traditional technologies.[78]

In this way, we jeopardise the possibility of the injured party successfully obtaining compensation for the damage caused by MHA with AI. From the point of view of civil liability, this is damage caused within the framework of a contract between the manufacturer and the user of the MHA. If the damage was caused by fault, the fault of the responsible person, the damage and the causal link between the fault and the damage would be proven.[79] However, as Ordish underlines, it also exists a different regime of liability—strict liability. There are some special situations where the legislation provides that a manufacturer may be liable for a user's harm even if he or she did not cause it. In this case, the manufacturer is not responsible for doing something wrong; instead, it deals with the fact that the manufacturer is responsible for something going wrong.[80]

The idea behind strict liability is that even if the use of a dangerous item is socially acceptable or even desirable, its operator should be liable regardless of any fault on their part.[81] Wendehorst claims that:

---

[77] Pesapane (2018).

[78] European Commission (2020), p. 13.

[79] Lohsse et al. (2019)

[80] Ordish (2018), p. 3.

[81] Schneeberger et al. (2020).

> [. . .] strict liability may therefore be justified for AI applications because the 'autonomy' and 'opacity' of AI may give rise to exactly the kind of difficulties strict liability is designed to overcome.[82]

It will be difficult to trace the damage back to human behaviour and prove causation. The concept of burden of proof, therefore, has been described as a nearly insurmountable hurdle.[83] The Association of Technology Organisations has sent a letter to the Commissioners explaining that the introduction of strict liability is not an appropriate solution as it could have a negative impact on innovation and consumer choice in the EU. On the other hand, is it ethically permissible to let the burden of proof to the MHA user considering the 'black box problem' if they are probably seeking help in the mental health field? The legislator should strongly consider whether using strict liability for AI in healthcare is permissible.[84]

4.2 De Lege Ferenda*: Better Protection of User?*

The European Commission's Report on AI Liability underlines the absence of a harmonised legal framework for AI liability. Within the current framework of the PLD, there appear to be no problematic issues on establishing liability. However, the PLD does not provide sufficient guarantees with respect to the users. Not paying enough attention may lead to under compensation for damages caused by an AI system. To overcome this issue, the Commission has prepared three proposals for a new legislative framework, which is aimed at regulating AI liability. These include the AI Act, the revised PLD and the Artificial Intelligence Liability Directive (AILD).

In the previous section, I drew attention to the problem of considering software as a product. Expert opinions are not unanimous as regards the question of whether the product can merely exist as the tangible software. The Commission identified a legal uncertainty in the product definition. Therefore, Recital 12 of the draft revision of the PDL declares:

> Products in the digital age can be tangible or intangible. [. . . .] In the interest of legal certainty, it should therefore be clarified that software is a product for the purposes of applying no-fault liability, regardless of the mode of its supply or usage, and therefore regardless of whether the software is stored on a device or accessed through cloud technologies.

The Commission points explicitly to applications as a current form of software. Clarifying the product definition will bring legal certainty, as the PLD will be applicable to AI systems, including these in MHA.

---

[82] Wendehorst (2020), p. 160.

[83] Schneeberger et al. (2020), p. 222.

[84] Navas (2020), p. 77.

The proposal also responds to my second criticism regarding the unsatisfactory definition within Article 9 of the PLD, where 'damage' is defined as damage caused by death or personal injury and does not explicitly state whether mental health falls within its scope. The Commission recognised this legal uncertainty and explicitly stated that '*personal injury includes medically recognised damage to psychological health*'. In the appendix of the impact study to the Proposal for revised PLD, the Commission mentions that it is necessary to clarify what will be considered psychological harm.[85] And it immediately claims that it should be diagnosed as psychological damage, not just stress or anxiety. Based on this legislation in progress, it is clear that MHA will be covered by the revised PLD.

The proposal for a revised PLD makes two critical changes that should make it easier for MHA users who have been injured to hold the manufacturer liable. The most important is the one defined in Article 9(4), which regulates the presumption of product defectiveness. Article 9 further establishes the claimant's obligation to prove product defect, injury, and causation. However, para 4 of this Article provides for an exception relating to the technical complexity of the product, which is well applicable in the case of damage caused by MHA:

> Where a national court judges that the claimant faces excessive difficulties, due to technical or scientific complexity, to prove the defectiveness of the product or the causal link between its defectiveness and the damage, or both, the defectiveness of the product or causal link between its defectiveness and the damage, or both, shall be presumed where the claimant has demonstrated, on the basis of sufficiently relevant evidence, that:
>
> (a) the product contributed to the damage; and
> (b) it is likely that the product was defective or that its defectiveness is a likely cause of the damage or both.[86]

The provision of this presumption unambiguously draws attention to the possibility of complexity not only of applications but of software in general, which is now considered a product. However, applying this provision can be complicated because the national court of Member States decides whether a given product is technologically complicated. Thus, there is likely to be fragmentation within the EU.

The second provision directly presents a software regulation is Article 10, para 2, letter c). Article 10 provides for exceptions to the liability of the manufacturer. Paragraph 1 letter c) would allow exemption from liability if there were no defectiveness of the product when placed on the market. In the case of the MHA, this would mean that if the app did not suffer from a defect when it was put on the market, it does not matter that the software was not subsequently updated, and the application became defective. The legislator was aware of this problem, so para 2, letter c) states that this exception does not apply for the lack of software updates or upgrades necessary to maintain safety. The proposal for a revised PLD represents an

---

[85] European Commission (2022).

[86] Article 9 para 4 of the Proposal for a Directive of the European Parliament and of the Council on liability for defective products.

improvement in MHA users' rights. Although the burden of proof lies with the user, and strict liability will not apply in the case of defective MHA, users gain certainty that MHA is also a product that can cause damage and that they can claim compensation.

The Commission, aware of the uncertainty of the algorithm's functioning—especially when talking about deep machine learning systems—proposed a supplemental to the Proposal for the Artificial Intelligence Liability Directive, which will directly address the responsibility of AI. The directive regulates the disclosure of evidence of high-risk artificial intelligence systems, which would enable a claimant to substantiate their non-contractual civil claim for damages based on fault. The directive applies only to high-risk AI, which comes as no surprise. Since these high-risk AI systems are most likely affected by the so-called 'black box' problem, which may prevent the user, who is seeking compensation for the damages incurred, from presenting proof demonstrating AI's fault. The AILD is based on the definition of the Proposal for AI Act, which the European Parliament adopted in June 2023.

AI Act designates high-risk AI systems if both of these conditions are met:

(a) the AI system is intended to be used as a safety component of a product or is itself a product, covered by the Union harmonization legislation listed in Annex II;
(b) the product whose safety component is the AI system, or the AI system itself as a product, is required to undergo a third-party conformity assessment with a view to the placing on the market or putting into service.

The critical question I asked is whether the AILD will apply to MHA. This is conditional on meeting the two mentioned conditions of the definition of highly dangerous AI within the framework of the adopted AI Act. Considering the first condition, in the framework of Annex II, the MDR is listed as a harmonisation regulation. At first glance, I again face the problem that if MHAs are not certified as medical devices, they do not fall into this harmonised area and will, thus, not be considered a high-risk AI system. Only a fraction of MHAs are registered as medical devices. However, to define MHA as high-risk AI, the second condition regarding third-party conformity assessment. Under Article 52, para 7, if MHAs are classified as class I medical devices, the manufacturers shall carry out the certification based on a declaration that the medical device meets Annexes II and III requirements. So there will be no third-party assessment. Given these conditions, both MHAs that are not certified as medical devices and MHAs that are deemed class I medical devices are not considered high-risk AI systems. Again, we encounter the problem of a glaring gap in legislation, which may subject similar MHAs, if not identically, to different requirements, primarily based on the manufacturer's sincerity.

If MHAs are classified as high-risk AI systems, they will fall within the scope of the Artificial Intelligence Liability Directive. The biggest question within this directive was whether strict liability for manufacturers should be applied when these AI systems bring such a high risk to the user. In the end, the Commission did not propose strict liability. Still, it reasoned that this liability applies to non-contractual civil law claims for damages caused by an AI system, which are brought under fault-based liability regimes. However, Article 4 introduces a presumption of a causal link in the case of fault, which thus provides a greater guarantee to the claimant, namely the use of MHAs. The presumption applies in three cases. First, if the claimant proves there was fault when the provider or user of MHA does not comply with their duty of care, a causal link between fault and damage is assumed. The second condition is met when it is reasonable to assume that the error generated the AI output or the failure to produce an AI output. The last condition requires that the claimant proves that the output generated by the AI system or the failure of the AI system to produce an output caused him harm.

The presumption of causality is a significant shift that complements the lack of transparency in the functioning of—particularly—machine learning AI systems. The question arises whether the chosen form of this piece of legislation, namely a directive, is the most suitable for harmonising the field of AI. I express this doubt mainly because the AILD contains in Article 1, para 4 the possibility of Member States adopting or maintaining more beneficial provisions for the contracting authority than those established by this directive. In this case, Member States may also adopt the concept of strict liability, which is more beneficial than the one proposed in the Directive. This idea of strict liability was rejected at the European level. Even if it is the highest possible guarantee for the user, it could have a liquidating effect on the manufacturers and discourage them from developing AI systems in the European market. However, the author notes that this line of reasoning is merely theoretical since it is difficult to predict whether the Directive will be adopted in this form and what adjustments the Member States will adopt as part of the transposition process.

The indisputable fact remains the lack of protection for MHA users. Since the AI Act does not define most MHA as high-risk AI, this Directive is inapplicable. Suppose the legislator would focus on the regulation of mobile health applications. In that case, it is still possible to intervene in the framework of the European Parliament's legislative process in the text of the proposals for a revised PLD or AILD. In the case of the AI Act, this would have to be changed in the framework of trialogue negotiations between the Council and the Parliament. Given that the legislator has not yet considered regulating mobile health applications, this possibility is rather unlikely. On the contrary, I see the potential for voluntary regulation of MHA through the Code of Conduct (CoC). The Commission already recognised the sensitivity of using mobile health apps. For this reason, in 2016, the Commission decided to issue a Code of conduct, mainly focusing on mobile health apps that will lead to the improvement of the practices used: *'The purpose of this CoC is to foster trust among users of "mHealth applications" which process personal data that includes data concerning health'.*[87] Although the CoC will not be binding for MHA manufacturers, following the recommended rules is also in their interest. The CoC shall be the guideline for safe MHA without the need for additional rigorous regulations. Concerning the forthcoming Regulation on European Health Data Space, the CoC would only specify the requirements for applications that can obtain

[87] European Commission (2016).

voluntary European certification. While this step will not remove risky MHA from the market, the legislator will guide users in choosing a safe application.

Be it through CoC or other means, the need to modify the MHA and health applications as such is a burning issue. I would like to suggest that until all regulations, such as AI Act, PLD or European Health Data Space, are adopted, there will be no legislator's interest in the regulation of MHA. As the MHA is directly related to this mentioned legislation, the situation from 2016 could repeat itself. Back then, the CoC became incompatible with GDPR and therefore was suspended. For this reason, it will likely be necessary to wait for the adoption of this legislation before proposing a new regulation of MHA.

5 Conclusion

Mental health applications (MHAs) have become ubiquitous in our society, serving diverse purposes, from aiding in the management of chronic illnesses to profit-driven ventures that may neglect user well-being. This article's investigation into the existing European legislation underscores the inadequacy of safeguards for MHA users. A notable practice employed by most MHA manufacturers is capitalising on the European Court of Justice's ruling, allowing them to not classify MHAs as medical devices, thereby avoiding the stringent certification requirements imposed on medical devices. This circumvention of rigorous medical device regulations leaves MHA users exposed to a higher probability of potential physical and psychological harm, as MHAs are not obligated to adhere to the latest scientific knowledge.

Moreover, unlike medical device manufacturers, MHA manufacturers are not mandated to maintain sufficient financial reserves to cover damages resulting from product defects. The avenue for compensation in cases of defective MHAs relies on claims arising from the Product Liability Directive (PLD). However, current discourse among experts diverges on whether the PLD applies to MHAs, given their software-based nature, further complicating the avenue for claims under the PLD. Consequently, there is an imperative need to establish comprehensive regulations that safeguard the health and well-being of MHA users.

Furthermore, the reluctance of some manufacturers to classify MHAs as medical devices, even when their functionalities align with such categorisation, significantly diminishes user protection. In the case of AI-based MHAs, the 'black box problem' exacerbates the challenge of holding manufacturers accountable for defective MHAs, as establishing causation between the product and resulting harm becomes increasingly arduous. In sum, it is evident that legislative protection for MHA users exists in theory but remains unenforceable due to exploitable legal loopholes. To address these issues, this article also delves into forthcoming legislation, including the revised PLD, the AI Act, and the Artificial Intelligence Liability Directive.

The forthcoming European regulatory frameworks hold the promise of enhancing conditions for MHA users. Notably, the clarification of the definitions of 'product' and 'personal injury' within the revised PLD unequivocally establishes its applicability to non-contractual civil law claims arising from damages caused by AI systems. However, the existing text of the AI Act, in conjunction with the Directive on the Liability of AI, appears inadequate in resolving the liability issues identified in this article. Although it offers heightened guarantees and transparency for users, the presumption of liability applies solely to MHAs certified as medical devices of class II or III. Since MHAs often fall within the category I classification, they do not benefit from this liability presumption. In the same way, the presumption of liability does not apply to MHAs, which, although they use AI, are not classified as medical devices.

It is crucial to acknowledge that this analysis remains theoretical, as the aforementioned proposals are still the objects of the legislative process, subject to potential alterations during their progression through the European Parliament and subsequent legislative procedures. This article unequivocally underscores the need for enhanced user protection in the realm of MHAs, highlighting that current safeguards are insufficient.

Legislation

Council Directive 85/374/EEC of 25 July 1985 on the approximation of the laws, regulations and administrative provisions of the Member States concerning liability for defective products. European Parliament and Council. http://data.europa.eu/eli/dir/1985/374/oj.

European Commission (2022) Commission Staff Working Document: Impact Assessment Report Accompanying the document Proposal for a Directive of the European Parliament and of the Council on liability for defective products, Annex 5. https://data.consilium.europa.eu/doc/document/ST-13134-2022-ADD-2/en/pdf.

European Commission (2016) Draft Code of Conduct on privacy for mobile health applications. https://digital-strategy.ec.europa.eu/en/library/code-conduct-privacy-mhealth-apps-has-been-finalised. Accessed 30 May 2023.

European Commission (2022) Commission Staff Working Document: Impact Assessment Report Accompanying the document Proposal for a Directive of the European Parliament and of the Council on liability for defective products, Annex 5. https://data.consilium.europa.eu/doc/document/ST-13134-2022-ADD-2/en/pdf.

European Commission Proposal for a Directive of the European Parliament and of the Council on adapting non-contractual civil liability rules to artificial intelligence. COM/2022/496 final.

European Commission Proposal for a Directive of the European Parliament and of the Council on liability for defective products. COM/2022/495 final.

European Commission Proposal for a Regulation of the European Parliament and of the Council laying down harmonised rules on Artificial intelligence and amending certain union legislative acts. COM/2021/206 final.

Report from the Commission to the European Parliament, the Council, and the European Economic and Social Committee. Report on the safety and liability implications of Artificial Intelligence, the Internet of Things and robotics. COM/2020/64 final.

European Commission Report from the Commission to the European Parliament, the Council and the European Economic and Social Committee: Report on the safety and liability implications of Artificial Intelligence, the Internet of Things and robotics. COM/2020/64 final.

European Commission (2020) White paper - On Artificial Intelligence - A European approach to excellence and trust. commission-white-paper-artificial-intelligence-feb2020_en.pdf (europa.eu).

European Union Agency for Fundamental Rights (2022) Bias in Algorithms-Artificial Intelligence and Discrimination. https://fra.europa.eu/sites/default/files/fra_uploads/fra-2022-bias-in-algorithms_en.pdf.

Directive 93/42/EEC of 14 June 1993 concerning medical devices. Council of the European Communities. http://data.europa.eu/eli/dir/1993/42/oj.

Regulation (EU) 2016/679. The protection of natural persons with regard to the processing of personal data and on the free movement of such data. European Parliament and Council. http://data.europa.eu/eli/reg/2016/679/oj.

Regulation (EU) 2017/745 of the European Parliament and of the Council of 5 April 2017 on medical devices, amending Directive 2001/83/EC, Regulation (EC) No 178/2002 and Regulation (EC) No 1223/2009 and repealing Council Directives 90/385/EEC and 93/42/EEC. European Parliament and Council. http://data.europa.eu/eli/reg/2017/745/oj.

Regulation (EU) 2017/746 of the European Parliament and of the Council of 5 April 2017 on in vitro diagnostic medical devices and repealing Directive 98/79/EC and Commission Decision 2010/227/EU. European Parliament and Council. http://data.europa.eu/eli/reg/2017/746/oj.

CJEU:CJEU Case C-219/115, Brain Products GmbH contre BioSemi VOF e.a, ECLI:EU:C:2012:742.

Online Publications

Associations of startups, SMEs, and technology companies (2022) The upcoming revision of the EU liability framework. https://ccianet.org/wp-content/uploads/2022/08/2022.08.24-Joint-Industry-Letter-on-the-PLD-and-AI-Directive.pdf?utm_source=POLITICO.EU&utm_campaign=b0e04edd2c-EMAIL_CAMPAIGN_2022_08_31_05_00&utm_medium=email&utm_term=0_10959edeb5-b0e04edd2c-190373637. Accessed 30 June 2023.

Bernardo A, Álvarez Del Vayo M (2021) Pay up or put it off: how Europe treats depression and anxiety. (CIVIO, 2021), Pay up or put it off: how Europe treats depression and anxiety | Civio. Accessed 30 June 2023.

Buchholz K (2020) Where Health App Usage Is Most Common. Chart: Where Health App Usage Is Most Common | Statista. Accessed 30 June 2023.

Deloitte (2017) Global mobile consumer survey: US edition. 246075 GMCS executive summary (deloitte.com). Accessed 30 June 2023.

E-hälsomyndigheten, Hälsoappar södertätt och ubandärung. (E-hälsomyndigheten, 2022). halsoappar%2D%2D-forutsattningar-och-anvandning.pdf (ehalsomyndigheten.se). Accessed 30 June 2023.

Edwards L (2022) Regulating AI in Europe: four problems and four solutions. ISBN: 978-1-7397950-0-9. Expert-opinion-Lilian-Edwards-Regulating-AI-in-Europe.pdf (adalovelaceinstitute.org). Accessed 28 June 2023.

Eurostat (July 2020) Aging Europe - statistics on population developments. (Eurostat statistics Explained) Ageing Europe - statistics on population developments - Statistics. Explained (europa.eu). Accessed 30 June 2023.

Haute Autorité de Santé (2021) Assessment of apps in the mobile health (mHealth) sector - Overview and quality criteria of medical content for referencing digital services in the digital health space and the professional service package. Assessment of apps in the mobile health (mHealth) sector -Overview and quality criteria of medical content for referencing digital services in the digital health space and the professional service package (has-sante.fr). Accessed 30 June 2023.

Kleinman Z (2021). Most healthcare apps not up to NHS standards. BBC News. Accessed 30 June 2023.

Lodie A, Celis JS, Karathanasis T Towards a new regime of civil liability for AI systems: Comment on the European Commission's proposals. Multidisciplinary Institute in Artificial intelligence. https://ai-regulation.com/eu-commission-proposals-on-ai-civil-liability/. Accessed 28 June 2023.

Mason P (2016) The racist hijacking of Microsoft's chatbot shows how the internet teems with hate. The Guardian, The racist hijacking of Microsoft's chatbot shows how the internet teems with hate | Paul Mason | The Guardian. Accessed 28 June 2023.

Ministry of Health and Social Affairs, Vision for eHealth 2025 – common starting points for digitization of social services and health care. (2016). Vision for eHealth 2025 (ehalsa2025.se). Accessed 30 June 2023.

ORCHA (May 28, 2021) ORCHA's digital health insights featured in national newspapers. ORCHA (orchahealth.com). Accessed 30 June 2023.

ORCHA (2021) Digital & mental health recovery actions plans. https://orchahealth.com/wp-content/uploads/2021/04/Mental_Health_Report_2021_final.pdf. Accessed 28 June 2023.

OORCHA (2022) The Peoples' view of digital mental health. Digital for Mental Health Attitudes and Behaviour Report.pdf (hubspotusercontent-eu1.net). Accessed 28 June 2023.

Ordish J (2018) Legal liability for machine learning in healthcare. In: 25 years making science work for health. University of Cambridge. https://www.phgfoundation.org/briefing/legal-liability-machine-learning-in-healthcare. Accessed 28 June 2023.

Roser M (2023) AI timelines: What do experts in artificial intelligence expect for the future? Our World in Dat. Accessed 30 June 2023.

SMER (2020) Artificial intelligence in healthcare. smer-2020-2-in-brief-artificial-intelligence-in-healthcare.pdf. Accessed 30 June 2023.

SMER (2017) The Quantified Human. Ethical aspects on self monitoring by wearables and health apps. Smer - Statens medicinsk-etiska råd. Accessed 30 June 2023.

Statista (2021) Market size of augmented reality in healthcare worldwide in 2018 and a forecast for 2026, Augmented reality in healthcare global market size forecast 2026 | Statista. Accessed 30 June 2023.

Statista Share of health app users in selected countries as of 2022. Statista. https://www.statista.com/forecasts/1181436/shareof-health-app-users-by-country. Accessed 30 June 2023.

World Health Organisation (2017) Mental health of older adults. who.int. Accessed 30 June 2023.

Worldometer (2020) Coronavirus, COVID - Coronavirus Statistics - Worldometer (worldometers.info). Accessed 30 June 2023.

bias In Last J (Ed) A dictionary of public health. Oxford University Press. Retrieved 2023. https://www.oxfordreference.com/view/10.1093/acref/9780195160901.001.0001/acref-9780195160901-e-404. Accessed 30 June 2023.

References

Journal Articles

Brault N, Saxena M (2021) For a critical appraisal of artificial intelligence in healthcare: the problem of bias in mHealth. Eval Clin Pract 27(3):513–519. https://doi.org/10.1111/jep.13528

Byambasuren O, Beller E, Glasziou P (2019) Current knowledge and adoption of mobile health apps among Australian general practitioners: survey study. JMIR Mhealth Uhealth 7(6). https://doi.org/10.2196/13199

Crawford K, Whittaker M (2016) The AI now report the social and economic implications of artificial intelligence technologies in the near-term. In AI now public symposium 2016, White House and New York University's Information Law Institute

Davenport TH, Glaser J, Gardner E (2022) Artificial intelligence in healthcare. Edward Elgar, Cheltenham

De Grove-Valdeyron N (2019) Lecture du droit européen numérique de la santé : conséquences sur les patients, l'accès aux soins, la circulation des patients, pp 79–105. https://doi.org/10.4000/books.putc.4133

Ernsting C, Dombrowski SU, Oedekoven M, O'Sullivan JL, Kanzler M, Kuhlmey A, Gellert P (2017) Using smartphones and health apps to change and manage health behaviors: a population-based survey. J Med Internet 19(4). https://doi.org/10.2196/jmir.6838

Gordon WJ, Landman A, Zhang H, Bates DW (2020) Beyond validation: getting health apps into clinical practice. Digital Med 3(14). https://doi.org/10.1038/s41746-019-0212-z

Lohsse S, Schulze R, Staudenmayer D (2019) New approaches: form of liability. Münster Colloquia on EU law and the digital economy IV, pp 185–228. https://doi.org/10.5771/9783845294797

Markowetz A, Błaszkiewicz K, Montag C, Switala C, Schlaepfer TE (2014) Psycho-informatics: big data shaping modern psychometrics. Med Hypotheses 82(4):405–411
Martelli N, Eskenazy D, Déan C et al (2019) New European regulation for medical devices: what is changing? Cardiovasc Intervent Radiol 42:1272–1278. https://doi.org/10.1007/s00270-019-02247-0
Miller E, Polson D (2019) Apps, avatars, and robots: the future of mental healthcare. Issues Mental Health Nurs 40(3):208–2014
Ming LC, Untong N, Aliudin NA, Osili N, Kifli N, Tan CS, Goh KW, Al-Worafi YM, Lee KS, Goh HP (2020) Mobile health apps on COVID-19 launched in the early days of the pandemic: content analysis and review. JMIR Mhealth Uhealth 8(9). https://doi.org/10.2196/19796
Morley J, Machado CV, Burr C, Cowls J, Joshi I, Taddeo M, Floridi L (2020) The ethics of AI in health care: a mapping review. Soc Sci Med 260. https://doi.org/10.1016/j.socscimed.2020.113172
Murphy K, Di Ruggiero E, Upshur R et al (2021) Artificial intelligence for good health: a scoping review of the ethics literature. BMC Med Ethics 22(14). https://doi.org/10.1186/s12910-021-00577-8
Nahy F, Williams AG (2021) Use of digital health tools in Europe - before, during and after COVID-19. World Health Organization. ISSN 1997-8073
Navas S (2020) Producer liability for AI-based technologies in the European Union. Int Law Res 9(1):77–84. https://doi.org/10.5539/ilr.v9n1p77
Orăştean R, Sava R, Mărginean S (2022) Measuring healthcare digitalisation in the European Union: trends and challenges. J Econ Financ Theory Pract 74(4):64–74. https://doi.org/10.56043/reveco-2022-0038
Parmar P, Ryu J, Pandya S et al (2022) Health-focused conversational agents in person-centered-care: a review of apps. npj Digit Med 5(21). https://doi.org/10.1038/s41746-022-00560-6
Pesapane F, Volonté C, Codari M et al (2018) Artificial intelligence as a medical device in radiology: ethical and regulatory issues in Europe and the United States. Insights Imaging 9:745–753. https://doi.org/10.1007/s13244-018-0645-y
Rajkomar A, Hardt M, Howell MD, Corrado G, Chin MH (2018) Ensuring fairness in machine learning to advance health equity. Ann Intern Med 169(12):866–872. https://doi.org/10.7326/M18-1990
Sawrikar V, Mote K (2022) Technology acceptance and trust: overlooked considerations in young people's use of digital mental health interventions. Health Policy Technol 11(4). https://doi.org/10.1016/j.hlpt.2022.100686
Schneeberger D, Stöger K, Holzinger A (2020) The European Legal Framework for medical AI. In: 4th international cross-domain conference for machine learning and knowledge extraction. Lecture notes in computer science, vol 12279. Springer, pp 209–226. https://doi.org/10.1007/978-3-030-57321-8_12
Schönberger D (2019) Artificial intelligence in healthcare: a critical analysis of the legal and ethical implications. Int J Law Inf Technol 27(2):171–203. https://doi.org/10.1093/ijlit/eaz004
Shusted CS, Evans NR, Juon H, Kane GC, Barta JA (2021) Association of race with lung cancer risk among adults undergoing lung cancer screening. JAMA Netw Open 4(4). https://doi.org/10.1001/jamanetworkopen.2021.4509
Singh A, Thakur N, Sharma A (2016) A review of supervised machine learning algorithms. In 3rd international conference on computing for sustainable global development, New Delhi, pp 1310–1315
Tat E, Bhatt DL, Rabbat MG (2020) Addressing bias: artificial intelligence in cardiovascular medicine. Lancet Digital Health 2(12). https://doi.org/10.1016/S2589-7500(20)30249-1
Turk M (2018) Explainable Artificial Intelligence (XAI). Defense Advanced Research Projects Agency (Darpa); Local Interpretable Model Agnostic Explanations (LIME): an introduction
Wachter S, Mittelstadt B, Russell C (2018) Counterfactual explanations without opening the black box: automated decisions and the GDPR. Harv J Law Technol 31:841–887

Wagner G (2017) Produkthaftung für Autonome Systeme. Archiv für die civilistische Praxis 217(6):707–765

Wendehorst C (2020) Strict liability for AI and other emerging technologies. J Eur Tort Law 11(2): 150–180. https://doi.org/10.1515/jetl-2020-0140

Wildenbos GA, Jaspers MWM, Schijven MP, Dusseljee-Peute LW (2019) Mobile health for older adult patients: using an aging barriers framework to classify usability problems. Int J Med Inf 124:68–77. https://doi.org/10.1016/j.ijmedinf.2019.01.006

Zednik C (2021) Solving the Black Box problem: a normative framework for explainable artificial intelligence. Philos Technol 34:265–288. https://doi.org/10.1007/s13347-019-00382-7

Zhang Y, Koch S (2015) Mobile health apps in Sweden: what do physicians recommend? Stud Health Technol Inform 210:793–797

Books

Bhaskar P, Rao S (2022) Role of mobile health in the situation of COVID-19 pandemics: pros and cons. In: Poonia RCH (ed) Cyber-physical systems, pp 37–54

Bohr A, Memarzadeh K (2020) Artificial intelligence in healthcare. In: The rise of artificial intelligence in healthcare applications. Academic Press, pp 25–60. https://doi.org/10.1016/C2018-0-04097-9

Thesis

Müllerová P (2020) The development of telemedicine in the context of cross-border healthcare services in the European Union: comparative approach France/Czech Republic. Dissertation, L'Université Toulouse 1 Capitole

Tegen A (2022) Interactive online machine learning. Dissertation, Malmö University

Trustworthy Artificial Intelligence and Public Procurement

Isabel Gallego Córcoles

Contents

Abstract The use of artificial intelligence by public administrations raises major legal challenges, given its potential to harm citizens' rights and freedoms. The risks that artificial intelligence systems may entail must be assessed when AI systems are procured, both in the design of the tender and in the establishment of the obligations of the contract.

In this context, even in the absence of a European legal framework on the use of artificial intelligence systems, a number of soft law documents have already been drafted to ensure that administrations procure trustworthy AI systems. From these, it is possible to extract a series of guidelines that should be incorporated in the public

The research has been conducted within the framework of the activities of the Research Project Public Administration and Artificial Intelligence: regulation and implementation of AI in the field of public procurement (TED2021-130682B-I00) funded by the Spanish Ministry for Science and Innovation.

I. Gallego Córcoles (✉)
Department of Public Law, University of Castilla-La Mancha, Albacete, Spain
e-mail: isabel.gallego@uclm.es

E. Gill-Pedro, A. Moberg (eds.), *YSEC Yearbook of Socio-Economic Constitutions 2023*, YSEC Yearbook of Socio-Economic Constitutions (2024) 2023: 311–330,
https://doi.org/10.1007/16495_2023_67, Published online: 28 Decmber 2023

procurement of AI systems, as these clauses derive without difficulty from the general legislation applicable to the use of new technologies by the administration.

1 Introduction: Public Procurement as Driver and a Gatekeeper of Human-Centred Artificial Intelligence—The Role of Soft Law

The use of artificial intelligence by Public Administrations raises important legal challenges, derived from the necessary adaptation of the techniques for the protection of rights and freedoms to a new technological reality with a special capacity to infringe these rights and freedoms. In the absence of specific regulation of the use of AI, as a large part of the development of artificial intelligence solutions incorporated by the Public Administrations shall be private, public procurement should adopt the role of integrating the different guarantees that are outlined in the different legal systems, playing a gatekeeping role of the acquisition of human-centred AI.[1]

On the other hand, public demand has a significant impact on this sector, as public sector may act as a driver of innovation and regulator of the AI market.[2] In other words, public procurement may be used to stimulate and develop the AI ecosystem and the private sector and is one of the tools available to the public authorities to finance innovation and ensure trustworthy AI.[3] Moreover, public procurement rules and practices have a strong influence on markets, especially in their early stages of development. This is highlighted in the World Economic Forum's Guidelines for AI Procurement.[4] As noted in this document, industry is currently debating setting its own standards for these technologies; the institutional authority of government and its credibility can help to establish baselines in this area.

In any case, the acquisition of artificial intelligence solutions is not a traditional technology acquisition. There are a number of challenges linked to the public procurement of artificial intelligence:[5] (a) the need for data to be used through machine learning (b) data ownership and data sovereignty; (c) potential for bias and discrimination in AI; (d) intellectual property rights and trade secrecy and their

---

[1] See Oluka Nagitta et al. (2022) and Sánchez Graells (2022a).

[2] McBride et al. (2021), p. 11.

[3] See High-Level Expert Group on AI, *Policy and Investment Recommendations for Trustworthy AI*, p. 20.

In Spain, see Estrategia Nacional de Inteligencia Artificial, according to which Public Administration may 'act as a demander of technology solutions, thereby driving the development of technology solutions, thereby driving the development of new programmes and capabilities by the private sector'.

[4] Available in https://www3.weforum.org. See also WEF (2020).

[5] McBride et al. (2021).

relation to the transparency of algorithms. Hence, at the international level, there are various initiatives that seek to establish a set of guidelines for the procurement of AI-based solutions.

At the strictly European geographical level, the first states to adopt their own guidelines on public procurement of artificial intelligence were Estonia[6] and the United Kingdom.[7] Of particular interest, however, are the 'the Standard Clauses for Procurement of Trustworthy Algorithmic Systems' developed by the City of Amsterdam[8] (hereinafter, Amsterdam City Clauses), which describe the obligations imposed on suppliers to ensure the safe and responsible use of algorithms. In this regard, they address the most important aspects in the design of the purchase of algorithms: risk management, data quality, transparency, data ownership and audits.

In the area of EU law, Action 6 of the White Paper on Artificial Intelligence[9] foresees that the Commission shall prepare a specific 'Adopt AI programme' that shall support the public procurement of artificial intelligence systems, and help transform the procurement processes themselves. While this shall apparently be more linked to the role of a public sector as a driver of AI procurement, the European Commission is also sponsoring an initiative to ensure the procurement of trustworthy AI solutions.[10] In this regard, the project is to adapt the aforementioned Amsterdam City Clauses into a European standard that is aligned with the proposed Regulation of the European Parliament and of the Council laying down harmonised rules on artificial intelligence[11] (Artificial Intelligence Act, hereafter AI Act). As noted in the document—which is not an official EU document—although the proposed AI Act is the subject of ongoing negotiations and the text of the AI Act is not final, it contains best practices in the field of AI regulation that can be used in AI procurement. Despite the fact that these model clauses are not binding, the importance of this initiative should not be underestimated, as it is not only aimed at ensuring a trustworthy use of AI, but also, indirectly, at avoiding market access restrictions. The legal basis for the AI Act is Article 114 of the Treaty on the Functioning of the European Union (TFEU), which provides for the adoption of measures to ensure the establishment and functioning of the internal market. In fact, the primary objective of this proposal is to ensure the proper functioning of the internal market by setting harmonised rules in particular on the development, placing

[6]Documentation available, only partly in English at Instructional materials, Krattide veebileht (https://www.kratid.ee/) translation.

[7]*Guidelines for AI Procurement* (2020), available in Guidelines for AI procurement - GOV.UK (www.gov.uk).

[8]Available in Contractual terms for algorithms - Innovation (amsterdam.nl).

[9]A European approach to excellence and trust. Brussels, 19.2.2020. COM(2020) 65 final.

[10]EUROPEAN COMMISION (2023) Proposal for standard contractual clauses for the procurement of Artificial Intelligence (AI) by public organisations. High Risk version. Available in https://living-in.eu/groups/solutions/ai-procurement, A new version has been published in September 2023, available in https://public-buyers-community.ec.europa.eu/communities/procurement-ai/resources/eu-model-contractual-ai-clauses-pilot-procurements-ai.

[11]Brussels, 21.4.2021 COM(2021) 206 final.

on the Union market and the use of products and services making use of AI technologies or provided as stand-alone AI systems. In this context, market barriers through the implementation of AI additional requirements in national public procurements should be avoided; EU model clauses can play an important role to fulfil this objective.

In short, there is currently no European legal framework for trustworthy AI. However, public administrations are already acquiring artificial intelligence systems both to better provide public services and to act as drivers of innovation. In this context, the purpose of this chapter is to reflect on the guarantees to be included in these public procurement processes, for which we shall analyse the emerging soft law rules that are being developed at the international level.

2 Key Issues in the Design and Preparation of the Procurement Procedure

2.1 The Needs To Be Satisfied and the Subject Matter of the Contract: When to Buy an Artificial Intelligence Solution?

One of the most important decisions in the tendering process is to determine the subject matter of contract. When buying information and communication technologies, it is crucial to decide whether AI is the solution to solve one of the needs identified by the public administration. To take this decision, complex factors which are not present in other types of public procurement must be considered. For this reason, in some countries such as Estonia[12] or the United Kingdom,[13] an attempt has been made to guide this decision through the publication of different questionnaires.

As in any type of innovation-related procurement, it will be useful to approach the market beforehand in order to find out about the different possibilities it offers. In fact, in the field of procurement of artificial intelligence solutions, knowledge of the market is a key element for the success of the project.[14] From this perspective, the carrying out of preliminary market consultation[15] shall make it possible to gather information of interest on the possibilities offered by the technology for satisfying the public need.

[12] Available partially in English in Instructional materials | Krattide veebileht (https://www.kratid.ee/).

[13] *Guidelines for AI Procurement* (2020) available in Guidelines for AI procurement - GOV.UK (www.gov.uk).

[14] McBride et al. (2021), p. 11.

[15] See Article 40 Directive 2014/24/EU of the European Parliament and of the Council of 26 February 2014 on public procurement and repealing Directive 2004/18/EC (OJ L 94, of 28.3.2014).

Preliminary consultations can be useful both for checking the available technology before drafting descriptive specifications (thus avoiding favouring specific solutions) and for establishing ambitious and realistic functional requirements.[16] They can also help to understand the structure of the market, so that the most appropriate tendering procedure can be selected according to its maturity. The knowledge gathered from the consultations will help to better define the problem statement and can be useful to determine the feasibility of AI as a solution to the public need.[17]

2.2 *Preliminary Risk Assessment*

The decision to initiate a procedure for the procurement of an AI-based solution should be based on an initial assessment of the potential risks involved in the use of this technology and how to mitigate these risks,[18] so that the decision is based on a proportionate approach.[19]

Indeed, given the risks involved in procuring artificial intelligence solutions, it is recommended that tender documents only require the implementation of an artificial intelligence solution where there are strong indications that this technology will solve the problem it is intended to solve.[20] The need to procure an artificial intelligence system should be derived from an analysis of different alternatives, so that it is compared with other potential solutions—provided that the artificial intelligence project is not specifically oriented towards research and innovation. If during the evaluation phase it becomes clear that another solution that is not incorporated will satisfy the public need it is recommended using the alternative option.[21]

2.3 *Does Quality Data Exist?*

Issues related to data feasibility and data governance should be carefully analysed in the tender preparation phase. Data availability is a prerequisite for the implementation of any artificial intelligence solution. Furthermore, it has been pointed out that

---

[16] See Commission notice, Guidance on Innovation Procurement, Brussels, 15.5.2018, C(2018) 3051 final.

[17] See British *Guidelines for AI procurement,* p. 26. See also WEF (2019) according to which: 'pre-market engagement is also often essential in helping you to describe your problem and narrow down the task that AI may be able to assist with' (p. 8).

[18] WEF (2019), p. 9.

[19] See a specific AI risk assessment tool: WEF (2020).

[20] WEF (2019), p. 8.

[21] WEF (2019), p. 8.

access to data should only be granted after careful consideration of data governance issues,[22] which should cover all data activities related to the project: access of data to project members, storage location and consent issues.[23] In addition, as proposed, the tender should encourage innovative technological approaches that make less intrusive use of data.[24]

As a result, the analysis of existing data and data governance issues is one of the first steps to be developed in the preparation of the tender, because if insurmountable obstacles emerge from this examination, there will be no justification for even continuing the procurement design.

2.4 The Need to Foresee Possible Incidents in the Performance of the Contract

The development of an artificial intelligence solution will sometimes produce results that do not meet the initial need. In fact, any difficulties that may arise in the performance of the contract may even make it advisable to terminate the contract early or adapt the content of the service. Nevertheless, the system of contract modification established in European Law[25] makes it difficult to introduce modifications in the contract if these are not foreseen in the specifications. Thus, the lack of foresight—at the time of tendering—of the incidents to which the development of a complex contract may lead will, in practice, trigger situations that are difficult to resolve. This is sufficiently illustrated by the CJEU Case C-549/14, Frogne, ECLI: EU:C:2016:634.

In this case, in the performance of a contract for the supply of a complex communications system, and in the face of obvious performance difficulties, the parties decide to terminate the contract early. One of the companies that did not participate in the tender appealed against this agreement, arguing that the reduction of the subject matter of the contract constituted an essential modification of the contract contrary to the procurement directives. Against this, contracting authority argued that when difficulties arise in the performance of a contract—which is not unusual for certain types of contracts, such as those concerning the development of IT systems—the contracting authority must be given a wide margin of appreciation, in order to enable it to arrive at a reasonable solution to the performance difficulties. Otherwise, the contracting authority is obliged either to forego reasonable adaptations or to break the contract, with the risks and losses that this entails.

In contrast to these arguments, the CJEU concluded that after the award of a public contract it is not possible to introduce a substantial modification to the

[22] WEF (2019), p. 10.

[23] UK (2020): *Guidelines for AI Procurement.*

[24] UK (2020): *Guidelines for AI Procurement.*

[25] See Article 72 Directive 2014/24/EU.

contract without opening a new procedure for the award of the contract, even if that modification objectively constitutes a compromise solution involving reciprocal waivers by both parties and is intended to put an end to a conflict with an uncertain outcome arising from the difficulties which the performance of the contract poses. A different conclusion would be possible only if the contract documents provided for the possibility of adapting certain conditions of the contract, even substantial ones, after the contract had been awarded and determined the manner in which that possibility was to be applied. In this regard, the CJEU has had occasion to state that:

> 36 Furthermore, the very fact that, because of their subject matter, certain public contracts may immediately be categorised as being unpredictable in nature means that there is a foreseeable risk that difficulties may occur at the implementation stage. Accordingly, in respect of such a contract, it is for the contracting authority not only to use the most appropriate procurement procedures, but also to take care when defining the subject matter of that contract [. . .]
>
> 37 Although the principle of equal treatment and the obligation of transparency must be guaranteed even in regard to specific public contracts, this does not mean that the particular aspects of those contracts cannot be taken into account. That legal imperative and that practical necessity are reconciled, first, through strict compliance with the conditions of a contract as they were laid down in the contract documents up to the end of the implementation phase of that contract, but also, second, through the possibility of making express provision, in those documents, for the option for the contracting authority to adjust certain conditions, even material ones, of that contract after it has been awarded. By expressly providing for that option and setting the rules for the application thereof in those documents, the contracting authority ensures that all economic operators interested in participating in the procurement procedure are aware of that possibility from the outset and are therefore on an equal footing when formulating their respective tenders (see, by analogy, judgment of 29 April 2004, Commission v CAS Succhi di Frutta, C-496/99 P, EU:C:2004:236, paragraphs 112, 115, 117 and 118).

In view of this case law, it is advisable that when tendering for AI-based tools of a certain complexity, the performance of the contract should be organised in successive phases and, if necessary, possible adaptations of the contractual object should be foreseen.

3 Key Issues in the Content of the Contract

3.1 Right to Good Administration: Should the Transfer of Ownership of Source Code Be Required?

3.1.1 Introduction

According to right to good administration, every person has the right to have access to his or her file, while respecting the legitimate interests of confidentiality and of professional and business secrecy. Furthermore, the administration has the obligation to give reasons for its decisions.[26]

As the use of AI solutions could not ignore the right to good administration, in the design of the procurement it should be foreseen the way in which transparency and accountability obligations shall be fulfilled. This aspect is reiterated in the different Guides that have been developed by different institutions with respect to the public procurement of AI solutions.[27] It has also been outlined in the literature.[28]

This being so, the debate that arises with some intensity is whether the obligations of transparency and accountability require the allowance of third-party access to the source code. The solution adopted in this respect will have to be reflected both in the clauses relating to the possible transfer of intellectual property rights and in those relating to the limits of the principle of confidentiality.[29]

3.1.2 Possible Access to Source Code in the Guidelines on Procurement of Artificial Intelligence Solutions

From a general perspective, and although some authors[30] maintain that there is an obligation to grant access to the source code, transparency and accountability do not necessarily imply total openness of the algorithmic system.[31] Transparency and accountability are linked to the legitimacy of the system, control of the decision adopted; and to fulfil these aims it will not always be necessary to make the interior of the system, the source code, known. What is relevant in legal terms, according to this author, is to disclose the existence of the system, the data on which it is based, the information on its technical operation and the reasons why the decision has been taken. In this way, the requirements of transparency and accountability would not be linked so much to systematically disclosing the way in which the system operates from the technological point of view, but to human interaction with the algorithm's output and the design criteria of the inputs in order to maintain the requirement of intelligibility of the decision.[32]

The various documents that have been developed in different legal systems on the procurement of artificial intelligence solutions contain the proposal outlined above: it is not necessary in all cases to give access to the source code in order to safeguard

---

[26] See Article 41 EU Charter of Fundamental Rights.

[27] WEF (2019), pp. 13–15.

[28] McBride et al. (2021), p. 11.

[29] Furthermore, access to the source code may also have implications from the perspective of compliance with public procurement rules: the absence of assignment of intellectual property rights may mean that extensions and developments not included in the initial object of the contract must be carried out by the same contractor may entail a breach of the principle of free competition. On this topic, see Sánchez Graells (2022b).

[30] At least, Spanish authors. See Boix Palop (2020), pp. 223–270; Gómez Jiménez (2021), p. 150.

[31] Martín Delgado (2023).

[32] Martín Delgado (2023). See also Ponce Solé (2019).

the guarantees of transparency and motivation. Thus, the UK Guidance, in relation to possible access to source code, notes that suppliers may not wish to disclose details of the inner workings of their solution in order to protect their intellectual property and commercial advantage. In addition, it is stressed that during the design and deployment of the AI system, it is likely that a new algorithm will be developed, or an existing one tailored (e.g. retrained through its data), so the administration will need to assess whether the supplier or itself should own the intellectual property rights, for which it will be essential to determine who can best exploit the intellectual property generated.[33]

The Amsterdam City Clauses provide for a very detailed regulation of issues related to the explainability and transparency of algorithms. To this end, a differentiation between procedural transparency, technical transparency and explainability is introduced. The concept of 'procedural transparency' refers to the provision of information on the purpose of the algorithmic system and the process followed in the development and application of the Algorithmic System and the data used in that context, which should in any event be deemed to include the provision of an understanding of the choices and assumptions made, the categories of data used in the development of the Algorithmic System, the way in which human intervention is provided for in the Algorithmic System, the method used to identify risks, the risks identified, and the measures taken to mitigate the risks, as well as the parties that were involved in the development of the Algorithmic System and their roles.

'Technical transparency' is defined as the provision of information enabling an understanding of the technical operation which may in any event be deemed to include the disclosure of the source code of the Algorithmic System, the technical specifications used in developing the Algorithmic System, the data used in developing the Algorithmic System, technical information on how the data used in developing the Algorithmic System were obtained and edited, information on the method of development used and the development process undertaken, substantiation of the choice for a particular model and its parameters, and information on the performance of the Algorithmic System.

Finally, the Amsterdam Clauses define 'explainability' as the ability to explain on an individual level why an algorithmic system leads to a particular decision or outcome, which shall in any case include a clear indication of the key factors that have led an algorithmic system to a particular result and the changes in the input that must be made to arrive at a different result. In this regard, it is added that making an algorithmic system explainable includes the provision of all technical and other information necessary to explain, in appeal or other legal proceedings, how a decision has been reached and to give the other party and any other interested party the opportunity to assess how a decision has been reached, in order to provide third parties with realistic legal protection.

---

[33] UK (2020), Guidelines for AI procurement. A summary of best practices addressing specific changes of acquiring Artificial Intelligence in the public sector, p. 29.

In this context, Article 5 Amsterdam City Clauses on the transparency of algorithms imposes different obligations on the contractor depending on whether the information falls under the concepts of 'procedural transparency', 'technical transparency' or 'explainability'.[34]

First, through the introduction of the concept of 'procedural transparency', a category of transparency is established which allows for the disclosure of relevant information on the algorithmic system without disproportionately harming the interests of the contractor. Thus, the contractor is obliged to document the information falling within the scope of the definition of 'procedural transparency' and to share this information with the contracting authority, which will have the possibility to disclose the information provided and share it with third parties. The regulation is based on the fact that this information is essential for the administration to provide accountability to the public in relation to the use of the algorithmic system.

On the other hand, it is stipulated that the contractor will provide 'technical transparency' only at the request of the administration. The purpose of this form of

[34] 'Article 5 Transparency of the Algorithmic System. (5.1) On demand of NAME OF ORGANIZATION, the Contractor will provide NAME OF ORGANIZATION with Procedural Transparency. NAME OF ORGANIZATION will be entitled to share the information provided by the Contractor in that context with third parties and to disclose it. On demand of NAME OF ORGANIZATION, the Contractor will complete a register for Algorithmic Systems to be designated by NAME OF ORGANIZATION. (5.2) On demand of NAME OF ORGANIZATION, the Contractor will provide NAME OF ORGANIZATION with Technical Transparency in order to enable NAME OF ORGANIZATION to carry out an audit as referred to in article 8. NAME OF ORGANIZATION will only request and use such information if and to the extent necessary for purposes of article 8. NAME OF ORGANIZATION will, pursuant to article 5.2, keep business-confidential information provided to it confidential and destroy it after an audit as referred to in article 8, unless a legal obligation on the part of NAME OF ORGANIZATION opposes confidentiality or destruction or NAME OF ORGANIZATION needs the information in the context of a dispute with the Contractor or a third party. (5.3) For purposes of article 5.2, the Contractor may choose not to issue the source code of the Algorithmic System to NAME OF ORGANIZATION, but to an independent third party to be designated and engaged by NAME OF ORGANIZATION who will perform the audit referred to in article 8 on behalf of NAME OF ORGANIZATION. Any additional costs incurred as a result will be payable by the Contractor. NAME OF ORGANIZATION may require that the Contractor pay an advance in connection with the costs of the independent third party. (5.4) NAME OF ORGANIZATION should at all times be able to explain the operation of the Algorithmic System (Explainability). The Contractor will be under the obligation to lend its full cooperation in making the Algorithmic System Explainable and to provide NAME OF ORGANIZATION with all such information as may be required in that respect. NAME OF ORGANIZATION will be entitled to share the information provided by the Contractor in that context with third parties and to disclose it. (5.5) During the term of the Agreement, the demands described in this article will constitute obligations to realize those demands and, unless the Parties agree otherwise, no additional fee will be due by NAME OF ORGANIZATION to the Contractor in consideration of the performance of such obligations. After expiry of the term of the Agreement, the demands described in this article will constitute an obligation to perform to the best of the Parties' ability and an additional fee will be due by NAME OF ORGANIZATION to the Contractor in consideration of the services to be provided by the Contractor in that respect. (5.6) In all situations where the information provided on the basis of the various paragraphs of this article overlaps, NAME OF ORGANIZATION will be free to choose the regime that is most favourable to it'.

transparency is to allow the administration to check whether the contractor has fulfilled its contractual obligations through the corresponding audits. However, in many cases, the information provided under the concept of technical transparency will be protected by intellectual property rights. Therefore, the clauses oblige the administration to preserve the confidential nature of this information and to destroy it once the audit has been completed. In any case, there is no obligation to keep the information confidential or to destroy the information if a legal duty imposed on the administration opposes this, or if the administration requires the information in the context of a dispute with a contractor or a third party. Furthermore, in order to strengthen the interests of the contractor, it is foreseen that the contractor may choose not to provide the source code of the algorithmic system, but to hand it over to an independent third party who will carry out the audit on behalf of the administration and, in that context, analyse the source code of the algorithmic system.

Finally, it is established that the administration must always be able to explain the functioning of the algorithmic system, and that the contractor is obliged to fully cooperate in making the algorithmic system explainable and to provide the administration with all the information necessary to do so. The administration shall have the right to share the information provided by the contractor in this context with third parties and to disclose it. The obligation to make the operation of an Algorithmic System Explainable is partly based on several decisions of the Dutch Administrative Jurisdiction Division of the Council of State.[35]

As a closing clause of the system, a sort of priority is foreseen between the different types of transparency. Thus, as the document points out, it is likely that, in many situations, the information provided in the context of procedural transparency, technical transparency, and explainability will partially coincide. The clauses therefore state that, in such a case, the administration may at any time choose the regime that is most favourable to it. This is intended to prevent the contractor from using the limits to technical transparency to prevent the administration from making an algorithmic system explainable. Therefore, if certain information falls within the scope of technical transparency and is necessary to make an algorithmic system explainable, the administration will be free to disclose the relevant information and share it with third parties.

To sum up, Amsterdam City Clauses do not impose the delivery of the source code. However, they contain high guarantees of transparency and motivation. In practice, the main weakness of this regulation is that it does not precisely define the obligations assumed by the contractor, which will depend in each specific case on the possibility of guaranteeing the explainability of decisions without disclosing its business secrets.

[35] As it explained in the document, those decisions show that, if an administrative body makes an administrative decision using an Algorithmic System, that administrative body must be able to explain how an Algorithmic System has arrived at a particular result. Furthermore, the administrative body must offer the other party the opportunity to assess the operation of the Algorithmic System, so that realistic legal protection can be offered to the other party.

In contrast to this model, in the first draft version of the model contractual clauses sponsored by the European Commission the guarantees regarding transparency and motivation are established with a markedly open character. As indicated above, these clauses are aligned with the substantive regulation of the AI Act. Article 70 AI Act obliges the national authorities to respect the confidentiality of the information and data obtained in the exercise of their functions, all of this—it must be understood—without prejudice to the stipulations established in the scope of each specific contracting procedure.[36] Nevertheless, in the second version of the proposal for standard contractual clauses for the procurement of Artificial Intelligence (AI) by public organisations (high risk version), Article 6 provides that:

> **'Article 6 Transparency of the AI System**
> 6.1. The Supplier ensures that the AI System has been and shall be designed and developed in such a way that the operation of the AI System is sufficiently transparent to enable the Public Organisation to reasonably understand the system's functioning.
>
> 6.2. To ensure appropriate transparency, before the Delivery of the AI System at least the technical and organisational measures described in Annex E shall be implemented by the Supplier. These measures should result in the Public Organisation being able to understand and use the AI System appropriately by understanding how the AI System works and what data it processes, allowing the Public Organisation to explain the decisions taken by the AI System to the persons or group of persons on which the AI System is (intended to be) used'.

[36] 'Article 6 Transparency. (6.1.) The Supplier ensures that the AI System shall be designed and developed in such a way to ensure that the operation of the AI System is sufficiently transparent to enable [NAME OF PUBLIC ORGANISATION] to interpret the system's output and use it appropriately. (6.2.) <optional> During the term of the Agreement, the Supplier is obliged to assist [NAME OF PUBLIC ORGANISATION] at [NAME OF PUBLIC ORGANISATION]'s first request to explain on an individual level how the AI System arrived at a particular decision or outcome. In any event, this will include a clear indication of the key factors that led the AI System to arrive at a particular result and the changes to the input that must be made in order for it to arrive at a different outcome. (6.3.) <optional> The obligation as described in article 6.2 comprises in any event the provision to [NAME OF PUBLIC ORGANISATION] of all the technical and other information required in order to explain how the AI System arrived at a particular decision or outcome and to offer the other party and any other interested parties the opportunity to verify the way in which the AI System arrived at a particular decision or outcome. The Supplier hereby grants the [NAME OF PUBLIC ORGANISATION] the right to use, share and disclose this information, if and to the extent necessary to inform natural persons about the functioning of the AI System and/or in any legal proceedings. (6.4.) <optional> Without prejudice to Article 4, the obligations referred to in article 6.2 and article 6.3 include the source code of the AI System, the technical specifications used in developing the AI System, the Data Sets, technical information on how the Data Sets used in developing the AI System were obtained and edited, information on the method of development used and the development process undertaken, substantiation of the choice for a particular model and its parameters, and information on the performance of the AI System'.

As can be seen, the solution adopted by the EU model clauses is open, in the sense that public entities shall describe the measures to be taken to guarantee the transparency of the AI System. However, it guarantees the requirements of transparency and accountability provided for in some national legal systems as Article 13 sets the obligation to explain the functioning of the AI System on an individual level. For instance, in Spanish Law, at the very least the tenderer should be required to provide the administration with the information necessary to make effective the obligations of active transparency set out in the Article 11.1 i) of Royal Decree 203/2021, of 30 March, which approves the Regulation on the performance and operation of the public sector by electronic means.[37]

3.2 *Supervision and Control of Algorithmic Systems*

3.2.1 Human Supervision

Article 14 AI Act foresees that high-risk AI systems shall be designed and developed in such a way, including with appropriate human-machine interface tools, that they can be effectively overseen by natural persons during the period in which the AI system is in use. In this regard, as explained in recital 48 of the proposal, high-risk AI systems should be designed and developed in such a way that natural persons can oversee their functioning. For this purpose, appropriate human oversight measures should be identified by the provider of the system before its placing on the market or putting into service. In particular, where appropriate, such measures should guarantee that the system is subject to in-built operational constraints that cannot be overridden by the system itself and is responsive to the human operator, and that the natural persons to whom human oversight has been assigned have the necessary competence, training and authority to carry out that role.

In parallel to the regulation contained in Article 14 AI Act, Article 7 of the EU model clauses sponsored by the European Commission (high risk version) states that:

> **'Article 7 Human oversight**
> 7.1. The Supplier ensures that the AI System has been and shall be designed and developed in such a way, including with appropriate human-machine interface tools, that it can be effectively overseen by natural persons as proportionate to the risks associated with the system.
>
> 7.2. The Supplier ensures that, prior to the Delivery, appropriate measures shall be embedded in the AI System and taken to ensure human oversight. These

[37] According to Article 11 i) RD 203/2021, Public administration shall report the description of the design and functioning of the automated administrative action, the accountability and transparency mechanisms, as well as the data used in its configuration and learning.

measures, which could include inter alia training of employees of the Public Organisation, shall enable the individuals to whom human oversight is assigned to do the following, as appropriate to the circumstances:

a. be aware of and sufficiently understand the relevant capacities and limitations of the AI System and be able to duly monitor its operation, so that signs of anomalies, dysfunctions and unexpected performance can be detected and addressed as soon as possible;

b. remain aware of the possible tendency of automatically relying or over-relying on the output produced by the AI System ('automation bias'), in particular if the AI System is used to provide information or recommendations for decisions to be taken by natural persons;

c. be able to correctly interpret the AI System's output, taking into account in particular the characteristics of the system and the interpretation tools and methods available;

d. be able to decide, in any particular situation, not to use the AI System or otherwise disregard, override or reverse the output of the AI System;

e. be able to intervene on the operation of the AI System or interrupt the system through a "stop" button or a similar procedure,

7.3. <optional>To ensure appropriate human oversight, the Supplier shall at least implement the technical and organisational measures described in Annex F before the Delivery of the AI System'.

This article practically reiterates the content of Article 14 of the AI Act. In addition, it allows for the implementation of technical and organisational measures to ensure human oversight; among those could be included training for public administration staff, which will be essential to ensure that this staff has the real capacity to supervise the system.

Otherwise, the EU model clauses go further than the precedent clauses of the City of Amsterdam. In these, the requirement of human supervision is included in the requirement of explainability. However, the EU model contractual clauses are more in line with some national laws,[38] as they do not focus on a specific decision but on the functioning of the system.

---

[38] According to Spanish Law 40/2015, of 1 October, on the Legal Regime of the Public Sector (Article 41), in the case of automated administrative action, the competent body or bodies, as the case may be, for the definition of the specifications, programming, maintenance, supervision and quality control and, where appropriate, auditing of the information system and its source code, shall be established beforehand.

An automated administrative action is understood to be any act or action carried out entirely by electronic means by a Public Administration within the framework of an administrative procedure and in which a public employee has not intervened directly.

3.2.2 Implementation of a Risk Management Strategy

Supervision should not be reserved exclusively for decision-making in the strict sense, but can also take place ex ante when analysing the risks inherent to the use of an administrative intelligence system,[39] or ex post when articulating ad hoc mechanisms for the control of decisions adopted in an automated manner. Particularly in cases where systems based on machine learning are implemented, the requirements and guarantees to be implemented should not only be subject to initial approval, but should also be subject to periodic evaluation systems, in order to ensure that the evolution of the algorithm itself continues to be in line with the initial premises.[40]

Amsterdam City Clauses require the contractor, in the first place, to develop a risk management strategy. According to Article 6:

> **Risk management strategy in the development of the Algorithmic System**
> 6.1 In the development of the Algorithmic System, the Contractor will pursue a common and up-to-date risk management strategy that is appropriate for the nature of the Algorithmic System. For purposes of application of such risk management strategy, the Contractor will identify the main risks that may occur when NAME OF ORGANIZATION uses the Algorithmic System and take measures to make the identified risks manageable. When identifying the risks, the Contractor will, where relevant, in any event pay attention to the risk of non-compliance with one or more of the obligations referred to in article 2 and article 4, risks related to discrimination, the possibility for NAME OF ORGANIZATION to control the Algorithmic System and data protection.
>
> 6.2 The Contractor will implement and document the risk management strategy described in article 6.1 in such a way that the audit referred to in article 8 can verify whether the Contractor has performed the obligation described in article 6.1.
>
> 6.3 If and to the extent that the Contractor has developed the Algorithmic System prior to conclusion of the Agreement, the Contractor warrants that the measures described in article 6.1 and/or article 6.2 have already been taken. The Contractor will produce evidence thereof on demand of NAME OF ORGANIZATION.

On the other hand, Article 9 AI Act provides for the establishment, documentation and maintenance of a risk management system associated with high-risk AI systems. In parallel, Article 2 European Commission's Model Clauses provides that the supplier shall ensure that, prior to the delivery of the AI system, a risk management system is established in relation to the AI system. This system shall comprise at least the following steps:

---

[39] Cerrillo I Martínez (2019), p. 296.

[40] Valero Torrijos (2019), p. 91.

(a) identification and analysis of known and foreseeable risks to health, safety and identification, estimation and evaluation of the known and reasonably foreseeable risks to health, safety and fundamental rights of the European Union that are likely to arise in the light of the Intended Purpose of the AI System and Reasonably Foreseeable Misuse;
(b) evaluation of other possibly arising risks;
(c) adoption of appropriate and targeted risk management measures designed to address the risks identified pursuant to points a and b of this paragraph in accordance with the provisions of the following paragraphs

As, a result, the content of the 9 AI Act is thus virtually reiterated, but with the addition of an obligation to ensure, prior to the delivery of the AI System, that the AI System is tested to verify whether it complies with the clauses and whether the risk management measures mentioned therein are effective in the light of the intended purpose. If requested by the public body, the supplier is obliged to test the AI system in the environment of this body. In addition, the obligation to deliver this risk management document is laid down in the standard clauses. This seems to be a highly recommendable practice, provided that this document is adapted to the requirements of the principle of proportionality.

3.2.3 Auditability

Auditability refers to the ability of an AI system to undergo the assessment of the system's algorithms, data and design processes. Auditability it is one of the seven requirements of trustworthy AI.[41]

Amsterdam City Clauses require certain audits to be carried out to verify whether the contractor has complied with all the obligations imposed by the public body in the implementation of the contract. This is therefore a technical control, which must be reflected in a report that may be published by the public administration. It is foreseen that the public administration may carry out annual audits, carried out in whole or in part by external auditors.

The content of the standard Amsterdam City Clauses has been transposed almost verbatim into the European Commission's proposal for standard clauses, albeit with optional content in the first draft.[42] In last version published of EU Model Clauses,

[41] AI HLEG (2019), pp. 14–19.

[42] 'Article 19 Compliance and Audit. (19.1.) At first request of the Public Organisation, the Suppliers must make available to the Public Organisation all information necessary to demonstrate compliance with these Clauses. (19.2.) The Supplier is obliged to cooperate in an audit or other type of inspection to be carried out by or on behalf of the Public Organisation to assess whether the Supplier complies with its obligations laid down in these Clauses at all times. Such cooperation will include providing all information required by the Public Organisation, providing an insight into the risk management system implemented, making Supplier staff available for interviews and providing access to the locations of the Supplier. (19.3.) The Public Organisation will prepare, or cause the preparation of, a report in which the conclusions of the audit are recorded. In the report, the Public

this content is mandatory in case of high-risk AI, which is preferable. The knowledge on how to carry out algorithmic audits already exists. Among other documents, see 'Auditing machine learning algorithms. A white paper for public auditors' by the Supreme Audit Institutions of Finland, Germany, the Netherlands, Norway and the UK.[43]

3.2.4 Clauses on Data Protection

Amsterdam City Clauses set out two articles relating to data: Article 2, which regulates data quality and Article 3, which concerns data ownership.

In relation to data quality, these clauses impose two obligations on the contractor: (a) to ensure that the development complies with the applicable laws and regulations[44] and (b) to ensure that the data used in the development of the algorithmic system will be collected, analysed, structured and/or edited in accordance with 'a reasoned approach'.[45]

As explained in the document containing Amsterdam City Clauses, the quality of the data used may be crucial for the performance of an algorithmic system. Where data is collected, it may contain socially constructed distortion, inaccuracies, errors and mistakes. The measures to be taken by the Contractor should focus on avoiding that. Another purpose of the requirement that data (collection), analysis, structuring

---

Organisation will record the extent to which the Supplier complies with the obligations under the Agreement. If the Public Organisation establishes that the Supplier does not comply with the obligations under this article, the Supplier will be obliged to remedy the defects identified by the Public Organisation within the reasonable term set by the Public Organisation in the report. If the Supplier fails to remedy the defects identified by the Public Organisation within the term set in the report for remedying such defects, the Supplier will be in default by operation of law. (19.4.) The Public Organisation will be entitled to publish the conclusions of the report referred to in article 19.3. (19.5.) The Public Organisation will be entitled to perform, or cause the performance of, an audit once per calendar year or in relation to any Substantial Modification. (19.6.) The Public Organisation may decide to have all or part of the audit performed by an independent auditor. (19.7.) The costs of the auditor to be engaged by the Public Organisation, if any, will be paid by the Public Organisation. The Public Organisation will pay the Supplier a reasonable fee for any costs to be incurred by the Supplier in the context of the audit. In no event will a dispute about the amount of such fee give the Supplier the right to suspend its obligations under these Clauses. No such fee will be owed by the Public Organisation if the audit reveals that the Supplier has failed to perform its obligations under these Clauses'.

[43] Available in Auditing machine learning algorithms (auditingalgorithms.net).

[44] Laws and regulations include the General Data Protection Regulation.

[45] 'Article 2 Data quality. (2.1) If and to the extent that the Algorithmic System is developed on the basis of data provided by NAME OF ORGANIZATION to the Contractor, the Contractor will take the measures that may reasonably be expected of it to ensure that the data used in the development of the Algorithmic System will be analysed, structured and/or edited: (a.) according to a motivated approach, the purpose of which includes, without limitation, the avoidance of socially constructed distortion, inaccuracies, errors, mistakes, and undesired prejudice ("bias") in such data to the extent possible; (b.) in a manner that is in compliance with applicable laws and regulations'.

and editing should take place according to a motivated approach is to avoid bias in the data as far as possible. Thus, it is added, the data sets used (both for training and for conducting the work) may contain inadvertent historical distortions, be incomplete or contain poor governance patterns. If such distortion is maintained, inadvertent direct or indirect bias and discrimination against certain groups or individuals may occur, which could reinforce bias and marginalisation in the use of the algorithmic system. Any demonstrable and discriminatory distortions should be identified and, where possible, removed by the contractor as soon as possible.

On the other hand, Article 3 regulates the ownership of the data, providing for contractual agreements on the use of the data, their delivery and their destruction. Thus, Article 3 distinguishes between the situation in which the administration provides data to the contractor (Article 3.1) and the situation in which data are collected or created in the context of the performance of the contract (Article 3.2). In both cases, the basic principle is that the rights to the data belong exclusively to the administration. The difference between Article 3.1 and Article 3.2 is that Article 3.2 expressly includes the possibility to derogate from this Article. The reason for including this possibility is that it is conceivable that situations may arise in which, given the nature of the arrangements made and the confidentiality of the data collected, it is reasonable and permissible for the contractor to use the data collected also for his own purposes.

The EU Model clauses do not comprehensively cover personal data protection law issues, as these standard clauses deal exclusively with the issues covered by the draft AI Act. However, Section D deals with rights to use the data sets and rules: rights to public Organisation data sets (Article 14); rights to Supplier data sets and third-party data sets (Article 15); hand over of the data Sets (Article 16) and indemnifications (Article 17). According to these articles, all rights, including any intellectual property right, relating to Publication Organisation Data Sets will accrue to the Public Organisation or a third party designated as such by the Public Organisation. On the other hand, all rights, including any intellectual property right, relating to Supplier Data Sets and Third-Party Data sets will accrue to the Supplier or a third party.

4 Conclusions

Public procurement can play an important role in the uptake of AI solutions. On the one hand, it can act as a stimulus for the deployment of this technology, if procurement is used as a driver for innovation. On the other hand, as a strategic market that is still evolving, public procurement has great potential to steer this market towards the most successful practices in terms of AI reliability.

In the absence of specific regulation on the use of AI in public administrations, the tendering procedure currently provides a somewhat appropriate channel for implementing some of the guarantees enshrined in legal systems. Thus, among other aspects, prior to contracting, risks and alternatives must be assessed, in addition to sufficiently justifying the need for contracting. Obligations for transparency and explainability of the algorithms used must already be foreseen. In addition, formal tendering allows for various relevant decisions to be subject to challenge. However, all this does not mean that it is not desirable to incorporate in national legislation a specific procedure for the approval of the use of algorithms, outside the procurement procedure. Otherwise, there is a risk that the contracting bodies will be the guardians of the trustworthy use of AI, when they may lack sufficient specialisation and experience, and decisions will be taken that do not have the necessary level of standardisation.[46] It would therefore be advisable to articulate an algorithm approval procedure that is sufficiently coordinated with the tendering procedure, or at least to articulate the necessary governance instruments to ensure the appropriate use of technical discretion in the adoption of different decisions. Otherwise, not all administrations will be able to incorporate AI solutions with the necessary guarantees.

Moreover, and in the absence of mechanisms such as those described above, it is difficult to dispense with the guarantees regarding the content of the specifications established in the international documents on standard clauses that we have had the opportunity to analyse. On the one hand, because most of these clauses derive without difficulty from the general legislation applicable to the use of new technologies by the administration. On the other hand, because circumventing the guarantees contained in these standard clauses may compromise the future use of the algorithm.

Finally, given the importance of public procurement in the development of the AI market, the development of standard contractual clauses for the procurement of AI under the auspices of the European Commission is really useful. Otherwise, there is a real risk of fragmentation of the market through national procurement rules imposing different requirements, a risk that the adoption of the AI Act seeks to avoid.

References

Boix Palop A (2020) Los algoritmos son reglamentos: la necesidad de extender las garantías propias de las normas reglamentarias a los programas empleados por la Administración para la adopción de decisiones. Revista de Derecho Público, Teoría y Método, vol I, pp 223–270

Cerrillo I Martínez A (2019) Robots, asistentes virtuales y automatización de las administraciones públicas. Revista Galega de Administración pública 61:279–309

EUROPEAN COMMISION (2023) Proposal for standard contractual clauses for the procurement of Artificial Intelligence (AI) by public organisations. High risk version

Gómez Jiménez ML (2021) Automatización procedimental y sesgo electrónico: el procedimiento administrativo electrónico desde la Inteligencia Artificial. Thomson-Reuters Aranzadi, Cizur Menor

HLEG AI (2019) Policy and investment recommendations for trustworthy AI

[46] Sánchez Graells (2022c).

Martín Delgado I (2023) La aplicación del principio de transparencia a la actividad administrativa algorítmica. Inteligencia artificial y sector público: retos, límites y medios. Tirant lo Blanch. Valencia

McBride K et al (2021) Towards a systematic understanding on the challenges of procuring artificial intelligence in the public sector. https://doi.org/10.31235/osf.io/un649

Oluka Nagitta P et al (2022) Human-centered artificial intelligence for the public sector: the gate keeping role of the public procurement professional. Proc Comput Sci 200(1)

Ponce Solé J (2019) Inteligencia artificial, Derecho administrativo y reserva de humanidad: algoritmos y procedimiento administrativo debido tecnológico. Revista General de Derecho Administrativo 50

Sánchez Graells A (2022a) Protecting procurement's AI gatekeeping role in domestic law, and trade agreements? http://www.howtocrackanut.com

Sánchez Graells A (2022b) Public procurement and [AI] source code transparency, a (downstream) competition issue (RE C-796/18). http://www.howtocrackanut.com

Sánchez Graells A (2022c) Interesting legislative proposal to make procurement of AI conditional on external checks. http://www.howtocrackanut.com

UK (2020) Guidelines for AI procurement. A summary of best practices addressing specific changes of acquiring artificial intelligence in the public sector

Valero Torrijos J (2019) Las garantías jurídicas de la inteligencia artificial en la actividad administrativa desde la perspectiva de la buena administración. Revista Catalana de Dret Public

WEF (2019) White paper. Guidelines for AI procurement

WEF (2020) AI procurement in a box: AI government procurement guidelines, Toolkit

AI and Sensitive Personal Data Under the Law Enforcement Directive: Between Operational Efficiency and Legal Necessity

Markus Naarttijärvi

Contents

Abstract In constitutional theory, the requirement of necessity is an integral part of a wider proportionality assessment in the limitation of constitutional rights. It fulfils a function of sorting out measures that restrict rights beyond what is required to fulfil the intended purpose. Within data protection, the requirement varies in strictness and interpretation—from 'ordinary' necessity to 'strict necessity'. Recently, the European Court of Justice (ECJ) has introduced what appears to be an even stricter requirement of 'absolute necessity' relating to the processing of biometric information under the EU Law Enforcement Directive (LED). In practice, however, the implications of those respective levels of strictness tends to vary, from a strict 'least restrictive means' test, to an analysis of whether a measure is necessary for a more effective or a more efficient fulfilment of the intended purpose. In this contribution

The original version of this chapter was revised: this chapter was previously published non-open access. The correction to this chapter is available at https://doi.org/10.1007/16495_2023_66

M. Naarttijärvi (✉)
Umeå University, Department of Law, Umeå, Sweden
e-mail: markus.naarttijarvi@umu.se

E. Gill-Pedro, A. Moberg (eds.), *YSEC Yearbook of Socio-Economic Constitutions 2023*, YSEC Yearbook of Socio-Economic Constitutions (2024) 2023: 331–358, https://doi.org/10.1007/16495_2023_57, Published online: 18 October 2023

the principle of necessity as applied by the ECJ is analysed as it pertains to the LED and the Charter, more specifically in the context of implementing AI supported analysis of biometric data. The gradual development of the interpretation of necessity is traced in the data protection case law of the ECJ. The study shows the increased emphasis placed on proportionality over time, highlighting both strengths and potential weaknesses of the requirement in relation to the use of AI supported decision-making in the law enforcement context.

1 Introduction

The possibilities and pitfalls offered by the implementation of AI in government decision-making are currently at the forefront of political, legal, and academic interest. The expanding implementation of AI-assisted decision-making in Europe has been evident in state functions ranging from the administration of public benefits,[1] to the prevention of terrorism and other serious crimes.[2] Several factors contribute to making full automation challenging in the policing context, and the continued role of human decision-makers exercising judgment and discretion has consequently been highlighted in previous research.[3] Even so, the stakes involved in police decision-making and the potential consequences for individuals affected by mistakes caused by algorithmic policing tools have called to the forefront the need for functional safeguards for individual rights as well as the rule of law in this context.[4] In line with this, the use of AI tools for law enforcement purposes has been highlighted in the proposed new EU AI-act ('AIA') as high-risk, with the proposal outlining several limits to its use.[5] However, there are already existing rules and principles relevant for the use of such tools in the data protection framework of the EU, more specifically in Directive (EU) 2016/680 ('the Law enforcement directive', or 'LED').[6] Recently, these rules have been subject to significant developments

---

[1] Schartum (2020), Suksi (2021), and Ranerup and Henriksen (2020).

[2] See, for example, Directive (EU) 2016/681 of the European Parliament and of the Council of 27 April 2016 on the use of passenger name record (PNR) data for the prevention, detection, investigation and prosecution of terrorist offences and serious crime.

[3] Enarsson et al. (2022).

[4] See, among other examples; Ferguson (2017), Brayne (2021), Harcourt (2007), Naarttijärvi (2019), and Joh (2016).

[5] See European Commission (2021) Proposal for a Regulation of the European Parliament and of the Council laying down harmonised rules on artificial intelligence (Artificial Intelligence Act) and amending certain union legislative acts.

[6] (2016) Directive (EU) 2016/680 of the European Parliament and of the Council of 27 April 2016 on the protection of natural persons with regard to the processing of personal data by competent authorities for the purposes of the prevention, investigation, detection or prosecution of criminal offences or the execution of criminal penalties, and on the free movement of such data, and repealing Council Framework Decision 2008/977/JHA.

through ECJ case law, which independently of the final form of the AIA will place certain limits on the use of AI for policing, particularly those pertaining to the processing of sensitive personal data under the LED.

To better illustrate these developments and put them into perspective, we can turn to the specific example of automated facial recognition. This technology is of particular interest as it pinpoints a core challenge of law enforcement—the identification of unique individuals—and thus, in the words of Kotsoglou and Oswald, 'has the potential to revolutionise the identification process, facilitate crime detection, and eliminate misidentification of suspects'.[7] Facial recognition technology thus represents a clear example of shifting technological affordances,[8] as technology now affords a type of rapid mass-identification of individuals which previously would have been impossible. This in turn shifts the implications of the wide availability of images and video.[9] The technology is therefore simultaneously associated with significant risks, due to the potential consequences of a misidentification.[10] For the individual, some of the most obvious risks relates to false positives, being wrongly identified as a suspect which may trigger further, potentially far-reaching intrusive investigative measures. For law enforcement agencies, false negatives imply a risk of failing to identify a suspect, while false positives on the other hand will divert investigative resources towards unfruitful avenues or worse, towards suspects that may wrongfully be charged with a crime.[11] The risk of false positives have been said to be higher for individuals belonging to overpoliced communities, adding a discriminatory potential to the technology.[12] There is also the risk that through automation bias, the outcome of the application of facial recognition systems may be favoured in the assessment of evidence, even faced with contradicting evidence.[13]

However, the potential harms of facial recognition technology go beyond false positives. The European Data Protection Board ('EDPB') has highlighted that the processing of biometric information implied by such systems constitutes a serious interference with the fundamental rights without taking the outcome of the processing into account. Indeed, so are legislative measures allowing their use under Articles 7 and 8 of the Charter.[14] The EDPB goes even further, pointing to how biometric data and facial recognition technology may impact the right to human dignity under Article 1 of the Charter, which requires that human beings are not

[7] Kotsoglou and Oswald (2020), p. 87.

[8] See Hildebrandt (2010), pp. 121–123.

[9] See, for instance, Afra and Alhajj (2020).

[10] See (2022) Proposal for a Regulation of the European Parliament and of the Council laying down harmonised rules on artificial intelligence (Artificial Intelligence Act) and amending certain Union legislative acts—Preparation for Coreper recital 48.

[11] Moraes et al. (2021), p. 165; see also European Data Protection Board, *Guidelines 05/2022 on the use of facial recognition technology in the area of law enforcement*, 26 April 2023, para 41.

[12] See Zalnieriute (2021), p. 301.

[13] European Data Protection Board, *Guidelines 05/2022 on the use of facial recognition technology in the area of law enforcement*, 26 April 2023, para 41.

[14] Ibid., paras 36–38.

treated as mere objects. This observation is based on how facial recognition technology 'calculates existential and highly personal characteristics, the facial features, into a machine-readable form with the purpose of using it as a human license plate or ID card, thereby objectifying the face'.[15] However, the EDPB does not mention the potential implications of this—the right to human dignity is inviolable, so should facial recognition technology be found to interfere with it, it cannot be justified under any circumstances.[16] Still, the risks involved have so far not been held to generally preclude facial recognition systems being put to use in law enforcement agencies, as long as their use can be justified as legitimate interferences under the relevant fundamental rights, with the relevant data processed in line with the requirements of the LED, and authorised by law.[17] However, certain applications of facial recognition technology have been highlighted as particularly invasive by the EDPB. These include remote automated biometric identification of individuals in public spaces, biometric profiling, emotion recognition, and populating facial recognition databases through scraping of social media accounts. While the specifics are at this point still under negotiation, many of these applications are likely to be specifically regulated by the upcoming AIA.[18] However, in the shadow of these more contentious applications of biometric identification exist a range of applications that could be considered as more mainstream. This includes the forensic matching of suspects between videos or photos appearing in a criminal investigation, to existing police databases. Such applications may not raise the specter of mass-surveillance to the same extent as those highlighted by the EDPB, but still involves the processing of sensitive biometric data of individuals, the risk of false positives (and negatives), and involve what is generally perceived of as AI technology to reach law enforcement objectives.

One such automated facial recognition system has indeed recently been implemented by the Swedish police authority and will serve as our example of some of the specific issues involved under EU law. This system was introduced following a review in 2019 by the Swedish Authority for Privacy Protection (at the time named 'Datainspektionen', henceforth 'the DPA'). The review came as a result of a request from the Swedish national police authority within the framework of 'prior consultations' required under the Swedish transposition of the LED before conducting processing operations of high sensitivity.[19] The request concerned the use of facial recognition software to forensically match suspects in crime scene

---

[15] Ibid., para 39.

[16] Both the European Data Protection Board and the European Data Protection Supervisor has however argued for a ban on automated recognition of human features in publicly accessible spaces, see EDPB-EDPS, *Joint Opinion 5/2021 on the proposal for a Regulation of the European Parliament and of the Council laying down harmonised rules on artificial intelligence (Artificial Intelligence Act)*, 18 June 2021, paras 30–33.

[17] See European Data Protection Board, *Guidelines 05/2022 on the use of facial recognition technology in the area of law enforcement*, 26 April 2023, para 105.

[18] See Sect. 2.3 below.

[19] Polisdatalagen ('The Police Data Act') Ch. 3, § 7, 2 para.

surveillance footage or other forensic imagery against the national database of criminal offender photographs ('Nationella signalementsregistret'). This would, according to the police authority be more effective than traditional and time-consuming manual analysis by human investigators.[20] Having considered the request, the DPA eventually found in October of 2019 that the use of facial recognition was allowed. It based this conclusion primarily on the judgment of the ECJ in Case C-524/06, *Heinz Huber*,[21] finding that the requirement of the processing being 'necessary' in the Swedish act transposing the LED should be interpreted as 'something that is needed to effectively carry out a task'. The DPA consequently found that it was 'clear that the planned processing using facial recognition technology to identify perpetrators is significantly more effective than individual officers making this selection manually' and approved the use of the software in this context.[22] Following this decision, the use of biometric matching was implemented within the Swedish police as a new forensic standard procedure in May 2021. Photos of unknown persons are now processed through facial recognition and matched against existing photos in the newly developed police database ABIS (Automatic Biometric Identification System).[23]

The finding by the Swedish DPA that enabled the implementation of this system raises, however, a few issues of both practical and theoretical importance, and highlights what appears to be a tension in the interpretation of the requirement of necessity under European data protection law, especially in relation to the processing of sensitive personal in the law enforcement context.

First, there is the question of what level of necessity should be applied in considering the processing of biometric data under the LED. Article 10 of the LED states that such processing should be allowed only when it is 'strictly necessary'. The Swedish transposition of these rules in the context of forensic investigations state that biometric data can be processed when it is 'absolutely necessary' for the purpose of the processing,[24] which includes forensic matching.[25] But the necessity level the Swedish DPA applied in its decision was that of ordinary necessity,[26]

[20] Datainspektionen (2019) Förhandssamråd om Polismyndighetens planerade användning av. programvara för ansiktsigenkänning mot signalementsregistret.

[21] ECJ, *Heinz Huber v Bundesrepublik Deutschland*, Case C-524/06, Judgment of 16 December 2008.

[22] Datainspektionen (2019) Förhandssamråd om Polismyndighetens planerade användning av. programvara för ansiktsigenkänning mot signalementsregistret.

[23] Swedish Police Authority (2022) Nytt forensiskt standardförfarande driftsatt. In: polisen.se. https://polisen.se/aktuellt/nyheter/2022/februari/nytt-forensiskt-standardforfarande-driftsatt/. Accessed 2 March 2023.

[24] Lag (2018:1693) om polisens behandling av. personuppgifter inom brottsdatalagens område, Ch. 6, § 4.

[25] Ibid. Ch. 6, § 1.

[26] The specific reference to necessity made by the DPA was to Ch 2, § 1, Brottsdatalag, which applies more generally to the processing of personal data within the police, rather than the specific rule on biometric data within forensic databases.

as was the requirement interpreted by the ECJ in *Heinz Huber,* which Swedish DPA relied on.[27] Meanwhile, the ECJ has in numerous cases held that *all* derogations from the right to data protection must be limited to what is strictly necessary,[28] and has recently established what seems to be an even higher level of necessity in relation to the processing of biometric data under the LED.[29]

Second, the decision by the Swedish DPA highlights the rather opaque relationship that seem to exist between the necessity requirement and effectiveness. Given that manual analysis of surveillance footage is possible, and indeed represents the way this has been done for years, one could argue that the use of facial recognition software is not so much *necessary*, as it is *more efficient*. But is comparable efficiency enough to satisfy the requirement of necessity in this context?

Third, the analysis by the Swedish DPA contained no further assessment of proportionality *strictu sensu*, where the interest of the Swedish police to effectively analyse crime-scene footage was weighed against the damage done to right to data protection. Indeed, no such requirement seems to follow from the wording of the LED, where Article 10 only mentions that processing of sensitive personal data should be 'allowed only where strictly necessary'. However, the ECJ has increasingly made use of proportionality balancing in relation to derogations from the right to data protection.[30] How could these developments impact the legal requirements surrounding the use of biometric data and AI technologies in this context?

Analysing these questions allows for a fourth and final question; what impact will this have on the use of emerging AI-technologies as decision support or analysis tools in the law enforcement context, and the intended function of the LED to protect personal data in this setting? This final question is of salience in light of the proposed AIA, as it will determine what role the act will play as a further necessary safeguard in relation to processing of sensitive categories of data through AI technologies.

In this paper, these questions will be analysed in light of case law from the ECJ interpreting the LED and the GDPR; guidelines from the European Data Protection Board; decisions from national data protection agencies; as well as literature surrounding proportionality as a principle of constitutional and data protection law. The discussion will be focused on semi-automated decision-making, rather than fully automated decisions, as the former is (still) more prevalent in the context of both criminal investigations and police intelligence operations where few decisions are taken without first having been reviewed by a human at some stage of the decision-making process. The focus on automation and the implications of AI in this context is thus on its role as potential decision-support tools and automated analysis, rather than on making final decisions without human input.

[27] ECJ, *Heinz Huber v Bundesrepublik Deutschland*, Case C-524/06, Judgment of 16 December 2008.

[28] See below Sect. 3.

[29] See below Sect. 3.1.2.

[30] See Sect. 3.2.2 below.

Before proceeding to the analysis of necessity, we need to take a quick look at the specific data protection context that surrounds processing of personal data within law enforcement agencies.

2 Data Protection in the Law Enforcement Context

2.1 The Law Enforcement Directive: A Very Short Introduction

The LED is part of the overall EU data protection framework along with its more famous cousin, the General Data Protection Regulation (GDPR).[31] Given the special context of prevention, investigation, detection or prosecution of criminal offences or the execution of criminal penalties, the directive served as a way of ensuring a more specifically tailored legal framework in that setting.[32] Implicitly this gave member states further autonomy in choosing how to implement the necessary level of data protection. The LED has been described as 'a major step forward' in data protection showing 'that it now will be possible to achieve high privacy and data protection standards while processing personal data for law enforcement purposes in a more flexible manner'.[33] In comparison to the framework decision it replaced, the directive has been seen as increasing harmonisation as well as data protection standards.[34] Yet some characteristics of the LED have also been described as challenging those positive outcomes, particularly 'the lack of specific guidelines on how certain general concepts such as necessity, proportionality and appropriateness are to be implemented and applied by member states to balance privacy with security and other civil rights'.[35]

2.2 The Relative (Ir)relevance of the Rules on Automated Decision-Making

Before delving into the specifics of necessity in relation to the processing of sensitive personal data in the LED, it is worth pointing out the specific rules existing on automated individual decision-making (including profiling) in Article 11 of the

[31] Regulation (EU) 2016/679 of the European Parliament and of the Council of 27 April 2016 on the protection of natural persons with regard to the processing of personal data and on the free movement of such data and repealing Directive 95/46/EC (General Data Protection Regulation).

[32] See recital 10 LED.

[33] Sajfert and Quintel (2017), pp. 21–22.

[34] Marquenie (2017), p. 328.

[35] Ibid., p. 329.

LED. This rule contains what at first glance may appear to be a prohibition against the use of such decision-making, but one which is subject to several exceptions. First, Article 11 only refers to decisions based *solely* on automated processing, including profiling. The operative terms used in this rule are the same as in Article 22 of the GDPR, where the consensus have been that automated processes fall outside of the field of application of the article when they remain decisional support tools, 'provided the human decision-maker considers the merits of the result rather than being blindly or automatically steered by the process'.[36] Second, automated decisions as defined in Article 11 LED are still allowed if authorised by union or member state law which provides appropriate safeguards for the rights and freedoms of the data subject. Third, although a specific mention is made in Article 11(2) LED of how wholly automated decisions should not be made using special categories of personal data referred to in Article 10, this prohibition contains a similar exception if 'suitable measures to safeguard the data subject's rights and freedoms and legitimate interests are in place'. While this type of decision-making is not the focus of this contribution, as the type of decision support and analysis tools that are discussed here only supports human decision-making, it is worth noting that the protections in Article 11 are circumscribed to the point where automated decisions, even based on sensitive personal data like biometrics, are fully possible to implement under the LED, although fundamental rights as interpreted by the ECJ may form an additional layer of protection.[37]

2.3 *The Likely Limits of the Proposed EU AI Act*

Before moving onto necessity under the EU data protection framework, it is worth to briefly mention the intended relationship between the LED and the proposed AIA in this context. In relation to the processing of biometric data, the latest draft[38] establishes new rules limiting the use of 'real-time' remote biometric identification of natural persons for the purposes of law enforcement in publicly accessible spaces. The rules do not include a complete ban against the use of AI technologies for this purpose but limits its use through draft Article 5d to specific situations, such as the targeted search for specific potential victims of crime or the prevention of a specific and substantial threat to the critical infrastructure, life, health or physical safety of

[36] Bygrave (2020), p. 533; Article 29 Data Protection Working Party (2017) Guidelines on Automated individual decision-making and Profiling for the purposes of Regulation 2016/679, pp. 20–21; Brkan (2019), pp. 101–102.

[37] The ECJ have begun asserting the fundamental rights implications of automated decision-making, see for example ECJ, *Ligue des droits humains ASBL v Conseil des ministres*, Case C-817/19, Judgment of 21 June 2022.

[38] (2022) Proposal for a Regulation of the European Parliament and of the Council laying down harmonised rules on artificial intelligence (Artificial Intelligence Act) and amending certain Union legislative acts—Preparation for Coreper.

natural persons or the prevention of a terrorist attacks. It would also, according to draft Article 5 d (3) be subject to prior judicial authorisation. In this context, the AIA would according to draft recital 23 become *lex specialis*, and the use of such real-time remote identification could therefore not be based on Article 10 LED. However, all other processing of biometric data and other personal data involved in the use of AI systems for biometric identification, other than in connection to the use of 'real-time' remote biometric identification systems in publicly accessible spaces for the purpose of law enforcement would, according to draft recital 24, fall under Article 10 LED. In other words, the LED will still form the main legal safeguard, with the AIA providing additional limits in certain high-risk contexts. As such, the forensic matching we are using as our example here, would, most likely, still be primarily governed by the LED, rather than the AIA.

3 Necessity and Data Protection

3.1 Necessity, Strict Necessity, or Absolute Necessity?: The LED Meets the ECJ

3.1.1 The Early Discussion Surrounding Necessity in the LED

One of the previously mentioned flexibilities implied by the LED is that in contrast to the GDPR, the processing of sensitive categories[39] of personal data is not prohibited as a rule, rather it is restricted through Article 10 of the LED to situations where it is *strictly necessary* and subject to appropriate safeguards for the rights and freedoms of the data subjects. This differentiates sensitive data from the less stringent requirement of 'ordinary' *necessity* required for processing of non-sensitive data established in Article 8 of the LED. This reflects the legitimate need for law enforcement agencies to process sensitive categories of data in some of their tasks, from the use of fingerprints (i.e. biometric data) to identify suspects at crime-scenes to the processing of data on the religious or ethnic background of victims in cases of hate crime. Given the sensitivity of this data, the requirement of strict necessity makes it clear that processing of such data should not be a routine measure.

This two-pronged approach to necessity stemming from the text of the LED has however for a long time become increasingly muddled in light of case law of the ECJ in the data protection context. The ECJ has over time established *strict necessity* as a basic requirement for derogations and limitations of the protection of personal data, without limiting this analysis to the protection of special categories of sensitive

[39] Defined in LED Article 10 as personal data revealing racial or ethnic origin, political opinions, religious or philosophical beliefs, or trade union membership, and the processing of genetic data, biometric data for the purpose of uniquely identifying a natural person, data concerning health or data concerning a natural person's sex life or sexual orientation.

data.[40] While the cases establishing this level of necessity has concerned primarily the previous data protection directive and the GDPR, the European Data Protection Supervisor ('EDPS') has concluded that this *strict necessity* applies as an overall requirement within the context of the LED as well.[41] But if 'plain' necessity should be construed strictly, what is then to be made of the specific reference to strict necessity in Article 10 LED? The conclusion of the Article 29 Working Party (the precursor to the current EDPB) was that 'the term "strictly necessary" in Article 10 must be understood as a call to pay particular attention to the necessity principle in the context of processing special categories of data, as well as to foresee precise and particularly solid justifications for the processing of such data'.[42] Recently we received some clarity in this matter, as the ECJ interpreted the requirement of necessity under Article 10 LED for the first time in a ruling that partly confirmed these views, but which arguably went even further—establishing what must be regarded as a new threshold of necessity *above* strictly necessary.

3.1.2 Absolute Necessity in Criminal Proceedings Against V.S.: Establishing a New Threshold

In Case C-205/32, *Criminal proceedings against V.S.*, delivered in January of 2023, the ECJ considered a request for preliminary ruling from a Bulgarian court on the interpretation of the LED.[43] With regards to necessity, the ECJ interpreted the question posed by the Bulgarian court as whether Article 10 LED (read in conjunction with general principles of processing personal data in Article 4 LED and the requirements of lawful processing in Article 8 LED) precluded national legislation which provided for the systematic collection of biometric and genetic data of any person accused of an intentional offence subject to public prosecution. Specifically, when no specific obligations were established in national law for the competent authority to determine and demonstrate the necessity of that collection for specific objectives pursued and that those objectives could not be achieved by collecting only a part of the data concerned.[44]

---

[40] See ECJ, *Tietosuojavaltuutettu v Satakunnan Markkinapörssi Oy and Satamedia Oy*, Case C-73/07, Judgment of 16 December 2008.; ECJ, *Volker und Markus Schecke GbR (C-92/09) and Hartmut Eifert (C-93/09) v Land Hessen*, Joined cases C-92/09 and C-93/09, Judgment of 9 November 2010.; ECJ, *Tele2 Sverige AB v Post- och telestyrelsen and Secretary of State for the Home Department v Tom Watson and Others*, Joined Cases C-203/15 and C-698/15, Judgment of 21 December 2016, p. 2.

[41] European Data Protection Supervisor, *Assessing the necessity of measures that limit the fundamental right to the protection of personal data: A Toolkit*, 11 April 2017, p. 7.

[42] Article 29 Data Protection Working Party, *Opinion on some key issues of the Law Enforcement Directive (EU 2016/680)*, WP 258, 29 November 2017, pp. 7–8.

[43] ECJ, *Criminal proceedings against* VS, Case C-205/21, Judgment of 26 January 2023.

[44] Ibid., paras 114–115.

The ECJ began answering this question by acknowledging the special sensitivity of both the data at issue and the context of their processing. These implied, the court held, significant risks to the Charter rights to respect for privacy and for data protection.[45]

Proceeding to the specific interpretation of 'strictly necessary' in Article 10 LED the ECJ focused on the difference between strict necessity in that article, and the requirement of necessity in the directive in general. Here, the court specifically highlighted certain linguistic factors. The court began by taking note of the French-language version of the LED, where the term used in Article 10 was *nécessité absolue',* which the court found established 'strengthened conditions for lawful processing of sensitive data'.[46] This led to two interesting conclusions:

> Thus, first, the use of the adverb 'only' before the words 'where strictly necessary' underlines that the processing of special categories of data, within the meaning of Article 10 [LED], will be capable of being regarded as necessary solely in a limited number of cases. Second, the fact that the necessity for processing of such data is an 'absolute' one [('absolue')] signifies that that necessity is to be assessed with particular rigour.[47]

The court then proceeded to tone down the significance of how the term 'strictly necessary' was used in certain other language versions, as those words also implied a strengthened condition. In this context the court also took note of how that requirement had been added late in the legislative process, implying an ambition to give greater protection to persons subject to such processing.[48]

It is interesting to note how the court in *Criminal proceedings against V.S.* has essentially established a brand-new standard of necessity, above strict necessity, thus resolving the terminological paradox of *ordinary* vs. *strict* necessity in the LED. In doing so, the court also made it clear that this level of necessity will only be reached in a limited number of cases, thereby signaling the exceptional nature of the processing of this type of sensitive data. The court went on to observe that this level of necessity entails particularly strict checking of that the requirement of data minimisation under the LED has been met. This interpretation also confirms one made by the EDPS in its proposed guidelines on the use of facial recognition technology in the area of law enforcement,[49] which were published for public consultation in mid-2022, prior to the ruling in *V.S.* Here, the implication of strict necessity under the LED was interpreted by the EDPS as the measure needing to be indispensable. 'It restricts the margin of appreciation permitted to the law enforcement authority in the necessity test to an absolute minimum'.[50] The EDPS also tied this to the requirement of objective criteria defining the 'circumstances and

[45] Ibid., para 116.

[46] Ibid., para 117.

[47] Ibid., para 118.

[48] Ibid., paras 119–120.

[49] European Data Protection Supervisor (2022) Guidelines 05/2022 on the use of facial recognition technology in the area of law enforcement.

[50] Ibid., para 73.

conditions under which processing can be undertaken, thus excluding any processing of a general or systematic nature'.[51]

There is one more significant thing to note in the ECJ ruling in *V.S*. The court held that given the strict review that is warranted, it is also necessary to consider the nature of the objective pursued, to ensure that the processing is connected to 'the prevention of criminal offences or threats to public security displaying a certain degree of seriousness, the punishment of such offences or protection against such threats'.[52] Implicitly, the court here moves beyond necessity and into proportionality balancing, but without making any explicit reference to the latter principle. To understand the significance of this, we need to look at how the ECJ case law on necessity has developed up to the present ruling. As we will see, proportionality has played an increasingly important role in this case law, going from largely absent to explicitly used to limit restrictions of the right to data protection.

3.2 *The Emergence of Strict Necessity and Proportionality in the ECJ Case Law on Data Protection*

3.2.1 From Strict Necessity as an Interpretive to an Overall Requirement

In most of the cases leading up to *Criminal proceedings against V.S.* where the ECJ has expounded on the necessity requirement, it has done so in relation to national or union legislative measures derogating from the right to privacy and data protection. In the first case where the court mentions this application of strict necessity, Case C-73/07, *Satakunnan*, it was in explaining the specific derogations allowed by specific chapters of the Data Protection Directive (DPD) as they were to be applied in the balancing against freedom of expression with regards to the publication of tax-records by a newspaper.[53]

> In order to take account of the importance of the right to freedom of expression in every democratic society, it is necessary, first, to interpret notions relating to that freedom, such as journalism, broadly. Secondly, and in order to achieve a balance between the two fundamental rights, the protection of the fundamental right to privacy requires that the derogations and limitations in relation to the protection of data provided for in the chapters of the directive referred to above must apply only in so far as is strictly necessary.[54]

This case can arguably be said to establish mainly that the specific derogations allowed by the DPD should be interpreted narrowly to ensure that they are limited to

[51] Ibid., para 73.

[52] ECJ, *Criminal proceedings against* VS, Case C-205/21, Judgment of 26 January 2023, para 127.

[53] ECJ, *Tietosuojavaltuutettu v Satakunnan Markkinapörssi Oy and Satamedia Oy*, Case C-73/07, Judgment of 16 December 2008, para 56.

[54] Ibid., para 56.

what is strictly necessary. The ruling in *Satakunnan* was however later referred to in case S-92/09 and C-93/09, *Volker und Markus Scheke*, which concerned the validity of regulations requiring the publication of beneficiaries of agricultural funds.[55] This time the ECJ did not limit its statement to the DPD, but rather held that derogations and limitations in relation to the *protection of personal data* must apply only in so far as is strictly necessary.[56] While widening the scope of the statement from the specific interpretation of the DPD to a more general statement, this ECJ also moved its analysis to the legislative level, i.e. an analysis of a requirement to publish information established by the EU in a regulation, which was not strictly necessary to achieve the aim of the public interest.[57]

In the subsequent case C-473/12, *IPI*, the ECJ referred to the requirement of strict necessity as 'settled case law' and related it to 'the protection of the fundamental right to privacy'.[58] Again, this case related to a question on the national legislative framework of data protection, specifically the possible exceptions established by that framework in relation to the activities of private detectives.[59]

Through these three cases, we have moved from the specific interpretation of the DPD to more general considerations about the fundamental right to privacy and data protection, but in doing so, the court has also moved towards an application of the requirement in the context of legislative measures rather than specific processing operations within a specific legislative framework. This continued through case C-293/12 and C-594/12, the *Digital Rights Ireland* judgment, which also relates to the legislative level, this time the EU data retention directive.[60]

In 2014 the ECJ produced one of the few exceptions to the tendency to discuss strict necessity on the legislative level, case C-212/13, *Ryneš*.[61] This concerned a specific processing, a home security camera installed by a private person which recorded the entrance to his home as well as a public footpath and the entrance to the house opposite, and whether this processing could fall under the exception in DPD Article 3(2) for 'purely personal or household activity'.[62] The ECJ again repeated its statement on the need for strict necessity, again in relation to the Charter right to

[55] ECJ, *Volker und Markus Schecke GbR (C-92/09) and Hartmut Eifert (C-93/09) v Land Hessen*, Joined cases C-92/09 and C-93/09, Judgment of 9 November 2010.

[56] Ibid., para 77.

[57] Council Regulation (EC) No. 1290/2005 of 21 June 2005 on the financing of the common agricultural policy (Article 44a).

[58] ECJ, *Institut professionnel des agents immobiliers (IPI) v Geoffrey Englebert and Others*, Case C-473/12, Judgment of 7 November 2013, para 39.

[59] Ibid., paras 14–21.

[60] ECJ, *Digital Rights Ireland Ltd v Minister for Communications, Marine and Natural Resources and Others and Kärntner Landesregierung and Others*, Joined Cases C-293/12 and C-594/12, Judgment of 8 April 2014, para 52.

[61] ECJ, *František Ryneš v Úřad pro ochranu osobních údajů*, Case C-212/13, Judgment of 11 December 2014.

[62] Ibid., paras 13–18.

privacy, but ended up with a more narrowly tailored implication of this strict necessity—namely that the exception in DPD Article 3(2) 'must be narrowly construed'.[63]

In C-362/14, *Schrems (I)*, the ECJ returned to the legislative level and applied strict necessity to the data transfer agreement between the EU and the United States, finding that a generalised storage, transfer, and access, of all the personal data of all the persons whose data has been transferred to the United States could not be strictly necessary for the objective pursued.[64] Again, as the court moved to analysing a legal framework surrounding the protection of personal data, the strict necessity criteria seems to be used more actively and with more expansive consequences.

These cases indicate a tendency by the court to look towards the fundamental right roots of data protection to resolve cases before them, rather than being caught in more specific articles of the data protection rules in question.

3.2.2 Necessity, Proportionality, and Automation

An interesting development in the ECJ approach to necessity came the following year, in the 2016 *Tele2* judgment (C-203/15 and C-698/15).[65] Here, the court again considered the legislative framework surrounding the protection of personal data, this time the Swedish and British national rules on data retention for the purposes of investigating and preventing serious crime. After having up until now touched upon the requirement of necessity as a distinct requirement, the ECJ now found it to be explicitly derived from the principle of proportionality:

> Due regard to the principle of proportionality also derives from the Court's settled case-law to the effect that the protection of the fundamental right to respect for private life at EU level requires that derogations from and limitations on the protection of personal data should apply only in so far as is strictly necessary.[66]

It is reasonable to assume that the ECJ here talked about proportionality as a wider analytical framework, within which necessity forms a distinct step before proportionality *strictu sensu*.[67] The ECJ went on to make observations surrounding the general and indiscriminate retention of all traffic and location data of all subscribers and registered users relating to all means of electronic communications.[68] In doing

---

[63] Ibid., para 28.

[64] ECJ, *Maximillian Schrems v Data Protection Commissioner*, Case C-362/14, Judgment of 6 October 2015, paras 91–93.

[65] ECJ, *Tele2 Sverige AB v Post- och telestyrelsen and Secretary of State for the Home Department v Tom Watson and Others*, Joined Cases C-203/15 and C-698/15, Judgment of 21 December 2016.

[66] Ibid., para 96.

[67] Barak (2012).

[68] ECJ, *Tele2 Sverige AB v Post- och telestyrelsen and Secretary of State for the Home Department v Tom Watson and Others*, Joined Cases C-203/15 and C-698/15, Judgment of 21 December 2016, para 97.

so, the ECJ did not stray from a more narrow definition of necessity as a means to sort out derogations that unnecessarily impacts the right to data protection, as the court did not begin to discuss balancing against opposing interests until later in the same judgment.[69] Still, the explicit reference to proportionality had not been made before, and once mentioned in the *Tele2* ruling, it returned in later cases.

In *Opinion 1/15* on the Draft agreement between Canada and the European Union for the Transfer of Passenger Name Record data from the European Union to Canada, the court again reiterated that reference to the principle of proportionality, adding that it requires 'in accordance with settled case-law of the Court, that derogations from and limitations on the protection of personal data should apply only in so far as is strictly necessary'.[70] Again, the statement by the ECJ was made in the context of analysing legislative level frameworks and safeguards of data protection, to ensure interference is limited to what is strictly necessary. Interestingly, the court here added that '[t]he need for such safeguards is all the greater where personal data is subject to automated processing [...] particularly where the protection of the particular category of personal data that is sensitive data is at stake'.[71] This statement is directly relevant for our understanding of necessity in relation to the automated processing of biometric data implied by facial recognition technologies.

Similar concerns of automated processing and sensitive categories of data were later repeated in *La Quadrature du Net*,[72] and in *Ligue des Droits Humains*,[73] respectively. In these cases, the court was more explicit with proportionality balancing forming an additional step after the assessment of strict necessity, adding some needed clarity in terms of its view on the process of proportionality analysis. Again, the court in these cases analysed the strict necessity in relation to legislative frameworks derogating from the right to data protection, this time surrounding the access of law enforcement agencies to communications data in *La Quadrature du Net*, and passenger name records from airlines in *Ligue des Droits Humains*.[74]

[69] Ibid., para 102.

[70] ECJ, *Opinion of the Court (Grand Chamber) of 26 July 2017 — Draft agreement between Canada and the European Union. Case Opinion 1/15.*, Judgment of 2015, para 141.

[71] Ibid., para 141.

[72] ECJ, *La Quadrature du Net and Others v Premier ministre and Others*, Joined Cases C-511/18, C-512/18, C-520/18, Judgment of 6 October 2020, para 130.

[73] ECJ, *Ligue des droits humains ASBL v Conseil des ministres*, Case C-817/19, Judgment of 21 June 2022, para 115.

[74] ECJ, *La Quadrature du Net and Others v Premier ministre and Others*, Joined Cases C-511/18, C-512/18, C-520/18, Judgment of 6 October 2020; ECJ, *Ligue des droits humains ASBL v Conseil des ministres*, Case C-817/19, Judgment of 21 June 2022; see also ECJ, *GD v The Commissioner of the Garda Síochána and Others*, Case C-140/20, Judgment of 5 April 2022, paras 52–54.

3.2.3 Some Preliminary Observations on Absolute Necessity and Proportionality

Summing up the case law discussed so far, it seems quite clear that the ECJ views strict necessity as an overall requirement for derogations in relation to the rights of data protection and privacy. However, as this analysis also shows, the application of that requirement seems most consistent whenever the court have been asked to consider the overall legislative framework establishing such derogations. In these cases, the court has also moved towards explicitly engaging in proportionality balancing as an additional step after analysing the strict necessity of the legislative framework allowing for restrictions of the right to data protection. In the few cases where the court expounded on the specific processing of data *within* such frameworks prior to *Criminal procedures against V.S.*, the court has similarly made mentions of the strict necessity requirement, but applied it somewhat differently, mainly as a dictum to narrowly interpret the specific rules allowing for such derogation. For quite some time this suggested the possibility that the two-pronged necessity requirements of the LED, separating 'ordinary' from 'strict' necessity could have held in the face of ECJ scrutiny, through the distinction between *legislative measures* that derogate from the right to data protection, which the ECJ requires to meet the threshold of strict necessity, and specific measures taken *within the scope of such legislation*, such as the LED and its national transposition the necessity requirement would still depend on the category of data. In the latter context the requirement would primarily have been a call for a narrower interpretation in light of the rights of the Charter. We now know that the ECJ instead chose a different approach in *Criminal procedures against V.S.* and instead elevated 'strict necessity' in the context of Article 10 LED to what amounts to 'absolute necessity'. Still, while the ECJ ruling answered some questions it created a few new ones as well.

A first question arises from the fact that the ruling in *V.S.* did not contain any of the usual references to earlier case law establishing the requirement of strict necessity in relation to restrictions of the right to data protection. This is noteworthy, as references to for example *Satakunnan*; *Volker und Markus Schecke and Eifert*; and *Digital Rights Ireland,* have become something of a formula when the court applies necessity in the data protection context. Also, the court never explicitly mentions the overall requirement of strict necessity repeated in those cases, choosing instead to differentiate between those articles in the LED referencing only 'necessity' from that of 'strict necessity' in Article 10 requiring strengthened conditions of scrutiny.[75] This may be explained by how these often-mentioned cases relate to the DPD and the GDPR rather than the LED, and the need to separate the different contexts of processing. Still, in doing so, the ECJ missed an opportunity to clearly establish that (or at least clarify whether) the requirement of strict necessity does in fact carry across to the LED context outside of the scope of Article 10. However, one could argue that by establishing that 'strict necessity' in Article 10 should, in fact, be

[75] ECJ, *Criminal proceedings against* VS, Case C-205/21, Judgment of 26 January 2023, para 117.

construed as 'absolute necessity', the ECJ implicitly suggest the need for something stricter than 'strict necessity'—a need that reasonably arises due to the overall requirement of strict necessity in the data protection context.

A second question arises from how the ECJ avoided explicit mentions of proportionality balancing, instead opting for incorporating the weight of the purpose underpinning processing of sensitive data under the heading of necessity. This constitutes a break from the trend established in ECJ case law ever since the *Tele2* ruling. A possible explanation is that given how the court is acting not on the legislative level, but within the framework of the LED, the court maintained its more cautious approach by incorporating some concerns that traditionally have fallen under proportionality *stricto* sensu into the requirements under Article 10, rather than adding proportionality as a separate concern based on the application of Charter rights extraneous to the LED. While such an application of proportionality based on fundamental rights would carry additional weight, it is also something the court has generally preserved for cases where it assesses general legislative frameworks derogating from the right to data protection, rather than interpreting specific rules in secondary EU law. Also, by incorporating these considerations *into* the requirements included in Article 10, this requirement is likely to assert itself further in the application of this article within law enforcement agencies that may be less inclined to consider the need for overall proportionality assessment under fundamental rights documents.

3.3 *Implications of Necessity*

3.3.1 Necessity and Least Restrictive Means

Having established the standard of necessity required, we may now move to consider the actual implications of necessity, strict necessity, and absolute necessity, in the data protection context and in relation to the use of AI as decision-support tools.

To do this, we need to further consider what the necessity test implies. As suggested by the name of the test, it requires that a limitation of a right can in fact be proven to be necessary to reach the aim. The intention is to sort out unnecessarily intrusive measures, without having to resort to more complicated and controversial balancing exercises as part of proportionality in the strict sense.[76] Implicit in this necessity analysis is also the *least restrictive means test*, which includes an analysis of whether alternative means exist which still contribute effectively to the intended aim but which would restrict the right to a lesser extent.[77] If we can find such alternative means this is a clear indication that necessity is not met.

---

[76] Barak (2012), p. 338.

[77] ECJ, *Volker und Markus Schecke GbR (C-92/09) and Hartmut Eifert (C-93/09) v Land Hessen*, Joined cases C-92/09 and C-93/09, Judgment of 9 November 2010, para 86. Barak has divided this test into two elements, (1) whether there is a hypothetical alternative means which equally advances

One example of where the ECJ has found a violation of necessity through the least restrictive means test concerned the public disclosure of penalty points for road traffic offences in Latvia. Asked to consider whether this system complied with the right to data protection, the ECJ compared the Latvian legislation to alternatives in other member states using less privacy sensitive preventive measures such as public awareness campaigns or driving tests to reach the same goal. Such measures did not carry the same risk of social disapproval and stigmatisation of the data subject, yet according to the ECJ there was no indication that the Latvian legislature had considered them. As such, the court found that the Latvian system was not strictly necessary.[78]

In other cases, such as those relating to data retention and access to communications data by law enforcement agencies, the analysis of necessity is analytically somewhat intermingled with more overarching proportionality concerns, but certain parts of the ECJ jurisprudence in this context are clear expressions of necessity and questions of least restrictive means. For example, the retention of *all* communications data, for *all* users of communications networks, goes beyond what is necessary for the prevention of serious crimes or the protection of national security.[79] As such, some type of criteria must be implemented that implies a possible link between the affected individuals and the crimes the measure is intended to prevent—otherwise it will impact a wider set of individuals than is necessary. The associated proportionality aspect of this equation is that the significant impact of these measures for the rights in question can only be motivated by the fight against serious crimes or the protection of national security.[80]

It is not entirely clear how this requirement would translate into the facial recognition context. The Swedish police authority has stressed that searching through video footage in preliminary investigations will necessitate a scan of all faces that appear in the footage to identify an individual of interest to the investigation.[81] In other words, the scan is conducted precisely to identify the possible link between an individual and the crime. To some extent this scan will, in the case of preliminary investigations, likely relate to a specific location relevant to the

the law's purpose, and (2) whether there is a hypothetical alternative means which limits the constitutional right to a lesser extent, see Barak (2012), pp. 323–328.

[78] ECJ, *Proceedings brought by B*, Case C-439/19, Judgment of 22 June 2021, paras 111–113.

[79] ECJ, *Digital Rights Ireland Ltd v Minister for Communications, Marine and Natural Resources and Others and Kärntner Landesregierung and Others*, Joined Cases C-293/12 and C-594/12, Judgment of 8 April 2014, paras 56–65; ECJ, *Tele2 Sverige AB v Post- och telestyrelsen and Secretary of State for the Home Department v Tom Watson and Others*, Joined Cases C-203/15 and C-698/15, Judgment of 21 December 2016, paras 105–108.

[80] ECJ, *Tele2 Sverige AB v Post- och telestyrelsen and Secretary of State for the Home Department v Tom Watson and Others*, Joined Cases C-203/15 and C-698/15, Judgment of 21 December 2016, para 115.

[81] Swedish Police Authority (2022) Opinion from the Swedish Police Authority concerning the EDPB's Guidelines 05/2022 on the use of facial recognition technology in the area of law enforcement, p. 5.

investigation of a crime. This could imply that there is a limit to the affected individuals and that at least a possible link exists between the person, through the location, to a possible crime. Geographical limits have been highlighted by the ECJ as a possible measure to make communications data retention conform to the necessity requirement of the Charter.[82] However, in situations where the crime being investigated through the use of facial recognition technology has been committed in a public space with larger crowds present, such as in the case of riots occurring in the context of a political protest, this limitation is rendered less functional. In such situations, the processed images may also reveal political opinions of participants in the demonstration which adds further concerns to the existing processing of biometric data.[83]

It should be said that the way in which the ECJ has expressed the least restrictive means test adds a certain note of confusion to the relationship between ordinary and strict necessity. In *Proceedings brought by B,* the ECJ applied a test established in the discussion of 'regular' *necessity* in recital 39 of the GDPR to explain the implications for the *strict necessity* requirement emanating from the Charter. This requirement, the ECJ held:

> is not met where the objective of general interest pursued can reasonably be achieved just as effectively by other means less restrictive of the fundamental rights of data subjects, in particular the rights to respect for private life and to the protection of personal data guaranteed in Articles 7 and 8 of the Charter, since derogations and limitations in relation to the principle of protection of such data must apply only in so far as is strictly necessary [...][84]

This may indicate that in terms of the least restrictive means test, the threshold is similar under the two levels of necessity. In other words, the standard of *just as effectively* for comparisons to other potential measures that could fulfil part of the legislative aim, is the same. If so, the level of strictness or scrutiny that distinguishes necessity from strict necessity would apply primarily to the care with which courts and public authorities are expected to perform their review of necessity and the safeguards surrounding the measure. Essentially it would limit the margin of

---

[82] ECJ, *Tele2 Sverige AB v Post-och telestyrelsen and Secretary of State for the Home Department v Tom Watson and Others, Joined Cases C-203/15 and C-698/15*, ECLI:EU:C:2016:970, Judgment of 21 December 2016, para 106; ECJ, *Digital Rights Ireland Ltd v Minister for Communications, Marine and Natural Resources and Others and Kärntner Landesregierung and Others*, Joined Cases C-293/12 and C-594/12, Judgment of 8 April 2014, para 59.

[83] European Data Protection Board, *Guidelines 05/2022 on the use of facial recognition technology in the area of law enforcement*, 26 April 2023, p. 45.

[84] ECJ, *Proceedings brought by B*, Case C-439/19, Judgment of 22 June 2021, para 110. There are some subtle differences in how the Court has expressed this requirement in different cases, here it was 'just as effectively' but in *TK v Asociația de Proprietari bloc M5A-ScaraA* [2019] ECJ Case C-708/18, which was the case the Court referenced as support for this interpretation, the Court expressed it as 'cannot reasonably be as effectively achieved by other means less restrictive of the fundamental rights and freedoms of data subjects'. While unclear, the addition of 'just as' in *Proceedings brought by B* may indicate a stricter interpretation.

appreciation permitted to the law enforcement authority in the necessity test to a minimum.

3.3.2 Effectiveness or Efficiency: Two Sides of the Same Coin?

The question of whether the standard of *just as effectively* within the test of the least restrictive means can present a functional safeguard against unnecessary restrictions of the right to data protection will, ultimately, depend on the closer definition of *effectively*. A particular concern in this context is that moving from necessity to effectiveness may invite another subtle shift, whereby effectiveness is confused with efficiency.

We can find an example of this conceptual confusion in our example of the decision by the Swedish DPA, as it highlighted operational efficiency—as in cost/time efficiency—in its opinion on the Swedish police use of facial recognition, stating that the use of the system would be 'more effective than traditional and time-consuming manual analysis by human investigators'.[85] In other words, the question was not whether the measure was essential to achieving the public interest, but rather that it was a more efficient way of reaching the same result.[86]

In contrast, the EDPS has in its toolkit to assess the necessity of measures limiting the fundamental right to protection of personal data, stressed that convenience or cost effectiveness is not sufficient to reach the threshold of necessity.[87] The EDPS expresses that necessity requires a measure to be 'genuinely effective, i.e. essential to achieve the objective of general interest pursued'.[88] Not only that, the toolkit holds that '[i]f the proposed measure includes the processing of sensitive data, a higher threshold should be applied in the assessment of effectiveness'.[89] Questions of operational efficiency, such as the saving of resources, are issues the toolkit instead highlights as part of the proportionality analysis, as it is a question that 'requires the balancing with other competing interests of public interest'.[90]

This analysis of the EDPS finds support in the theoretical literature on necessity as part of an overall proportionality assessment as well. Aharon Barak, for instance, holds that questions of costs are questions dealt with under the proportionality *stricto sensu* step of analysis.

---

[85] Datainspektionen (2019) Förhandssamråd om Polismyndighetens planerade användning av. programvara för ansiktsigenkänning mot signalementsregistret.

[86] One explanation for this may be that the Swedish word for effectiveness is the same as for efficiency ('effektivitet'). The translation of the requirement of comparable effectiveness in ECJ case law into Swedish may in other words blur the distinction the EDPS wants to maintain against efficiency.

[87] European Data Protection Supervisor, *Assessing the necessity of measures that limit the fundamental right to the protection of personal data: A Toolkit*, 11 April 2017, p. 17.

[88] Ibid., p. 16.

[89] Ibid., p. 17.

[90] Ibid., p. 17.

> Whenever the new means, whose limitation of the constitutional right is of a lesser extent, require additional expense, we can no longer conclude that the means originally chosen are not necessary. [...] The issue, therefore, is whether the state's choice of avoiding the additional expense in order to prevent the further limitation of a human right is constitutional. The necessity test cannot assist us in attempting to resolve this issue; indeed this discussion should be conducted within the framework of proportionality stricto sensu, which is based on balancing.[91]

As previously mentioned, there has been a move towards more explicitly acknowledging the need proportionality balancing by the ECJ in the data protection context, which could contain these matters of efficiency as well. However, it could be argued that the ECJ has recently adopted an even stricter approach to necessity and operational efficiency.

In Case C-184/20 *OT*, the ECJ was asked to consider the publication of personal data of persons in charge of establishments receiving public funds, in a publicly accessible database on the Lithuanian Chief Ethics Commission's website. The publication of this data was intended to allow for discovery of conflicting interests and combat corruption in the public sector. The disclosure forms published contained information about the declarant's spouses, cohabitees, or partners, as well as information about presents received and transactions between partners, which may reveal sensitive personal characteristics, including sexual orientation.[92] In its preliminary ruling, the ECJ focused extensively on the necessity in terms of whether the measure was the least restrictive means to reach the aim. This, the court held, was a question that had to be assessed 'in the light of all the matters of fact and law specific to the Member State concerned'.[93]

One part of this discussion is particularly salient in this context. On the question of why the information in the database had to be available to the public rather than used only by anti-corruption authorities, the Lithuanian government had argued that the state it did not have sufficient human resources to check effectively all the declarations that were submitted to it.[94] Essentially, the Chief Ethics Commission counted on a form of crowdsourcing to allow for a more efficient use of human resources. The ECJ response to this approach was blunt and to the point.

> However, it must be pointed out that a lack of resources allocated to the public authorities cannot in any event constitute a legitimate ground justifying interference with the fundamental rights guaranteed by the Charter.[95]

On its face, this statement by the ECJ could essentially exclude concerns of efficacies of human resources or cost saving measures to underpin a claim of necessity. If so, this could carry far-reaching consequences for many different applications of

[91] Barak (2012), p. 326.

[92] ECJ, *OT v Vyriausioji tarnybinės etikos komisija*, Case C-184/20, Judgment of 1 August 2022.

[93] Ibid., para 86.

[94] Ibid., para 88.

[95] Ibid., para 89.

technological methods of analysis, as many are implemented as cost-saving measures, or to reduce dependencies on limited human resources.

A more cautious reading may however be warranted. In the context of policing, as well as in other sectors, many cost-saving measures can plausibly be reframed as effectiveness-measures. As an example, the police may rightfully argue that the use of facial recognition is the only effective way to *quickly* identify potential perpetrators in crime-scene footage. However, implicit in this argument hides the fact that the police will always be resource constrained in comparison to its many tasks, with an associated need to prioritise resources.[96] The argument can thus be reframed; the only way to *quickly* identify potential perpetrators *within existing resource parameters*, may be to use facial recognition technology. This reframing does not however answer the question of whether this identification is accurate, or forensically valid,[97] which ultimately will determine whether the method is in fact effective.

Furthermore, in the context of automating certain tasks, comparisons to manual processing may also invite arguments relating to tensions that may exist between different principles and values within the LED as such. One example can be found in the Swedish Police Authority's opinion on the previously mentioned proposed EDPS guidelines on the use of facial recognition technology in the area of law enforcement.[98] First, the Swedish Police Authority opined that the implications of the EDPS's interpretation of 'strictly necessary' would be that the scope to use facial recognition technology would be limited to an absolute minimum. This would, the authority pointed out, 'conflict with efforts of lawmakers and authorities to use the possibilities offered by technology to more effectively prevent and investigate crime and in doing so protect people's fundamental rights and freedoms'.[99] The Authority also pointed to secondary effects of manual processing:

> In the Swedish Police Authority's view, it should be taken into consideration that the alternative in certain cases to using software for image analysis to assist in search and analysis, for example, may instead involve a large number of officers going through huge quantities of images manually. Even if it is possible in theory (in some cases), this would mean needing to actually access a large number of irrelevant images and would require the images to be saved for a considerably longer period of time, which is difficult to reconcile with the general principles in data protection regulations.[100]

This argument is interesting as the use of facial recognition also requires access (by automated means) to a large number of irrelevant images, as well as biometric processing of all photos included in a database intended for comparison. Still, these arguments illustrate how issues of cost-efficiency can be restated as matters of

---

[96] Landström et al. (2020).

[97] Kotsoglou and Oswald (2020).

[98] The proposed guidelines are still in the public consultation phase.

[99] Swedish Police Authority (2022) Opinion from the Swedish Police Authority concerning the EDPB's Guidelines 05/2022 on the use of facial recognition technology in the area of law enforcement, pp. 4–5.

[100] Ibid., p. 5.

effectiveness in relation to more overarching aims of crime investigations, such as the positive obligations of the state in safeguarding fundamental rights through the protection of life through effective measures to detect, prevent, and investigate crime.

Almost every part of policing, regardless of member state, is affected by the need to prioritise limited resources. The drive to implement technological systems will inevitably take place against this backdrop. As such, the impact of the statement by the ECJ in *OT* is still uncertain, but it is clear in the sense that arguments of cost-efficiency cannot singlehandedly justify limitations of fundamental rights under the umbrella of necessity. However, systems that can be argued to also improve effectiveness—reaching the aim faster, or with better accuracy—while still having positive effects for cost-efficiency—are likely to be accepted under this necessity analysis and need to be analysed further, through balancing *stricto* sensu.

4 Conclusions: Necessity and AI-Supported Decision-Making Under the Law Enforcement Directive

The recent case law from the ECJ has added much needed clarifications on necessity under the LED (see Fig. 1). While there are reasons to believe that EU data protection law can provide meaningful limits to the use of AI in the law enforcement settings, the conflation of effectiveness and efficiency is likely to remain a risk. This is due to the way the requirement of necessity has been expressed in the LED and the GDPR, not only in the context of sensitive data—with no mention of proportionality although such a requirement is implicit in the limitation of fundamental rights. As we have seen, there are increasingly explicit mentions of proportionality balancing in ECJ rulings on necessity under data protection frameworks, as well as in the current guidelines from the EDPB. This is in line with how proportionality theory stress that necessity is one (important) threshold requirement, before moving onto proportionality balancing. Still, the absence of proportionality in the relevant sections of the LED and the GDPR may—as we can see in our example from the Swedish DPA—lead to proportionality balancing potentially becoming lost in practice. This highlights the need for DPAs and courts to continuously acknowledge that 'human rights cost money',[101] and guard against strict necessity devolving into simple cost effectiveness.

When the ECJ baked in certain aspects of proportionality balancing into the analysis of necessity under Article 10 LED in *Criminal proceedings against V.S.*, it may have countered that risk to some extent. It is a clear signal that the LED is not immune to proportionality considerations. It is also likely that the new threshold of 'absolute necessity' established in *V.S.* implies the need for a much stricter scrutiny of necessity, particularly in connection with the emphasis on data minimisation.

---

[101] Barak (2012), p. 326; Alexy (2002), p. 400.

Date	Case	Context	Development
2008-12-16	Case C-73/07, *Satakunnan Markkinapörssi and Satamedia*	Publication of tax tables.	Strictly necessary is established as a requirement relating to the data protection directive.
2010-11-09	C-92/09 and C-93/09, *Volker und Markus Schecke*	Validity of regulations requiring the publication of beneficiaries	Requirement of strict necessity repeated, not with reference not to the directive, but to data protection and privacy in general.
2013-11-07	C-473/12, *IPI*	Activity of a private detective acting for a professional body in order to investigate breaches of ethics of a regulated profession.	The requirement of strict necessity is repeated, designated as "settled case-law" but now connected to the fundamental right to privacy.
2014-04-08	C-293/12 and C-594/12, *Digital Rights Ireland*	Data retention directive requiring the undifferentiated storage of communication data.	Repeated as settled case-law.
2014-12-11	C-212/13, *Rynes*	Home security camera capturing parts of public space.	Repeated as settled case law, now in relation to the EU Charter right to privacy in Article 7.
2015-10-06	C-362/14, *Schrems I*	Transfer of personal data between EU and the US which could be subject to interception by US national security agencies.	Repeated in connection to the fundamental right to respect for private life at EU-level.
2016-12-21	C-203/15 and C-698/15, *Tele2*	Compatability of national rules on communcations data retention with the charter, based on the findings in Digital Rights Ireland.	Repeated, but now explicitly connected to the principle of proportionality.
2017-07-26	Opinion 1/15 , *Draft agreement between Canada and the European Union*	Transfer of Passenger Name Record data from the European Union to Canada for the purposes of automatic analysis for crime prevention and national security.	Repeated with connection to proportionality, first reference to greater importance when automated processing is at hand.
2019-12-11	C-708/18, TK v *Asociaţia de Proprietari bloc M5A-ScaraA*	video surveillance system installed in the common parts of a residential building, for the purposes of ensuring the safety and protection of individuals and property.	Definition of the requirement of least restrictive means.
2020-10-06	C-511/18, C-512/18 and C-520/18, *La Quadrature du Net*	Bulk access to communication to investigate and prevent serious crime and protect national security.	Repeated with connection to proportionality, now with a more explicit mention of the need for a proper balancing between the public interest and the fundamental rights. Risk of automated processing repeated.
2021-06-22	C-439/19, *Proceedings brought by B*	Public disclosure of personal data relating to road traffic offences.	Repetition of the least restrictive means.
2022-06-21	C-817/19, *Ligue de Humaine*	Automated processing of airline passenger data for the purposes of detecting serious crime and protect national security.	Repetition of the need to proper balancing between objectives of general interest and the rights at issue.
2022-08-01	Case C-184/20, *OT v Vyriausioji tarnybinės etikos komisija*	Publication on the internet of (sensitive) data contained in the declarations of private interests of natural persons working in the public service or of heads of associations or establishments receiving public funds	Repetition of least restrictive means connected to article 7 and 8 of the Charter. Adds that a lack of resources allocated to public authorities cannot in any event consitute a legitimate ground for justifying interferences with fundamental rights under the Charter.
2023-01-26	Case C-205/21, *Criminal proceedings against VS.*	systematic collection of biometric and genetic data of any person accused of an intentional offence subject to public prosecution	Establishes 'absolutely necessary' as a standard for the necessity of processing sensitive categories of data under the LED.

Fig. 1 Development of necessity in ECJ case law

However, the emphasis the ECJ placed on how processing of sensitive data should be a very clear exception rather than commonplace is likely to conflict with the ambitions of many member states in the law enforcement context.[102] Through the ruling in *OT*, the ECJ has also highlighted how considerations of lacking resources cannot itself be enough to warrant restrictions of fundamental rights. Taken together, the rulings in *V.S.* and *OT* have planted seeds that hold the potential to grow into effective legal limits for the implementation of AI systems that impact the fundamental right to data protection, particularly in contexts where sensitive categories of data are used. However, to what extent those seeds will grow depends on the extent to which DPAs and courts engage in critically examining the purported benefits of AI-supported decision-making.

Looking at the development of the principle of necessity in ECJ case law, it seems clear that it has, over time, become a focal point of the court's reasoning in data protection cases. Simultaneously, the primary source of interpretation has shifted towards its fundamental rights foundations rather than its expression in secondary law. This is significant as it mirrors how the ECJ over time have emphasised data protection rights in the face of large-scale data processing and surveillance measures established in secondary law (such as in Digital Rights Ireland and *Tele2*) or international agreements (such as in *Schrems* and *in Opinion 1/15*). While the ECJ has not been entirely consistent, it is still clear that the interpretation of the requirements of the LED will need to be taken against this broader backdrop of fundamental rights.

A lot of attention as of late has been placed on the prospects of the upcoming AIA. However, the developments outlined here shows that data protections concerns are likely to remain highly relevant in relation to AI use by law enforcement even as the AIA arrives on the scene. There are several strengths brought by this framework as compared to the AIA. First, unlike the AIA, the data protection framework is largely technology agnostic and is not dependent on establishing the presence of a specific AI-technology. Second, data protection can come into play at the earlier stages of data gathering as a form of processing, rather than through the deployment of an AI-system. Third, it will remain relevant across the different categories of risk proposed in the AIA. While the AIA is likely to express that some uses of AI technologies, such as live 'remote' facial recognition of public spaces should be forbidden (at least as a main rule),[103] it should be noted that those same uses are likely to run afoul of the current data protection principles as well. It is in any case fair to say that the strength of the current data protection framework has not yet been

[102]The Swedish government initiated a public inquiry in May 2021 that is to propose new rules holding that more people suspected of crimes must be able to be identified using fingerprints, DNA, facial images, or similar information about individual characteristics. The inquiry will deliver its proposal in June, 2023. Justitiedepartementet Biometri i brottsbekämpningen.

[103](2022) Proposal for a Regulation of the European Parliament and of the Council laying down harmonised rules on artificial intelligence (Artificial Intelligence Act) and amending certain Union legislative acts—Preparation for Coreper. Recital 18 & 19.

fully tested in relation to emerging AI technologies, but it has the potential to act as a meaningful safeguard against the risks of such systems.

In another sense, however, the developments outlined in this contribution might be able to tell us something of what to expect of future interpretation of the AIA. As many of the articles of the act is built upon foundations found in fundamental rights such as the respect for privacy and human dignity, we should not be surprised if those foundations will slowly begin to emerge and influence the interpretation of the act as well. Perhaps it is through this process, rather than in any specific statutory addition to the current data protection framework that the real potential of the AIA will be located.

Acknowledgements This work was supported by the Swedish Research Council under Grant number 2020-02278. The author would like to thank Therese Enarsson, Johan Lindholm, Lena Enqvist, Jan Leidö, Isak Nilsson, and Felix Bockel, for comments on an earlier draft of this paper.

References

Afra S, Alhajj R (2020) Early warning system: from face recognition by surveillance cameras to social media analysis to detecting suspicious people. Phys A: Stat Mech Its Appl 540:123151. https://doi.org/10.1016/j.physa.2019.123151

Alexy R (2002) A theory of constitutional rights. Oxford University Press, Oxford

Barak A (2012) Proportionality: constitutional rights and their limitations

Brayne S (2021) Predict and surveil: data, discretion, and the future of policing. Oxford University Press, New York

Brkan M (2019) Do algorithms rule the world? Algorithmic decision-making and data protection in the framework of the GDPR and beyond. Int J Law Inf Technol 27:91–121. https://doi.org/10.1093/ijlit/eay017

Bygrave LA (2020) Article 22 automated individual decision-making, including profiling. In: The EU General Data Protection Regulation (GDPR). Oxford University Press

Enarsson T, Enqvist L, Naarttijärvi M (2022) Approaching the human in the loop – legal perspectives on hybrid human/algorithmic decision-making in three contexts. Inf Commun Technol Law 31:123–153. https://doi.org/10.1080/13600834.2021.1958860

Ferguson AG (2017) The rise of big data policing: surveillance, race, and the future of law enforcement. NYU Press, New York

Harcourt BE (2007) Against prediction: profiling, policing, and punishing in an actuarial age. University of Chicago Press, Chicago

Hildebrandt M (2010) Proactive forensic profiling: proactive criminalization? In: Duff RA, Farmer L, Marshall SE et al (eds) The boundaries of the criminal law. Oxford University Press, Oxford

Joh EE (2016) The new surveillance discretion: automated suspicion, big data, and policing. Harv Law Policy Rev 10:15–42

Kotsoglou KN, Oswald M (2020) The long arm of the algorithm? Automated facial recognition as evidence and trigger for police intervention. Forensic Sci Int: Synergy 2:86–89. https://doi.org/10.1016/j.fsisyn.2020.01.002

Landström L, Eklund N, Naarttijärvi M (2020) Legal limits to prioritisation in policing – challenging the impact of centralisation. Polic Soc 30:1061–1080. https://doi.org/10.1080/10439463.2019.1634717

Marquenie T (2017) The police and criminal justice authorities directive: data protection standards and impact on the legal framework. Comput Law Secur Rev 33:324–340. https://doi.org/10.1016/j.clsr.2017.03.009

Moraes TG, Almeida EC, de Pereira JRL (2021) Smile, you are being identified! Risks and measures for the use of facial recognition in (semi-)public spaces. AI Ethics 1:159–172. https://doi.org/10.1007/s43681-020-00014-3

Naarttijärvi M (2019) Legality and democratic deliberation in black box policing. Technol Regul:35–48. https://doi.org/10.26116/techreg.2019.004

Ranerup A, Henriksen HZ (2020) Digital discretion: unpacking human and technological agency in automated decision making in Sweden's social services. Soc Sci Comput Rev 1–17. https://doi.org/10.1177/0894439320980434

Sajfert J, Quintel T (2017) Data Protection Directive (EU) 2016/680 for Police and Criminal Justice Authorities. SSRN Scholarly Paper ID 3285873. Accessed 10 February 2022

Schartum DW (2020) From legal sources to programming code: automatic individual decisions in public administration and computers under the rule of law. In: Barfield W (ed) The Cambridge handbook of the law of algorithms, 1st edn. Cambridge University Press, pp 301–336

Suksi M (2021) Administrative due process when using automated decision-making in public administration: some notes from a Finnish perspective. Artif Intell Law 29:87–110. https://doi.org/10.1007/s10506-020-09269-x

Zalnieriute M (2021) Burning bridges: the automated facial recognition technology and public space surveillance in the modern state. Columbia Sci Technol Law Rev 22(2):284–307. https://doi.org/10.7916/ZW5G-GC57

Correction to: AI and Sensitive Personal Data Under the Law Enforcement Directive: Between Operational Efficiency and Legal Necessity

Markus Naarttijärvi

Correction to: Chapter 57 in : Markus Naarttijärvi, https://doi.org/10.1007/16495_2023_57

Chapter "AI and Sensitive Personal Data Under the Law Enforcement Directive: Between Operational Efficiency and Legal Necessity" was previously published non-open access. It has now been changed to open access under a CC BY 4.0 license and the copyright holder updated to 'The Author(s)'. The book has also been updated with this change.

The updated version for this chapter can be found at https://doi.org/10.1007/16495_2023_57

E. Gill-Pedro, A. Moberg (eds.), *YSEC Yearbook of Socio-Economic Constitutions 2023*, YSEC Yearbook of Socio-Economic Constitutions (2024) 2023: 359–360, https://doi.org/10.1007/16495_2023_66, Published online: 12 January 2024

The manufacturer's authorised representative in the EU is Springer Nature Customer Service Centre GmbH, Europaplatz 3, 69115 Heidelberg, Germany. If you have any concerns regarding our products, please contact ProductSafety@springernature.com

Printed and bound by CPI Group (UK) Ltd, Croydon, CR0 4YY
01/10/2026
02225897-0013